BOYS THEMSELVES

BOYS
THEMSELVES

A Return to Single-Sex Education

Michael Ruhlman

Henry Holt and Company ■ New York

Henry Holt and Company, Inc.
Publishers since 1866
115 West 18th Street
New York, New York 10011

Henry Holt® is a registered
trademark of Henry Holt and Company, Inc.

Library of Congress Cataloging-in-Publication Data

Ruhlman, Michael, 1963–
Boys themselves: a return to single-sex education/Michael Ruhlman.—1st ed.
        p.   cm.
1. University School (Hunting Valley, Ohio)—History.
2. Same-sex schools—Ohio—Hunting Valley—History.   I. Title.
        LD7501.U68R84   1996
    370′.9771′32—dc20   96-17114
                CIP

ISBN 0-8050-3370-X

Henry Holt books are available for special
promotions and premiums. For details contact:
Director, Special Markets.

First Edition—1996

Designed by Paula R. Szafranski

Printed in the United States of America
All first editions are printed on acid-free paper. ∞

1   3   5   7   9   10   8   6   4   2

For Donna

ACKNOWLEDGMENTS

First, my thanks to Rick Hawley for allowing me into University School without preconditions and for innumerable hours answering my questions. I'd like to thank the administrative staff and faculty at University School; all were generous and candid in their conversation. I would especially like to thank Nancy Lerner and Paul Bailin, who did not once turn down a demand from me for their time. My thanks also to the students, especially to those portrayed in this book.

Deep thanks to Elizabeth Kaplan, a literary agent who is enormously patient and also a gifted reader. I am very lucky to have a fine editor, Bill Strachan, and I'm grateful for the work of assistant editor Darcy Tromanhauser. I am indebted to this book's copy editors, Don Kennison and Jeanne Tift. Thanks also to Lee Kravitz for his insights and help.

I would like to thank Reynolds Price and Daniel Stashower for guidance and support.

I would also like to thank John Schambach of Live Publishing Company and Michael von Glahn, former editor of *Northern Ohio Live,* for giving me work during and after the writing of this book.

Two acknowledgments must stand at a remove from the others.

I have magnificent parents, and I am grateful to them. As far as the writing of this book is concerned, I am especially beholden to my father for his enormous generosity.

Finally: Donna. M.L.C. Thank you. For everything.

CONTENTS

Part I

FALL

1

The letter began, "Dear Mr. and Mrs. Fletcher, My purpose for writing this is to indicate to you that the faculty has serious concerns about Kristopher's academic standing at the school. As you know from Kristopher's report cards and from conferences with his sponsor and others of us here, we are convinced that his performance fails to represent his ability and falls below our expectations.

"It is therefore impossible for us at this time to enclose the registration materials for the 1990–91 academic year."

The letter proposed that Mr. and Mrs. Fletcher consider enrolling their thirteen-year-old in a summer program. But warning prevailed: "We also suggest that you begin to consider other schooling options for the next year in the event that Kristopher's performance does not improve sufficiently to warrant his returning to University School in the fall."

The letter was dated February 22, 1990, and signed "Sincerely, Kerry P. Brennan, Director of the Lower School."

While not unexpected, this was nevertheless exactly the sort of mail parents do not want to receive from the school their son attends. Kris was none too happy about it either. Report cards often initiated parental fireworks, and the letter, some serious decisions—namely, did Kris want to stay in this school or go back to public school? Everyone knew Kris was smart. He consistently tested in the top 1 percent of kids his age. But the test scores did not translate to class work. At public school Kris was near the top of his class and he didn't have to do homework to get there, a tactic that proved less effective at the new school.

A few days after the letter was sent, Kris exacerbated his shaky standing at the school by smashing a raw egg into the face of a classmate. There had been a lot of eggs that day, a requirement for a science experiment. After school, Kris still had his egg. As many thirteen-year-olds will tell you, you never know when an egg will come in handy. Indeed, in front of the school waiting for the bus, when a classmate made a derogatory remark about Kris's mother, handy it was. The egg incident required a formal apology from Kris and money for dry cleaning.

It did not keep him out of school, however. Nor did his performance over the next three months. He was readmitted the following year, and the year after that, and the year after that. In the end it had come down to a personal challenge: "I didn't want to admit defeat," Kris says.

On September 2, 1993, Kris awoke at 5:15 A.M. to begin his final year of high school.

Kris's room, about the size of a standard walk-in closet, contains a narrow bed and a small bureau. One wall is given over to shelves jammed with sci-fi books, magazines, and plastic toys, mainly Dungeons and Dragons figures and miniature vehicles. What little space is left for moving about is taken up by a barbell, two guitars upright in their stands at the foot of the bed, assorted sheet music, and the blade of a plastic broadax. The walls are decorated with posters of heavy-metal stars—shirtless, anemic, androgynous. Kris, like these stars, grows his hair long, a heavy brown mantle of it, straight, nearly shoulder length, with bangs that curl fanglike from a sharp widow's peak around his wide, angular cheekbones. His thumbnails are likewise long, typically measuring an inch or so from cuticle to rim.

It's not easy these days to be a metalhead, especially at a private school. Many people consider the music annoying; others claim the music is inextricably linked to Satan worship, drug abuse, and suicide. But Kris, whose love of baseball has recently metamorphosed into a love of music and books, can now articulate a defense against such claims. He will tell you that Iron Maiden's "The Rime of the Ancient Mariner" led him to read Coleridge. "How can a music be void of education if the words of Tennyson's 'The Charge of the Light Brigade' are on screen during a video for a song about war?" he argues. "How many types of music groups write a musical biography of Alexander the Great? Or have a Winston Churchill speech at the beginning of one of their tapes? The vocalist of my favorite band has written two novels, both published, and is the seventeenth-ranked fencer in England."

Kris pushes past the curtain that separates his room from the upstairs hallway, heads toward the shower, and, when he's finished washing, he wakes his brothers. Nicholas begins ninth grade today. Kris is genuinely proud of Nick: "He's going to do a lot better in school than I did," Kris says. Nick's round face has the color and apparent elasticity of dough, slivers for eyes that are disproportionately small in such a large head, and clipped blond hair. Nick listens to heavy metal, too, but he prefers classical music. When asked who his favorite composer is, he says he doesn't know, hoping you'll leave him alone; when pressed he says, "probably Tchaikovsky." Nick seems almost never to speak, at least when in school. All his teachers, while admiring him, remark on his apparent shyness. His backpack, when loaded to capacity with books, is roughly half his size and weight, and as he hefts it, he must angle forward, apparently to avoid falling backward.

When Kris enters the room, silent, scholarly Nick appears unconscious beneath the bedsheets until Kris tries to rouse him. Nick says, "Get away you fucker, I'm up already!"

Every morning, says Kris, shaking his head, every morning for the past three years. Get away you fucker, I'm up already. Kris then wakes his youngest brother, Adam, who shares the room and, as he begins sixth grade, is a less irreverent riser.

At 6:09 A.M., Kris, Nick, and Adam, three private-school boys, leave the house in which their mother was born, the house their great-grandfather built before the turn of the century. Often they walk to the bus shelter, but on this their first day their dad gives them a ride. Most of the houses that line their street, packed tightly as teeth in this working-class neighborhood on the West Side of Cleveland, Ohio, are unlighted at this hour. Mr. Fletcher turns left at a grungy Dairy Mart at the end of their street and drives about a half-mile to deposit his boys at the intersection of Denison and Fulton. There, they wait for the No. 79 bus across from a gas station above Interstate 71, which buzzes lightly with pre-rush-hour traffic. The bus deposits Kris, Nick, and Adam at Public Square, the center of downtown Cleveland, marked by the Terminal Tower, now referred to as Tower City, a complex of offices and a vast, three-level concourse of fancy shops and mesmerizing fountains. Beneath Tower City, the three lines of the Rapid Transit converge. Kris, Nick, and Adam board the Green Road line.

Cleveland is bisected by the Cuyahoga River, which separates the East Side from the West Side. Some people have observed that this is the actual dividing line between America's East Coast and Midwest; moreover, the difference between East Side and West Side in the collective mind of this city is distinct and evokes the heated analysis and debate that typically attends great sports rivalries. The East Side is largely middle- to upper-class, white-collar, racially integrated; the West Side, generally middle- to lower-class, blue-collar, and predominantly white with ethnic roots in Eastern Europe, though it has recently accommodated a huge influx of Asian and Latino immigrants. When Kris is with a group of East Siders and someone says the words "West Side," his chin rises slightly and his lips form a sly, competitive curl.

The Rapid Transit, as the Cleveland train system has been called since it began operating in the 1920s, will carry the Fletcher boys along the decrepit southern edge of the city, and up into the lush eastern suburbs, where great houses spread out between deep, well-tended lawns and massive oak and maple trees.

Kris used to resent this daily trek into territory so distinctly foreign to him, but after six years, he's gotten used to it. Moreover, many of his old neighborhood buddies are in detention centers or jail for petty theft and assault and battery, and the ones who stayed in school say the violence has gotten so bad, sometimes they simply don't go. The thought of this helps him tolerate the hours on buses and trains, and anyway he's got only one more year of it left. A girl named Kathleen helps too.

At the first school stop, Courtland Boulevard, girls from Hathaway Brown gather their books and descend to the platform. Kris has been watching Kathleen—a tall, pretty Filipina and fellow West Sider—disembark here for a couple years, but that's all, and enough, for now. He had tried to make some small talk before they got on the Rapid, but their relationship remains courteous and formal. At the final stop, a second cluster of girls, Laurel School girls wearing green plaid skirts and white blouses, will disembark. Between these two stops, Kris, Nick, Adam, and about a half dozen other West Siders and city boys leave the train to walk a half-mile to the lower campus of University School. While Adam goes to his classes here, Kris and Nick board another bus—a proper school bus this time—for the last leg of their journey to the school's upper campus seven miles farther east in a village called Hunting Valley, a wealthy, rolling patch of land seven miles square, population 850. Signs marking Hunting Valley's borders used to include the addendum "No Hunting," but so many people made fun of it that city officials changed it to "Observe All Ordinances."

Though extravagant residential real estate has thrived in Hunting Valley during the past twenty-five years since construction of University School's upper campus began (the median home price here exceeds half a million dollars), the town remains mostly wooded. The upper campus of University School, which houses grades nine through twelve, is not visible from any road. Except for the playing fields which spread out like a pasture at the rear of the school's two hundred acres, all other space used for school business—seven tennis courts, the building itself, the drives and pathways—appears to have been carved out of the woods as if from a linoleum block. The rectangular student parking lot, just past the front of the school, is walled by trees so tall and even that, when viewed from above, it might be a giant shoe box filled with matchbox cars.

The air is humid this morning, and a soft rain begins. A steady stream of cars pours down the winding entrance drive. Upperclassmen drive their own vehicles if they have them. Underclassmen arrive via parents in cars ranging from Lexuses and BMWs, short, pig's-tail antennas affixed to the back windshield, to Chryslers and Toyotas. At eight A.M., the yellow school bus motors around the small oval in front of the school and deposits the dozens of students who boarded at the lower school. For Kris and Nick, it's been a two-hour commute that will be retraced at 3:30 every school day for the next nine months.

Were it not for the hundreds of kids advancing toward the doors, a visitor might not be sure that he's found the front of the upper school. Private and public schools once proclaimed their identity with expansive steps rising to formidable entrance doors, graced by Doric columns and massive bell towers, but University School's upper campus was built in 1969, an era that prized openness and adored simple geometrical shapes. Here, students descend to the glass front doors, which are neatly framed by brown metal trim against the red brick façade. No school name or motto is chiseled in marble; there are no columns, no tower. At its highest point, the school is two stories—giant square blocks of brick plunked down in the middle of woods.

The main lobby is openness itself. Seventy-five yards long from the entrance doors to the glass wall of the faculty lounge, and twenty yards across at its widest point, the vast corridor can simultaneously accommodate several hackey-sack games, a band of seniors lounging on the steps of the locker area, two dozen freshmen wrestling or batting wads of paper in an area called Monkey Island (a connected expanse of carpeted platforms and seating spaces), and one meaningful footrace across the smooth brown

7

carpet. Or a four-man jazz band rocking the house, fifty faculty, and 370 students—a living experiment in chaos theory—arriving for the first day of school. More specifically, 370 boys.

Only boys. Boys only. A mob of boys, stuffing themselves into jackets and knotting ties for the first assembly of the 1993–94 school year. Crowds, generally, tend to erase identities and individual differences. Throw in a dress requirement and the identities are further hidden. Wipe out an entire gender, teenage girls, and the mob-effect is near total. Kris Fletcher, dressed in black and having spent the first chunk of his day riding public transportation out of a dilapidated pocket of the West Side and into the eastern splendor of Hunting Valley, slips into the crowd as if into a pond, vanishing.

Every now and then, the newspaper reports that some East Coast fisherman has hauled up in his net a slimy, black fish with the head of a lizard and the vestiges of squat legs instead of pectoral fins, a species thought to have become extinct a million years ago—but there it is, flopping around in the net looking confused. Scientists scratch their heads in wonder, point to the creature's fossilized relatives, and call the discovery remarkable, while readers hover over their newspaper with perverse fascination at the ungainly, prehistoric fish.

For many people an all-boy school is little more than this—a quirk, an evolutionary oversight, unless they went to one, or worked at one, in which case it's not quite so weird. Or maybe weirder. But fewer and fewer people go to boys' schools because fewer and fewer exist. Public all-boy schools are illegal, so most all-male schools exist in the independent sphere of American education. Though they had once been plentiful, by the mid-1980s, most were gone, and few people cared that they were; those who did care were mainly glad.

This disappearance, and the public perception of the single-sex school, is something of a paradox. Beginning in the late 1970s and growing steadily, research has described clear advantages of single-sex education over coeducation in both cognitive and social outcomes. Indeed, the evidence grew so strong that many prominent researchers began to ask what were the benefits of *coeducation?* Two leading researchers, for instance, noted in one study that "rarely did attending a coeducational secondary school prove advantageous." Diane Ravitch asked, "Why should single-sex education have to prove itself when coeducation can't?" As secretary for Educa-

8

tional Research and Improvement and counselor to the United States Secretary of Education in the Bush administration, Ravitch convened a group of experts in Washington, D.C., specifically to ask "whether our society should reexamine its received attitudes about single-sex education—especially the belief that it is antiquated and irrelevant—and should reconsider those public policies that contribute to its decline."

Cornelius Riordan, a professor of educational sociology at Providence College in Rhode Island and an educational researcher, wrote a book in 1990 called *Girls & Boys in School: Together or Separate?*, in which he evaluates all known studies comparing single-sex and coeducation. Riordan wrote, "The scales tip, I conclude, in favor of single-sex education." Then he asked, "Does it not make sense to learn more about the potential efficacy of single-sex educational environments before they become historical artifacts?" In a foreword to Riordan's book, the sociologist James Coleman noted that conventional wisdom is often "strong enough to inhibit research into the area in question." The perception that single-sex schools were anachronisms, often harmful ones, and that coeducation is obviously better because it's more equal and democratic, he suggests, may be part of the reason so little research has been done on the subject. Coeducation, for a century taken for granted as the best way to educate children, is the only option available to 99 percent of the public; who cares about single-sex education anymore? This reaction was borne out in 1992 in the United States Department of Education itself: Diane Ravitch was replaced in the new administration, and her project to evaluate the efficacy of single-sex educational institutions was scrapped.

For me, these paradoxes were my initial reason for arriving on this rainy September day for the opening ceremonies of a contemporary all-boy school. I was here not simply to watch the ceremony; I planned to stay all year. The all-boy school was not strange to me because I'd graduated from this place more than a dozen years earlier. Today was not simply an entry into an all-boy school, a single-sex laboratory, it was also a journey into my past. And I'd arrived with questions. Was there something distinctly different and good about the all-boy school? Or did it instead conform to the blue-blooded, elitist, sexual-pressure-cooker stereotype, boys twisted into cruel shapes by this unnatural situation? The general notion in America was that the single-sex form was bad, and yet there was no evidence to suggest that this was true. Why the paradox? If research over two decades had confirmed the benefits of coeducation over single-sex, or if national opinion paralleled the research, what would be the interest in confirming what was already known? This paradox needed to be addressed; both positions could not be right.

There was one more curious knot in this situation. All of the researchers had carefully separated out white boys from single-sex benefits. All noted that single-sex education had proven enormously effective for girls and minority boys, but white boys fared less well than their white coed counterparts. No one bothered to address why this should be so. How could single-sex education be good for every variety of child except white boys?

The first thing that struck me upon my return to high school was that so little had changed. I spotted several old teachers of mine; some said hello, others sent uncertain double-takes. No one, curiously, asked me what I was doing here. So little had changed, in fact—including myself, I suspect—that the morning seemed timeless. I half expected to see my old classmates emerge from the locker area at the opposite edge of the commons. It remained unthinkable to walk into the off-limits faculty lounge. The band, immediately inside the front doors, was the only unusual element of the scene. The boys were *cranking.* It was like a party, everyone milling about, shaking hands.

At one point a stranger approached me, a big fellow, but young. I didn't know if he was a student or a teacher.

"Evan Luzar!" he bellowed, holding out a beefy hand.

I said my name, but had to concentrate on my hand.

"Are you a teacher?" he continued.

"No. Are you?"

"Yeah! This is my second year! What do you do?!"

"I'm a writer."

This seemed to confuse him, but he recovered and said, "I graduated from here! I love this school! This is a *great* school!"

I said I'd like to talk to him about it later. He said, "I'd love to!" and moved off. It really was like a party.

I was looking for someone. Over the summer, I'd met with some incoming seniors: Tyler Doggett was one of them, but I couldn't spot him.

Doggett, a classmate of Kris's, also vanishes the moment he enters the school. To judge by his sandy-blond hair and wire-rimmed glasses Tyler is either a model prep-school boy or the weary stereotype of one. Whereas Kris is vintage West Side with metal-inspired hair and thumbnails, Tyler Doggett is Eastern prep, the antithesis of Kris. They are as different as their journeys to school. Tyler lives a mile away and can leave for school in his 1990 Dodge Daytona at eight, park, walk to the building, and still have enough time to slip on a jacket, knot a tie, and take his seat before the doors to morning assembly close at 8:10.

While Kris is liberal, Tyler is the school's archconservative. I'd been told he was "wildly opinionated." Most of Tyler's classmates, Kris included, defer to his intelligence; he rarely speaks in class but when he does the room is silent. He's prone to bizarre outbursts.

"Camille Paglia says if women ruled the world, we'd all be living in grass *huts*," Tyler announced on one occasion to no one in particular and for no apparent reason when his English teacher entered the classroom.

In addition to his post as vice-president of the senior class, he's a member of the debate team, plays varsity tennis, is one of a dozen boys who have received a Davey Fellowship, for which he intends to complete a collection of six short stories this year, and he attends AA meetings twice a week.

These meetings give him a great sense of serenity, but he can't stand, he says, "the bile of old women who say, 'I used to put all my faith in alcohol and now I put all my faith in God.' . . . How can you give yourself over to a baser thing and then give it over to God? God isn't the thing. We're on earth. We're responsible for what we do. They say they're off booze, but they're hooked on coffee, cigarettes, groups."

Tyler spent the summer traveling with a school group from Morocco to Jordan, during which he visited the home of, and interviewed, Yassir Arafat before returning to the United States and University School.

"Major culture shock," he says in a low soft voice that's part mumble and part effort to conceal braces. He shakes his head, directs his gaze at his feet, and taps out a nervous beat on his collarbone. "I spent some time in the Gaza Strip and had rocks thrown at my head. There was gunfire. I saw people fighting and killing for what they believe in. And then I come back to US . . . ," he trails off cynically.

By 8:05 on opening day, the school commons teems with so many people that Tyler, a reclusive bundle of passions, insecurities, and opinions, is invisible. Instead, I see Geoff Morton and his wife Emily hustling to pass out strips of paper with students' schedules on them. Keith Green, a native of Birmingham, England, who teaches French and German and runs the foreign-exchange program, rushes to and fro through the crowd in a mild panic. "I'm looking for a Japanese boy," he says, British inflection intact. "Have you *seen* him? Doesn't speak a word of English, you know." And Kerry Brennan is darting back and forth attending to last-minute details. He's carrying a large leather duffel bag.

Today, Kerry Brennan, who stepped in seven years ago at age thirty to lead the lower school, begins his first year as director of the upper school. He's the point man for this campus, the mediator between students and faculty, faculty and headmaster. The faculty are glad to have someone in charge of what had been, as one put it, a rudderless ship, but they're nevertheless nervous about Kerry's style. He has been likened to a commandant by former colleagues. One wouldn't think this judging from appearances. His large round brown eyes, plump dimpled cheeks, his thick, brown, perfectly coiffed hair and short compact frame make him seem, well, adorable rather than formidable.

One of Kerry's first aims as he steps into the new post is, in his words, "to establish anew, or again, a sense of ritual and decorum" that many felt had frayed during the past few years of shifting administrators. This will include a reenforced dress code for the students. Kerry himself is the model of sartorial decorum, whether in an olive green suit and snappy tie or, today, gray flannels and tasseled loafers. As one friend put it after Kerry read announcements to morning assembly on the day of a big football game, "He's the only person I know who can look nattily dressed in a football jersey."

Kerry's somewhat nervous today. On Monday, when the faculty reconvened for opening meetings to listen to the financial state of the school, some stirring remarks from the headmaster, and other school news, Kerry, the suspected commandant, explained that the day was indeed a portentous one for him as a great historic moment aligned with a personal one: his first day as director of the upper school, he explained, just happened to be Jay Leno's first performance as host of NBC's "Tonight Show" and David Letterman's first, and much ballyhooed, night on CBS. Coincidence? Kerry shrugged. And for opening day ceremonies, he's got some unusual, parallel plans. The band, for one—that was his idea.

Nowhere to be seen, however, is the headmaster of this school, Richard A. Hawley. Hawley, forty-eight years old, is an unusual headmaster. If he does indeed show up for work today, he will be well on his way to bucking one set of odds. He is beginning his sixth year as headmaster of this school; headmaster tenures, once measured in decades, now average seven years.

Within the school community—students, teachers, parents, alumni— Hawley is controversial, considered by some to be a dangerous radical (at one point, he was nicknamed Robespierre). Others see him as an ultraconservative with hopelessly archaic, perhaps harmful, notions of right and wrong, a moral absolutist among boys who need leniency and compromise when they make mistakes, not Grand Inquisitor–style discipline. Many adore him, stand in awe of his erudition, his literary work, his intelligence. Others scoff behind his back, expressing nothing but mistrust and distaste. The man evokes strong feelings. I know some people who've never met Hawley and hate him anyway.

Hawley is also unusual in that he's a literary administrator with a ten-year faculty tenure at the Bread Loaf Writers Conference and a dozen books to his name, including an epistolary novel, a libretto, a memoir, poetry, a psycho-social tract—drawing from electroencephalogram studies and Greek philosophy—on the purposes of pleasure as it relates to adolescents and drugs, and a new book published this past summer entitled *Boys Will Be Men: Masculinity in Troubled Times,* a thoroughly eccentric volume intertwining Jungian and feminist psychoanalytic theory, Western myth, and stories of boys he's known as a teacher and headmaster. Over the past few years he's been writing and speaking about boys' schools, has become, in fact, a sort of boys' school guru.

I might have gone to any number of boys' schools—had these most private and media-wary institutions allowed me to—but Rick Hawley was here.

Now, only a few minutes before the opening-day ceremony is to begin, the headmaster appears at the top of the stairs, a wide, carpeted expanse of steps and landings that turns three times between the second-floor classrooms and offices and the downstairs commons area. Hawley is wearing a blue blazer with the school crest which reads "A Lasting Legacy" on the breast pocket. His striped tie is knotted tightly at the collar of his crisp white shirt.

When the headmaster reaches the center of the bottom landing, he stops and stares out over the vast commons which thrums with boys. His aspect is not that of the proud, fatherly headmaster overseeing his charges, nor of the sly, clever revolutionary. He looks a little disoriented. His straight dark hair is tousled. His gaze is vacant. He squints, somewhat addled, at the loud music pumped out by keyboard, saxophone, guitar, and drums half a football field away at the far end of the commons.

Only when a student tentatively approaches does he seem, momentarily, to snap out of it. Working up a smile, the headmaster says, "Hi, Kevin."

From head to foot, Kevin Casey is wrapped in folds of canvas, covered with pockets and straps and buckles. He's wearing a droopy, khaki-colored rain hat which nearly obscures his wide eyes and fluttering eyelashes. His long dark hair curls out from behind his ears. He's shouldering a large backpack. A plastic coffee mug dangles at thigh level from one of its straps. From the looks of him, Kevin might be heading off on a trek through the Adirondacks.

Hawley appears glad to see Kevin, has always liked him for his eccentric interests and energy. Kevin's a talented actor, and will soon begin rehearsals for a play at one of the oldest and most respected community theaters in the city, run by his mother. Last year, as a junior, he won the Sherman Prize speaking contest, a tradition at the school since the early 1900s and the most prestigious competition open to juniors. His knowledge of the Civil War is so voluminous that when he was a sophomore he was asked by a history teacher to teach upperclassmen on the areas of his expertise.

Hawley extends his hand to Kevin and says, "Welcome *back.*"

The band, on an extended riff, has managed somehow to segue out of jazz and into a rendition of the Grateful Dead's "Lovelight"; it's almost hard to hear conversation.

Kevin shakes Hawley's hand and mumbles, "First day of school. *Whoa.*" Hawley smiles tensely at Kevin—he senses something is wrong—and Kevin shuffles off to drop his backpack in a corner of the landing.

Vaguely troubled, seemingly confused, the headmaster disappears into the crowd.

2

In November 1991, a month after taking a job as an editor at a local magazine, I drove out to Hunting Valley to interview this headmaster. I'd graduated from the school on June 5, 1981, and the last words I remember anybody saying to me that hot bright day—my final day as a US student—came from the previous headmaster. I, like every other seventeen-year-old on the quad, wore a blue blazer and white carnation, white slacks and a maroon tie. I'd been at the school since sixth grade but had never once spoken to the headmaster, a fearsome man named Rowland McKinley who stood, in my memory, six-foot-seven in white bucks and silver military brush cut. He was revered as a great orator; indeed, his booming speeches were all most students knew of him in his last decade as head. Even the quaint argot of a previous era—"BY GUM," for instance, punctuated most of his speeches—seemed formidable given enough volume. McKinley was the sort of man who spoke only in all capital letters. It had been my impression that the man had never in his life called anybody by their first name, and he could scare the bejesus out of any adolescent who crossed his path.

My best friend once did cross his path, literally, and got knocked on his back in the middle of the school commons near the student lockers one morning after assembly. Dave, then a ninth grader, would later claim that McKinley deliberately went out of his way to deliver the blow, but at the time he managed only to push himself off the carpet and gawk at McKinley with drop-jawed indignation. McKinley said only that he'd been on earth longer than my friend and therefore no apology was forthcoming.

By graduation, having forgotten this small injustice visited on my friend and bounding about the sunny quad in my graduation outfit, I could not contain myself. Diploma in hand, brimming with good spirits and love of the school, I waited till McKinley was alone, carefully organizing words of gratitude, then pressed quickly through the churchlike mob of blazers, brothers, sisters, parents, and relatives, to shake his hand.

"Mr. McKinley—um—I just wanted to tell you that I really loved this school." His smile was fierce; it could almost sear your skin. "It's a really great school—um—and I just wanted to thank you."

"GIVE MONEY!" he said and strode into the crowd. I never saw McKinley again.

I don't know that I expected him to blubber with affection, but I was nonplussed, so the memory took some time to ripen. The guy was all efficiency. No bullshit. Just like his bucks and crew cut. Granted, he'd never flattened me, but even if he had, I think what would remain even now would be the certain knowledge that I'd been in the presence of both an original and an archetype, the quintessential headmaster, the very sort of no-nonsense, bigger-than-life authority that had been presiding over boys' schooldom since Thomas Arnold cracked his cane at the Rugby School in the 1830s.

I left Cleveland and stayed away for a decade, first at college, then in New York, a brief trek through Europe and Africa, then Palm Beach, where I'd fallen in love with a local news photographer. In 1988, McKinley retired and the new headmaster, Richard A. Hawley, was installed.

Shortly thereafter, having an address of some permanence, I began to receive mail from the school which often contained quirky little essays by the new headmaster on boys and scholars and civilization. I would sit beneath a giant banyan tree on the front patio of our ramshackle, bungalowlike rental on Cocoanut Row to read them. At first I thought they were simply school boosterism, fancy, promotional, feel-good articles and inspirationals, but when they kept coming, I suspected they were something more. The new headmaster was saying some of the oddest things.

One memorable essay, delivered in morning assembly, described a US graduate named David who returned to the school briefly to teach history. Students hated him for assigning reading so abstruse that sometimes the faculty in the English department couldn't understand it. He was let go after two years for chronic absenteeism.

"David, I believe, has no money," Hawley told the assembly. "He lives in a garret room on the West Side with his books and plans." In his mid-thirties at the time, David had already written hundreds, if not a thousand pages on the Russian Front in World War II, Hawley told the school; he had finished a book-length, epic poem on what went wrong with Jefferson's democracy. Hawley often wondered how David lives, how he eats, whether or not David even has health insurance. David's story, Hawley said, "bears no relationship to the dominant types of his age." His Princeton classmates must think he has not come to much, he told the boys, but "the fact of the matter is that while he has not lived a life a late twentieth-century, middle-class person would likely imitate or even understand, it is nonetheless a life very much like those lived by the few, truly great souls we teach about in schools. It's a life rather like Socrates' or Keats's or Henry David Thoreau's or Emily Dickinson's." This headmaster of a private boys' prep school was elevating an apparent crackpot, who'd been fired from the school, to heroic proportions.

In the spring of 1989, Hawley spoke to the eighth graders graduating from the lower school to the upper school. "For all the talk about it, I really don't know what the term 'teenager' means," he told them. "I think I do know what it means to be a 'boy,' also what it means to be a 'young man' and what it means to be a 'man.' The passage from boy to young man to man is significant. Civilization depends on it. This afternoon we acknowl-edge a progressive step forward in the maintenance of our culture."

I had no idea how other people talked to a crowd of thirteen-year-olds, but Hawley was telling them that civilization depended on their gradua-tion from his school. And he *meant* it.

At another graduation, Hawley told the kids that culture doesn't typi-cally hold thirteen-year-olds in high regard. "It is really strange," he said, "that boys this age should be so regarded, as it is a time of unprecedented physical growth, of achingly intense feeling, and of astonishing capacity for new learning." He then noted some famous adolescents. Buddha and Christ, for instance, had done some fairly serious thinking as teenagers. David was an early adolescent when he slew Goliath. Juliet was thirteen and Romeo a couple years older when, Hawley said, "they commenced the most inspiring love story in the Western record. At fourteen, Mozart was an accomplished performing artist and esteemed composer. At the same age, young John Stuart Mill was one of the most acute political theorists in history." Hawley then told the boys that it's not enough to be smart—Hitler was smart. "Please remember," he concluded, "and help *us* to re-member, what smartness is for."

A few days later, he told an assembly at the upper school graduation that "we will be asking our boys—as we have asked these graduates—to align themselves with what is true; to recognize its elegance in science and mathematics; to see what is fixed and true behind so much that seems to be shifting and muddled in the news of the day."

Odd and passionate, these public addresses. To me, surrounded by tropical lushness and the decay of southern Florida, Hawley seemed a sort of reverse-image Kurtz, dispatching soulful messages from a reverse-image wilderness. Odd and presumptuous as those essays were, I found something compelling about them. Particularly when he shot off on a new, odder-still tangent: he began to argue the unlikely resolution that the boys' school was a good thing *because* it was all boys.

In 1990, he put down his views in an essay he would publish in Columbia University's *Teachers College Record.* He argued that "there are no objective data of any kind to support a negative appraisal of boys' schools *qua* boys' schools. The data suggest, if anything, the opposite conclusion."

"Structuring schools so that they realize what is deepest and truest and best in females," he continued, "is currently regarded as a progressive educational attitude. Structuring schools so that they realize what is deepest and truest and best in males is not currently regarded as a progressive educational attitude (to put it mildly)." Further addressing a political climate that railed against an oppressive patriarchal society and rampant sexism, he wrote, "Far from being the culprits, single-sex schools, as some feminists have begun to suggest, may be the way out of the trouble."

It was the early nineties and gender had become an explicit topic of the day. *Iron John* sat atop *The New York Times'* best-seller list and the William Kennedy Smith rape trial buzzed at the Palm Beach County courthouse half a mile away from my door. Guys' retreats became a fad, and *Esquire,* as ever, ran its yearly analysis of what it means to be a man in whatever year it happened to be. The very existence of the guys' retreats—a curiosity to some and an embarrassment to others—the *Esquire* features, and many of the men's-issues books all seemed founded on the same premise: that masculinity could somehow be *fashioned,* that its components could, every five years or so, be picked apart, scrutinized, then popped back together like so many Lego blocks to form a shape that would match whatever mores happened to be in vogue that day. Books and articles on gender problems accumulated. Gender, once a lowly grammatical term for nouns, had expanded into the realm of biology. In the fall of 1991, Anita Hill accused Clarence Thomas of impropriety so unbelievably lewd it would have been hilarious had it not been the business of the United States Senate and the

Supreme Court. Issues pitting men and women against each other were on broil. I headed out to my old high school to talk to Hawley to see what he had to say about gender and schools, figuring it might make a good local story with a national-issue angle.

Ann McGovern, Hawley's secretary, a stately Brit who doesn't mince words, called out "Rick" to say I'd arrived for the interview.

The headmaster who had replaced the bigger-than-life McKinley appeared at the door of his office and said, "Hi, Mikey," smiling and holding out his hand.

The new headmaster was about as unlike Rowland McKinley as anyone could be. First impressions would tell you Hawley was a very lifelike five-feet-eleven; straight dark hair with exactly the amount of gray you'd expect of a fortysomething father of three; a brainy fellow who talked too fast.

He got us both a mug of coffee from the Mr. Coffee next to the fax machine on the file cabinets behind Ann's desk.

Ann's office is all white and pulses with neon office light. The first thing you see when you enter Hawley's office is trees. The entire back wall, which runs about thirty feet, is nearly all window. You can see a four-acre, V-shaped pond called Lake Kilroy and, with the leaves off the trees, the dirt-and-gravel path to the athletic fields winding along its perimeter. At one end of his office, a desk and a maroon leather chair sit in front of shelves jammed with books, framed photographs, and students' visual-aid projects—a replica of the Rosetta stone, a medieval catapult made of balsa wood and glue, a replica of an ornamental Egyptian dagger. At the other end is what could as easily be a lunch table as a miniature conference table where Hawley's classwork piles up. The center of his office is what might be called "the Parlor"—a coffee table, a couch, three rose-colored sitting chairs, and a table lamp glowing warm and homey.

I set my mug on a coaster embroidered with the school insignia—the letter *U* superimposed over an *S* (inevitably one student or another notes that if you cut off the bottom of the *U,* a dollar sign remained)—and mumbled something about being interested to hear more about his ideas on gender and the boys' school. Before I could sit, he said gender was really important. He said it was deeper than humanity.

I asked him to expand on that last bit.

"Gender is a *big deal,*" he said, more or less hovering over me. "Gender is deeper than race, it is deeper than culture. Deeper than humanity, all the way down to plant phylum. The basic polarities of life. . . ."

Listening to Hawley, when he gets going, is like trying to speed read; you feel as if you're missing as much as you're taking in. And when he talked about gender, he could really smoke.

"It *is* a coed world, but it's not a *unisexual* world," he continued. "The fact that it is a gendered world and that genders interact differently is a very different thing than saying there's only one kind of person. There are distinctive features of each kind that have to be understood and responded to.

"Nobody likes to think about gender," he continued. "The most unnatural thing in the world is to be reflective about gender. I don't think we really like to think about ecology either. We want to breathe clean air and to have to be reflective about what seems to be innate and natural and right is a pain in the ass. The only reason we do think about ecology is because of peril. And that's the way I feel about gender."

When he moved into the subject of gender and education he spoke so fast I kept looking at my little tape recorder, half-expecting to see steam rising from it. As our time wound down, Hawley veered off the subject altogether. He didn't sound like a headmaster at all.

"Romeo wasn't *pals* with Juliet," he said. "They didn't go to *school* together. She was an amazing alien. She was an other. She was a *Beatrice*. One of the things I'm most worried about is that we're losing that wonderful discovery of the other gender, wonder and admiration and respect. That's the most profound journey in life—the finding of the other. The finding of the exquisite otherness."

Nearly two years later, shortly before his book on boys was to appear, his passion undiminished, I wrote to Hawley asking if I might spend a year at his school, attending classes, talking to people, and taking notes, with an eye toward writing about gender in an all-boy school. He wrote back to say he thought it a wonderful idea. And that, more or less, was that, though I suspect there were times when he questioned his decision. I asked a lot of questions, and at one point Nancy Lerner went to Rick and asked, "Are we supposed to tell him the *truth?*" Hawley said, "I don't *know*. I *thought* so."

Hawley may have been a little surprised, and occasionally annoyed, by my presence during some of the darker moments of the school year because he'd assumed that since I went here and liked it, I therefore thought the boys' school *qua* boys' school was good. In fact, I came with no conclusions whatsoever. Hawley was making some pretty big claims; I wanted to question those claims. And I wanted to ask my own questions. What were the societal ramifications of schooling boys together? Were boys, once they left this sheltered and comfortable boys' world, prepared for life outside it? Could I learn something about gender, about the development of boys' attitudes about themselves, specifically, and about women generally? Heated debate on how schools might be organized during a time of despair in American education had been going on for years. Could a careful, protracted scrutiny of one single-sex school address issues on how schools should or should not be structured? And finally, this: what *happens* to boys day to day when you cloister them in a school?

On September 2, 1993, I found myself in a thronged school commons on the first day of school, hundreds of boys and men smiling and greeting one another, the air buzzing and crackling with the electric adagios of the Grateful Dead.

A few minutes before 8:10, the jazz band stops playing and the speakers, hung at ceiling level above the commons, begin to blast brass marching music, "When the Saints Go Marching In," Sousa, and then Tchaikovsky's *1812 Overture*. With Pavlovian predictability, the students (myself included), file through one of four doorways into assembly. Time for school.

Morning assembly is the linchpin of the day at this school. Invariable. Bedrock. Every school day, at ten after eight, for anywhere between sixty seconds and sixty minutes, the entire school gathers for announcements, occasional addresses from the headmaster, outside speakers, or a student performance. If there are no speakers, addresses, recitals, or announcements, *that* is the announcement.

The assembly seats 454 boys and teachers in six sections; seating is assigned by class in alphabetical order. Nick Zinn has the penultimate seat in the senior section, front center, and sits beside the headmaster every day. Kris Fletcher, Tyler Doggett, and Kevin Casey find their seats almost without thinking. Freshmen fill the back ranks behind them, separated by an aisle. Above the freshmen is the technicians' booth, where boys monitor lights, microphones, and music. Four sections of sophomores and juniors flank the seniors and freshmen.

This morning, a battered upright piano has been wheeled to stage right. A podium, a modest vase of cut flowers at its base, and two captain's chairs are at center stage for Brennan and Hawley, who will sit against the background of the lowered maroon curtain. At the last minute, the aisles clogged with students moving toward their seats, Mike Logsdon, who oversees operations of the entire upper school facility, squeezes through the crowd toward the stage with an unwieldy flagpole the size of a knight's jousting lance, nearly decapitating several stragglers in his haste. It would be an awkward moment for Kerry to have the entire school stand and pledge allegiance to an empty flag stand—teenagers being particularly attuned to ironic symbolism—and Logsdon has remembered just in time.

Brennan and Hawley stride across the stage as the music fades. Brennan sets his leather duffel bag at the side of the podium. He did not begin writing his opening-day remarks until eleven last night, but as always he appears wrinkle-free. Hawley sits and Brennan takes the podium, gazes sternly to the left, to the right, taps the microphone, waits for assembly to quiet, then utters the first words of his upper school career.

"I'm not *only*," he says forcefully, *"president* of the Hair Club for Men. I'm a *client* as well."

Brennan pauses, scans the audience.

"I'm not *only* director of the upper school," he continues, "I'm a wearer of *belts,* and *shoes,* as well." He bends over his leather duffel and holds up a fistful of belts, ties, and shoes. "If anybody needs any, I've got some for you right here." He returns to the podium and says, "Good *morning."* He takes a breath as if to speak, but stifles it, turns some pages of his notes. Dimples form in his plump cheeks; still staring at his notes, he appears to chuckle.

The audience has just been clubbed into a did-I-miss-something? silence. No one expected a gag from the new director, avatar of ritual and decorum. Eventually a couple of bona fide har-hars ring out, and Brennan moves from late-night talk-show host to school administrator.

"Masters and scholars of the *largest* and most *distinguished* K-through-twelve school for boys in the United States"—apparently he can't help himself—"welcome to the opening of University School's one-hundred-fourth year." Brennan, a singer and musician, clearly loves a stage, but an eight A.M. audience of boys is not the most pliable of crowds. After his next gag, a little annoyed that he's not getting more laughs, he tells them, "You gotta be ready for these, fellas. They'll appear periodically."

All this is so new to the boys they sit through it with a kind of numb obedience. Kerry asks that all stand to pledge allegiance and sing "America the Beautiful." Brennan and Hawley really belt it out.

The rest of opening-day assembly proceeds almost perfectly. Brennan welcomes ten exchange students from Europe and thanks the boys whose families they'll be living with all year. He introduces three new teachers—a physics teacher and swim coach, a history teacher, and a classics teacher who arrives from a coed independent school in Baton Rouge. He reads off the names of new teacher apprentices, notes faculty anniversary years, summer marriages, summer accomplishments, and concludes by introducing the headmaster. But here, he commits a significant error, one not lost on Emily Morton and Nancy Lerner, who are watching from the wings of the auditorium, two of approximately ten women in the audience of 420.

"It's no surprise that Dr. Hawley has a few words of wisdom for us," Brennan says. "Nor is it a surprise, frankly, that at the end of another summer, we can announce proudly that another book, *Men Will Be Boys,* written by this most prodigious of scholars, has found its way to print and has already earned impressive praise."

Nancy and Emily turn to each other, mirror images, mouths gaping, four eyebrows high on the forehead.

Hawley takes the podium, opens a manila folder, thanks Mr. Brennan, and before moving into his address, says, "I hope this isn't churlish, but it's *Boys Will Be Men,* not *Men Will Be Boys. Men* will be *boys* . . . would be . . . um . . . a *terrifying* . . . ,*" and he mumbles into his chest. Emily turns to Nancy and says, "Yeah, but it's more often the case!" and they silently howl.

"First days," the headmaster says to the audience, "are always about getting back together, finding out your courses, for those of you who are new, establishing a map of the place and getting on with the business, and that's exciting business. In some ways, although we want so much to talk to you here this morning, that's what you're waiting for and that will certainly happen soon. But I didn't want to let this assembly go without adding—because this is the best time, really, to do it—some statement, some picture, of what we're *doing* here and what it's *for.* And I can promise you I will be brief."

This is a relief to many of the boys who have listened to the headmaster before. (Kevin Casey, speaking for most of the students, says delicately, "He tends to ramble." Many of the boys will sink in their seats, their heads falling back, eyes glazed at the ceiling, when he approaches the podium. Hawley himself knows he is sometimes speaking to cement—"You can *die* up there," he says.) Unusually, the headmaster has prepared nothing for this important day. His folder is typically stuffed with a dozen pages of handwritten, eloquently crafted words which he reads. But he and his wife, Molly, spent all night driving home from New York, having delivered their middle daughter to her first year of college, and Hawley's had no time to write a word.

"This is the one-hundred-fifth year of University School," he begins, getting the year wrong by one. "When it was formed a hundred and five years ago on Hough Avenue in the city of Cleveland, there was no other school like it in the United States, no other school like it in the world, because it was a novelty. It was a *theory*, a theory of a founding man named Newton Anderson who thought—there were at that time some great schools, not too many, great schools in this country that prepared boys and girls, some of them, in classical learning so that they could attend universities and then fulfill those sorts of positions in life that university training was necessary for—law, the clergy, medicine, engineering, and so forth. But there was no school that passed on classical learning and what we call here applied learning.

"Think of the country in 1889 if you can. Electricity was new, internal combustion was new, or just on the horizon. All the things that really determined the shape of modern life were just beginning. And this young bright engineer said, 'You can have a school in which you pass on classical learning, literature, and language and so forth, and *also* have people, boys, roll up their sleeves and *do* real things, *make* real things, make real things that *work*, and you can do that all in one setting. There can be clubs, there can be sports, you can eat together, and you can prepare for the best universities in the land without having to go away to board,' which is the way the situation had always been before. And he founded a school. He convinced the richest people in Cleveland to give him a little backing and University School began a hundred and five years ago."

Hawley reminds the boys of the school's mission. "The mission of the school," he says, "is to take boys of good to superior promise and to take them as far along their personal and intellectual and physical range as they can go." He does not complete the mission statement, the one printed in school catalogues. It makes a lot of people nervous. "We believe," the formal statement concludes, "that this is best achieved in an environment in which each boy is known and loved." The word "love" is charged, particularly at a boys' school. But the headmaster likes it. He wrote the mission statement himself.

"In some ways," Hawley continues, "you are the most privileged and fortunate high school boys in the United States. Perhaps you have read something or heard things about the condition of American education generally. It is *technically* and *officially* in *crisis*. There's never been more

24

concern and disillusionment with schools, especially at state or public schools, and no matter how little you've been paying attention, you know that this is no golden age in American education. *You* represent a very small and a very select minority. You have chosen this school, you and your families have, and we have chosen you. Even you boys who have been here before and are returning—we make an annual contract, make an annual choice. The fact that your schooling is a matter of choice is something of a novelty. It means we have a voluntary contract to do well by each other. Our part of the choice is obvious."

He wants to talk about their choice, the students' choice. He says many may have chosen the school in order to get into a good college, a valid choice. Some have chosen it because it's small, and they think they'll do better in a small school. Some have chosen it because the teaching is good.

"These are *reasons* to attend school," Hawley says, "but good as they are, they're tiny. They almost don't matter compared to what I think is the best reason for choosing this school. *Best,* but it's also a very strange reason.

"I think at the heart of things, you have chosen, or somebody has chosen, University School because it's very *hard.* Even the brightest and the highest tested students sitting out there in this audience are going to find school at some time, if not several times, *hard.* It's going to ask more of you than you think you've got sometimes. More time, more homework, more depth, more effort. You're going to be asked to serve, to help out, to clean up. You're going to be asked to behave differently in some ways than your friends elsewhere are going to have to behave, and even dress a little differently than your friends elsewhere are going to have to dress. You're going to have to do all these unusual things, make this special effort, which at various times in this year, believe me, is not going to feel easy or pleasant. And if you follow through, if you follow through on this choice that you've made, and take responsibility for it, and do it because you've chosen it and not because you have to, or somebody's making you do it, you are going to finish up with an irreplaceable and a very rare gift.

"You're going to *know,* as few other schoolchildren in the United States know, that you can do *anything.* That you can meet any challenge a college would put before you, or that a workplace would put before you, or that life itself would put before you."

The headmaster then tells the audience the story of two boys, real boys, he says, to support his claim that school is hard. One of the boys in the story left this school because it was too hard, and was glad he left; he had been an athletic and academic star at his old school, Hawley says, but here he was only average. Another boy arrived and stayed because it was hard—he too had been a star at his previous school, but the stardom had come too easily. Hawley has no intention of trying to give today's students a pep talk, because he knows most of them are already excited to see who their teachers will be and who's in their classes. If anything he's throwing out a challenge—boys want a challenge. Some of you in this audience, he implies, might very well be like the boy who didn't make it. Some of you won't be able to handle the load. Some of you are going to have to struggle to be average. It's going to be hard and you're going to want to quit. "It's going to feel," he concludes, "like you're swimming upstream."

Brennan joins in the polite applause, then returns to the podium asking for the audience's help. He wants to try something new. Something he hopes is symbolic of this "community," as he often calls it, a confirmation that this is a place of contact and intimacy. After a brief prayer in which he asks for blessings for the boys and the faculty, especially during hard times, and after the singing of the school song, "Hail, University!," all veterans, he says, will exit the auditorium; the rookies—freshmen, new members of the upper classes, and new faculty—will remain while the others form a line outside assembly. He'd wanted the line to form outdoors but, given the rain, he asks that the seniors who leave first go upstairs to the door of the lecture room. Juniors follow, and so on, until a single chain of students and faculty winds from one end of the school down the stairway, past Monkey Island and the lockers, to the front entrance doors. He then instructs each person new to the school this day to walk the line and shake every person's hand.

Individually, this idea gets mixed results. Some of the faculty think it's a little odd, wondering if it's an ominous portent of what's in store from the new director; others simply bristle. The seniors, of course, cringe at any formal, mass bonding ("You could ask them to stand in line to receive dollar bills and they'd get mad at you," says Hawley).

Even Kerry is downcast. As the boys are filing out, Hawley approaches him at the podium and before Hawley can speak, Kerry, looking down and away from the headmaster, whispers, "Kind of a downbeat ending."

"Huh?"

"Kind of a *downbeat* ending."

Hawley chuckles warmly and says, "Because there's no *hall* out there." Hawley doesn't like the lobby/party area. "At the upper school meetings, did you go through the drill with the faculty?"

Kerry shakes his head, "No, I didn't." He shakes his head again, and leaves the stage.

But this is a polite crowd and no one says a word. The assembly is eerily hushed, as hundreds of boys file out to form the chain, so that cumulatively the effect has the weight of an initiation or passage. One almost imagines it, in retrospect, to have been staged in candlelight. And no matter how limp some of the handshakes are, the students for whom this ceremony is acted out, smiling and embarrassed, seem oddly thrilled by it. Even the three new faculty members wear goofy grins as they pass down the line. Yet the chain remains, jacketed shoulder to jacketed shoulder, until each student and faculty has shaken the hand of each new member of the school. For Hawley, the ceremony has ended with liturgical force.

3

"I am the *most* uncoordinated woman in the *world*," says English teacher Nancy Lerner.

This is entirely possible, though it may just seem that way to her as she begins her third year teaching in a boys' school, where large motor skills are everywhere on view. Her claim says more about her than how far she can throw a baseball, however. Nancy speaks in absolutes; her statements have the grand, sweeping style of the literature she teaches. She is expert at raising the ordinary to a level of credible melodrama.

As the bell, a series of four and a half electronic *pings,* sounds the start of fourth period, Nancy maneuvers out of the crowded English-department office. She is dressed in a long skirt and blazer. The carpeted corridor thrums with boys heading to class, and Nancy pushes into it tugging behind her a Radio Flyer red wagon—the Mercedes Benz of the wagon industry—loaded with books, critical texts, reproductions of artwork from ancient Greece, a scarf, stacks of Xeroxes, a black cape, a hockey mask, and Fagles' translation of Aeschylus' *The Oresteia.* Her part-time schedule comprises two sections of Advanced Placement English, the room in which she teaches is fifteen feet away from the English office, and she is the only teacher in the school who requires a red wagon.

"Gentlemen, I am in a foul and wretched mood today," Nancy says. Her books land with a thump on the table and the students hush. She drops her keys—*clank*—on a stack of papers. She uses a large key ring attached to a Lucite butterfly with "Nancy" lettered on it; she loses it all the time anyway, but it's an effective silencer when dropped purposefully on tables.

Nancy sweeps her brown bangs off her forehead with the back of her hand. Her eyes are dark brown and anchored in her narrow face with a lidded depth that brings to mind the actress Susan Sarandon. It's difficult to guess Nancy's age—anywhere between thirty-seven and fifty. Her attire is elegant, conservative, professional. The students call her Dr. Lerner. "Gentlemen, I am in a *foul* and *wretched* mood today," she says. "It has nothing to do with you—but you may suffer for it."

Room 270 has recently been redecorated. The walls, once off-white institutional paneling, have been sheathed in oak. A closet has been added, and Nancy occasionally uses it to store her larger props. What appears to be another closet beside the blackboard opens onto a console containing a television and VCR. When the class moves from ancient Greece to Renaissance England, she will view *Hamlet*'s play-within-a-play scene to compare the reaction of Claudius as interpreted by several different actors, most notably—"in my opinion, a *brilliant* interpretation," she tells the seniors— the angry, combative reading by Patrick Stewart (this before he assumed the helm of the starship *Enterprise*).

In the center of the long, rectangular room, five wood tables have been pushed together to create an island around which the students tilt in their captain's chairs. Built out from the walls are oak benches for extra seating; these run the length of the classroom, from either closet to the windows at the far end. The back wall is nearly all glass and looks down on a small courtyard.

This is also the room in which Hawley teaches philosophy. The headmaster had for years coveted the room of a teacher at Hathaway Brown (a nearby "sister" school), one with the ornate warmth of a Cambridge tutorial chamber. Hawley wanted his school to have at least one room whose interior was commensurate with the study of Greek philosophy, Aeschylus, or Shakespeare, and he was so intent on getting it right that he sent a photographer to Hathaway Brown to capture images of the room from which the carpenter-designer would work. He had in mind a room worthy of the students who would inhabit it for a full year, students who were enrolled in one of the most advanced humanities courses offered by the school—the joint AP English/Philosophy course. Only these students would be assigned to this room. It would be perfect. The walls themselves would almost exhale knowledge and truth.

Due to intricate scheduling requirements, language-department chairman Roger Yedid, who's in charge of matching 370 students to appropriate classes, and appropriate classes to appropriate rooms, has created in Room

270 one of the most trafficked areas in the school. Hawley grimaces when he enters the room and stoops over scraps of paper. Tattered notebooks and paperbacks are abandoned by juniors. Even Nancy, whom Hawley esteems like no other colleague, occasionally brings to the room vegetables and tree branches. This was not what Hawley had in mind, but after the initial shock and peevishness inevitable upon recognizing flawed excellence, he has taken it well. Now, flawed or not, it is referred to not as Room 270, but rather as "Hawley's Room."

The most uncoordinated woman in the world has an agile, improvisational classroom style. During the past fourteen years she's taught hundreds of students in both public and private high schools and has learned to move to the students' rhythms, to direct them forward by using their questions and responses as a springboard to plunge deeper into a text. She tells the class she's not an entertainer, but she can even use an interruption to great theatrical effect. Ken Sable, the boy who records fourth-period attendance each day, knocks on the door to Room 270 on the day of Nancy's foul and wretched mood and pokes his head in. Nancy turns and, with a sweep of her bangled left arm, shouts, "Be gone! Avast thee!" The boy, bowing his head, backs away, closing the door as he disappears. Nancy drops her gaze to the books before her and says softly, "I don't even know his *name,* and I'm *terrible* to him."

Nick Zinn sits immediately to her left, watching this scene. He's rocking back and forth, and side to side, rather like a barge on a choppy sea. Without speaking, he's creating an isolated disturbance.

Nancy turns to Nick, her mouth open, then says, "The more you go on with these *windy suspirations* of *forced* breath . . . ," and that is all it takes to raise a self-conscious smile from Nick. He leans back in his chair, becalmed for the moment.

Most of the eighteen students in this class stick to general areas of the room. The wildly opinionated Tyler Doggett sits somewhere to Nancy's direct right, leaning forward on his elbows, tugging the T-shirt beneath his button-down over his mouth, brooding. Kris Fletcher is at the back tilting against the window, silent and wary. Mike Cohen, Ryan Alexander, Wilkie McKelvey are also at the back. Always in the middle is Philipp Hanfland, an exchange student from Bonn, Germany. Jason Koo, head cocked to the side and staring inscrutably at a blank page of his spiral notebook, sits middle left. Across from him, middle right, low in his seat and tucked up to his chest at the table, is Viswam Nair. Igor Lyubashevskiy, who arrived in the States from Kiev less than two years ago, sits on either side of the room, but always at a latitude close to Nancy, as does Eugene Gurarie, another native of the Ukraine who arrived in the States about the same time as Igor. Eugene usually sits across from Igor, which lends an even keel to the Ukrainian influence.

While many many boys sit silently, whether pushed up to their chests at the tables or feet crossed on top, tilting back, hands behind their head, the cumulative feel of a classroom of boys compared with a classroom of girls is tangible. During the year, I visited classes at other schools; one class was the AP English class at Hathaway Brown, held in the very room Hawley had tried to re-create in this room—a girls' equivalent to this class. There, girls filed into the room and took their seats quietly, arranged their books and notebooks and pens before them just so, sat straight with even intervals between them; they appeared ready to work, their gazes directed immediately at the teacher; what conversation there was was subdued. Perhaps they were on their best behavior for a visitor, but I don't imagine they ever fill a room the way these boys do. Boys take up as much space as possible. Indeed, this difference in how boys and girls fill space played out almost in caricature during singing auditions for Carol Pribble's spring musical later in the year. Pribble's custom is to bring groups of five into the empty auditorium, alternating boys and girls to reduce audition jitters. As group after group entered, the boys draped themselves across the entire first two rows of the center section, arms taking up seats on either side, legs slung over back rests; the girls invariably packed themselves side by side, elbow to elbow and perfectly straight, into the same five seats in the back row of this section.

Nick Zinn is an extreme example of how a boy uses space. Nick always sits in the same chair, almost hanging on Nancy's left arm. Or if it's Tuesday-Thursday philosophy, on Hawley's left arm. Nick is rarely still in this seat beside the teacher. He lists to the right, he lists to the left. He taps his heel rapidly on the floor. He heaves and sways and lurches as though the chair is too small for him, too tight, too confining. If Nick arrives late and someone is already in his customary spot, he says, "Hey, you're in my seat." Most times the trespasser moves, but the once or twice that he doesn't, Nick tilts his head from side to side, a shrug begins low in his wide back and rolls like a wave cresting at his shoulders, and he says something that requires a lot of breath like *"Geeeez"* or "All right, all right, shhhh," and takes the next closest seat to the front.

No matter which seat he is in, though, Nick is always ready with a comment the moment Nancy walks through the door. He is so relentless that one morning, Nancy simply looks up at the class and says, "Why are *men* so difficult?"

"Why are you making a generalization about m-m-men?" Nick responds. "Why don't you say, 'W-w-why is Nick so difficult?' "

"That was my *next* question."

Nick smiles, heaves, and rocks in a cloud of sibilant suspirations.

Nancy has begun the fall term with García-Márquez's *Chronicle of a Death Foretold,* and will move from that into a close reading of Aeschylus' *The Oresteia,* which takes its characters and events from Homer and is considered to be among the first tragedies written. She chose *Chronicle* because, she says, "It provided the springboard. I felt I could go from this behavior in one community in the modern world in Latin America back to ancient Athens."

If she has any problem with *The Oresteia,* it's that she loves it too much. "I'm *insane* about this stuff," she says. "I could stay in *every* line." When she reads to the class, for instance, *"And once he slipped his neck into the noose of fate,"* one feels that she truly could spend all semester on just that line, following myriad tributaries throughout the whole of Western literature. The text is also appropriate for seniors because, as she puts it, "this stuff nails the adolescent sensibility." On another level, she loves the story because, she tells the class, "sexual roles and gender questions permeate the whole play." Having taught both coed classes and boys' classes, she's fascinated by questions of gender. She reads to the class a description of Clytemnestra, who kills her husband Agamemnon, king of the Greeks, when he returns from the Trojan war: " 'And she maneuvered like a man.' What is he saying about gender?" she asks the class. *The Oresteia* also allows for effective class participation in the acting out of various scenes.

When she asks for volunteers to read the part of Clytemnestra, Mike Cohen, one of the more experienced actors in the school, raises his hand. Mike is a stocky boy with short, dark, wavy hair, and is one of the most ebullient presences in the class. Through fall and the endless winter, he remains the daily embodiment of cheerful willingness; even when he's mad, it seems his happy choice to be that way. Nancy gathers the hockey mask, scarf, and cape from her wagon. Mike accepts the garb gladly, dons cape, slips on the mask, ties the scarf like a babushka over his head, grabs his book, and stands on one of the wall benches to read aloud, gesticulating with his free arm, though he has a bit of trouble because he's wearing glasses which are ill-accommodated by a hockey mask. When he finishes, Nancy says to the class, "You're getting to be *good* Greek actors." For

Mike, she adds a special compliment. "You make a wonderful queen," she tells him.

"Thank you," he says, returning to his seat against the window.

"And, you look *good* in a scarf."

"Oh," he says, surprised. "Thank *you.*"

For all her skill at making opaque texts not only understandable to teenagers but also drawing shrewd parallels between ancient literature and her students' lives, and for all her obvious adoration of the students—sometimes, when she talks of them, her dark eyes sparkle with tears—Nancy is not happy this fall. The emotional and physical demands of teaching, combined with the time it devours, are wearing on her. She doesn't have enough time for her husband. She doesn't have enough time for herself. There's so much yet to read. When she took this job two years ago, it was to be part-time only; she intended to spend the afternoons grading papers and reading. Her daughters are grown and her husband makes a comfortable living as an interventional radiologist, so she doesn't have to work at all. Yet her colleagues have watched her parlay this part-time schedule into a full-time job.

The most time-consuming task for Nancy is grading papers. She assigns a lot of them to her thirty-eight students and because she allows them as many as three rewrites, grading and regrading and discussing them line by line with the boys can result in as much as eighty hours of work a month, in addition to teaching, preparing for each class, grading tests and quizzes, Xeroxing, and miscellaneous school duties. Students call her at home at night and on the weekend to ask questions and beg extensions. When she sleeps, she dreams she is teaching.

As Nancy tells her classes, in-depth reading of *The Oresteia* is not to teach them about some Greek myth, "it's to give you a reading experience that will allow you to read *anything* this way, to plumb it to its depths." "Are you reading this?" she asks on a day when the boys' attention seems to flag. "If you can read *Hamlet* and Aeschylus you can read anything. But this isn't easy. The language has to be *penetrated.*" She reels off a train of simple-sounding sentences. " 'I shall in all my best obey you, madam.' 'So much for him.' 'A little more than kin and less than kind.' 'Nay, madam, I know not *seems.*' " She tries to show there's gold in these lines if they're prepared to dig. It has recently occurred to her that Shakespeare's most potent lines are monosyllabic, and her most effective argument in teaching them that there is reading and there is *reading* lies in one of the most famous lines ever uttered on stage. It has been attempted by thousands of actors, by

Barrymore and Olivier, Derek Jacobi and Kevin Kline. Yet it's rarely delivered in exactly the same way, so deep and subtle are its nuances. Six one-syllable words—two of which are repeats, and none of which is more than three letters long—form what may be the most celebrated line in all of Western literature. She speaks the words for them, as blandly and as monotonously as possible, without inflection, and with long, even spaces between each word: "To . . . be . . . or . . . not . . . to . . . be." She halts, scans the faces of her students, and repeats it: "To . . . be . . . or . . . not . . . to . . . be." And again. She then asks each person in the class, starting with Tyler Doggett on her right, to recite this potent, four-word combination, without repeating it once. They are able to accomplish this without too much difficulty, though a couple try twice and thrice before hitting on a meaning no one else has offered.

It's this same attention that she wants them to bring to their own writing, and thus she reads rewrite after rewrite. When they succeed, when in class they penetrate a text, she can say to them honestly, "Do you realize what an incredible level of reading you're doing? I was just beginning to do what you're doing beginning *graduate* school." And you can see the boys smile.

When she returns papers, and she's not pleased, she tells them so. She announces that "those of you who have abandoned the apostrophe, ended the career of the semi-colon," did not do well. She then brings up the word *plagiarism,* the thievery of ideas from critical texts without attribution, she says. "I'm an absolute *demon. Be paranoid* about plagiarism."

Depending on the mood of the class, she's just as likely to use a drastically different tone when talking about an essay assignment, this one a personal essay of their choice; people have been asking her how long it should be. "You've all heard the old male-faculty miniskirt response to that? No? 'Essays should be like miniskirts—short enough to be interesting, long enough to cover the subject.' " The class laughs, but she doesn't; she seems momentarily annoyed, and adds, "A feminist shouldn't say that, though I suppose there's a grain of truth in it."

When asked about this remark after class, she explains, "I'm a feminist in that I believe in equality, but I'm not militant." She adds, "I'm more of a humanist." At her last school, she offered a women-in-literature course, but she found it limiting, in large part because only girls signed up for it. She is a teacher and scholar who has taken the recent politicizing of the Western canon seriously, and found it tiresome.

"If I stopped and addressed every feminist issue we'd never get through anything." And if they avoided everything that has, she says, "an un-PC slant—Eliot's anti-Semitism, Shakespeare's misogyny—I'd have to throw out all of culture. I can only teach literature as literature. I've seen enough great literature get lost."

When I approached Nancy, asking to sit in on her classes, she said, "Sure."

This preliminary meeting took place, not unsurprisingly, at the copying machine in the administrative wing, actually a peninsula of offices in the center of the second floor of the building, a central command post. Nancy has a preternatural affinity for paper and staples, and she runs her days according to the principle why-do-two-things-at-once-when-you-can-do-three-things-at-once, so as she dealt various pages to the machine, loaded an empty tray with paper, and pressed buttons, we talked. I mentioned my interest in the boys' school.

"It's like walking into an alien *world*," she said with a grin. "Boys are *different*."

When I brought up her boss, she said without hesitation, "Rick is formidable. *ForMIDable*." She admitted that were it not for Hawley, she might never have surprised herself and taken a job at a boys' school in the first place. But this headmaster was like no other school administrator she'd encountered. He was foremost a committed teacher, but he was also a scholar who could match her level of discourse on literature, as well as a writer she admired. From these shared passions, a friendship grew; throughout the school year, she and the headmaster would talk for hours, during school and after, about nothing but books and students.

Hawley had explained to the faculty who I was and what I would be doing, and Kerry Brennan had introduced me to the entire school at morning assembly, so I assumed that everyone was clear about why I was here. But when Nancy asked me to stand and tell her class about myself and about my work, and I detailed my intent, she felt a serious jolt of surprise: *Wrong, not in my class, not this year, last thing I need, somebody chronicling my bad-hair days, I'm swamped as it is with obligations I didn't choose.*

As it had happened, she was not at the aforementioned faculty meeting and assembly, and thus had no idea what I was doing at this school when she said "sure"; she figured I was interested in teaching and wanted to observe some of the veterans.

After class, she suggested we have lunch.

■ ■ ■

We planned to meet at a place called The Cheese Cellar in an upscale mall a couple miles from the school. Nancy was late. This unsettled me somewhat because she'd hinted that this was to be a sort of Dear John lunch, and hers was one class I was especially interested to watch. I knew already that she was widely admired by the students. She was one of five faculty who have doctoral degrees and is the only female Ph.D. There are a total of three women who teach in the five major academic departments, and the other two, who double as administrators, teach only one section each (psychology and math). I believed it important to watch a class of boys taught by a woman; in an English class, issues of gender relations, romantic and sexual love, and student attitudes would be close to the surface. Since I had already arranged to sit in on Hawley's philosophy course, it made sense to watch the other half as well. Furthermore, Nancy was a veteran of three different types of schools: public, coed private, and boys' private. She could bring some perspective to my return to this all-boy school.

I studied my watch and made periodic, lost-look cruises through the restaurant to make sure she wasn't already seated, wondering if Nancy would throw a wrench into my plans.

She pushed through the glass doors of the mall carrying what seemed to me at the time a purse the size of a small suitcase, apologized for being late, and said she'd have to leave early because she was meeting her husband. We were seated in a booth in the dimly lighted restaurant and, after ordering, she launched immediately into why she didn't want me sitting in on her classes. "I'm not a representative teacher. I'm only part-time." Second, she already had so many demands on her time, time that the school would continue to squeeze out of her, including Bob Davis, a teacher apprentice working toward his master's degree and sitting in on her classes for the first trimester and for whom she acts as teacher-counselor-mentor. It's disruption enough to have one non-student in her classes—I was asking to be the second, and she saw me as yet another obligation. "I've already accepted this committee because of one charismatic man," she said, referring to Hawley. "If I can't go to the orchestra some night, or just be with my husband, because of another . . ."

Nancy's absolutes and extremes extend to flattery as well, and I did my best to explain that not only was I not charismatic, but also that I would be all but invisible in her classroom. Invisibility was the goal. I wanted the students, and her, to forget I was there. I wanted only to observe. It was not her time I required.

Oddly, then, she segued into a story. In conversation, Nancy seems to be exhaustively discursive, moving from one subject to the next with no apparent motive or end in sight; gradually, though, one begins to sense a complexity at work as a series of unrelated topics forms a cohesive web noticed only after it's been spun. So, when she began to tell me about an education conference a couple years ago, it seemed at first to be an extended non sequitur.

Her story concerned a national meeting of the Independent Schools of the Central States, held in Cleveland, where hundreds of teachers and administrators gathered to talk about school. The speaker was Samuel Freedman, who'd recently published *Small Victories*, a highly regarded book about a crowded school in the Lower East Side squalor of New York City and a remarkable teacher who worked there. Freedman, a former *New York Times* reporter, is a good writer, an even better journalist, and given his recent immersion in school, promised to be a galvanizing speaker.

He was, too, but not for the planned reasons. This conference was to be a boost, a cumulative applause for these teachers' and administrators' hard and diligent work, and a penetrating conversation on ways to make that work even more fruitful. Freedman had just spent a year in a decaying high school in which the kids struggled to surmount unbelievable hardships— lethal crime; poverty; many were without adult family; the school building was a wreck, the neighborhood choked with drugs and gangs—odds none of the teachers at this conference could possibly understand. They were private-school people, teaching privileged children in lush surroundings. And here came Freedman, who'd spent a year of his life living in the war zone of a depleted inner-city school.

Nancy recalled Freedman, and his words, as clear as yesterday:

"He got up there and said, 'I don't know *why* I'm here. I don't know why you *invited* me. I don't know why I *accepted*. You are putting *caviar* on a table that's already *full*.' "

Nancy paused, then ground her fist into her chest. "Those words twist in me like a *blade*."

Here was a woman who loved teaching, who adored her students and adored the man who was her boss, and who clearly loved the school where she now worked, yet she still felt something was seriously wrong. When I asked her about this, she responded, *"Yes, I feel guilty. People are starving."*

So here was a deeper reason for not wanting me to sit in on her classes: she did not want even to be noticed.

Nancy's not morose about the guilt—most of the time she's too exhausted to let it bother her—and she's not a poser, styling herself as secretly racked by self-recriminations that she is not working for the good of society. In lighter moments she can say to herself it's all right to teach in this privileged world because, "while I'm here, my husband is saving lives in the real world." But a thorn exists nonetheless and, as she told me at lunch, she often thinks that her career might have been better spent teaching in the inner city, where the effects on students can be more profound. There are plenty of excellent teachers willing to teach at private schools, far fewer willing to endure the struggle of inner-city teaching and inner-city problems. Yet she knew if she had chosen this, she would have been teaching, on the whole, kids who were less talented than those at Shaker Heights High, Hawken, or US, less dedicated, and that she would do less teaching and more disciplining. At bottom, one simple, inexorable need ruled her decision: "I *had* to have Shakespeare."

The conversation grew increasingly elliptical after that. She spoke of the school and its demands, various faculty and students.

Jim Lester, she said, recently missed two of her classes, and this pissed her off. Jim, by his own admission, is something of a wild man among the seniors, prone to taking risks without much thought. This past summer, for instance, he was at a concert at Blossom Music Center, an expansive outdoor theater with a towering band shell that spreads out over the stage and 5,200-seat auditorium. Jim convinced a couple of his buddies to distract the nearby guards. They did and Jim scampered up the huge steel girder of the band shell on to the sloping roof, whose lip descends to about sixty feet above the audience. Jim then began to jump and dance as the crowd below, reclining on blankets across the lawn, cheered. Security eventually convinced Jim to descend and escorted him out of the park. The following spring, he would spend a night in jail for dashing into the outfield of Jacobs Field during an Indians game.

That sort of cavalier behavior is all very interesting outside Nancy's class, but when you blow off two consecutive AP English periods and thus miss being placed in a group that's required to give a presentation, and furthermore do nothing to fix the problem, Nancy's going to take it personally. She told Jim he would now read the entire *Oresteia*, all three books, and give an *individual* presentation to the class. Jim was mad and sulked away. Nancy cooled off and reconsidered. She'd been way too hard on Jim and tracked him down the next day to say, "Jim, you don't have to present on the whole thing, just part of it, and I've got some articles on it if you need help." Nancy smiled as she recalled this. He looked her dead in the face and said, "No, I can do it." Jim was defiant. He wasn't going to let anyone tell him something was too hard, that he couldn't handle it. She adored this defiance, the insistence on accepting a challenge.

The conversation circled through many students—all of the stories pointing up her contention that the all-boy school tolerates the eccentric student far better than did coed schools where she'd worked—until Nancy realized that she'd have to rush to meet her husband. Nothing more had been said regarding my place in her class. I paid the check and hustled with her to the parking lot. As she stood at the door of her car, fishing for her keys, I nearly said, "Well? Do I pass?" I didn't need to, as it turned out. She looked at me, rolled her eyes, and shook her head at the car. She disappeared into her white Toyota and zoomed out of the parking lot, thinking, *And he's made me late besides.*

Thus I would sit in on Nancy's classes, which met Monday, Wednesday, and Friday during fourth and fifth periods—on a normal schedule, from 11 to 12:20. I sat in the same spot every day, off to the side perched on the room-length bench built out from the wall. I never spoke unless Nancy addressed me directly which, on occasion, she did, typically asking me to confirm what she'd just claimed colleges would expect of students in the way of reading and writing. I would nod, and she would carry on.

After our lunch, my desire to watch her teach boys had increased. This was partly because of her answer when I asked why she was a teacher.

"I went into teaching because I had to live with literature and discuss literature," she said, "and where was I going to do it?" There were no jobs available at colleges in town when she completed her dissertation in 1976, and family rooted her in Cleveland. "But I had no idea I would like kids," she continued, "let alone teenagers. Then one day about a month after I started teaching at Shaker, I was walking through the hall and I had this epiphany. It was literally as if the sky opened up and I thought, 'Oh my *God,* I *love* them.' And I never knew that.

"I adored *them,*" she went on. "It wasn't just the literature. I adored *them.* . . . I regard it as—don't tell Rick this—a *gift* from *God* that has nothing to do with me." She laughed as if she herself couldn't believe it. "I just loved them. I swear to God. In a crowded, mobbed, hallway with noisy teenagers. When I first got to Shaker I thought the noise levels in the hallways would do me in. But, it's always been true."

Almost hidden in this reason was something revealing. "Don't tell Rick this." More than the reason she didn't want me to tell him—"he'll say it proves I believe in God"—was that, first, she cared one way or another what he thought, and second, that he was so close to the surface of her thoughts that when she described the epiphany that has driven her career, Hawley was somehow interwoven with it.

This, I was beginning to understand, was the nature of the headmaster. He wasn't omnipresent in the thoughts of Nancy Lerner alone, but in every teacher at the school, in every crevice of the building itself. You could like and admire Hawley, it seemed, or you could hate Hawley, but you could not dismiss him. Nancy, of course, went further: "Rick is my Oedipal father," she told me, rather matter-of-factly.

During a year in Nancy's classroom, even on her foulest and most wretched days, her gift, as she calls it, never failed her once. It was in this classroom that I sat, one Tuesday, expecting Hawley to stride in with his books saying, "OK men!," when Nancy appeared instead, explaining that she was unprepared but Dr. Hawley was out of town and had asked that she take his class. As headmaster, Hawley is out of town about once a month at conferences and tending to administrative obligations. He tries to schedule trips on non-teaching days, but when this can't be done, such as today, a day in early November, when he is in Chicago keynoting an alumni gathering to raise money for the school, he asks Nancy to flip-flop and she always obliges.

She arrives with a stack of Xeroxes and begins handing them out. She wants to give the kids a break from the syllabus but at the same time keep them on track, and she's chosen a twentieth-century link to the ancient literature they've been moving through all fall. She's decided on two poems by Yeats—"Leda and the Swan" and "The Second Coming," works they'll need to have under their belts when they take the Advanced Placement exam in the spring.

"Leda and the Swan" is particularly apt, as it describes the mythical act that set in motion all the events they're currently reading about—the birth of Helen, whose capture ignites the Trojan war, which leads to Agamemnon's murder upon his victorious return. According to myth, this historical drama was set in motion by a rape Yeats describes in his poem about Zeus, who transforms himself into a swan to have his way with the mortal Leda.

Nancy asks the class to read the poem first, and then, not entrusting her favorite works to the unsteady cadences of the students, she reads it aloud. *"How can those terrified vague fingers push the feathered glory from her loosening thighs? And how can body, laid in that white rush, but feel the strange heart beating where it lies?"* When she finishes, she asks, "Now, who can analyze this poem?"

There's a moment of silence, and Ryan tentatively begins, "It's a very sexual poem."

"We use the word sexual a lot," Nancy says, "but what's the particular quality of this poem?"

Slowly the kids warm up, talk openly about the sexual nature of the event. Ryan maintains that the poem is terribly violent; so violent in fact that he can't understand why Nancy even likes it. "What do you find beautiful about it?" he asks.

Nancy, seated at the head of the class, *Norton Anthology of Poetry* dangling from a hand resting on her crossed leg, is taken aback. She's unprepared to defend the beauty of the poem in which Leda is violated and dropped indifferently to the ground. She takes a stab at describing what she had thought was self-evident, but the boys are skeptical. " 'The great wings,' " she says. " 'The dark webs.' 'The feathered glory.' " She pauses for a moment. "I don't know *why* I think it's so beautiful. I think it's the most sensual poem I've ever read. Do you know the difference between sensual and sensuous?"

No one ventures an answer. Nancy explains, but the boys remain stuck on the fact that this is quite frankly a rape. "It's chaotic and violent," Ryan continues.

Scott Seidelmann agrees: "It is a violent act."

Nancy remains surprised by their response, how they've stuck on the literal event. She wants to show them that it's more than a rape. "In Yeats' hands," she says, "it's not a rape by a highwayman or a brute. It's a sacred, violent, epiphanal moment in which the course of a great war and the fall of the Trojan civilization is all but guaranteed. *'A shudder in the loins engenders there,'* " she reads, *'the broken wall, the burning roof and tower and Agamemnon dead.'* "

A soft knock sounds at the door. Nancy turns abruptly to find Ken Sable, poking a sheepish head in, wanting attendance. "I have *no* idea," she says, and returns to the poem.

Ryan asks, "Are you saying, like, he did her a favor, almost?"

Nancy sighs, starts at the beginning and runs through the poem stanza by stanza in a valiant attempt to separate this from a made-for-TV melodrama. In her hands the sexual violence isn't the crass description of a woman's defilement because, with body and voice, Nancy conveys her personal love of the material directly to the students, and they respect the material absolutely because of this. Even the potential booby trap of the line *laid in that white rush*—how easily an adolescent wheeze might make something of that in a class of boys—is scrutinized beyond what is explicit. They wouldn't think of venturing a crude remark, not aloud anyway, and yet they want to talk about it, analyze it, are excited by the poem.

What is also apparent in a single-sex classroom—and during this class particularly—is that the students respond to the teacher as if it is a one-on-one situation. Sociologists who have studied the male-female dynamics of coed classrooms have noted that boys tend to shout out answers, demand a teacher's attention, posture before the class, and that girls often yield to the elbowing boys and suppress comments for fear of appearing too brainy. In Nancy's class—indeed, in all the single-sex classes I watched—the students directed questions to the teacher all but regardless of their peers. Hawley had told me that his goal in each class he teaches is to have at least one eye-to-eye exchange with every student in the room; this is possible because the kids are trained on him and not on each other. The main disadvantage of the single-sex classroom, of course, is that boys and girls together would approach "Leda and the Swan" differently and, ostensibly, learn more about each other in discussing the poem. Would their questions and responses, though, be screened, the discussion more careful, less open, less charged? Were there girls in this classroom, Ryan would likely have screened his question. But when Ryan does ask such a question, one that's dangerously off the mark no matter how ingenuous his reasons might have been, Nancy can address it immediately, steer the class in the right direction. Here the boys continue to cling to the facts, down to Nancy's discussion of the final line, *Before the indifferent beak could let her drop?*

"So you're saying he just orgasmed, and that's *it?*" Eric Hermann blurts out, his eyes wide, almost disbelieving.

"Well," Nancy answers, "those great, epiphanal moments end. They must end." She thinks for a moment and asks the class, "What matches the ecstasy of a great sexual union?"

Kris Fletcher has so far remained silent. Often he doodles in his notebook during class or composes lyrics to heavy-metal songs. At Nancy's question, though, Kris looks up. *"Skydiving,"* he says with a grin. "Bungee jumping."

"Right," Nancy says, rolling her eyes. "Leda and the Bungee Jumper."

■ ■ ■

No one who knows Kris would call him the typical US boy. No one ever defines this species exactly, yet everyone seems to know what it is; at least, when a student says, "you know, your typical US boy"—a phrase invariably uttered with ironic disdain—he assumes you know what he's talking about. There's even a bronze statue in the entrance to the lower school *called* "The US Boy."

In 1893, four years after the school opened, the art teacher, or master, Herman Matzen, created a life-sized plaster figure of a boy dressed in a short tunic and leather thongs lashed at the ankles—the uniform of a young athlete in ancient Greece. The right hand grips a large stone-carver's hammer; the left rests on a scroll beside an oil lamp. While its accoutrements are symbolic of the principles on which the school was founded—athletics, manual labor, and scholarly pursuit—the figure was modeled on an actual boy, the first boy enrolled in the school, and the first graduate of the school to graduate from college. He played baseball and football. In a school with a capacity enrollment of two hundred, he was elected not only president of the first graduating class, but also vice-president, secretary, and treasurer. His name was James Goodwillie. Evelyn Waugh could not have thought of a better name for a boys' school emblem. It's a handsome statue by classical standards, yet not twenty-five years after its creation, its importance in the eyes of the school had diminished; it stood, rather more in storage than in view, beneath the balcony in the main assembly hall until 1956, when school alumni had it cast in bronze and moved to its current post. James Goodwillie would have been eighty then, had he not died of pneumonia at age twenty-six.

The statue is a century old when Kris Fletcher claims that bungee jumping matches the ecstasy of a great sexual union. Goodwillie himself, if he returned today, likely would be just as surprised to find his form immortalized in bronze in the lower school's entrance as he would be to learn that people now attach themselves to elastic cords and fling themselves from high places for fun. But such contrasts between the old and new, tradition and fad, create a tension, a tautness, in the life of the school that prevents staleness and rot. This notion of buffing a century of tradition was in fact symbolically enacted when four zealous middle-schoolers on work detail approached the statue. The statue had over the years developed a rich ebony hue creased with verdigris—a beautiful façade that took years to

43

achieve—and the boys scrubbed young Goodwillie till he shone like a newly minted penny.

Kris echoes many students here when he says he likes going to an all-boy school, though his belief that it's "an incredible opportunity" is somewhat stronger than most. A majority at US, not surprisingly, will tell you they would rather have girls here; but this desire decreases with age. Seventh- and eight-graders would kill to have girls here. When asked, freshmen generally say that, if you put it like that, well then, of course we'd rather have girls here. For a seventh-, eighth-, or ninth-grader to say that he prefers not to have girls here would be a potentially dangerous comment. But as the students grow, their craving to be in school with girls is less pronounced. Not every student wants to be here; I talked with some who said they were here only because their parents made them go. The majority, however, seemed to value the school more than they desired girls in the school. There were two ways to ask this question: "Would you rather US were coed?," or, "Would you rather be going to a coed school?" The responses again were in favor of the school over its gender policy, even though given their druthers, they'd rather have girls around. It's important to remember that this is not a boarding school miles from civilization. They see girls all the time. US is a day-school; boys go home to their families, their sisters, they meet girls after school; Kris, for instance, sees Kathleen every day on the Rapid, though he's still more or less watching from a distance.

Furthermore, any talk about the school's actually going coed ended long ago, and the subject is rarely discussed among students or faculty, especially with Hawley going great guns about the all-boy institution.

It's impossible to know the sort of student Kris would be in a coed school. I'd be surprised, though, if he'd have much energy for girls at all. Most days, he's exhausted even as he leaves morning assembly. Most days, he has not a single period free. Given his twice daily crosstown commute, Kris's school day is longer than that of most students. This, too, parallels tradition. In 1890, the school day ran from 8:45 to five, apparently an unusual practice at the time. Today, athletes typically don't finish their day before six. An athlete acting in one of the three plays produced during the year won't finish till after nine.

Following his two-hour commute and morning assembly, Kris pushes through the mobbed senior lounge to his locker, which he shares with his friend Tim Watkins, loads books into his backpack, and jostles through the doors, beneath a sign reading "Designated Smoking Area"—the school suspends anyone caught smoking—to Doc Strater's Latin 4-5 class. Doc, a thirty-year veteran who spent most of his career in a public school, is Kris's favorite teacher, so this is a good way to start the day.

The door to the classroom is locked and Kris waits. His friend, Tyler Soltis, the other Tyler of the senior class, meets him here. Tyler, a bit on the chubby side, has short dark hair and wears glasses. He's manic, and often seems ready to explode.

"I can't be*lieve* it," he's saying.

Kris asks, "What?"

Tyler is staring incredulously at an essay he's just gotten back from Mr. Garrett. "He says it's the best writing I've done all year," Tyler tells Kris. "I wrote it at three in the morning." Students do this often—denigrate their effort in something they've been marked well on; conversely, when they've gotten a bad grade on a paper, they tend to say, "But I really tried. This one I worked hard on."

"Three in the *morning,*" Tyler repeats.

"Wired on coffee," Kris says.

"Well, *yeah.*" Tyler stares at his paper, an essay on citizens' right to free speech, as though it's a mirror. He's made twenty-seven copies of it, and plans to expand it for entry in the annual political essay contest.

English teacher Kevin Kay opens the classroom door which has been locked since the night before, and several boys file in. Tyler takes his seat in the back row but notices the empty blackboard.

"What should I write?" he says, and then, ah-ha—he seizes the chalk: "Looooook Ooooooout!!! Kris Fletche is now driving." He's still writing when Doc waddles in with his battered briefcase and sets it on the desk. *"Good* morning, Tyler," says Doc.

"Good morning, Doc."

Doc stares at the blackboard. "Mr. Fletcher is a *driver,*" he says.

Tyler runs back to the board having forgotten the "R" in Kris's last name as Doc wanders the room, starring the boys' daily homework assignment so that he knows, when they're handed in at the end of class, they were not completed during class.

"Everybody in here is above average," says Doc, continuing the rounds.

"If everybody is above average," Kris says, "where do we get the average?"

"Ah, figure that out," Doc responds, and chuckles.

"That's a question for your sophists club," says Tyler.

Doc sits at the desk in front of the blackboard and delivers a brief preamble on the Catullus poem they're reading, then says, "Mr. Fletch, would you read the first line?"

Kris would have second period free, but as part of his financial-aid deal, he works in the library, first sensitizing books so that they'll set off an alarm if someone tries to sneak one past the electronic gates, and then shelving books with call numbers ranging from 306 through 399—books whose titles include *Schools for All, Education in America, The Politics of Guaranteed Income, The Right to Lifers, Chemical Dependency: Opposite Viewpoints,* and *The Environmental Interest.* He'd much rather be in the lower stacks with Freud and science fiction, but the choice wasn't his. Last year his job was attendance taker. His brother Nick sets lunch tables in the dining room.

Kris arrives in the library as usual except that today he has to clear something with the librarians, Polly Cohen and Frances Hanscom, who work at desks in a glassed-in office area overlooking the group-study tables. He must apologize—he didn't show up yesterday second period. "I was taking my driving test," he tells them.

"Oh," says Frances, with maternal interest.

Polly, who, after twenty years here, knows boys and speaks her mind, says, "Uh oh, another *maniac* on the road."

"Did you pass?" asks Fran.

"Yes."

"Are you going to be a *good* driver?"

"Yeah," says Kris, and gathers a stack of newspapers and magazines that need to be reshelved. Kris is seventeen. He's put off this test, the once quintessential rite of passage for American teenagers, because, he explains, "I was afraid to fail." The drawbacks of waiting were small; he doesn't have a car and usually one of his friends does. The rest of the time, he's a public transportation guy. Also, waiting a year had one small, bright shimmer of good fortune. He took driving classes over the summer. For the first class, he rushed home from his job to shower and wash his hair. He knew another student driver would be in the car. Maybe, just maybe, this fellow student driver would be a girl, and just maybe she'd be cute. It was worth it to hustle home, shower, and put on clean clothes even though he knew it was a long shot he'd have any luck. The car arrived at his house, he hopped in the front seat, and there, in the back, was Kathleen, a junior at Hathaway Brown, the girl he'd been watching on the Rapid for two years now, the girl who lightened his dreary commute each day simply by boarding the train.

They became, he thinks, good friends, but license or no license, summer is over and he still hasn't "screwed up my courage to talk to her" on the Rapid.

He returns from the magazine shelves—pristine tilting oak racks filled with more than fifty periodicals from *Audubon* to *Popular Mechanics* to *Rolling Stone* to *Time* to *The New York Times* and *The Christian Science Monitor*—then loads his arms with books to be reshelved at section 306 to 399, bindings facing up, not out. Frances will check that Kris understands proper numerical ordering, looking for mistakes. This annoys Kris—do they think he doesn't know how to count?—but he's fatalistic.

Kris likes this school, he says, but notes that his only other option is the Cleveland public school system, which his buddies go to but often cut so they don't get beat up, and where his dad, an occasional substitute teacher, has been physically threatened by students. He is also cynical about US. "They make a big deal about this place being diverse," he says and, with a grimace, shakes his head *not true.* And the students, particularly the rich kids, he loathes. "I really couldn't care if half of them dropped off the face of the earth today," he says of his contemporaries. "I can't tell you how many times I've just wanted to *pummel* somebody here. I know it sounds barbaric and primal, but there have been some people that I just really want to hit around."

The dislike and distrust is, he feels, the result of economics. He's a financial-aid kid. "Just getting into this school was a trial for me," he says. He feels there's a double standard for him. He's got to watch his ass or he's out. The rich kids don't have to worry like he does, he believes. He's here because he's smart; rich kids don't have to be smart. "I resent it, yeah, because I think it makes for a weak individual." In ninth grade he turned in one such classmate for cheating; had it been anyone else, he would have kept his mouth shut, and the event still makes him smile.

What Kris believes regarding how the school operates may or may not be accurate, but his convictions are genuine. He pads through the school quietly in his baggy pants with bulky pockets at the thigh and "Bugle Boy" stitched on the leg in a looping script. He's removed the laces from his soft-soled black shoes. As he walks to the shelves with books, he tosses his long heavy hair to one shoulder and then to the other. Kris is tough. He doesn't care.

Kris is supposed to spend about an hour a week "reading" the shelves to make sure everything's filed correctly and is neatly aligned, but today he procrastinates, talking with friends hanging out in the stacks—Bill Shepardson, Odum Pich, a refugee from Cambodia, and Tyler Soltis. Nick Zinn, too, lurks hidden in the stacks and spies on the conversation, eyes peering over a row of books.

The talk moves toward girls, as usual. While girls are not physically present, their influence is always in effect. Odum is quiet but Bill likes to talk about his exploits, which usually have to do not merely with whom but with how many. He's recently got a bad name at some schools, though, because several girls discovered that they were all supposedly dating Bill. Kris listens to them as he runs fingers over book bindings, and he and Tyler continue the conversation when Kris returns to the front desk.

Kris shakes his head in solidarity. "Generally," he says, "guys can care about more than one person. And girls can't. They go nutty."

"Nutty, that's a good word for it," says Tyler, his eyes wide and bulging behind his glasses. "I don't believe in love," Tyler says. "Love exists the way you love your mom or dad or best friend. There are girls that I love that way, too. When it becomes something more—" he balks, searching for words. "Everybody wants to be loved but once they *have* it, it's *terrible.*" He's referring to a girl he dated for ten months and he says he was miserable the entire time. "I did things that I didn't think I could *do.* Like checking up on her. I was actually *checking* up on her. I *hated* myself for it."

Hate, Kris and Tyler agree, is much easier than love.

When Kris has finished in the stacks, he does homework at the front desk, until he's interrupted by Tyler—in which case Frances will eventually appear to stage-whisper something like, *"Gentlemen"* or, "These ceilings echo; we can be heard all the way in the silent study area"—or by someone checking out a book. Each student has a card with a coded strip, kept on a Rolodex at the desk. Kris runs an electronic, pen-shaped device over the book's strip, the student's card, and the "check-out" strip taped to the desk. The computer beeps acknowledgment. At the bell, Kris stuffs his homework into his backpack and heads off to calculus, which he hates.

"I understand how it was created and why it was created," he says, "but at some point I just lost it. It was like being pushed out of a car." Every day from 9:52 A.M. to 10:32 A.M., he sits in math class as if on some highway pavement in Nevada, watching the car get smaller and smaller.

Between third and fourth periods is a twenty-six-minute block of time called "Break," designed for someone with Kris's schedule. During the Break meetings are held—the yearbook staff, the news staff, teams and clubs, the Cultural Awareness Society (which, when I was a student, was the Black Unity Society), or the Asian Awareness Society (which, when I was a student, would have been a very small group, had one existed). Later in the year, a fringe group, the Frank Zappa Appreciation Society, will also meet at the Break.

Kris is a member of the Asian Awareness Society, though he's not Asian; usually he hangs out during the Break with Tyler, Bill, Odum, Tim Watkins, and J. C. Bigornia. Tyler hands Kris a copy of John Guare's *House of Blue Leaves* and asks him for help memorizing the soliloquy that ends Act One, which Tyler must recite in Mrs. Pribble's fourth-period drama class, when Kris is in his double-period English/Philosophy class.

"And Kris," says Nancy Lerner returning to the class essays she's just finished grading, "who was the *darling* of my class last week, has written *the* most *disgusting* paper." This raises respectful murmurs throughout the classroom, and Kris smiles slyly at the attention, looking away from the inquiring glances of the class, then at the essay Nancy hands him—92%, minus 1% for dangling participles. Nancy's comments usually run the gamut from *"incredible"* and "I was *blown away"* to "I could *kill* him." Today, as she's returning the personal essays, and while she shames "all you vipers who wrote about your mothers," they have never heard Dr. Lerner call any paper *disgusting*—*anything* disgusting for that matter, but for one or two of Hamlet's more inspired outbursts. It's high praise as far as they're concerned. They ask "what?" and "why?" Nancy says, "If I let you read it, you would be *nauseated,"* and carries on.

Nancy has assigned the personal essay partly as a writing exercise in a form other than critical writing, which they will do all year, and partly to prepare them for the college essay. Everyone in this class is in the process of applying to college and most of the forms will require an essay on themselves—thus this effort in mirror-gazing. Also, she knows that they want to write about themselves in their own voices—in critical papers, Nancy says, they too easily fall back on formulaic prose, and she wants to encourage a more personal approach to writing.

Kris in his essay has cast his gaze on a subject, he says, that was born of a summer idyll, his newest love: Cleveland sewers. Or, as he calls it, "The wonderful world of sewers."

He's titled his paper "Exodus: The Journey of a Lurp," and it begins, "Wilderness. The name is self-explanatory. Wild, untamed, unexplored—

the unknown. It's where I spend hours upon hours, day after day, and the way I like my life. For someone like me, growing up in the city, it's not always easy to find an unexplored region, but my friends and I try."

It began in "the sun-dappled park" where Kris and his friends, he writes, "enjoyed being alive, and all of the games that we played stressed quickness, cunning, daring and above all, recklessness." They'd carved out an overgrown and unused edge of the park on the bank of a shallow stream that runs behind the Brooklyn Library and Kris's old nursery school. At the end of a serpentine path, through tunnels of thickets and brambles, they cleared brush and dead trees to build a fort area. They dug a fire pit. A nearby landmark, a rusted, skeletal car, with brush and trees growing out of it, remains, he says, "an enduring mystery." When there were enough people at the fort, they'd post sentries at either side to keep watch for cops. When they'd venture away from this base, it would be up the creek, barefoot on the sharp rocks and cans for anyone being initiated. After a hundred yards or so, the banks widen to form a waist-deep pool which they've named "The Arena," sided respectively by a steep, dirt bank and a spread of green lawn. Here they would wrestle and fight, like ancient Romans. They'd take sides on either bank for acorn battles in the shade of towering oaks; acorns are perfect artillery, Kris explains, because they hurt like hell if you really whip them at an opponent. They would swing from tree branches into the water with incredible splashes.

"It was a time when all pressure was gone, and we were something more primal," Kris writes. "With the breeze roaring in your ears, the smell of fresh earth in your nostrils, and sweat dripping down your back, you can truly feel alive."

Yet, he continues, "It was not long before we became disenchanted with our little corner of paradise and began to crave more." Thus, the band of miniature Marlowes traveled up the creek, passing a garden hose mysteriously tied to an overhanging tree branch, past rising shale banks, under bridges, through leech-infested water—as if into the heart of some impenetrable Metropark.

It was after the second large bridge, Kris writes, "that we stumbled upon what I now regard as one of the most influential factors of my life."

His first sewer.

None of his band, he admits, was under the illusion that this creek was clean. They even knew that recently E. coli bacteria had been found in the system. But this was just a "starter sewer," as they would come to call it—roughly two hundred feet long and about a yard in diameter, more an overflow pipe than a sewer, really, and when they crawled through the darkness and emerged into the light at the other side, they found that "the feeling of relief and the joy of being alive is like a drug when you get out." They wanted more.

Kris and his friends—Tom, Nate, Tim, Mike, Droopy—explored ten different sewers throughout the summer. Each is named—the "Nate and Tom" sewer (after its discoverers), for instance, the "Grandaddy" (for its size). A terminology developed around their expeditions. Those who crawl in sewers are "lurps"; lurps go "lurping"; when two lurps enter a particularly foul sewer, they execute a "two-man muck." Kris and his friends logged many miles through the sewers last summer. When the water is deep, they occasionally feel something slither past their ankles. "Feminine hygiene products," as Kris delicately puts it, occasionally float by. Sudden surges of water engulf them.

"One of the most influential sewers that I have ever entered is the Hills Sewer, so called because it runs underneath a Hills Department Store for about six hundred feet," he writes. "The first time I ever encountered this sewer, I was led by the Orange Waterfall. I later found out that the beautiful orange color came from a certain bacteria found in human fecal matter. . . ."

Nancy has underlined this last sentence and written "another disgusting moment" in the margin.

"Climbing the long, sloping waterfall," he continues, "I stopped in awe as I saw the entrance: large, square, and glorious. . . . That day, I only got twenty-five feet into the sewer for lack of light, but it was not long before I was back. Since then I've been through the sewer backwards, forwards, with light, without light, and even in my good shoes."

Here, Nancy can't help but comment, "I think I'll call your mother to offer my sympathies."

In all, Kris completed seven lurps through the Hills' sewer, but one particular venture stands out, the one he made in early June. The one he made in his good shoes.

"Right after school had let out," he writes, "I went up there with Tom and Droopy. It had rained recently so the water was swift and higher than normal, but we debated for mere moments before splashing in. . . . The Hills' sewer is not an incredible labyrinth by any stretch of the imagination. The only side tunnels it has are little two-and-a-half-feet by two-and-a-half-feet passages leading to drains from the parking lot. Since we were feeling dangerous, we clambered into one of these side tunnels, army-crawling our way through the muck to where light shone on the other side. To make a long story short, the three of us opened the grate and climbed up onto the asphalt of the parking lot, much to the surprise of on-looking patrons. The incredible rush of lurping into the sunlight and running at full speed to avoid any punishment is unbelievably intense."

Nancy has stapled an evaluation sheet to the front of the essay; the sheet has a line for the student's name, a line for the grade, a drawing of a smiling monkey hanging from the top of the page, and three questions along the left side: "Does it work? If so, Why?," "What doesn't work and why?," and "What might have worked?" For Kris she has abandoned these questions completely and has written instead, "This is the most nauseating, disgusting, and revolting description I've ever read, and I'm very happy I'm not your mother even if you do read Greek! (It's also quite well done— although it could use some editing and condensation, especially in the first two pages.)"

Kris's essay came as a surprise to Nancy, alternately delightful and disgusting, because the week before, Kris had indeed been the darling of her class. He had given a reading of *The Oresteia* from the original. He had mentioned to Nancy that he was comparing the various translations to see how they matched up, and she asked would he read to the class the words, the very sounds actors uttered on stage in 500 B.C. Greece? Kris bowed his head to the book and read passable Greek, and when he'd finished, Nancy said, kidding, "You only made two mistakes, but that's great."

"When you guys get tired of being at US," she told the class, "just think how many high schools in the United States offer a chance to study Greek." She seemed genuinely jealous that one of her students could read her beloved Aeschylus in the original.

Lunch is served both fifth and sixth periods; tables are assigned each trimester; students' waitering duties alternate weekly and include bringing lunch to the table in a large plastic tub and clearing the table afterward. Warren Siekman, class of '54 who returned to teach math in 1960, says grace before sixth-period lunch and reads announcements after, excusing the boys about fifteen minutes before the start of seventh period. Kris usually wakes Tyler Soltis, who sleeps in the library sixth period. They talk till the bell rings, and Kris heads off to Mrs. Mason's psychology class. Eighth period Kris lifts weights in the weight room, next to the wrestling room, which is directly beneath the swimming pool—a relatively painless way to fulfill his field requirement. He finishes up the day as he began it, with Doc Strater and the classics, Greek 2.

Kris kicks himself for not beginning Greek earlier. If he'd taken Greek in tenth grade, he would have been able to read *The Odyssey* in the original for eleventh-grade English. Now he's trying to make up for lost time.

"I love the classics," he tells me one fall afternoon. "I was reading Homer this morning. I was translating some of *The Odyssey*. It was just such a thrill to me. I've done parts of *The Iliad*. We're talking about the oldest extant piece of Western literature. There's just something about that, that you don't get when you pick up Fitzgerald's translation of it. I don't know why I really love them. I've always had a love of mythology, but we haven't read a lot of mythology except in tenth grade when we read Ovid.

"It might just be because I'm good at it," he continues. "I don't mean to brag or anything, it's just one of those things that when we started studying it in seventh grade, I just found out that, hey, I can do this kind of thing. And Greek always fascinated me because it's a different alphabet." He explains that he feels obligated, personally, to learn these ancient languages.

Heavy metal, sewers, and the classics. For Kris they are not contradictory; each feeds the other. Iron Maiden led Kris to Coleridge. In the sewers—"a modern form of spelunking," he calls it—he acts out his own Greek-inspired myths.

I ask Kris what his goals are.

He pauses for only a moment, then says, "I have many goals on many different levels. When I was younger I used to want to be a sports star, baseball star in particular. But I haven't played baseball in the longest time. And as I tend more toward academia instead of athleticism, I've realized what sports are, and I've really come to dislike sports. Um. Childish. I think they serve a purpose and everything, but I don't think they serve a purpose that's ultimately that important. I guess in a way I would still be fulfilling a fantasy if I were to become a baseball player or a football player. I would like to become a heavy-metal star. I would like to have a band that made it on a record label and sold a million copies and got to tour the world. That would be great. I've thought about being a teacher in many subjects, mostly English, history, or the classics. I've thought about writing, because I love creative writing, so I've thought about being a writer. Those are the main ones. And I'd be happy with any of them." He pauses momentarily. He looks at me, still tough, slightly disdainful but serious, and says, "But I think the one thing I really want to do is I want to be President."

I raise my eyebrows. Kris, a boy who was nearly kicked out of this school three years ago for crummy grades, offers the faintest trace of a smile but doesn't look away. "Of the United States," he adds. "I've given it a lot of thought."

4

All teachers at University School seem to have their own metaphors for the demands of school. Latin teacher Karl Frerichs says, "The nature of the body-snatching differs, but it's rape and pillage at all private schools." He notes that at public schools, duties are also heaped on teachers, but they're paid for extra assignments. Private schools demand such extra work as yearbook adviser, literary magazine adviser, coaching, and any number of special events that need orchestrators, offering no remuneration, because this is, after all, a business—nonprofit, but business nonetheless. What these schools offer in return is a steady raise (most years), loyalty to those teachers who extend themselves for the school, an enormously comfortable teaching environment, orderly classrooms, and, generally, courteous and respectful students. Karl says, "They want people who will kill themselves for very little money."

One headmaster I spoke with happily called it slavery, nine months of outright slavery.

Fall is always like this at schools—a combination of extreme busyness and excitement, high hopes and a clutter of details. The move from languorous summer into vigorous fall is jarring.

School and weather are inseparable, and in Cleveland, the weather is big. While winter here is famously dreary, fall is spectacular. Azure summer skies darken to charcoal gray, against which the orange and red maple leaves seem electrically bright. The ground, baked by summer, is hard and cool. The air absorbs the smell of dry leaves. The wind snaps.

Seasons do more to a school than dictate what sports tear up the fields or pound the gymnasium floor. They define the mood and tone of the place in ways so powerfully routine that the effects become profound. If you leave school, as most people do, never again will life be measured by the September to June cycle, but the memory of that calendar, for many, remains indelibly marked on one's consciousness. Even for those long out of school, for those whose work is constant regardless of seasons, the sudden emergence every September of yellow school buses in suburban neighborhoods and children clustering at street corners on chill mornings are perennial reminders of school days. So it is in Cleveland, a city of suburbs; houses of every kind spread out through one thousand neighborhoods in a semicircle along a thirty-mile diameter of Lake Erie shore. Though the cycle—once an economic concern in agrarian America when boys were needed to work the summer fields—is no longer a practical necessity, and while many have questioned its wisdom, it remains fixed as the seasons that once governed it.

Part of the reason this back-to-schoolness remains embedded in our minds may be because in any given September, more than a quarter of America is heading to school. In the fall of 1993, 3.7 million teachers instructed 63.9 million students in schools organized and maintained by 4.2 million administrators and support staff. In other words, of 258 million people now alive in the United States, 72 million of them go to school.

Fall may be the most productive time of year at school. Hemingway pronounced that writers work best in fall because they feel death coming on, but at school, it's just the opposite. There's a liveliness in the air. The routines feel new; books are unknown and promising; sports are no longer played in sweltering heat as they were during summer practice; all grade sheets are clean, and anything is possible. Sentiment attaches itself to the crisp exuberance of fall: students with their books walking into school as the bell tower sounds eight; the bracing air and autumn leaves; burgundy sweaters and tan bucks, apples, wood smoke, and books.

That's fiction—good fiction, certainly—but the fact is, schools are so phenomenally busy that when you find yourself suddenly inside this miniature society, it feels more like being abandoned in a carnival midway than taking a smooth tour through culture's citadel of order and tradition, even in this all-boy school, which is small and unusually orderly compared with most high schools in America.

Karl Frerichs, new to the school this year, remarks on this apparent order. Karl has the straight white-blond hair, ice-blue eyes, and chiseled Nordic features not uncommon in the Great Plains, where he grew up a preacher's son—most of it in Russell, Kansas, home, Karl will tell you, of Bob Dole and Arlen Specter ("When you're from the Midwest you cling to even dubious fame," he says). Karl left a small coed Episcopal school in Baton Rouge to take this job. Second period finds him proctoring the downstairs commons. The school is quiet at this hour; students read the sports pages of Cleveland's *The Plain Dealer* at a table on the lower landing, get extra Latin help from Karl, sit and study or talk on the stairs of the locker area. Leaning against the rail overlooking the dining room, Karl says that here, "teachers *expect* students to study hard, and they *expect* them to behave." At Karl's previous school, when he gave a test and a student didn't show up for it, Karl would have to search for the kid and haul him into class. Expectations of students there were low. If a student of his misbehaved, Karl, not the student, was more likely to be taken to task for it.

For the thirty-year-old classics scholar it's still early in the year and the job, the new school, and the new city are fresh. He teaches five sections of Latin One, Two, and Three (for most teachers outside the language department, the maximum load is four sections), he proctors one period, oversees a lunch table of freshmen fifth period, coaches cross-country after school and in the spring will coach track. This gives him two free periods in the day to prepare lessons, give extra help, and grade tests; what he doesn't complete then will have to be done between six P.M. and 7:30 the next day, when he leaves for school.

Because schools are so busy, and demands on teachers and students are constant and intense, both physically and emotionally, everyone stakes out their own territory to provide them with a sense of order within the chaos. Many faculty mark their place in the faculty lounge, a room with polished hardwood floors and elegant furniture. Looking out as it does through a large window at the vast entrance corridor of the school, it gives one the sense of being removed from the bustle without being distant. The faculty lounge is also the most unusual place in the school. So unusual, so fascinating, in fact, that Debbie Nash, the coordinator of the Teacher Apprentice Program, has organized her morning schedule around it.

"I would not miss it for anything," she says. "That's why I get there at quarter to eight." She arrives with *The Plain Dealer,* and she turns on lamps. Men don't turn on lamps, she says. "If it weren't for Kerry and me, those lamps would stay off all day." Kerry is an exception to the men-and-lamps rule, but more important, he took it upon himself to remove one of two central tables around which most of the kibitzing is done and where most of the stories are told. Kerry thought the room looked better without two tables taking up all that space. He might just as well have detonated a small bomb in the lounge. Uniform and vituperative dissent followed, then a petition, and Kerry, with a sort of gee-whiz mystification, returned the table.

The missing table had upset the unofficial caste system at work here, without which the chaos outside creeps in. Chuck Seelbach, who graduated from the school in 1966 and returned to teach history after two years as a relief pitcher for the Detroit Tigers, is the uncontested anchor of the lounge. He sits at one end of the tables, the lounge's central post, his back to the window overlooking the entrance commons, before morning assembly and then for the duration of the first period. All other free periods he will spend here, too, grading papers and reading history texts which he keeps in his scuffed leather briefcase. If someone happens to be sitting in his chair when he walks in, they move. Keith Green, Polly Cohen, and Dick McCrea, all with twenty or more years at the school, sit on either side of Seelbach. Deb Nash has recently moved to these ranks, but she says it's taken her twelve years to migrate from the far end of the tables to this inner sanctum, advancing about one chair every two years. New faculty typically hover behind Seelbach in the lamp area of the lounge, which contains two rose-colored sitting chairs, a small sofa, and coffee table on an Oriental area rug. If there is an advantage to sitting at the far end of the tables it is only to be near the coffee. Teas are also available, as are packets of cocoa, and in the fall and winter, hot spiced cider. A bowl of fresh fruit is placed at the center of the tables each morning.

After assembly the lounge bustles and a line for coffee forms against the back wall. Talk inevitably includes sports; in the fall that means the Cleveland Browns. Seelbach is cemented in his chair, defending Browns' coach Belichick. Dick McCrea, the school's preeminent eccentric—odd unmatching clothes, shirttails half tucked in, and a throat-clearing laugh so unusual it has made him the annual focus of the students' faculty parody at the fall variety show—is wandering randomly through the lounge in search of his coffee mug. He's mumbling to himself, scratching his bristly white hair, and absently patting his coat pockets on the off chance his mug will be here. He spots an unused mug by the sink. "Arr*hem!* I sometimes use this as a back-up," he says to himself.

Kerry, who has just entered says, "So does everyone else."

"Arr-ggk-ha-ha!" says McCrea.

Meanwhile, Seelbach is delighting in the University of Minnesota's loss over the weekend. "Evan was *hooting* on Saturday about that," he says. "And they got *beat!*"

McCrea slurps his coffee and says, "Evan will just have himself a third lunch and he'll be all right."

All right, perhaps, after the requisite doughnuts. Throughout the morning, doughnuts are sold in the dining hall and when Evan Luzar, who had greeted me so vigorously the first day of school, is in the faculty lounge, it is usually before a tower of doughnuts and the sports pages. Flipping newsprint, Evan sees an ad for a new movie, *The War Room,* and tells his friend and fellow English teacher Craig Lapine that he wants to see it. Craig hasn't heard of it, and it doesn't sound like the kind of movie he'd want to go see, especially if it interests Evan. Evan says it's the documentary about Carville and Stephanopoulos during the Clinton campaign. "Stephanopoulos was at the Cedar Lee for the opening," Evan tells Craig.

"Didn't Stephanopoulos go to US?"

"Lower school," says Evan. "He graduated from Orange."

McCrea is pacing the floor with his coffee. He remembers Stephano-poulos. "Scotty Weiss wrestled him," says McCrea. Evan and Craig turn to the veteran. "Remember Scotty Weiss? Scotty was a good wrestler, and before the match, Stephanopoulos came up to Scotty and said, 'Scotty, just don't *pin* me in the first *period.'* " McCrea laughs. "Aaarrgh, already the perfect politician!"

Students take over specific areas of the downstairs commons according to grade, very much as the faculty organize lounge seating according to tenure: seniority begins at one end and moves west, away from the entrance doors. The seniors have an actual lounge of their own, a section of lockers that has been glassed in and decorated with Grateful Dead emblems. The juniors corral at the middle section of lockers, and sophomores at the far end. Freshmen reign on the blue-carpeted platform seats of Monkey Island, directly across from the senior lounge. This is the only domain that is truly theirs, and they group in large numbers here throughout the day, gaming with paper and baseball bats, studying and talking. No one person or class is ever instructed to congregate in the historically appropriate area but it follows like the seasons.

It should be noted that when I use the words "busy" or "chaotic," their meaning is particular to this school. To a visitor, these qualities are invisible. As a rule the hallways and common areas of the school are hushed. One teacher visiting from a private coed school, for instance, was asked how this school differed from his own—a question that might have been answered a hundred different ways. He immediately remarked, "It's *quiet*," adding that noise in the upper decibel range was noticeably absent. Of course, a loud debate erupts every now and then, a race ensues down a corridor, or a junior will heave his stuffed backpack at another junior, who will, in turn, jump on the heaver's back so that they both tumble to the carpet. Still, other than the two minutes between each period, the school remains all but silent. Even those two-minute class changes are relatively orderly; two minutes is too short a time even to get to one's locker for the appropriate books (thus the ubiquitous forty- to fifty-pound backpack), let alone allow time for determined roughhousing.

But add a single girl to this boys' stew, and its entire complexion changes. Girls are almost never in the school, so when they are, the halls seem to crackle with energy—a drop of water in a pan of hot oil. Add swarms of girls and the effect is ecstatic. The first time I saw girls in any number here this year was at the fall variety show, which raises money for United Way and features more boys playing electric guitars than most people will ever see, or want to, in their lifetime. On this night every year the downstairs commons teems with teenage girls who cluster, whisper, cling to each other's arms, dart in groups, and add an unfamiliar pitch to the cacophony of crowd noise. Boys who spend their days shuffling blank-faced from one class to the next suddenly strut and posture, are mainly solitary, and gather rarely in groups of more than two or three. Having seen only boys together, it was exciting to watch boys and girls together the night of the variety show. They seemed to shoot and glide on a thin film above the carpet. It was like a giant air-hockey table.

When school was in session, though, the entire building was library quiet.

Where then, in this hushed atmosphere, is this sense of extreme busyness if visitors are immune to it? I can only say that it's present like gravity; only the effects are visible. To understand the events that will happen during the coming year, it is essential to understand the nature of this force. The effects vary from person to person; routine, such as Seelbach's anchoring the faculty lounge, diminishes the effect. But everyone recognizes it. Margaret Mason, dean of students, counselor, and psychology teacher, once reminded me that I had requested an interview with the school psychologist. I gave her an expression, one she'd evidently seen before, to say I was presently too busy.

Happily, she cried, "You've got the US disease!" and threw her head back, mouth gaping in a silent scream and fingers, frozen into claws, scratching at the air.

I don't mean to suggest that this force is horrible or even a bad thing; it may be inevitable when you marshal four hundred adolescent boys into a building where they must be quiet and industrious for seven hours. Yet the weight and pressure of the air is different here. You will feel something similar if you swim to the bottom of a twelve-foot-deep pool and don't clear your ears. One teacher, moving his palms gradually closer as he spoke, said to me, "You come down that driveway, and you can feel the place *swallow* you."

The peculiar forces, some suspect, result in head colds, flu, and, occasionally, back problems. When you try to leave the school, you must add an unaccounted-for ten- to twenty-minute delay. It's never been measured, but I would not be surprised to find that teachers weigh more here than they do at home.

Paul Bailin's metaphor for the busyness is unnoticeable, painless bloodletting. This is his second year teaching; there were no surprises this year. He had prepared for his classes—three sections of ninth-grade Western Civilization I and one section of tenth-grade Western Civilization II; he was rested from the summer, and even enjoyed a week in California at a teaching seminar, paid for by the school, learning a Socratic-dialogue technique for teaching which he was eager to put into action.

He and three other teachers, however, have created a class called Reason and Rhetoric, in which formal debate and writing skills are taught to upperclassmen. Paul wishes he hadn't been so ambitious—he really didn't *need* to take on a fifth class, let alone help create one that didn't previously exist. He's coaching debate after school, and he's also the chess club coach. None of this would be so difficult were it not for one forty-minute chunk of soul-draining struggle each day immediately after lunch—seventh period. His final section of Western Civ I comprises a thoroughly unruly mob of freshmen. Miscreants, troublemakers, perpetually distracted gabbers, note-tossers, and flunkies. Of the thirteen total, there are a few solid students, but the bad-apple ratio is unusually high. The very thought of seventh period each day is, Paul says, "just *terrible.*"

Shawn will not sit down and will not stay quiet. Jay and Chris, Tim and John talk throughout class. Sang Back, who's used to the urban bustle of Seoul, Korea, where it was not unusual for him to take ten or twelve classes a day, says American school is more fun—but his written English is weak and Paul has to compensate by allowing Sang Back extra class periods to write his tests in English (he has a pocket computer that helps him translate); when Jonah complains about this—"How come he gets more time?"—Paul says, "You can have more time too if you want to take the test in Korean." And *Kevin.* Paul is reasonably certain that he and Kevin will be enemies the entire year—it's something he knew right away. Normal demands—classes, students misbehaving at the usual rate, parents demanding to know why their son got an 87 and not a 90 on the last test, sponsor meetings, debate, chess—push Paul to the limit even before the seventh-period sparring match.

"It's like paper cuts—you get paper cuts all over you," Paul says, pressing two slender fingers to his forearm. "And you can't tend every one, and you don't really notice them at the time. But by the time you get home, you've lost two quarts of blood."

Paul is an old boy—in two respects as it turns out. He is what the British sometimes call, with gruff jocularity, an Old Boy (though "alum" is the preferred term here)—a US Boy who graduated six years ago. Paul doesn't look much like the "US Boy" statue either, but he was in his day a star of the school in academic matters. He was the 1987 class valedictorian; he and his brother Mitch, a year behind him, made it to the national finals in debate; and he won the Greek prize (though Paul has always felt rotten about the Greek prize; his brother Mitch, deserved it, Paul feels, because *he* cheated to get by in Greek, copying his brother's homework most days before Doc Strater's seventh-period class; it's been nagging him, and he's promised himself he'll confess to Doc before the year's out).

Though he's returned to his alma mater to teach, Paul doesn't remember being all that happy as a student. "Maybe I just didn't like my childhood and blamed it on US. Maybe I was just insecure, like most high school kids are, and blamed that on people around me. . . . I was sort of nerdy. I had some friends but I wasn't all that popular."

Paul remains somewhat nerdy by appearance. His hair is orange Brillo. A wispy little moustache quivers over his small mouth and small, pointed chin. Wire-rimmed spectacles perch on a prominent, aquiline nose. And his ears—well, better not to describe them, better simply to say that, hanging from the lamp above his narrow bed at home are two large cardboard ears attached to a semicircle of wire, cartoon ears his former girlfriend wore when they once dressed up as twins. Paul's intriguing physiognomy rests upon a tubular neck, Adam's apple commanding the full runway, and a feather-thin body.

Paul says he never felt all that comfortable at US and doesn't feel all that comfortable now. But he says there's *no* place he feels truly comfortable. He certainly doesn't appear comfortable in school clothes. His are mostly faded, thrift-shop threads, a green tweed jacket, worn leather patches at the elbows, or a black jacket cleaned so many times—in a washing machine, from the looks of it—it's become gray, and faded green or faded black pants that reveal an inch or two of green or black short, cotton socks.

He varies this attire once each year, and on this day, in the fall, he does appear completely at home. After lunch, he repairs to the history department office directly across from the English department and, as he did twice earlier in the day before first period and before fourth period, he removes his jacket and slips it over the back of his desk chair. He unknots his tie, unbuttons his shirt, slips off his socks and stuffs them in his shoes. He unfastens his belt and removes his trousers.

The bell ending sixth period sounds—*ping . . . ping . . . ping . . . ping . . . p*—and the humanities corridor is suddenly jammed with students leaving class and, moments later, with new students arriving for seventh period. The hallway is mobbed.

Paul emerges from the history department office wearing an orange Buddhist-monk's robe. The river of students, amazed, parts for him as he walks barefoot along the carpet, books held at belt level with both hands, head bowed, meeting no one's eye, to Room 260.

Conversation ceases. Shawn, bewildered, takes his seat immediately. Kevin and Jonah are looking around smiling hilariously but not speaking. Paul sets his class materials on the desk and stands at the center of the room. He faces the blackboard. He kneels on the carpet, back curved, closes his eyes, presses his hands together, and begins to rock slightly. The room is dead silent. Paul bows three times, once for the Buddha, once for the dharma, and once for the sangha, or community. Then he speaks:

Namo tassa bhagavato arahato sammasambuddhassa.
Namo tassa bhagavato arahato sammasambuddhassa.
Namo tassa bhagavato arahato sammasambuddhassa.

This is a Buddhist chant which translates, "Homage to the Exalted One, the Arahant, He who is perfectly Enlightened by himself."

When he finishes, he pauses for several seconds, eyes still closed, then stands abruptly and strides to his books. "Good afternoon, gentlemen," he says.

The silence broken, boys fire questions: "Mr. Bailin, what are you wearing?" "Why?" "What was that thing you just said?" Paul does not answer, but instead writes on the blackboard:

> Need to know: Hinduism
>   Polytheistic
>   Circular view of time vs. Judeo-Christian
>   linear time

The students lean forward in their desks, which are pressed against the walls in a semicircle. They appear to be galvanized by this break in routine, all but one, who sits smiling peacefully along the back wall. Hen Nyugen doesn't seem at all surprised. He seems glad, in fact. His family, Vietnamese immigrants, is Buddhist. His father and uncle bought a boat in Vietnam in the late '70s and sailed it to Malaysia. When the entire family had moved safely to Cleveland, shortly after which Hen was born, the grandparents founded a temple called Dragon Light.

"Today, we move into Buddhism," says Paul. "The central idea of Buddhism is suffering. No pain, no gain—but in a spiritual sense." The boys open their notebooks. He will answer their questions in good time. It is the most orderly seventh period since school began, and he moves methodically through the first lesson in Eastern philosophy. The biggest interruption comes from outside, when students passing by the large window halt to stare at Mr. Bailin dressed in the weird toga. Then, just before the bell rings to end class, the fire alarm sounds.

"OK guys," Paul says. "On your way to the fire drill pick up tomorrow's assignment." Then they all file out, followed by Paul, through the corridor, down the brick stairway at the back of the humanities wing, and into the brisk fall air. The sun is bright and Paul, in his orange robe, seems almost to glow. Carol Pribble spots Paul in the crowd—not difficult today—throws her head back and howls. Paul loiters peacefully, barefoot, hands clasped at belt level, goose bumps raised on his slim pink arms, and stares at the ground.

It's an unusual sight, the faculty in their ties, the boys in their button-downs and Dockers, and Paul, looking to all the school like a Jewish-American Gandhi.

I had not yet got to know Paul all that well, so the image set in my mind on that cold bright afternoon. For the rest of the year, even when he wore his green jacket and faded black pants that were two inches too short, he seemed to me to be floating through the corridors in his orange monk's robe.

"Hawley basically hired me through the mail," Paul says. "I'm not sure why he hired me."

Paul graduated from Stanford University, having studied primarily philosophy and religion; he wrote his senior thesis on a Dominican preacher who lived in the early 1300s and was accused of heresy by the Archbishop of Cologne for his controversial teachings on, in Paul's words, "how one comes to know and speak about God." Immediately after, Paul traveled for half a year through the Far East and lived for three months in a Buddhist monastery, Wat Pa Nanachet, in the village of Beung Wai in Thailand. Here he meditated, rarely spoke to anyone, and wrote long letters "on the floor of my meditation hut with the spiders running around on the walls by candlelight." Shortly before his return, knowing he would not be ready to plunge into graduate studies (his eventual goal), he wrote to Hawley, and they discussed salary and terms by phone.

Paul eventually met with Hawley. He was nervous about this because the last time he talked with Hawley in his office, in fact the only time he remembers talking to Hawley at all during his nine years as a student, was when he was being disciplined for driving his car across the front circle of the lower school, through the middle of a soccer game, on a 25-cent bet. This time Hawley conducted a formal interview, addressing Paul's assets and possible problems, which seemed to Paul a little odd since he already had a contract. Hawley asked if Paul would be interested in teaching summer school, in addition to teaching during the academic year, which would help the school and help Paul find his teaching legs. For this, Hawley offered Paul more money than the school could afford to pay him. Paul accepted.

When Paul showed up for the summer classes, he was informed by Margaret Mason that he didn't necessarily have the job and if he did get it, it would be at a salary lower than the one Hawley had quoted him.

This is apparently an unwritten tradition at the school that goes back at least as far as 1968, when the headmaster himself looked for a job here. Even today, Hawley scowls at the memory.

Hawley was just finishing up his doctorate at Case Western Reserve University in Cleveland at the time, he told me, recalling his twenty-three-year-old self, and among the schools he was applying to for a job was US. He had a good impression of the school, what is now the lower campus, remembers that the place felt "sturdy," which he liked. On Geoff Morton's recommendation, Rowland "BY GUM" McKinley met with Hawley and offered him a job on the spot, and at a salary generous enough to allow Hawley to marry his college sweetheart. Hawley was ecstatic and called Molly, then an art student in Boston, to propose. Molly accepted and began planning a move to Cleveland.

A few days later, Hawley called McKinley to inquire about some details. Hawley remembers the conversation well. Before he could say why he was calling, McKinley said, "SON! I'D LIKE TO OFFER YOU A *JOB!*"

"I—I thought you already offered me a job."

"DID I? WELL, I'M OFFERING AGAIN!"

Same job, different salary. Hawley took the job, and the different salary.

Paul, too, accepted all terms the school offered, but Paul didn't propose to anyone; he bought a car instead.

With Paul, as with Nancy, the specter of the headmaster always hovered just over his shoulder. Hawley was the reference point. In class, when a boy raised a tricky philosophical question that contradicted, say, the notion of the existence of objective truth, Paul would grin and say, "You should ask Dr. Hawley that question."

The fall is a busy time for the headmaster, and because the year began so smoothly, I saw him only occasionally outside the classroom. There he was on a sunny Saturday afternoon, dressed in bright yellow turtleneck, camel coat and wearing his studious-looking round spectacles, cheering on the football team; or speaking to a group of parents in the library in the evening about his boys book and theories of gender development, boys' stories, and single-sex schools (always the teacher); or relaxing in the faculty lounge after lunch.

These occasions amounted to glimpses, however, and did not account for his presence. So strong were the effects of this headmaster, even when he was nowhere to be seen, I couldn't help but wonder why and how this could be so? Was it the nature of this school, its size and structure? Did it have something to do with its being a boys' school? Or was it the result of Hawley's personality, his absolute answers, his absolute authority in the school?

In the late 1960s, Peter Prescott returned to his boys' school, Choate, and wrote a book called *A World of Our Own*. In it, he makes an observation that has stuck with me. "The Age of the Great Headmasters is over," he wrote. "The species is extinct, dead as a dinosaur. . . . The Great Headmasters are gone, killed off by a crisis of confidence in the two articles of faith that sustained them as they built their schools: a belief in the natural and stable order of society, and a belief in the truth of Christian Humanism."

The year I'd arrived, 1993, was decades beyond the cultural maelstrom of the 1960s, decades beyond the forties and fifties when schools such as Choate and US thrived, unquestioned by society. Was Hawley that same sort of dogmatic autocratic headmaster of a past age, the sort an old-fashioned boys' school seemed to demand? Or was he truly progressive in his arguing for single-sex education, as he contended, just as female educators arguing for single-sex for girls were considered progressive? Was a boys' school's success and effectiveness dependent on such a strong and rigid figure? I had returned intending to watch the boys in this school, how they played off teachers and each other in this unusual world; but it quickly became apparent that this headmaster, the very sort Prescott had pronounced dead, was the elemental force driving this century-old school, and the thoughts and actions of everyone in it could not be fully understood without taking into account their headmaster.

Even Paul, who had a razor-sharp intellect and who was not only fiercely independent in his thinking but couldn't be more different from Hawley, was pressed upon and directed by this headmaster's presence.

Unlike the headmaster, Paul doesn't plan on making a career of teaching, but it's been a rewarding interim before graduate school. At least, that's what he's thinking as the 1993–94 year at US begins—and it's an especially comforting idea whenever he thinks of seventh period. In fact, he finds it a bit surprising that he's teaching. At his graduation, Paul's history teacher said to Paul's parents, "Paul would make a terrific teacher if he didn't mind living in poverty." Paul was standing right there and remembers thinking, "Yeah, *right*. I'm gonna be a rich lawyer, sucker."

As it turns out, Paul doesn't mind poverty as much as he thought he would. Of course, it's not actual poverty. His salary, he says, is $20,500, $1,000 more than it was last year, and about $10,000 less than he'd make at a public school were he to have the proper credentials, which he doesn't. He rents a house, for which his share is $180 a month, with three women, two of whom are grad students, the other a social worker. He lives mainly on broccoli and rice, and occasional take-out from the Chinese restaurant at the end of his street in Cleveland Heights. With rent, bills, and car payments balanced with a frugal style, he's been able to save some money, but he's banking on significant financial aid from a grad school.

Paul can see himself as a college professor somewhere down the line, maybe at a small rural school where academic back-biting is minimal and where he'd have more time for reading and reflection than he does at this high school. He also says he'd be perfectly happy picking up trash at a very good national park. Some days, he considers opening a cat shelter. Paul loves cats.

"You know those people you read about who die and they find a hundred-eighty cats living in the house?" he says. "I'm one of those people." He pauses. "But I don't think there's a lot of money in cats."

Paul enters Room 260, sets his books on the table, and as he removes his green tweed jacket says, "It is the nineteenth of October and we have a lot to cover." Paul names the date each time he enters a classroom as a reminder to the students that they're expected to keep daily class notes; periodically, the notebooks will be turned in to Paul to be checked and graded. As they arrive for class, students lay pink and blue exam booklets on the desk by the blackboard; after each reading assignment, they're required to write two questions regarding the material. As they're taking their seats, Paul returns yesterday's question books. Students are also expected to highlight their reading each night, and during tests, Paul will check their books to make sure that they're doing this also.

Ninth graders, of course, don't simply file into class, rest their question books on the desk, and take their seats. They more or less storm a room. On any given day, two-thirds of them arrive huffing, their faces scarlet and glistening. Many of them, immediately after lunch, the very moment Mr. Siekman says "You're excused," bolt from their chairs to the gym. If they're fast, they'll get in twenty minutes of pick-up basketball before the end of sixth period. The gym is open most of the day and many teachers consider this absolutely essential in maintaining order in the school. You have to let these boys exhaust themselves physically, or they'll be hell in class. The open gym also results in chronic lateness to Paul's seventh-period Western Civ and a heightened sense of disorder during the first five or ten minutes. Shirts are untucked. Kids change at their seats from gym shoes to street shoes. The room grows slightly steamy.

Drew just makes it as the bell rings, looking like he's run a marathon.

"Gentlemen, take your seats. Please take your notebooks out. We've got a lot to cover today. The Quest is tomorrow and we haven't gone through a good deal of the material yet, so we've got to move quickly."

Jonah, looking cool and kempt, is about ten seconds behind Drew. Jonah enters the classroom and beelines for his seat, hoping Mr. Bailin won't notice him amid the ruckus.

"You need a KA," Paul tells Jonah softly, and tries to begin the lesson.

A KA, or "Kindly Admit," is required from whichever teacher made you late. If you don't have one, it's one demerit. After five demerits, you're locked in silent study for three hours Friday after school. The psychological weight of demerits—handed out for anything from an unexcused absence to chewing gum in class—decreases steadily as the boys get older, but they are effective with freshmen. Once, when Drew arrived at the bell, he appealed to Paul before the bell rang. "Mr. Bailin," he said. "I forgot my question book in my locker, can I go get it?" Paul explained that he could get his question book, but that it will make him late and result in a demerit. Drew desperately spelled out the situation for Paul, as if pleading before a judge. Paul told Drew the decision was up to him. You could watch Drew's inner battle: *If I get my question book, I get the homework point, but I also get a demerit; if I don't get my question book, I don't get a demerit, but I don't get a homework point either. How many demerits do I have? How many homeworks have I missed?* Drew stood in the center of the room, biting his lower lip, his eyes glassy and distant. Paul watched, and watched, then smiled and shook his head. "Come on, Drew, it's too late now, take your seat." As if released from bondage, Drew's body sagged in defeat—he had not made a decision—and he slunk to his desk.

The moment Jonah hears Paul say "You need a KA," he breaks from the beeline to his seat by 90 degrees till he's smack in front of Paul. "I *can't,*" he implores, arms stretched down at his sides, palms out.

"Talk to me after class," Paul says quietly.

"I left my highlighter in the library," Jonah pleads. "I *had* to go back."

"Talk to me after class," Paul says, then, loudly, "We left off yesterday with the first two noble truths." Jonah falls heavily into his seat, slaps his books down at the injustice of it. "The first one, very simply, is that life is suffering. All life, whether it be things that seem to be unhappy or things that seem to be good, are suffering deep down. Everything is impermanent, everything ends, everything changes. The second noble truth is that the reason this happened is because we are ignorant of the way the world is, and because we have desires for it to be other than the way it really is. Where do you see this in Ajahn Chaa's parables?"

Western Civilization is the bedrock of the US humanities curriculum, and while the years and events a teacher must cover are clearly defined, the course allows enough flexibility for Paul to spend a week or so on Eastern philosophy and personages. He is the only teacher this year qualified to teach the subject, the only glimpse a US student is likely to get of it here. Mindful of the general construct of the course, he's able to parallel the themes of ancient Asian history with those of Western history.

The course—designed by the headmaster in his early teaching days, along with his friend and then-colleague the Rev. F. Washington Jarvis, who's now headmaster of a boys' school in Boston—begins with geography. The students must learn and memorize the layout of the Middle East, the geographical epicenter of their studies. They move from geography to Hammurabi's Code and Mesopotamia, where writing and advanced agricultural and governmental systems developed in what is now Iraq. They are responsible for knowing the general characteristics of paleolithic and neolithic life, which leads them to the civilization of Egypt, and from Egypt to Israel with Abraham, the ancient Hebrews, and the Kings of the Old Testament. Here the theme of suffering arises and stays, through their introduction to Buddhism to their reading of *Night,* Elie Wiesel's memoir of the Holocaust. They then move to ancient Greece. In all, the course covers about 11,350 years of history, from 10,000 B.C. (or "B.C.E.," in Paul's classes—"before the common era," which, he explains to the boys, is now considered a more inclusive, that is, a less-Christian-centered orientation) to 1350, when the Black Plague ravaged Europe.

A facility to memorize names, dates, and places comes in handy in Western Civ—the boys are regularly grilled on geography (throughout the year Paul will ask students to go to one of six world maps taped to the walls and point to Assyria, say, or Egypt, or Athens), they must commit to their souls a regular vocabulary list which includes words such as "dynasty," "metaphysical," "patriarch," "dualism," "bureaucracy," "hierarchy," and they must remember a slew of pharaohs and kings. But memory is not the goal. "I don't really care if they don't remember the names of the pharaohs at the end of the year," Paul says. "I don't remember them myself." What he wants them to develop is good "problem-solving ability" and clear writing.

"If there's one thing US does," says Jonah, "it's teach you how to write essays." The boys write like mad here. Alumni remark on this as well—US taught me to write, they invariably say.

"Good afternoon, gentlemen, today is October twenty-fifth and we've got a lot to cover."

Paul is beat. It was supposed to be an easy week, because he had little grading to do, and he promised himself he'd get to bed at 10:30 every night. He's got to make use of this light week. He describes a night during a typical week fatalistically: "To come home at four o'clock, or six o'clock if there's debate, and fix dinner and watch a half hour of CNN, and then to realize you've got four or five hours of work to do, fall asleep at some point and wake up early and do it again . . . ," he trails off as if exhausted thinking about it. Minutes of sleep are so important that he sets out his clothes each night so that they're fireman-ready when he wakes. He can remain in bed till 7:20, leap out, wash his hair under a faucet, dress, drink a cup of tea, and make the twenty-two-minute drive to school by two minutes after eight. On Mondays when he's returning with his load of weekend work, he'll be hefting what he calls his "Ox Box," his old debater's briefcase, which looks big and sturdy enough to carry an anvil. The one week when he's able to get to bed by 10:30, his friends in California decide to call and keep him up till all hours. Lack of sleep makes class murder. "If you come in when you're tired, everything seems to break down," he says hopelessly.

It's an important class today. He's got to make sure they're prepared for a test on Friday on the Kings of the Old Testament.

Jay takes advantage of the fact that Paul's spending a lot of time at the blackboard. Early in the year, Jay sits on the left side of the class against the window that looks out into the hallway, alphabetically stationed between Matt, the class brain, and Tim, a husky athlete who could be a good student if he weren't so disorganized. Also in this row is Paul's seventh-period nemesis, Kevin, who is playing with his blue retainer, making monster faces and trying to balance it on his nose.

Throughout class Jay appears to struggle hard in his notebook. He comes from an Italian background and has a dark complexion, dark brown eyes, and a large grin packed with wide short teeth. He's smart, and he can be arrogant about it—like today. He's not feverishly taking down notes. Instead, his pencil is meticulously scribbling on scraps of paper the size of silver dollars. The scraps soon will be tightly balled and placed casually on the left side of his notebook. He keeps watch on Mr. Bailin; when Paul turns his back to write on the board, Jay grips the leaded end of his pencil, pulls it back, releases, and the paper nugget sails to the opposite corner of the room where his buddy Chris, also pretending to listen to Mr. Bailin, is ready to pounce for the note before Mr. Bailin turns around.

This is not the sort of writing Paul seeks to encourage. Its effect is not dependent on a clean prose style. The notes contain few verbs; in fact, they are almost entirely composed of the names of girls. Jay writes diligently:

Scale 1–10.
Anna   10 who cares if she's flat
Kristi   9 no comment
Marsha 8 not amazing
Hilary   10 Wow!

All four scraps of paper fired today from one side of the room to the other are filled with the names of girls, except for one, which reads, "Now let's rate guys."

Opposite Jay is Shawntae. Shawn spends most of the period looking around the room, looking everywhere but at Mr. Bailin. He, too, is proving to be a case for Paul.

Shawn, one of two African Americans in this class, is the largest freshman at six-foot-three and 250 pounds. He wears, he says dismally, size-15 shoes. He wishes he'd quit growing. He also wishes he could quit Western Civ; he'd rather be reading *Sports Illustrated.* Shawn has a big grin and an infectious laugh—his heee-heee-heee resonates through the classroom clamor, but his eyes, bright white against his dark complexion, never seem to fix on anything. They are perpetually rolling from the ceiling to the floor, to the right and to the left—a movement that parallels his scholarly pursuits.

By the end of the first term, Paul will be forced to write Shawn's mother that "his lack of organization and attention to his studies, as well as his behavior, have been a constant handicap for him this term. Shawn has turned in only half of his homework assignments, and the weekly book checks reveal that he often does not complete his nightly reading. In class, I have repeatedly asked Shawn to take his seat at the beginning of class, to raise his hand, and to attend to class discussion." Paul goes on to say that Shawn failed the major test on Mesopotamia and that he didn't show for their meeting to discuss his mistakes. "The course will grow increasingly challenging," Paul concludes, "and if Shawn wishes to make the most of his high potential, he must buckle down and devote full time and attention to his work."

The only student who seems genuinely worried is Jonah. He's been talking to the people in Paul's other classes and says, "We're like a *month* behind."

"We're only one week behind," Paul answers, "but we've really got to fly through this stuff."

Here is the second way Paul is an old boy: he graduated from this school just six years ago and he's forty years old, or so it seems. Nancy told me, "We all heard Rick was bringing in this guy who was going to have a nervous *breakdown* before the end of the year. But he had this aura of *peace* around him."

Ask Paul what his goals are, and he'll tell you, in all seriousness, "To find the meaning of life." He pauses and says, "But that's something you're supposed to do as an undergraduate."

He's more concerned right now about uncovering an ethical system of behavior that will incorporate various cultures and cultural practices. Because of this, he's tagged as a relativist. In a school run by a very non-relativist headmaster, this can make waves. Paul himself will concede, when pressed, that he's an "ethical relativist," but that, too, is oversimplifying the matter, because religion *is* important to him. "Otherwise," he says, "I wouldn't have spent all these years studying it." And yet, he says, "I'm not sure I could *ever* have a religious conviction. I mean, I'm just not the sort to be convicted about things like that. I talk to Life sometimes, and sometimes it makes sense to call it Life and sometimes just to call it To

Whom It May Concern. Every once in a while it sounds right to call it God but not usually."

This spiritual struggle seems to have begun in college. Paul was raised as a Jew, but at one point, he joined a born-again Christian group and went to Bible studies. "I really, really wanted to have faith," he recalls, "thought that was the neatest thing in the world. But it's just not in my grain, I just couldn't do it. There were times when I thought that these were really neat, nice people, and I thought it would be *great* if I could have Jesus as my savior and all that stuff. But I just couldn't, it just wasn't there, *anywhere*.

"I read Nietzsche as a freshman and at that point I was pretty much converted."

Paul seems constantly to struggle with the big issues, and while his outward demeanor is indeed peaceful, I could *watch* the struggle in the minute details of his life at the school. He rarely spends time in the faculty lounge, though he likes the room and will sit there when it's empty. But when he hears a conversation he doesn't like, he leaves the room. "It's so *male*," he says of the lounge, squinting with an expression of comical distaste. He wonders what on earth they'd talk about if they didn't have sports.

Among Paul's, and all other faculty's non-teaching responsibilities is acting as sponsor, a sort of counselor and advocate, for the ten students who choose him, and he meets with them throughout the year during his free periods. Andy Wagner, a junior, is one of the few upperclassmen who have chosen Paul. He's taking Paul's Reason and Rhetoric class and is on the debate team. In the fall, after interim grades have been recorded, he arrives at Paul's office for a third-period meeting. Kerry has asked all teachers to meet with every sponsee to evaluate progress and goals.

Andy drops his books on the two-seater couch adjacent to Paul's desk, and slumps, tossing his long, heavy, dark bangs out of his eyes. Paul sits directly in front of Andy in his desk chair and opens a folder containing Andy's interim grades. "We just want see if there's anything we should be horribly concerned about," he says to Andy with a gentle bedside manner. Paul suspects that Andy is something of a party animal, but says, "He's a good kid working pretty much at his potential," though he asks Andy to address what he calls Andy's "academic nonchalance." Andy smiles in agreement, and tells Paul that his goal is first honors, an 88 average.

"OK," Paul says, writing down this first goal.

The meeting is casual and conversational. Andy's delighted to hear

74

Laurel girls might be joining the debate team. He wants to work harder at debate. He also wants to play tennis every day to get ready for the spring. Paul writes these goals down, and asks, "Anything else? What else is going on outside school?"

"My dad and I are going hunting," Andy offers, though he's sort of sheepish about it. "My dad wants me to kill something first. I think it's kind of inhumane." Andy explains that he and his dad are planning to go to a duck farm where ducks are corralled in front of you. "They're trained to fly *at* the hunters, and the ones that aren't shot are trained to fly back to the lake," he explains to Paul, where they're caged up again. Andy tells Paul that he likes the idea of hunting, but only in a natural setting.

Paul nods, looks down at the list of goals he's writing for Andy, and says, "Well, we'll just put down killing your first innocent animal."

Andy smiles and nods, satisfied.

Paul wears rubber bands on his right wrist. When he catches himself being judgmental, or thinking in a way he doesn't like, he snaps the rubber bands just below the heal of his palm. He clearly disapproves of many things that happen at US, and of many conversations he hears—talk of the killing of animals, for instance—but he refrains from judgment. Or tries to. When he can't he gives himself a little zap with the rubber bands.

Every day, three or four green, Papermate ballpoints jut in all directions from Paul's shirt pocket. Green pens, he believes, are the one mark he's made on the school. When he arrived there was not a green pen to be found. The supply office refused to stock them. Recently, Paul had read a study that suggested green was a better color for grading tests and essays. It's less violent, less intimidating to students, than red, which can make an essay look like a battlefield. He enlisted several faculty to support him, and now, Bridget, who buys supplies, stocks plenty of green pens.

This concerned gentleness extends beyond his school life. In addition to a heavy work schedule, Paul volunteers once a week for Cleveland's Free Clinic Together Hotline, answering questions about drugs and AIDS, counseling people considering suicide, and attending to other urgent phone requests. The only room in his schedule for this is late Friday, or Saturday rather, from midnight to four A.M. This often means he will only get a few hours of sleep before he joins the debate team on Saturday mornings, coaching students and judging the Lincoln/Douglas-style competitions.

Paul's mother, Iris, a local food writer, agrees that Paul's spiritual age is indeterminate. She says he was born ageless—and skinny. "He was five and a half pounds," she says, "and it was *all balls.*" Paul does have the odd, cartoonish look of someone who could well have been born looking exactly as he does today. One can almost imagine the doctor arriving at the side of Iris, who's exhausted from labor, and handing her a swaddled Paul with spectacles perched on his formidable beak, moustache damp and glistening, the distinctive Adam's apple cruising a long tubular neck. "Congratulations, Mrs. Bailin, it's a forty-year-old."

"OK, we're going to have a discussion today, so put away your notebooks," Paul tells the class. "Let's move in closer."

"Can we meditate first?" Shawn asks. Paul had recently taught his classes some simple techniques of Buddhist meditation.

"No, we don't have time for that today, Shawn."

In several classes throughout the year, Paul has the boys scoot their desks toward the center of the room, till they're all almost touching, for a discussion. Here, the boys are not supposed to raise their hands. They're expected to hold an even and respectful dialogue with each other on an important topic.

Paul crosses one leg over the other, leans toward the circle of boys and says, "The reason I wanted to have this discussion is because we're moving into some material that can cause some confusion, and students often have a lot of questions on some of the material. We're beginning to study Ancient Greece and the subject of homosexuality has already come up. Some of the leaders we're learning about were homosexual. For instance, when your reading said that Alcibiades had male lovers it meant just that. And students often feel uncomfortable about this, so I just wanted to discuss it. A lot of people think it's OK. And many people think that it's unacceptable. So we're going to be talking about it. And because we don't know if there's anyone in the room who might be gay, I don't want anyone to use derogatory language." The boys look silently around the room as though someone is evidently concealing a dread secret. "I only want people to use the words gay or homosexual. Again the rules in discussion are that no one has to raise his hand but you do have to let other people talk."

The ground is set, and Paul opens the floor: "What are some of the thoughts people have about homosexuality?"

Throughout an entire year at this school, I rarely hear homosexuality discussed, so what Paul does today is unusual. There is a lot of joking about it throughout the school. One senior told me that were a student to be pegged as actually being gay, he would be an absolute pariah, though this never happens unless a student comes out publicly, which is rare. Each year, a couple of boys talk with Margaret Mason, who acts as an in-house psychologist and counselor; typically, they're lonely and looking for support and friendship, she says, or they're concerned about how to tell their parents. Given that these four years here are also the four years during which each student will gradually come to understand his sexuality, a student who might be gay will not necessarily understand it as such. Margaret admits that the subject may cause more tension at a boys' school because without girls, boys can't prove their sexuality during school. And she imagines it must be difficult for a boy to be gay here, given all the rote put-downs—"fag," "faggot," and "fairy" are common slights.

"If they went to Hawken or Heights," she says, "I think that same sort of banter that boys do, 'Oh, you fag' or that kind of put-down statement is going to happen. I don't think it's expressed more here than it would be at a coed school. But again I don't know that."

Seniors, of course, can talk about the subject more openly than freshmen. The opinionated, intellectual Tyler Doggett can discuss it at length without a hint of discomfort. In fact, he seems to like it, as do most boys, I think. Talk of sexuality, any kind of sexuality, is instantly and thoroughly engaging to them. Tyler raises the stakes a notch. Sometimes Tyler wears skirts to school.

"I just periodically wear skirts," he says, referring to his kilt. "My parents don't like it at all. They don't mind it. They roll their eyes, but they don't protest against it. One thing, it's a reaction against myself. It's a reminder to myself to be more tolerant. Because I can see that I'm intolerant and I know it's not a good thing. It's something I'll have to deal with. But I think homophobia is wrong the way racism is wrong."

When Tyler discussed his variety show act (the closest thing to performance art by a student the school has seen, Tyler simply appeared on stage as the last act of the evening wearing an ankle-length skirt and a T-shirt with the word "lesbian" written in large black letters across the front—in the ensuing silence the show ended), he explained that it was a last-minute idea, "a reaction to all the people who muttered, like, 'fairy' to me when I was wearing a kilt. It says, I may wear a kilt but I still like girls . . . I'm not homosexual at all, I'm pretty comfortable with my sexuality, so I'm willing to get on stage. . . . What they have to deal with is *why* are they saying this stuff? I mean *why* are you calling someone a fairy?"

Freshmen are not as sophisticated or forthcoming as Tyler; many *seniors* are not as sophisticated or forthcoming. But freshman, most of them fourteen years old, react to the subject with ingenuous excitement. Now when Paul opens the floor for discussion with an open-ended question—"What are some of the thoughts people have about homosexuality?"—the atmosphere is instantly pressurized. The room has never been, and never will be, so silent. And Paul's going to wait. He's opened the forum—it's their turn now. The tension creates a house-of-cards effect—one breath and the class will topple into nervous laughter. Which is exactly what happens.

Five, ten, fifteen seconds of silence and John, sitting in the corner, begins to squirm. He's got something he wants to say. John is energetic in classroom discussions though not a diligent student. He's short, has close-cropped, reddish-brown hair, wears braces and his face is carpeted with dark freckles.

The silence is exciting, thick and getting thicker, and then John stops squirming and says, "Uh," and the class topples. John looks right, looks left—right, left, right, left—*whadIsay?*—grinning wildly.

"That's OK," Paul says. "This can be a difficult subject to talk about and it takes time to get going. John?" This sufficiently quells the boys and John speaks.

"I'm taught in my religion that it's wrong."

"OK, what religion are you?" Paul asks.

"Roman Catholic."

"OK, and you're taught that it's wrong, anything else?"

"It's all around," John says. "You hear about it a lot."

Kevin, his retainer for once properly secured upon the palate, says, "I think when you, when people, hear the word, they have a lot of thoughts about it. Personally I'm not in favor of gay people."

This results in more laughter, but a different sort than John got; it seems less sympathetic, slightly derisive. The boys are intuitively attuned to what's acceptable and what's not. Kevin seems undaunted, though he says nothing, allowing John to continue along this new line he's opened up.

"When you think of yourself with another man it's," John says, fidgeting and holding his stomach, smiling, "it's gross."

"OK, you think it's gross," Paul clarifies.

Jay says, "In the media you don't hear a lot of good things about gays. In the government, and gays in the military."

Paul again clarifies the response, telling the class that the media often cover the subjects Jay has mentioned, giving equal weight to the various views people have on the subject.

John agrees. "They're showing a lot about gays in the media," he says, then brings the conversation back to a personal level, suggesting that your own views are your decision.

"I don't think there's anything you *decide,*" Kevin says. "It's either you like them or you don't."

Some laugh at this and several shout out that "accept" is a better word than like or dislike.

"OK, we should discuss this," Paul says. "How can you not like them but accept them? John?"

"Well, it's like Jonah's Jewish, and I'm Catholic, and I accept that he's Jewish but I don't have to believe what he does."

Kevin says it's different.

"OK, Kevin," Paul says. "Is there some food that you really don't like, that really—"

"Spinach," he says, definitively.

"OK, spinach. Now that makes you feel ill to think about eating it, but does that mean you don't think other people should eat spinach?"

"Well, no," Kevin says. He thinks for a moment and the class waits. "That's a good analogy but being homosexual is different than food." Several students nod approvingly. "Being a homosexual is probably the biggest thing in their *lives.*"

"People don't like them because of the stereotypes," says Jay.

"How do you know those stereotypes aren't true?" Kevin responds.

"OK, this is good time to talk about stereotypes," says Paul. "What are some of the stereotypes of gay people?"

"That they act feminine," Shawn offers. "They don't—" he lifts his shoulders, puffs his chest, clenches his fists and says, *"Masculine."*

Other stereotypes are called out. They have high-pitched voices. They walk funny.

Paul repeats their remarks, uses the word "flamers," and makes goofy motions with his hands to point up the silliness of stereotypes.

"But they are treated differently," says Kevin. "If someone in this school said that they were gay—"

"What would happen?" Paul asks.

A number of voices call out from around the circle saying that such a person would be ostracized, that people would make fun of him.

Jim, seated beside Paul, says, "If someone in this school said they were gay, they would be *very* lonely."

"When I was at US," Paul says, "a couple people were openly gay and they got both reactions."

This comes as a shock to several students. Kevin can't fathom it. "Why?" he asks. *"Why* would they *say* that?"

"OK, why would that happen?" Paul asks.

Chris says, "It's their freedom to do that." Others focus on the names an openly gay student would be called, and the notion of prejudice comes up. Paul asks what is the difference between being prejudiced against blacks or Jews and being prejudiced against gays? "If you used the word 'nigger' or 'kike' in this school," Paul says, "people would be *all over* you. But people use the word 'faggot' all the time."

Jay suddenly wants to know if people choose to be gay or not. "Because," he says, "it would be different if you *chose* to be that way."

Jonah says, "I can't even *think* about it."

Paul notes that there are some studies that say it's genetic and linked to a specific part of the brain. He notes that some researchers have suggested that ten percent of the population is gay. "That would mean there are thirty-five or forty gay people at this school."

This raises some eyebrows, and again the boys look suspiciously around the room at their classmates.

"A lot of people think it's a choice of lifestyles and criticize it for that," Matt offers.

John wants to know, "Do gay people feel repulsed at the—"

Paul interrupts quickly, "OK, do they have negative feelings—"

"Yeah," John says, "do they have negative feelings when they think about a man and a woman?"

"I don't know the answer to that," Paul says. "I've never asked any of my gay friends if this is the case. Does anybody know the answer to this?"

No one does and Paul continues.

"So it's uncomfortable for you to think about two men together, but is it the same with lesbians? Do you feel the same discomfort when you think about two women together?"

The boys look around, exchanging glances—no, they don't think that's so bad, not at all.

"Why is that?" Paul asks.

This question strikes a chord in John. He grins in amazement. "Yeah," he says. "Yeah, that's right, why is that? That's kind of weird. I *do* feel that way. That's *so weird.*"

Shawn says, "It's a mind set," and contends that women are equally repulsed at the thought of lesbians.

"We can think of two women because we can put ourselves in their shoes," says Jonah.

"That's *so weird,*" John says, happily.

"OK, here's another question," says Paul. "What do people think of interracial marriage?"

Chris says, "I don't think it compares. It's still a man and a woman."

Kevin says, "I mean, my niece is half black and I think that's OK."

"Would that have seemed OK a hundred years ago?" Paul asks. Everyone calls out *no.*

"So, Chris, is this just a stronger bias that might take time for people to get over, like interracial marriage?"

Chris doesn't respond verbally, but gives Paul a concessional shrug and nod.

Drew has been silent, thinking, and suddenly bursts out with his thought. "Every homosexual has to have a mother and father, right?"

The class explodes into laughter.

Paul says, "Quiet down. Drew's posing a question."

Drew continues: "If they have a mother and a father, wouldn't the *parents* teach them *not* to be a homosexual?"

"This goes back to what Jay was saying about choice," says Paul. "They didn't teach you to be straight—I'm assuming that you're straight."

Drew puts his hand on his chest and says, "Yeah, of *course.*"

"You're parents didn't *teach* you to be straight did they. They didn't hang a picture of Christie Brinkley in your room and say, 'That's what you want.' "

"No," says Drew, seeing Paul's point.

"OK, Matt's been waiting to get in here. Matt?"

"You can look at the biases logically," he says in a soft voice that seems almost pleading, "but some people just have *feelings* about it."

"OK, it seems most of you do have a gut feeling that there's something negative about homosexuality. Let's talk about some philosophical issues. What are some of the negatives from a philosophical standpoint?"

"That it could happen to *you,*" says Kevin.

"That you could become gay?" Paul asks.

"No," he says. "That someone would *approach* you." This seems to be Kevin's biggest concern, being approached sexually. It makes him shiver and scowl. He says if a gay person approached another gay person, fine, but if one approached him, there would be *consequences.*

One student brings up the subject of dreams in relation to homosexuality, and Paul tells the class that straight people sometimes have "gay" dreams; this might suggest, he says, that everyone has some deep desire for all people, and he explains that some people are openly bisexual.

"I had a gay dream," John bursts out. And the class again laughs uproariously. "No, no," John corrects quickly, with his right-left, right-left grin. "I *did,* I had a gay dream, but it was about two other people. I did. It was. And I woke up." John puts both hands on top of his head, and says, "And I was, like, disgusted."

Paul quiets the class down and changes direction. "What are some of the arguments that it's immoral?"

"Religion," says John.

There's some discussion about gay Christians and gay Jews and Paul asks, "How can someone be gay and still be a Catholic?"

Before anyone can answer, the bell rings. In unison, the students bend to the floor to gather their notebooks and backpacks. Shawn asks, "Mr. Bailin, is the Quest tomorrow going to be all period or just half?"

It's as though nothing had happened; the boys are already hustling to their next class. Paul leaves the room looking downcast. The boys really surprised him, though with that class maybe he shouldn't have been so surprised. He suspected he'd have problems with seventh period. In his first-period class, not a single student voiced a negative impression. "I actually tried to *lead* them to say negative things about gays and couldn't," he says. "The closest they came was admitting negative feelings about the thought of gay sex but realizing it was something that you had to work out." Leaving today's seventh-period class he says, "That was the most homophobic discussion all day."

5

One morning during the fall, I head to the office of Kerry Brennan. It's a small, corner room in the administration wing. One wall is bare-brick, another is glass overlooking lake and woods. It contains two bookshelves, a couch, a chair, and, most days, stacks of Broadway sheet music, which spill out from beneath the desk. Almost as many framed photographs as books line the shelves—pictures of Kerry with lower school boys, with whom he spent the past seven years before being named upper-school director. The photographs show he once wore a moustache, looked twenty-four years old, and doesn't appear much older than that now.

When I arrive at 8:45, he's just finished dialing the phone. He motions me in.

"Joyce," he says into the receiver, leaning forward to prop himself on his desk. "Kerry Brennan. . . . Is he up yet?"

Kerry nods, covers the mouthpiece and says to me, "She *warned* Kevin I'd be calling."

Kevin Casey, the Civil War scholar, is different this year. He walks and speaks, when he speaks at all, more slowly than he did last year. His face is a wall. His eyes won't meet yours. He's not completing his school work and he's failing math. In a faculty meeting to discuss students' problems and progress, his name came up. Dick McCrea, who began as a fourth grader at this school during the Roosevelt administration, is Kevin's sponsor and Civil War buddy and was the first to suggest aloud what many suspected.

"I don't know if he's off smoking something *other* than cigarettes, but he always looks under the *weather*. After Kevin got back from the trip to Gettysburg he became a *very different* person." McCrea, besides being worried for Kevin, is personally upset—Kevin had once been his "jewel," he said, the best scholar of the Civil War he'd encountered in his thirty-five years of teaching.

Carol Pribble, the drama teacher, reminded the faculty gathered in a circle around the desks of Room 270 that Kevin is acting in a community theater. "He works five or six nights a week," she says with an edge of protectiveness. "Maybe *that's* why he looks tired."

Roger Yedid said, "I agree with Dick. He's involved in something else."

Kevin, roused from sleep, reaches the phone.

"Kevin," says Kerry. "Good morning. You coming to school? . . . Uh huh. Uh huh. . . . What do you have this morning? . . . Who do you have for French? . . . Well, you're in luck, because he's not here this morning, so you got a bit of a break. . . . Are you doing your paper on a word processor? . . . Good. Can you bring your work *in?* . . . Try and get into school so you can make it to math and English. Doc Thomas will cut you some slack on the paper. . . . All right, Kevin. . . . See you soon."

Kerry hangs up the phone and says, "I've *got* to get him into school or I've got to *suspend* him."

Kerry Brennan would rather be talking about educational theory, about ideas for improving the curriculum and the school, but dealing with daily glitches, such as Kevin's unexcused absence, students' defiance of the dress code, and other minutiae such as the faculty's uproar at a table that disappeared from their lounge, seems to swallow an increasing amount of his time. He wants to talk about the geographical survey course, which combines the creation of computerized topographical land surveys of Cuyahoga and Lake counties with field trips to gather soil and water samples for a comprehensive environmental studies–computer science course, or the experimental Reason and Rhetoric class. He wants to discuss what the ideal mix of traditional and cross-disciplinary classes should be in a school's curriculum. But during his first months as upper school director, he has been one person: The Enforcer.

"This morning at eight fifteen," he tells me, "I want to greet kids, and say good luck on your test and how ya doing, but instead I'm saying 'Please take your hat off' to kids three or four times."

■ ■ ■

The only person within the school who seems truly immune to the weird-gravity effect is Kerry Brennan. Perhaps it's the excitement of the new job, or maybe he runs on some special fuel, but his wash-and-wear appearance never varies. He's unflappable.

In a way, it's surprising that Kerry is even here. Eight years ago, he was twenty-nine years old and an English teacher/music director/basketball coach at Roxbury Latin, a boys' school in Boston headed by Tony Jarvis. Kerry had just spent a year at Columbia University as a Klingenstien Fellow where he studied educational theory. Since he took the job at Roxbury Latin at age twenty-three, he had taught by intuition; at Columbia, for the first time in his career, he learned about the art and science of teaching, about the way schools were run and how school cultures were built, about the significance of independent schools in American education. He returned to Roxbury Latin with a master's degree and on fire to put a slew of new ideas into action. He wanted to change the school.

"We're just fine the way we are," he was told in no uncertain terms. The headmaster of the school ran the show, and Kerry remembers that Jarvis, in a school whose enrollment is roughly 270 boys spread over six grades, was able to put his indelible stamp on everything. Jarvis did see a genuine spark in Brennan and suggested he look for work in administration at a school that might be more receptive to the fresh ideas of an ambitious young schoolmaster. He said he knew a school in Cleveland that was looking to find a director for its lower school. Jarvis handed him a US brochure and told him, "You *owe* it to yourself to go there. Rowland McKinley is one of a kind. And, besides, you'll never get the job."

Counting on that, Kerry went to a headhunter to discuss various options. Kerry mentioned the job opening at US. "You're ten years away from that job," the headhunter said dismissively. Kerry was too young and didn't have enough experience for a director's post. The headhunter said perhaps an administrative "helper" would be more realistic. These things take time; one needs to build slowly and carefully. The headhunter suggested that if Kerry was determined to advance through the administrative ranks of an independent school, it wouldn't hurt if he were married; he and his wife might form a "partnership." Kerry says the headhunter stopped just short of telling him to buy a golden retriever.

Kerry had been ambivalent about the US job in the first place, so he wasn't all that upset after meeting with the headhunter. When he told Jarvis about it, though, Jarvis phoned his old boss and asked him to see Kerry. The school flew Kerry in for an interview. He loved US, as it turned out—*here* they were talking theory and development. Kerry and McKinley hit it off, and McKinley offered him the job.

Now, after seven years of working with boys ages five through fourteen—and, more often, their parents—he's once again working with teenagers, and on a new campus, which has its own equally complex dynamics, disciplinary matters among them. No longer are infractions relegated to mild academic dishonesty, bad language, disruptive classroom behavior. Occasionally, the problems are serious and could not be further from his interests in education.

A few weeks ago, for instance, toward the end of September, the school received an anonymous phone call informing them that one of its students, Chris Petro, had gotten into a fight at a party that led to a police report and a formal charge of assault and battery against him.

Chris does not look like a gentle soul. He is so big that his head seems disproportionately small. Chris is co-captain of the football team, the defensive linchpin at middle linebacker, a position that he, at six-foot-two, 235 pounds, is suited for. Chris is such a powerful athlete that as a freshman he played on the varsity team, something that's almost unheard of at the school. Nick Zinn, in a school newspaper article, described Chris as having "the agility of a yoga master and the brawn of the towel guy from those commercials." Of all the players on this year's squad, Chris is the person you least want to see on the other side of the line.

After Margaret received the anonymous phone call about the event, what Chris calls simply "a beef," she finds Kerry and describes the situation. So far, all is hearsay, and Kerry and Margaret head to the athletic fields and pull Chris out of practice. He confirms the story. He seems to Margaret almost inhumanly large in his massive shoulder pads, not a boy at all, until, as he recites the details of the night in question, he begins to cry. The sight of this brutish boy, dressed in football armor, weeping, jars Margaret.

Kerry and Margaret meet with Hawley and come to a decision about what must be done. The event happened over the weekend, not during school hours and nowhere near the school. The school is not required by law to do anything. Chris will appear in Juvenile Court to answer the charges. But Kerry, Margaret, and Hawley agree that Chris's behavior was grossly inappropriate for a student at this school and decide that Chris will not be permitted to play in this week's game.

Chris and the team are devastated. In an already shaky season, it's a crucial game against Columbus Academy, their biggest and toughest opponent. If there's one game they need Chris for, it's this one. What's more, Chris has been told that Big-Ten college scouts are planning to attend; this game could lead to a football scholarship, possibly determine the course of the next four years and beyond. The school stands its ground.

The football team, with a 2-1 record going into the game, is not only physically diminished but emotionally bruised by the school's decision. Quarterback Nick Caserio, the other co-captain, must rally the team and compensate for a weakened defense with a powerful air show. He does. Nick completes ten of fifteen passes for 287 yards and racks up 26 points. As the game moves into the closing minutes of the fourth quarter, with US ahead 26–25, Columbus Academy gains control of the ball in time for one final drive. Caserio and the offense can do nothing but watch as Columbus Academy plows through the US defense toward the end zone. US loses, 31–26.

For Chris, it is the turning point of the season. "I got down and the team got down," Chris says. The team, after a 9-1 record last year, will finish with a mediocre 5-5 record.

The decision is consistent with the way Kerry Brennan intends to run the upper school and is revealing of both the convictions of the school and the variety of problems with which the new director must contend.

"There are certain things I think a school should stand for," he says. "And that's part of why we're having some problems over the last couple of weeks up here. I do believe a school should be a model for certain things for kids."

Kerry must grapple daily not only with students but also with faculty. They press their own demands and problems on him. Many want longer class periods, periods that are frequently truncated by special assemblies; this continual debate grew hot in late October when an outside speaker gave a powerful—and long—presentation on how even liberals condoned the mass slaughter of a race of people during World War II. Gus Pla, the only Hispanic faculty member and a veteran boys'-school Spanish teacher, wanted more time after assembly and during class to digest the words of the speaker. Scott Smith, a math and computer teacher, was furious that his class had been shortened to 36 minutes on the day of an important test. It required some diplomatic "two-stepping," as Kerry puts it, to calm them both.

Hawley stops by Kerry's office later that day to ask if everything is all right. Kerry says he believes it is.

Hawley says, "I still think you should have locked Scott and Gus in a room till they came out hugging."

Kerry laughs—his brown eyes sparkle, and dimples form deep in the cheeks of his large oval face. For an instant, the tension of the day vanishes.

Hawley often stops by to chat with Kerry. He's grateful that Kerry's here; Kerry is relieving him of a boatload of work. His only concern, in fact, is that Kerry is too ambitious, will try to change too much too fast. He stops by Kerry's office often, mainly because he likes him and likes to talk about school business with him. Obviously in a hurry, but still standing in the doorway of Kerry's office as though he doesn't want to leave, Hawley thinks of something else that's bothering him.

"I want to talk to you about," Hawley says, then lifts his eyebrows and intones a French accent, "Rene Salozar."

Kerry quickly asks what's wrong.

"He was *asleep* in assembly again," Hawley says, his tone now serious. "That's the *third* time." Hawley looks at the floor and shakes his head. Then he makes strangling motions with his hands. "I'm going to talk to him." He pauses. "When I'm not so *mad,* I'm going to talk to him."

Rene, a senior, is new to the school this year. He's moved from Texas in order to participate in a joint program the school has with the Cleveland Institute of Music, in which students spend half a day at US, and the other half at the Institute. Rene plays viola, and Kerry, a musician and singer himself (and also president of the board of Lyric Opera Cleveland, a respected local group), is sympathetic. He knows the boy is having a tough time adjusting not just to a new school but to a new city as well, away from family and friends, and he comes to Rene's defense.

"Rick, he sleeps in the *dorm* at CIM," Kerry says. "And he's up practicing until one thirty or two thirty in the morning."

Hawley shakes his head, says, "I still think it's something else," but he waves goodbye and saunters off, heading to the lower school, where he's promised to attend the youngsters' Halloween parade.

Of all Kerry's problems, of all the debates and decisions—in addition to teaching a section of sophomore English and administrative juggling—one issue has made a smooth immersion into this new job, into this new campus, impossible. One command has become *the* most contentious concern of his new post: the dress code.

At first, this seemed to me a bit odd. Open it to a national perspective, and the issue sounds rather small, even a little silly. While here, debate surrounds white T-shirts and the exact definition of a sweater as opposed to a sweatshirt, in some public schools in the country, students are mugged and beaten—even murdered—because of, and for, their clothing. The principal of a school in Brooklyn implemented a dress code at his school because, the *New York Times* reported, "he was weary of attending funerals of students slain for their clothing."

From New York to California to Texas, *public* schools have begun enforcing rules of dress, barring such things as Doc Martens boots, Oakland Raiders jackets, and accessories associated with gangs; they're also banning non-violence-related apparel, such as T-shirts with crude messages, sneakers with blinking lights, and underwear worn outside the trousers. One can only imagine what Kerry would do if a boy walked into morning assembly wearing coat and tie and white Jockey briefs stretched over his chinos.

Also, many schools throughout the country are considering dress codes in order to encourage the students to be more attentive in class and to raise their self-image. Some studies suggest that students who must conform to a dress code often earn better grades. Many students, and even more parents, like the idea of dress codes; others call their nearest civil-liberties union, contending that no one can interfere with their freedom to dress as they wish, and demand that the courts decide. Some consider dress codes, especially those of the coat-and-tie variety, to be elitist. Others argue that *not* having a dress code creates visual, sometimes painful, class distinctions among students, that dress codes are therefore egalitarian rather than elitist. Next year, the Long Beach, California, public school district will become the first in the nation to require its students to wear uniforms.

An independent school, on the other hand, can legally require whatever sort of dress it wishes. And an independent *boys'* school, one would think, would be free of student pressure; whom do the students want to dress up, or down, *for?*

This appears not to be the point at US. The dress code has always been coat and tie for morning assembly, no tennis shoes or jeans, collared shirts that button down the front, and only white T-shirts. It used to be that coat and tie were required for lunch as well; this resulted in a greater number of soiled coats than are found at the school today. Over the past few years, as the administration of the school shifted, faculty and administrators stopped enforcing the few requirements the school had kept. The boys grew sloppy and most of the faculty didn't like it. So Kerry reacted, sending a letter to parents reiterating the rules and making it clear from his very first appearance before the student body that things would be different this year. He was personally in favor of it, but says it was not something he had planned to enforce himself.

"I, frankly, was willing to say, 'What is important? Can we reexamine this?'" Kerry tells me. "And people for the most part, said, 'No, kids should learn that there are certain ways to behave in certain settings.'"

Shortly after school began, one of the seniors most angered by Mr. Brennan's rules organized a petition to relax the dress code and obtained fifty signatures, which he brought to Mr. Brennan. Nothing happened. Soon after that, bulletins began to appear throughout the school with "DRESS CODE" written in bold laser print across the top—another petition, written and organized by the same senior, Franz Maruna.

"When the school year was about to start I was very hopeful that with the new blood in the administration we could get some new and interesting things done," it read. "Instead I find US's senseless policies are increased with no explanation to the people they affect, the students. Increasing the dress code in this day and age isn't the act of a school that wants to stay up to date with the real world, but the desperate act of an over-conservative institution that's trying to hold on to out of date values. No one cares if you wear nice boots or have long hair in many companies. Indeed some of US's own faculty have facial hair, hair over their shoulders, and probably don't wear white undershirts. So what's US's point? Guess they just want us to look good for their alumni."

This is a secondary and common subtext of student ire. They believe that the way they look and behave is not for their benefit, or the school's, but rather for graduates of the school, potential money-givers. It's true that when alumni return, the school goes out of its way to impress them. Some students seem to feel that alumni are the people for whom the school exists; for all the students can figure, they might not even have to *come* to school were it not for alumni.

The subject is even referred to in bathroom stalls. Granted, what one finds written in bathrooms probably does not represent the strongest minds of the school at work, but the opinions are likely honest. In the fall, I wrote down a couple of examples from admittedly slim pickings (most of the stalls, miraculously it seems to me, were graffiti-free). Amidst some references to drugs (pro and con), sex (exclusively pro), an unflattering remark about Mr. Brennan, and the all-purpose "Fuck you" floating like a lone balloon in a clear sky sent up by some angry-at-no-one-in-particular student, I found two revealing dialogues:

"Alumni suck."
"We'll be one soon retard."

And:

"Do you smell the paint? It was used to cover obsene [sic] graffiti, (just before Open House!) Do you feel taken?"
"That was a pretty pathetic job to make our school look good."
"Why not have it look good buddy?"

For every negative appraisal of the school, there would be a positive one, even in the bathrooms.

Franz's bulletin continues: "Flannel shirts, boots, colored undershirts, facial hair"—beards and moustaches are verboten for students, as well—"and hair over the shoulders can all be worn and the student will still look clean and neat. If a student looks dirty and lacks personal hygiene, of course the administration should be able to tell him to trim or clean his hair, and clothes, or get demerits, but not cut it off and throw out clothes that have worked fine for the school in the past."

Mr. Brennan's response: I appreciate your spirit, Franz—but no dice. They negotiate an agree-to-disagree stalemate, and Franz lets it drop.

This is all very frustrating, not to mention time-consuming, for Kerry. First, he explains, there's nothing *new* about the dress code; he had merely enforced the existing code. Second, after bowing to the majority of faculty who asked that it be enforced, he now has to listen to them explain that *they* won't enforce it because it's not their job.

"The bottom line on all that business," Kerry says, sounding a bit weary of it all, "is that there is an important value in distinguishing for kids what's appropriate in certain settings. I happen to think that a certain civility in dress is important, but I also don't want to *define* myself that way." To the faculty who contend that enforcing a dress code is not their job, Kerry responds, "If that's *just* my job, then I don't *want* this job. So that's not been fun, but in the scheme of things it's not that big a deal."

It does, however, confirm what any parent of a teenager already knows: that for teenagers, the most prolific narcissists in the world, appearance is the chief means by which they create, or inform people that they are creating, a self that is distinct from parents, school, and even friends. Also, teenagers need a fight. Doesn't matter what kind, where, what issues are at stake—the struggle is the thing. If Kerry were to permit boots, but only so long as they were fully laced with pant cuffs worn outside, the laces and cuffs rule would be, if not debated, then egregiously disobeyed; if all shirts, not just button-downs, were permitted so long as they were tucked in, odds are high some students would buy shirts that weren't designed to be tucked in, then protest the unfairness of the tucked-in rule.

Math teacher Warren Siekman describes the dynamic succinctly: "I don't care *where* you put the boundaries, *that's* where they'll fight you."

Kerry's new job provides him an unusual vantage point. He has been reunited with boys he knew as eight-, nine-, and ten-year-olds. He can, with some students, witness the conclusion of the boy-to-young-man transformation. Tyler Soltis, now a senior, is a significant example. Tyler is a lifer. He began US in kindergarten twelve years ago, and Kerry has known him since fourth grade, when Tyler was ten.

That first year, when the new, thirty-year-old director of the lower school arrived from Boston, he surprised little Tyler. "He knew my name right from the beginning," Tyler recalls. "The first time he saw me he said, 'Hi, Tyler.'" This gave Tyler a serious enough jolt that he remembers the moment vividly eight years later; it wasn't so much how the new director knew his name, but rather why he would care in the first place.

The other surprise Mr. Brennan gave Tyler happened in the spring of his eighth-grade year. Tyler had just finished gym class, and waited in line outside the dining hall where Miss DeSilva checked them before lunch. Hair combed, shoelaces tied, shirt tucked in, belts on and buckled. Miss DeSilva, possessed of raven hair and stiletto voice, had been terrifying boys for decades, and her powers had only increased with age. As Tyler waited to get past Miss DeSilva, Mr. Brennan pulled him out of the line.

"Tyler," Mr. Brennan said, "I'd like you to speak at graduation."

Tyler was flabbergasted. "My eyes bulged out," he recalls.

Traditionally, three boys speak at eighth-grade graduation—one lifer, one who began in fifth grade, and one who began in seventh grade. Mr. Brennan had chosen Tyler to represent the lifers. Tyler thought, "You have got to be kidding." It didn't make any sense, he remembers. "There were so many kids smarter than I was. I wasn't class president. I didn't do *anything*. There were so many people he could have picked."

What's more, Tyler was the butt of his classmate's jokes, and he knew it. He was the sort of awkward, unlikable kid who tried so hard to be people's friends that they made fun of him, knowing he'd always come back for more. Tyler was an outcast. Today he remembers that that speech became "the only thing I did in eighth grade that I put my heart into." When he delivered this speech at eighth-grade graduation to classmates, to faculty, to parents, he wore a special gift from Mr. Brennan: a limited-edition, 100th-anniversary, commemorative school tie in honor of the school's centennial that year.

By appearances Tyler Soltis has changed in ways one might expect; he's bulkier than he was in eighth grade, and now, newly eighteen, a swarthy shadow of whiskers coarsens his plump cheeks. He's not athletic, and, given his short, rotund body, you wouldn't expect him to be. He's an average student. His dark hair is short and thick. Other boys don't pick on him the way they used to; mainly they ignore him.

"I'm one of those people who don't necessarily belong here," he told me, "don't fit in, per se. I just can't *relate* to anyone around here. There are a few of us."

More significantly, though, the weight he's gained over four years, the new physical bulk, seems to have engendered a new energy. While once Tyler was insecure and passive at school, now everything about him seems likely to bust out. His dark eyes are protruberant behind thick glasses. His body lurches when he speaks, like a car whose driver hasn't mastered a stick-shift, whether he's talking about girls with his friend Kris Fletcher, the dress code, or the Cleveland Cavaliers (he's missed only three home games in three years), or when he attacks the blackboard before Doc Strater's first-period class to write his daily message.

This year, his thirteenth and final year at the school, Tyler must meet with Mr. Brennan about another public address, his senior speech. Every senior is required to deliver a speech to the school in order to graduate, and these speeches must be approved by a faculty member to ensure that none of the boys broadcast anything unseemly while on stage. Miss O'Donnell, who was to approve Tyler's speech, wouldn't. "It doesn't *conform*," she told him. "See Mr. Brennan." Tyler couldn't believe it. "You have got to be kidding," he said to Miss O'Donnell. For the first time in twelve years Tyler has something important to say, and now he's not allowed to say it.

Tyler's senior speech is a thinly veiled allegory concerning "a small, exclusive private school" he calls Benito Springs High School; Benito, as in Mussolini, which, coincidentally, makes the school's initials BS. Kerry read the speech and didn't like it any more than Miss O'Donnell did. Tyler sat in Mr. Brennan's office and listened to Mr. Brennan's list of proposed changes. Tyler, adamant, conceded to only one. Mr. Brennan asked him to take out the many references to the "fictitious" school as "BS" (some of the people actually like their school and what they do here, Kerry reasons, and he doesn't want any student standing on stage calling their work bullshit). Kerry asks Tyler to *consider* several other changes.

If a senior wants to be crafty, he gets his speech approved at the last minute; that way, extensive overhauls are impossible and he can keep his revisions superficial, which is what Tyler has done.

The following morning, Tyler slumps in one of three captain's chairs on stage well before assembly begins, silent and waiting. He appears to be so nervous he can't move. The mood of the morning, though, is lively. The speakers are blasting "Another Opening, Another Show," from *Kiss Me, Kate.* This is step-and-kick music, Kerry's choice, in honor of the fall play which opens tonight, and he's waiting at the edge of the auditorium, grinning and rocking from heel to toe along with the music.

He looks so bubbly, I give him a double take as I move to my seat.

"The headmaster's away," he says. "I'm goin' crazy."

At 8:10 the song fades, the last boys slip into their seats, and Kerry strides across the stage stuffing morning announcements into his coat pocket.

"Good morning," he says. "To introduce this morning's senior speaker is Bill Shepardson."

Tyler's buddy stands and greets the assembly. Bill, too cool to be nervous, cocks his head to one side and then to the other, shifts from right foot to left, as he stumbles and mumbles through the intro—a brief collage of his friendship with Tyler, a relationship that dates to second grade. "We share girl problems," Bill recites from his note cards, "late-night dinners at Denny's, concerts, Indians games, Cavs and Thunderbolts games along with millions of other exciting experiences." Bill concludes with the resounding loyalty and support that may only be possible among deep boyhood friends: "Tyler hasn't done much for this school but manage the one-and-fifteen freshman basketball team and host this year's variety show. In fact, Tyler hasn't done much but complain and complain about everything from this school to his hamsters Beavis and Butt-head having babies. Here to talk to you about something I had absolutely *nothing* to do with is Tyler Brandon Soltis the first."

Tyler scarcely seems to have heard Bill's introduction as he lunges at the podium. Kerry is seated directly behind him. Tyler spots Miss O'Donnell scowling at him from the audience. His parents are in the audience, as well.

Tyler recounts the story of Bob, who attended Benito Springs High School. Bob had a hard time. "You see," Tyler tells the school, "it seems that Bob had a trait that the administration didn't approve of: he thought for himself." This was not good at Benito Springs, Tyler explains, where, after eighth grade the administration hypnotized all the students so that they believed peculiar things. "Suddenly," Tyler says, "a person's length of hair directly affected their intelligence, and the wearing of cowboy boots made it more difficult to do math." Bob, unluckily, was not hypno- tized, so in order to maintain his individuality, he had to keep his true beliefs hidden. But eventually Bob was broken and forced to conform. This was Bob's downfall. "His college life," Tyler explains, "was terrible because he couldn't stop agreeing with everyone. . . . His nonexistent backbone made it very hard to walk, thus making it impossible to find any kind of job." For ten minutes, Tyler barks out a story of the destitute and lonely Bob: a harangue against Mr. Brennan, Dr. Hawley, and the faculty so thorough that even his classmates don't avoid a good drubbing for their passive acceptance of rules and the mindless, spineless cliques they form.

"Conformity is an awful thing," Tyler concludes. "It feigns order and makes the society that rules over us think that everything that they do is fine. Well, everything they do is not fine, and not enough people under- stand that."

The speech, like all speeches, receives polite applause from everyone except Franz Maruna, who had recently forfeited his dress-code war. Franz gives Tyler a vigorous one-man standing ovation. Mr. Brennan claps, though only for a moment and with a sour face. When Tyler falls into his chair on stage, clutching his speech, Mr. Brennan notices something that lends an ironic twist, and a note of continuity, to the performance. Tyler's last words to the lower school were those of humorous adoration; his final address to the upper school is an angry-young-man polar opposite on the evils of conformity. Yet there, dangling neatly from his shirt collar, is the limited-edition, 100th-anniversary commemorative school tie Kerry had given him back in eighth grade before his last school speech. Tyler had not worn it by accident.

Then an unusual thing happens to Tyler. For the first time in his life, he enjoys a shimmering moment of celebrity, even of minor notoriety. People he doesn't even know are stopping him in the hallway to respond to his speech. "That was the best speech I've heard here," one junior tells him. Ricky Smith, a sophomore, shakes his head afterward and says, "If people don't like the rules, they can go somewhere else." Tyler's classmate, Dan Petrov, tells him, "I don't agree with what you said, but you said it well." One of his teachers, somewhat ambiguously, says, *"Tyler,* I didn't think you had it in you." Tyler's words have had repercussions.

Tyler bobs slightly as he walks, the feet of his stout legs spread wide. Because his eyes seem always on the verge of popping against the insides of his glasses, he gives the impression of perpetual, intense alertness. On the day of his speech, this effect is enhanced. Walking the halls, he senses he's being talked about. He's never had so much attention, something I consider when I ask if he has some time to talk. I've always had a soft spot for misfits and outcasts, and Tyler is clearly one of them—awkward in appearance and movement, not immediately likeable, somewhat abrasive, otherwise nondescript, but high energy. Like an untimed piston. More than any senior I'd so far met, Tyler is clearly on the cusp of some kind of change, physically developed but with a voice that's not yet in sync with his body. This becomes clear as we talk, though in an odd way: Tyler can't stop contradicting himself. You can watch the tensions butting each other as he tries to reconcile the conflict, to find some objective balance, never successfully. One of the first things he tells me, for instance, is that he doesn't belong at US. He has, of course, been here as long as or longer than any other student in the school. During sixth period, approximately five hours after he publicly excoriated the school, he says to me, "I keep a low profile about how I feel."

"This school is such a *small* part of my *life,"* he says. "When I go home, this school is the *last* thing in my mind. I would like to sever myself from this place as much as I can. I don't go to sporting events, I don't do school functions, I don't do dances." Immediately, then, he tells me he went to last year's prom and that he'll probably be at this year's. "But prom is different. Prom is something you *have* to go to, something you want to tell your kids about." He smiles.

If he wanted to sever himself from the school, I wonder, why did he emcee the fall variety show, a job that put him on stage for an entire evening in front of hundreds of his fellow students and scores of girls from other high schools? It was a whim, Tyler says, he doesn't know why he did it. This evening he will appear in the opening of *To Kill a Mockingbird*. "I have a really small part," he argues. "I just wanted to be in a play."

"I'd like to be accepted once in my life," he continues. "I'm accepted by the administration because I'm *extremely nice* to teachers. I try very hard not to make enemies, but I'm *weird*. That's how I'm regarded by the students. I don't care what people think about me. I *do* care what *some* people think, but not what *these* people think." *These*, meaning his classmates, or as he might phrase it, the other people who go to this school, which is one reason he has his heart set on getting into Syracuse University. The people he met there, now those are his kind of people—nonconformists.

All his life he's been a good boy, he says, never complaining out loud, never saying anything to anyone, keeping it all inside. It has been a career, by his own reckoning, of passive fatalism. "I don't usually speak up because I know people who *do* speak up and it *doesn't matter*," he says. "Since the beginning of the year, we've had good ol' Franz trying to do our little petition thing and it's never gonna *work*. It should be tried, but it's never gonna work. And besides, dress code isn't significant. I don't mind coming here wearing what I have to wear. The dress code is something we have to live with, and I don't have a problem with it." But, he says, "I *do* have a problem with the *rules* they've changed this year. Things like we're not allowed to wear *these*." He points to his new Timberland boots. They don't conform to the dress code that he doesn't have a problem with.

Tyler is more complex than even these contradictions suggest. Last year, he confides, a psychiatrist labeled him a manic depressive and prescribed medication that eventually induced seizures and forced him to endure a barrage of tests and occasional hospitalization. Tyler missed a month of school. He's certain it was the drugs and he now refuses all medication, determined to fight depression on his own. What makes Tyler worth watching, though, is not that he ties himself in knots during conversation, nor that he has become, for a day at least, an unlikely emblem of student discontent. It is, rather, what these things describe. While Tyler appears grown, he is actually still forming. The obedient eighth-grade Tyler, desperate to be popular, now battles with an emerging hunger for independence. He is in mid-morph.

■ ■ ■

The senior speeches, about seventy of them during the course of the year, are usually an entertaining way to begin the school day. Though occasionally dull or awkward or unmemorable, each speech becomes a remarkably personal moment for the boy on stage. These aren't speeches on NAFTA or health-care reform. The boys almost invariably talk about themselves. A short, chubby boy named Brian describes for the school his freshman year, when he was suspended for inhaling whippets—nitrous oxide—in the woods, was cut from the lacrosse team, and how, during that bad time, a foreign exchange student who lived with the family threatened to steal his brother's affections from him, and the terrible jealousy that created.

Andrew Eakin, a lanky six-feet four-inches tall, discusses his decision— after a doctor told him that his projected height of at least six-feet eight-inches could be medically prevented—not to take a growth-stunting hormone.

Another senior describes his decision not to commit suicide.

Brother stories are big this year, and Kevin Feder's speech about his older brother surprises those who only know Kevin as a class clown and habitué of Thistledown Racetrack.

Kevin is eighteen years old and thirty-five pounds overweight. His trousers hang about three inches below his waist—not a fashion statement—the backs of his cuffs drag on the carpet, and his shirts sag and fold. Kevin doesn't look you in the eye for more than a moment at a time. Most of his transactions during a school day are completed sideways. He speaks as though he's wearing a green visor, a cigar wedged in the corner of his beef-red lips. When the doorknob to the lecture room is slathered with Vaseline before Mrs. Mason's seventh-period psych class, it's not surprising to see Kevin Feder in the distance doubled over in laughter as hand after hand reaches for the greasy knob.

"Hey, Mr. Seelbach," Kevin calls out to his favorite target, the former Detroit Tigers relief pitcher turned history teacher. "I tried to buy one of your baseball cards but I didn't have anything smaller than a quarter."

Kevin's sense of nuance and subtlety is forever battling with an innate craving for sexual innuendo. "Wes Koontz," he intended to announce to the school in his speech to boost support for the hockey team, "gets off more shots than Joey Buttafuoco." That one didn't pass

Kerry Brennan, who makes sure to read carefully everything Kevin intends to say on stage.

"Do you think people are going to laugh?" he asks me the day before his senior speech. He tells me that a lowerclassman asked him if his speech was going to be funny. Kevin said no. "Can I laugh anyway?" the lowerclassman asked.

Kevin's nervous eyes betray his reflexive smile when he takes the stand in his blue blazer and droopy pants to deliver his senior speech. He ignores a few chuckles that spurt from the crowd even before he opens his mouth. Kevin begins with a poem, then, quoting from it, tells the audience, "All of my life I will have a sweet memory and an aching void of my brother Darin."

Darin, Kevin says, was born mentally and physically handicapped and regularly developed malignant tumors throughout his body as a result of neurofibromatosis; when he died last May, Darin had far exceeded his life expectancy. Kevin describes Darin's courage and happiness in the face of horrible pain. Kevin used to be embarrassed to bring his handicapped brother to school functions and now feels permanently ashamed of himself. It is an almost mawkishly personal speech, but this effect is sharpened by the fact that the boy describing the most wrenching and powerful relationship in his life is Kevin Feder. Far from being a rote requirement, the senior speech, for many boys, becomes a public confession of their deepest feelings.

Few at school, for instance, will forget the speech by Sam Woo. Hawley told me Sam was "the oddest boy in North America." The nature of Sam's speech is both personal and philosophical, and he has had a hard time completing it. His speaking date has been pushed back several times. Speeches aren't necessarily titled, but Sam's might be called, "How the Duck-Billed Platypus Has Changed My Life."

It seems that the duck-billed platypus is everywhere in Sam's vision of the world, and it brings him great joy. When at last he gives his speech, he tells the school that he negotiates almost no experience in which somehow the lowly, egg-laying mammal from Australia and Tasmania does not come to mind. "For example," Sam explains to his classmates, flipping straight dark hair out of his eyes like a metronome, "while in France this past spring break, I awoke in beautiful Paris, got out of bed to gaze at the incredible city, when I noticed a pile of ham on the floor. I had no idea what it was doing there. How strange and awkward, I thought. Much like the platypus."

Only the day before, Sam had been to the Louvre, where he gazed at "the Mona Lisa and noticed she had no eyebrows. Which, I remembered, the platypus also lacks."

"The platypus features a short brown coat of fur," he continues. "This will always remind me of times after the swimmers have shaved their heads, and I would see them roaming the halls, and I would think to myself, 'They would look much like platypuses if they dyed their hair dark brown.'"

For Sam, every characteristic of the platypus is somehow linked in his mind to the human condition. Even the platypus's cheeks, he says, "remind me of an eating contest held at the lower school dining hall when a friend stuffed a whole banana in his mouth and found it impossible to swallow or spit out. Yes, his puffy face was much like a platypus. And I can't help but think if only he had a duck-bill, he could've chewed much more easily."

Sam receives whooping, resounding applause.

On Thursday, November 11, I arrive as usual around eight, buttoning my shirt collar and knotting my tie as I move to my seat in the auditorium. Freshmen, sophomores, juniors, and seniors file in. Class deans tell boys that ties go *under* shirt collars. Music pumps. Weary boys fall into their seats like sacks of grain. Kerry waits at the side for 8:10, talking with Phil Thornton. Essential routine.

I take out my notebook, though more often than not, there is little to record—a list of sports scores, groups meeting at the break—but, with two boys slumped in chairs on stage flipping through note cards, there might be a decent senior speech. This too has become fairly routine, so when Kerry arrives on stage and says, "To introduce this morning's speaker is Brad Krupa," I have every reason to believe that assembly will carry on as it does most every day of the school year until it occurs to me that the atmosphere in the assembly, like a slack cord, has suddenly pulled *taut.*

The air seems to hum. Then small pops of suppressed laughter sound out. Then snickers. I hear delighted whispers of "Oh, my God" behind me. Seated on stage behind Brad, Kerry Brennan begins whispering something that is clearly unpleasant as Brad speaks into the microphone. Kerry's face has darkened like a thundercloud.

Brad is a heavy-set senior with preppy, straight brown hair, a golfer like his friend Rob, whom he will be introducing. It was of golf that Brad then spoke, explaining to the audience that his friend Rob "beats his balls harder than anyone else." Brad had put some thump into those words, and when he followed with "stroke . . . after stroke . . . after stroke," lingering lovingly on each word, the audience began to stir and snicker. Boys sat up, paid attention, and Kerry grew darker and darker and darker, as Brad went on, methodically moving through a seemingly endless litany of masturbation innuendo.

Kerry begins to speak more loudly—*"Siddown, Brad,"* he says—and Chuck Seelbach, in the audience, who's listened to hundreds of students speak, thinks to himself, "My God, when is Kerry going to *sit* him *down."* Polly Cohen, the librarian, simply stands and leaves the auditorium. Brad, courageously, and with perfect enunciation, is committed, however, and he plows through to the end, explaining, *in* conclusion, that his friend Rob can usually be found on the weekends "playing his organ" or, in the driveway, "waxing his truck."

Brad, at last, sits and Rob takes the podium to deliver his speech. Brad stares at his lap as Kerry whispers more harsh words. Brad looks unhappy, as though surprised to have been caught.

Immediately after Kerry excuses assembly, Nick Zinn bolts from his seat, which is easy to do this morning because the headmaster, who sits between Nick and the aisle, is not in attendance. Nick spots his sponsor, Mr. Kay, runs to him and says, "Hey, Mr. Kay, w-w-what did you think?"

Kevin Kay, a kind and serious English teacher in his mid-thirties, tells Nick that Brad might just as well have dropped his trousers and gotten the same response.

"But didn't you think it was *funny?"* Nick asks, grinning like a madman.

"Nick," Kevin says, "how do you think Rob's *parents* felt?" Rob's parents had come to hear their son's speech.

Nick wags his head from side to side in solemn agreement; Mr. Kay has a point. Then a smile spreads across Nick's face and he sprints away.

Kevin Kay shakes his head and moves toward the exit with his colleague Phil, who is steaming over Brad's intro. "They should kick him the *hell* out," Phil says to Kevin.

Apparently, none of the faculty appreciate Brad's humor. With the exception, perhaps, of old McCrea, who's yucking in the faculty lounge afterwards about famous student speeches through the decades, reaching back three headmasters to Harry Peters, who in the mid-1940s walked onstage after a boy had uttered the name of a Cleveland burlesque house.

Headmaster Peters just stood there, according to McCrea, shaking this kid furiously by the lapels and terrifying the entire school.

A rumor spreads almost immediately that Brad is suspended. In the senior lounge, Franz and Viswam recline on tattered couches, laughing. Brad's intro was hi*lar*ious, they say. Oh, yeah, *sure*, he ought to be *punished*. "But with demerits," says Viswam. "He shouldn't be suspended."

On the downstairs landing, Nick Zinn is practically running in circles. "W-w-what did you think, Mr. Ruhlman?" he asks me, his grin undiminished.

Brad trots down the stairs. He's just left Mr. Brennan's office. Yes, he is suspended.

He stands smack in front of me, and Nick steps aside but listens in. "What did you think?" Brad asks me. He is dead serious.

I tell him I thought his introduction was interesting.

"But how was my delivery? How was my *delivery?*" He is right in my face, his eyes glistening almost to the point of tears.

I tell him his delivery was clear.

"Nothing has *happened* this year," he says. "Absolutely *nothing.*" He explains he wanted seniors to have something to remember and, defiantly, he heads down the long commons, like a ballplayer heading toward the showers having been wrongly ejected from the game.

Throughout the morning and into the afternoon, the school buzzes.

It just isn't fair, students say. The speech had been *approved.* How can Mr. Brennan suspend someone for reading something that had been *approved* by a *teacher?* Bob Hanson, the guilty party, admits "I approved it," but he claims that what he heard on stage was not what he'd approved. Brad had caught Bob at 4:30 the day before; Bob, an English teacher of some three decades, says he was worn down from a long day. More likely, Brad's delivery to Mr. Hanson was not so loving as it would be in morning assembly. Bob says that Brad added a few words as well. Still, it *had* been approved. And the criticism that it offended the parents is so much more palaver, according to students, because the parents *knew* about it—Brad and Rob told them what was going to happen. What's more, Brad didn't even *write* the thing. The afternoon before, the brooding Doggett and the wily Kevin Feder had, with a gleeful mixture of laughter and passionate intensity, combined forces, while Feder marshaled every slang phrase for masturbation he could think of.

None of this alters Brad's fate. That evening, Brad will return to the school for the fall sports banquet, when awards and speeches are given and next year's team captains are announced over a hearty dinner. When Kerry sees that Brad has shown up, he will shake his head—Sorry, Brad—and instruct him to leave immediately.

When you're suspended from school for the day, it means the entire day.

After Kerry sends Brad home, he would like to prepare for his fourth-period English class. School work might help to remind him what he's doing here. But he's got to finish a letter first. A chore, really, but he'd promised some parents the night before that he would write it immediately.

11 November 1993

Dear Parents of Seniors:
At the Senior Retreat on 31 August Doug Lagarde, the Senior Dean, Margie Mason, the Dean of Students and I expressed our hope to the seniors that they would consider ways in which they might help to shape their senior year and, in particular, ideas for building class solidarity. . . . We also indicated that there would be no Beaverfest this year and no Senior Cut Day. These events are ill-advised for legal, educational, and safety reasons. In no way could we condone unsupervised events at which illegal and unsafe activities might take place.

When on 27 October it came to our attention that a version of Beaverfest, a campout on the campus without adult supervision, was planned, we reiterated to seniors that they could not hold such an event here. Late that morning we activated the parent phone tree in order to alert you to the possibility of seniors' attempting such an event and our opposition to it. . . .

About half the class did congregate on that evening. They did not camp out on campus; however, they did drive extensively through the eastern suburbs, apparently stole some campaign, realty, and security signs from front yards, and briefly ventured onto the campus. A few boys in cars were asked to leave the campus by Hunting Valley police at 3 A.M. and 5 A.M. Apparently the boys who got together had a good time. I'm not sure, however, that what they did was safe and I am sure that the timing was bad and boys who could not participate felt left out.

In this letter I hope to reiterate our stand: we will not condone a Beaverfest or Senior Cut Day this year. Should boys choose to participate in such events, they will face disciplinary action. We will continue to work with members of the class to help them design viable, safe alternatives. In the meantime I hope that you'll discuss this issue with your son and that you'll be willing to enter into a partnership in order to honor what I think is a justifiable position on the School's part and in order to avert a potential tragedy. Some of the boys perceive our stand to be an unfair denial of a 'tradition' to which they're entitled. Indeed what they're entitled to is our responsible teaching and parenting. I regret their disappointment, yet I'm more than willing to endure that if in the process an injury or death might be avoided. . . .

Thank you and all best wishes for a joyful Thanksgiving.

Sincerely, Kerry P. Brennan.

The Beaverfest to which the letter refers is a relatively recent "tradition," begun happily and spontaneously several years back on the night before the big football game against archrival Hawken. Apparently US had a beaver in its lake and had claimed it as the school's unofficial mascot. Word spread that Hawken players, the night before the game, intended to capture the beaver, and the US football team organized a night on campus to protect their mascot. A fine evening of boy bonding, the event was repeated the next year and the year after that, and the night-long campout on school grounds transformed into a class-wide "tradition." Last year, however, students climbed about on the roof; there were rumors of on-campus drinking; and several boys broke into the school and wrote crude comments on the blackboards of several teachers.

When Kerry took over as head of the upper school he decided that Beaverfest—a name that offended some at the school (regardless of the tradition's origin, there seemed to be little disagreement, from teachers or students, about why the name appealed to the boys)—would not occur. The name was unseemly, and the night had become little more than an excuse for the boys to stay out all night on their own, making mischief on campus, many of them drinking. The school stood to gain nothing by allowing, or even turning a blind eye to, such shenanigans. They had plenty to lose. Boys at this school have broken their legs, fallen from high places, crashed their cars, and smashed through plate-glass windows *during* school hours. If the school was to condone, even tacitly, an off-hours occasion, and something along these lines happened, they could easily find a student in the hospital and themselves in a lawsuit.

Thus this year's Beaverfest prohibition and the necessity of clandestine communications among the seniors to pull it off. But on the morning of the 27th a parent called the school to say how wonderful it was that the school was having a senior-class campout. Little in this school remains a secret for long.

Kerry Brennan was able to prevent all members of the soccer team from joining the night's festivities—they had a tournament game that night—but most other seniors met as planned in the parking lot of the Embassy Suites Hotel in the nearby suburb of Beachwood. The night was cold and rainy. Kris Fletcher, dressed in black and wearing his steel-toed boots, had trouble convincing his parents to let him out of the house, then had to get a ride with Bill Shepardson across town to Nick Zinn's house, who was their driver for the evening. Lumbering Nick was ready, donning a coonskin cap and hefting a thermos filled with something he called "The Brew," a goopy mixture of instant coffee and molasses intended to keep them alert till dawn. From the parking lot of the Embassy Suites, a swarm of cars departed for destinations throughout the city's east side with a mission: steal as many signs as possible.

Dozens of signs were stolen, a few boys were escorted off school grounds by the Hunting Valley police, who had been asked by the school to make special patrols, and many seniors spent the rest of the night hanging out at an all-night Dairy Mart a mile from the school. It *was* a good time, according to those involved. The next day, though, sleepy boys missed morning classes. Those whose names the police had taken were given Friday detention, including Nick Zinn, who was caught dozing in his car in the parking lot, "The Brew" notwithstanding.

The matter might have ended there, but a week after Beaverfest, the US Parents Association, a group of about two dozen parents, primarily mothers, met at the school at seven P.M. for one of its regular meetings. As usual, Kerry gave a brief state-of-the-school address and school business was discussed, Beaverfest among the items. Some of the mothers still weren't clear about where the school stood. Others were critical of Kerry for not making the school's position clear in the first place.

In his office, Kerry recalls this meeting with the mild disbelief he has suffered on many occasions this fall.

105

He says he tried to explain to the mothers that "my first inclination with eighteen-year-old boys is to afford them the respect of saying to them directly what I expect, and then presuming they all understand that, and abide by it and, if they needed to communicate with me, that they would be truthful about it. That's my first inclination." When he said this at the meeting, though, it elicited stern, silent gazes, so he added, "But if you want me to write a letter, I'll write a letter *now.*"

It irks him, this reaction of the mothers. He—along with the faculty, he's quick to point out—thinks the whole notion of Beaverfest is bad. But, he adds, "I like the fact that the kids are examining what it is they stand for and what we stand for. What I don't like is that they are quick to judge, and quick to presume." Once Beaverfest was over, with no one hurt and no one sued, Kerry wanted to drop the whole thing and get back to school, but the mothers persisted. "Make it clear to us," they told him, "so we know what we have to do in response."

"I think that's an abiding challenge at this school and in America generally," Kerry tells me. "Parents need *permission* to be parents. They want *us* to say that these are the things you should prevent your child from doing." Many parents, he says, are too worried about being liked by their kids. At the meeting, he asked one mother, "Did you think it was *odd* that your son was leaving your house at two in the morning on a school night?"

"Well," she responded, "he said it was a school-sponsored thing."

Kerry didn't want to be critical or hostile, so he said, simply, "If ever there's a problem like this again, *call* the *school.* Call me at *home.*" But he was thinking, *What kind of idiot are you to think that something school-related would be going on at two in the morning?*

6

The day after the Krupa introduction, Kerry convenes morning assembly as usual. This fall has been contentious; student tension has continued to bubble to the surface. Kerry and Doug Lagarde, the senior dean, have been shaking their heads about the senior class in particular; the boys have become sour and cynical in just a few months. Some faculty told me the seniors always get like this and attribute the mood to fatigue, fretting over colleges, or the building anxiety of leaving a comfortable and familiar world for something unknown. Others say this is an unusually sour class. When Kerry's finished reading sports scores and announcements, he reiterates to the students the rules of the dress code. Standards are slipping, he says, but, after a written brief from Doggett arguing for specific dress-code changes, Kerry has decided to amend earlier rules. He's trying hard to show the kids that he's not completely rigid and that their voices are heard when expressed in a civil manner. Even though Doggett's written request was a little snotty, Kerry wants to use it to make a point. He has, he tells the boys, overturned the no-turtlenecks rule. He holds fast on boots, however. Kerry then calls an impromptu meeting: "Will faculty please meet in the boardroom after assembly."

As the boys head to their lockers and to their classes, a stream of faculty pours into the boardroom immediately off Monkey Island. The room is furnished with chairs and sofas; several tables are arranged in a square in the center of the room, a makeshift conference area; a three-foot-long model of a dirigible, built of balsa wood and onionskin paper by a past student, hangs from the ceiling in the center of the room; the far wall is adorned with five large oil portraits of the school's past headmasters; the adjacent wall is covered with photographs of board members past and present. Nancy Lerner inevitably remarks on this each time she enters the room: "All these *men*. Can you *imagine* what would happen if they actually put a *woman* up?"

Kerry, standing at the far end of the room as faculty find seats and prop themselves against walls, gets immediately to business—not much time before first period—beginning with what he calls "Exam Security." First trimester examinations are approaching, teachers have begun to fashion tests that cover material from the first third of the year, and massive Xeroxing is done. Kerry cautions all gathered, "Be careful where you leave papers." He wants to run a tight ship.

Next on the agenda is discipline. Several seniors are pushing the demerit envelope. The school had originally planned to suspend anyone who racked up more than twenty demerits, but several seniors have as many as forty-five demerits and he hasn't acted on the suspension threat. "None of these kids has done anything awful," Kerry explains, "but they've been nickle and diming us on the demerits and I think we've got to respond somehow."

Kerry wants to keep the faculty abreast of what's going on in the school, and he feels it's important to do so now, given the unusual string of events during the past few weeks.

"About the Brad Krupa introduction," he says. "I know it upset a lot of people, and some of you would like to see a harsher penalty. But he *was* sent home from the sports banquet last night. It was an awkward moment, but I think we've responded appropriately."

The outspoken Polly Cohen, who was so offended she'd walked out of assembly, holds her tongue. (Later in the day, Brad, hanging out in the library, will prod Mrs. Cohen further. She *had* to think his intro a *little* funny, he said. No, Brad. "I still think it was funny," Brad said with a pout. "Yeah," Mrs. Cohen responded. "You think it was funny because you're seventeen and you're a *jerk.*" Mrs. Cohen is a straight shooter.)

Kerry asks if there is any other business to discuss?

Warren Siekman wants to know procedure on the anonymous student poll regarding faculty opinion on the demerit system.

"Poll?" Kerry says. "I don't know anything about a poll."

A teacher hands Kerry a copy. He reads it, and the faculty wait.

"Who did this?" Kerry asks. Someone suggests it might be an experiment for Margie's psychology class, but no one knows for sure.

Kerry shakes his head. "I don't know anything about this, but I recommend that you don't fill it out."

Siekman, who's got a booming voice, sounds off as though he's just been duped: "I already filled mine *out.*"

Deb Nash says, "So did *I.*"

Polly Cohen, two fingers pressed laconically into her cheek, lifts her eyebrows and says, "I filled *mine* out. I said I don't *answer* anonymous *polls.*"

Kerry closes with some reminders about the dress code: "Let's enforce it," he says. Frances, Polly's library coworker, asks for a ruling: "Are turtlenecks OK by themselves, or do they have to be worn beneath a shirt?" Kerry thinks but a moment and says, "No, by themselves is all right." Phil wants to know about the so-called moon boot, a tricky boot-shoe hybrid which seems to be reappearing. More definitions are required, more decisions, and the meeting disperses as the bell for first period sounds.

Kerry has sensed that the edges of this fall are fraying. He will be away from school for the first three days next week. The weeks between September's opening day and Thanksgiving break are a long, uninterrupted sprint. Without breaks, the air is unable to purge itself of student and faculty stress. Beaverfest, the dress code, the Soltis speech, the Krupa introduction and then suspension, the rising number of demerits, and pervasive senior cynicism coalesce into a sort of pressure in the air. Everyone feels it. School will shortly adjourn for the weekend, but weekends are not enough at this point.

At 7:30 A.M. the following Monday, November 15, a lone boy enters the commons. The school is deserted. He walks quickly, bobbing and lurching, and wears an expression of alert purpose. He's carrying twelve hundred sheets of paper stapled the night before into four hundred identical packets. He climbs the stairs to the second-floor landing. To the left stand two large elevated wood boxes, divided into hundreds of slots. Above each slot is a sticker with a student's name and grade on it. Most days students will find marked tests and homework assignments in their slot. The boy works quickly, slipping one packet into each slot. His heart races; he doesn't have much time. When he's finished, he scoots downstairs, soon to slip unnoticed into the crowd of boys arriving for school.

This morning, the beginning of the last four days of classes before trimester exams and Thanksgiving Break, is like any other except for two important differences. The headmaster and Kerry Brennan are in separate cities, part of school-evaluation teams working for ISACS—rarely are both gone from the school at the same time. Second, every student who stops by his mailbox finds a document that begins "I know this is a lengthy letter, and I know that you probably have a very busy schedule, but this is extremely important, and I urge you to read it through." The letter, six dense paragraphs, covers an entire page. Stapled to it is Exhibit A, a copy of Mr. Brennan's Beaverfest letter which had been mailed last week to parents of seniors.

Gradually, the packets begin to litter tables of the upstairs commons; they're folded and stuck in notebooks, then abandoned in classrooms. Their content is discussed quietly between students, between faculty. There's a soft crackle in the air. No one knows who wrote the document. Classes proceed, bells continue to ring every forty minutes.

Shortly before second period the following day, Nancy Lerner crosses the upstairs landing on her way to the English office. She stops to talk with one of her students and notices at her feet some folded sheets of paper. She doesn't stop speaking when she picks them up, as though she only wants to get garbage off the floor. But she unfolds them, reads the first couple lines, and decides to wedge them into the stack of books she's supporting with her hip.

Nancy is taking the headmaster's fourth-period class today, and she opens with a surprise. Yesterday, she tells the class, "I was in a state of crisis. Either I'm a terrible teacher, or you're not reading. . . . I think what can I do? And then I think, this is an AP course, and I don't have to beat my head against the wall."

The rigors of fall are weighing on the students. They're slipping behind, not completing their work, with exams three days off. They're tired and so is Nancy, but she wants to arrest further decay. "I'm giving you a pop quiz," she announces. A brief, brow-wrinkling moment follows; most of the boys sit up abruptly. "It will not count," she continues, "and I don't want your name on it. I don't give pop quizzes." Brows smooth, shoulders droop, chairs tilt back again. "Take out a sheet of paper," she says, and opening her copy of *Hamlet,* reads several lines and asks the students to write down who said what and to whom.

" 'It is a custom more honored in the breech than in the observance,' " she reads, her glasses perched on the tip of her slender nose. She licks a finger and turns some pages. " 'Grapple them into thy soul with hoops of steel.' " She reads six in all, and though she seems to be plucking these jewels willy-nilly, her last choice clearly has some method in it. "And number six, let's see, 'Youth to itself rebels, though none is near.' "

That last line is Laertes's concluding advice to his sister Ophelia, warning her about young Hamlet, patron saint of double business. Nancy has some double business of her own; after running through the answers, she moves suddenly, out of nowhere, it seems, into the anonymous letter.

"I don't know if any of you wrote this," she tells the class, flapping the copy she'd picked off the floor, "but my feeling is you *blew* it." The letter's not bad, she says, until it ended with that "snotty tone." "If you want to make an impact," she says, "you have to be more serious." She feels its very anonymity a shabby thing, and backs up the claim with a line that could have been part of the quiz: "As Hamlet says, 'Conscience doth make *cowards* of us all.'

"Look, cut day is a game," she continues. "If you play the game you have to take the penalties. So cut, if you want to so bad. What will they do? They'll give you some hassles, sure. But then you'll graduate and go off to college. They're not going to expel the whole senior class." She scans some papers scattered on the table, lifts her book. "My unsolicited opinion, there it is. Acting this way allows them to treat you like babies. I'd like you to rewrite the letter and ask for something serious."

Nancy's appraisal of the letter is pretty much my own and I'm glad that at last someone has brought it up, however fleetingly.

Whoever wrote this letter was apparently very upset by the one written by Mr. Brennan—whom the letter writer calls "our fearless leader." The anonymous letter thoroughly rebuts each of Brennan's points regarding Beaverfest, taking him to task for his alleged concern, and insisting that just as they had Beaverfest they would have a senior cut day. This section is reasonable, more or less, given the emotion with which the anonymous author wrote. Only in the last two paragraphs does the writer really get going:

> *Don't let anyone fool you, we're being deprived of our right to tradition and of our rights as individuals. . . . Mr. Brennan does not realize that he is no longer dealing with the snot-nosed lower school kids that he believes we all still are. . . . When we were in the lower school, the teachers encouraged individuality and nurtured it, now the same person is trying to stop what he started. . . . Don't believe the administration. They are deceitful, and they care about nothing but money, their beloved alumni, and how this school looks to the outside world. . . . The seniors refuse to listen to their crap, or take their*

letters at face value. . . . {W}e are not going to sit on our asses and
let ourselves be whores of Mr. Brennan. . . .

The day this letter was distributed I spotted Tyler Doggett in the library hovering over a book, his blond bangs obscuring his face as he talked with his friend Matt Jackson across the table. Doggett's elbows rested on the two-man study table, his hands cupping his chin, a stray finger concealing his perpetually chapped lips. There was an off chance that Doggett was the letter writer, but if he wasn't, I figured he'd know who was.

"Did *you* write the letter?" I asked him.

"No, I did not write the letter," he said. He seemed miffed that I would so impugn his writing style. It *wasn't* his style, but I still thought he knew who'd written it and hoped to goad him into telling me. Matt Jackson, across the table, followed Tyler's lead and remained silent. The dialogue hadn't lasted ten seconds when a third boy sidled up to make our group a foursome. It was the other Tyler, Tyler Soltis. He stuffed his hands in his pockets and began to rock back and forth on the balls of his feet. His wide round eyes and open-mouth smile suggested he'd appeared for a reason.

Doggett then said, "I *think* I know who wrote the letter."

"OK, *OK*," Soltis said, needing no further prodding. "*IIIIIIIII* wrote the letter. It was me." He yanked his hands out of his pockets and held them out, stubby fingers splayed, as if to push back air. "I want it to spread, but I don't want it to spread *too* quickly." He smiled a manic little smile, his eyes bulging.

On Wednesday, Tyler Soltis drives home from school as usual. The house is empty; his father, with whom he lives, is out of town on business. He's finished his early-admission application to Syracuse University and needs only to remember to bring it into school tomorrow to give to Mr. Lloyd, the college guidance counselor, who will send it off along with transcripts, test scores, and teacher recommendations. Though trimester exams are only a day away, Tyler is feeling pretty confident about his classes so no school work is pressing. One more day of school followed by exams, and then it's an easy glide through Thanksgiving vacation. The long Christmas vacation is three short weeks later—which means, for a senior, the year is practically finished. All he has to do to graduate is show up. The future seems all but certain. He has but a single concern: while he's confident he'll get into

Syracuse, he may not be accepted by the division of the university that he desperately wants. His heart is set on Syracuse University's S. I. Newhouse School of Public Communication.

He's done all he can, and with the trimester nearly done, and his application ready to be mailed tomorrow, everything's under control. He's going to take it easy tonight. He deserves it. It's been a busy two weeks. His speech, the play, and then the letter, and last night a *second* letter, an apology of sorts. Though neither the headmaster nor Mr. Brennan has seen his first letter it has not gone unacknowledged by the administration.

Margaret Mason called Tyler into her office to discuss it. Mrs. Mason has a maternal, sympathetic manner with students and is adored by most of them. When she sat Tyler down and stared at him, she seemed more cross than anything else. Disappointed. "Why would you *say* these things, Tyler?" she asked him. He was honest. He told her that when his father showed him a copy of Mr. Brennan's letter, he started to tremble, he was so mad. It was a lie, he said, an insincere effort to make the senior class look bad, and someone had to answer it. Mrs. Mason, Tyler said, reminded him that he's on financial aid—the school's giving him money so that he can be here—how could he be so nasty? Tyler explained that he didn't mean to be nasty, but her question irritated him. Does financial aid prohibit his having an opinion? he asked.

Mrs. Mason told him she wanted him to write a letter of apology to Mr. Brennan. Tyler agreed and also decided to write a letter of apology to the school. The anonymity of the first letter had raised implications of cowardice that he wanted to address. He's also upset that people think he's an ingrate, and, in retrospect, it had been rather more nasty than he'd intended. The second letter—which began "Well, it's been two days since some jerk wrote that darn letter and stuck it in everyone's mailbox"—was not so much a contrite apology as a clarification of what his first letter said, and included a couple of things he said he'd learned "during my transformation from senior to public martyr." For example: *"never, never, never* use the word whore when writing a letter to anyone about anything, because the sight of such a word seems to make everyone who reads it forget what the letter is about." His letter of apology concludes, "Once again, I am sorry if I offended anyone, I did not mean to be personal, and I hope this letter gets me back some of the respect I supposedly lost. If some faculty members are still mad at me after this, however, maybe their respect is not something that I want. I, for one, am willing to talk to the administration about a possible agreement, because something has to be done before this school becomes a thing that nobody will be proud of. Love always, Tyler B. Soltis."

Tyler figured that should take care of everything. Just to make sure it was clear to the headmaster that he, Tyler B. Soltis, has taken full responsibility for the anonymous letter, he had taken a copy of it to Ann McGovern. She told Tyler and Kris Fletcher, who'd joined Tyler on the errand, that she'd make sure Dr. Hawley got it first thing.

All clear. Tyler plunges into some cushions to watch a little TV.

"Tyler, this is Dr. Hawley."

Wednesday, six P.M., and the TV's background drone slowly fades to silence. The *headmaster* is phoning him at *home*. When Tyler hangs up the phone, he's not quite sure what to do. Some deep breaths. Assess the situation. He runs through the conversation. Pretty one-sided. Yes, Dr. Hawley did say, "I have never read anything so offensive in twenty-six years of teaching." Yes, Dr. Hawley was clearly piqued. He hadn't given Tyler much chance to respond. In fact, Tyler hadn't said a word other than a grunt or two to acknowledge he was still vertical. Dr. Hawley also said, "Don't come to school tomorrow." But that's not the scary part. Dr. Hawley had not said when to come *back*.

Hawley had been in Toledo for three days evaluating St. Francis de Sales, a Roman Catholic boys' school that's eligible for ISACS accreditation this year. When the last meetings are concluded, he heads down I-90 for the hour-and-a-half drive due east to Cleveland. Night is falling as he pulls into his driveway.

Evaluating a school is exhausting work according to most who've done it, and Hawley would like nothing more than a quiet evening at home with his wife and daughter. But he's already late and has time only to wash his hands and change his shirt before returning to school. The Tower Society, a group of alumni who donate $1,000 or more a year, is honoring retired faculty, and Hawley must preside over the ceremony. He stops by his office first. Ann has gone home, but she's left a stack of papers several inches high on his desk, priority business to attend to tomorrow. On top of this stack is the Soltis letter. Ann has stuck a Post-it on top explaining that Tyler and Kris Fletcher dropped it off this afternoon. Thus Tyler's letter is the first thing the headmaster reads upon returning to his school, a return he always cherishes. The letter—"I know this is a lengthy letter" . . . "They are deceitful" . . . "they care about nothing but money" . . . "not going to sit on our asses and be whores of Mr. Brennan"—reverses his mood.

Hawley's reaction is sudden. He's so mad he doesn't hesitate before reaching for a student directory and phoning Tyler. He's so furious he doesn't even let Tyler speak. He tells Tyler not to come to school until they decide what to do. Tyler is still stammering a response when the headmaster hammers the phone's receiver into its cradle.

Hawley leaves his office to attend the Tower Society reception, but the sour mood stays with him through the evening; later that night, ensconced at last in his home, his anger is stoked when Tyler's father calls him long distance. Mr. Soltis can't believe it. Suspended for writing a letter? Mr. Soltis suggests that Hawley is overreacting. Hawley tells Mr. Soltis that when a student calls one of his colleagues deceitful and says that his work is crap, he's going to get a little mad. Mr. Soltis tries to be reasonable, says *he* read the letter, and *he* didn't think it so very awful; in fact, he even made some *suggestions* on how his son might improve it. Hawley says maybe you and your son should consider a different school.

Occasionally, the headmaster agonizes about decisions when something at school goes wrong. Hawley has seen so many kids go wrong in far worse ways that he's realized, with the deep sympathy possible at his writing desk, that "a boy's most passionate, most forceful acts are often carried out without reflection of any kind," that boys almost always feel more a helpless *witness* to their misdeeds rather than a participant. Having thought so long about boys and watched so many of them pass through his life, he often struggles under the weight of each case's unique complexity. Because being kicked out of a school has repercussions that can extend long after a boy leaves high school altogether, Hawley's decisions, his alone, can change irrevocably the course of a young life. "In every disciplinary case," he says, "there is a great argument for mercy, and there is a great argument for standards." But in the Soltis case, perhaps because it did *not* involve anything illegal, nor anything prohibited by the school, there is no agonizing whatsoever.

In the midst of the ordeal, Hawley told me his view of the situation: "If a student walked up to me and said, 'Fuck you,' I'd say, 'Go home.' " I had never before heard the headmaster use an obscenity, and I never would again.

■   ■   ■

The fact that Hawley has not told Tyler when he will be allowed to come to school has Tyler in something of a spin. He can't think clearly. His Dad's out of town and he's alone. The ramifications of the suspension become clear only as the night progresses.

When Tyler has regained his breath, he tries to call his father. The next person he calls is Tyler Doggett. Doggett is class vice-president and a member of the Student Discipline Committee, a group of officers from each class who meet to recommend student disciplinary action to Mr. Brennan and the class deans. By his own admission, Tyler Soltis doesn't have many friends in school, especially not those involved in student government. He's already acknowledged that he wants to separate himself from the school and most of the people in it as much as possible, and that most people, furthermore, think he's weird. But Tyler Soltis can at least *talk* with his intellectual classmate.

Doggett's not home.

Tyler then calls Jim Lester, a boy who likes to reduce himself to a dancing speck in front of concert crowds by climbing massive outdoor band shells. Jim's not a class officer but Tyler calls him because, he says, "when something's going on at school, Jim's usually in the middle of it," and he wants Jim's advice and vocal support. He also calls Dave Kaval, a senior and president of the Student Discipline Committee. Dave has been at the school for as long as Tyler—they began kindergarten together—and Tyler says he has never sustained a hatred for one person as long as he has for Dave. Dave, who used to bully Tyler repeatedly between sixth and eighth grades doesn't hate Tyler and never has; he just ignores him.

When Dave hears what's happened, he's flabbergasted. Dave senses fear in Tyler's voice. Everyone Tyler calls, in fact, is stunned. Word of Hawley's response spreads fast on Wednesday evening. Tyler's phone begins to ring—yes, he tells callers, it's true—I know, I can't believe it *either*.

Between calls, a thought occurs to Tyler. "My application!" he thinks. "It's due tomorrow, and I'm not allowed on campus!"

His big effort in public communication might, through a bizarre series of events and unfortunate timing, block his admission to the Newhouse School of Public Communication.

Tyler calls his favorite teacher, Henry Strater.

Doc Strater, on first impression, does not seem a formidable personage on the faculty, one who would command respect from a classroom of boys.

He wobbles along the hallways with a healthy portliness, baggy school-teacher clothes and briefcase, wispy white hair astray—an affable old grandad. One would think he's simply too old and too agreeable to carry any weight with cynical teenagers. Yet Kris Fletcher, the heavy-metal sewer king, calls Doc his favorite teacher. Tyler had told me earlier, "Doc Strater has got to be the coolest teacher I've ever had in my life. He's so great. He reminds me a lot—and this is going to sound so bad—he reminds me a lot of me."

Doc is at home and, to Tyler's great relief, is as incredulous about Hawley's reaction as his classmates have been. Tyler explains his college-application dilemma. Doc tells him this is all ridiculous, that Tyler should come to school, and he will personally stand up for Tyler. Tyler is cautious though, and Doc agrees that caution is best. They plan a covert rendezvous in front of the school, eighth period. Tyler will drive to the school and hand the Syracuse documents to Doc, then bolt. Tyler hangs up, but a few minutes later, the phone rings again. It's Doc Strater's wife, known to all as Mrs. Doc. She's been talking with her husband and is worried someone will recognize Tyler's car. Tyler agrees this could cause trouble. It's decided that Mrs. Doc will drive him; that way he should be safe, and he'll get his application in before the deadline.

Tyler feels strangely exhilarated. "Doc is *so cool*," he thinks. "He's *there* for me." And for the first time in his high school career, Tyler's telephone is ringing off the hook. With *concern*. For *him*. All his classmates are on his side. Even Kofi called.

Kofi Anku is only a junior, but his black, stoney face radiates control. Kofi is from a well-off family, originally from Ghana, which makes him different from the many black students who are on financial aid. This fact, however, seems not to distance him from them, but rather to strengthen his commitment to issues of race at the school. His gaze alone—humorless, steady, and unmoving—can bore holes; and when he says, softly, "Race means *everything* to me," you know he means it. His eyes hold yours till *you* leave. This is exactly why Tyler has had a problem with Kofi. Kofi is a reverse racist, Tyler has always thought, and he and Kofi have tangled over this since they've known each other. While Tyler doesn't know what Kofi thinks of him—probably not much, he figures—and while he doesn't agree with Kofi about 100 percent of the time, Tyler says, "Kofi is someone I respect."

Now Kofi calls *him*. Kofi's not worried about Tyler, but he wants the story firsthand because he's concerned about the way the school makes decisions. Kofi and Tyler talk, and before Kofi hangs up, he tells Tyler that the students are behind him on this one.

Dave Kaval has promised to talk with Hawley personally first thing in the morning. Tyler's enemy, nemesis, and former bully is going to bat for him.

It's a remarkable show of support—utterly unexpected, and therefore all the more powerful, a force matched in intensity only by Hawley's reaction and the sudden turn of events that followed. In fact, Tyler's elation almost surmounts his fear until the phone rings again. It's his father calling back. He's just talked with Dr. Hawley. It's more serious than either of them at first believed.

Mr. Soltis tells his son that he doesn't know what is going to happen, and Tyler realizes then that, incredible though it seems, expulsion from the school is a possibility.

The following evening, I call Tyler to see how he's holding up. He's been home all day and has a meeting with Hawley tomorrow. He remains, he says, in "total shock."

"It's not like I drink or do *drugs*," he says. "I just wrote a *letter*."

Plus he's gotten more bad news. Dave Kaval called to describe what had happened.

As Hawley strode out of this morning's assembly, Dave rushed up behind him and asked for an explanation for Tyler's suspension. Hawley didn't even stop walking. He said, "A boy with those opinions does not belong at this school." Dave, without thinking, called out, "That's a pretty petty thing to say." Hawley halted. In the crowd leaving assembly, Hawley turned and glared at Dave but said nothing, then walked away.

Dave couldn't believe he said that—"He is the headmaster, if you know what I mean."

Later in the day, Dave continued to baffle himself. For Tyler Soltis, a kid about whom he could not care less, he went to Hawley for more. "The letter insults me," Hawley told Dave, "and it insults the school." The conversation was more complete than their first one, but Hawley's emotions were undiminished. You could tell from the sound of his voice, Dave said. The words were reasonable, but the voice was weird. Dave described it as the sound of someone talking while you're grinding a knife into their back.

When Dave finished his story, Tyler hung up the phone. The words rang in his head: "A boy with those opinions does not belong in this school."

"I *do* care about this school," Tyler tells me over the phone. "I really *do*. And that's why it concerns me. I don't blame the administration for everything that goes wrong. A lot of people here do things wrong. It's just the way we handle it. I see such a great school. What they say the school is like is such a great idea. It's kind of a utopian belief. But that's *not* the way it is. . . . Dr. Hawley says he wants us to be individuals which I find *extremely* hard to believe."

Tyler is a snarl of emotions. On one hand is Dr. Hawley. On the other, practically the entire school is supporting him, most importantly, Doc and Mrs. Doc. The secret delivery had gone as scheduled, and Tyler says, "I feel *fantastic* that somebody *cares* about me so much."

"I'm not sure how I'm going to handle it," Tyler says when I ask about tomorrow's meeting with the headmaster. He sounds exhausted. "I'm trying not to give up what I think, but I don't want to screw things up." He believes so far he's managed to remain true to himself, claims he's still not afraid to express his views, but adds, "I'm more afraid to express them *now.*

"I've learned my lesson about life. I guess they're teaching me about how the *real* world works. It's the *negative* part."

Before I get off the phone, I ask Tyler if he has any regrets about the situation, about what he's done. He thinks, then says no regrets except one: "I wish I hadn't been so mean."

The school is muted when I arrive the next day, the morning wet and cold, a day of perpetual dusk. There is no assembly. Most boys are dressed in sweatshirts, jeans, and sneakers. Kris Fletcher arrives wearing a black heavy-metal T-shirt, a cross dangling from his left ear lobe. Franz Maruna looks as if he dressed in a dark closet then walked through a neon-paint-spray machine.

Boys are prostrate on the carpet cramming over notebooks for their first exams, conferring purposefully in the locker area, spread evenly from the bottom of the stairs all the way up to and across the second-floor landing. At 8:30 history exams begin. Tyler Soltis's Am Cult test has started and he should be here, but he's not. He is not permitted on school grounds until 10:15, the time of his appointment with the headmaster.

I've come to school because I'd scheduled a meeting with Hawley immediately following his Soltis appointment. Throughout the week,

I'd tried to remain impartial, but I couldn't help myself from siding with Tyler. Like most of the students, I was surprised by the sudden gravity of the situation, created entirely by the headmaster himself. Both the letter and the "apology" were crass, but talk of whether or not Tyler would be expelled seemed a bit much. I knew that Hawley was not a psychotic dictator, raging within after a mutinous dispatch from a disloyal subject; he was a reasonable man, and a reasonable man would not expel a boy for writing a letter, no matter how disrespectful. Tyler after all—and Hawley had to realize this—was not simply rebelling against authority, or attempting to hurt anyone. He was, deep down, testing the sound of his own voice.

I'd been thinking that there was more premeditation and strategy in Hawley's actions than he was letting on. In the larger scheme of things, the Soltis letter wasn't that big a deal; I figured Hawley just wanted to scare Tyler, and that he knew everyone would be buddy-buddy in the end and school would go on as always.

I head to Hawley's office shortly before his meeting with Tyler.

Hawley is seated at his desk in his red leather chair looking over some papers. When I appear in the doorway, he swivels toward me.

"I have a request," I say. "With your and Tyler's permission, would it be possible for me to sit in on the meeting?"

I know this is a touchy thing to ask and that Hawley is in a bad mood for a number of reasons, the Soltis appointment only one among them. Given the nature of the meeting, I'd hoped that catching him off guard would give me a slight advantage. I want to be a part of this.

Hawley's face tightens at my question. I know him well enough by now to see this is his answer, and I wait for the curt refusal. He says, "Mike, I understand why you would want to sit in, for journalistic purposes." His face remains tight, eyes asquint, mouth stretched into a lipless grimace. Then he says, "I don't think so. We're really deciding Tyler's *place* at this *school.*"

I have underestimated Hawley. The letter in his mind *is* bad, really bad, and he himself, I realize, does not know if Tyler will remain at the school. In this, I see, his mind is completely open. Tyler's expulsion is possible.

Leaving his office, I pass Tyler. He has posted himself like a terrified guard, bolt upright against the window of Ann McGovern's office. I say hello and ask him how he's doing. He mumbles an answer, which is incomplete and nonsensical. He is smiling, though it's the sort of smile you'd expect from a disgruntled postal worker. His eyes are huge—too nervous to blink.

Hawley opens his door, leans out and says, "Tyler?"

Tyler charges the office. Hawley closes the door. Taped to this door is a quotation from Aristotle's *Ethics:* "We are not conducting this inquiry in order to know what virtue is, but in order to become good, else there would be no advantage in studying it."

Thus neither Tyler nor Hawley knows how the meeting will end. All that's known is that they're going "head to head," as Hawley put it, to find out if Tyler in fact will finish the year at this school.

I cruise the school for a while, look out over the dining hall where a couple hundred boys are hunched over blue and pink and green essay books; most boys scribble at a feverish pace, and those who don't look none too comfortable. Teachers stroll among the tables, hands clasped behind their backs, keeping watch. Every now and then I walk back to Hawley's office to see if he and Tyler are finished. Through the narrow, vertical window in the door, I can see Tyler, sitting on the edge of the couch, forearms on his knees, facing Dr. Hawley, who sits across the coffee table in the rose-colored chair nearest the window. Until then, I had not realized someone could be so animated and still remain seated. Tyler is talking, by the looks of it, nonstop. He bounces in his seat as he speaks; his body jolts with each sentence. I ask Ann McGovern, who's at her desk trying to concentrate, how it's going.

"I don't know," she says. "Tyler's doing a *lot* of talking."

When I return again, I find Tyler standing in the reception area of the administration offices. His feet are planted wide apart, arms stiff at his sides; he stares straight ahead toward Monica, the school's receptionist. He looks like he's just stepped off a carnival ride, determined to keep his balance. He still isn't blinking. I stand near, but don't say anything. I suppress an urge to wave my palm in front of his face.

Then Tyler speaks. "I'm not kicked out of school, at least." His unblinking eyes remain fixed on a distant point.

A few moments later, Mrs. Mason appears. She gives Tyler a hug. He receives the embrace with the warmth of a two-by-four. Mrs. Mason doesn't know all the details, but she knows it has worked out well, and she tells him with a big smile that she's arranged for him to take his three-hour history exam immediately.

■ ■ ■

Hawley looks twenty pounds lighter. He had been ready for Tyler to walk in and defend his letter: "If he said, 'This letter, the sentiments, the crass language, that's me, that's who and what I am,' I was prepared to say that he has no place in this school, people don't have dialogues this way, opinions aren't expressed this way." If that had been the case, Hawley continued, he would have been impressed by Tyler's integrity, and he would have felt justified in letting Tyler go.

But Tyler was not about to get himself kicked out of school because Mr. Brennan wrote a letter he didn't like. Tyler had said to me, "I really *do* care about this school," and that, in the end, is what mattered to Hawley.

"Tyler's sorry, and I'm satisfied. He was even a little obsequious." Hawley says "obsequious" with evident disappointment, though one can hardly blame Tyler for that.

Hawley has returned to his chair, and I have taken Tyler's place.

Now that it's over, now that the event has found a satisfactory closure, Hawley speaks without emotion. Tyler is expressing himself for the first time in his life, he explains, as if to convince *me* of Tyler's innocence. Hawley recalls Tyler's junior year, when medicine for depression resulted in seizures and hospitalization and weeks out of school. "He'd lost confidence in himself," Hawley tells me, adding with the distance of a clinician, "Depression is anger directed on the self, turned inward. Tyler's now turning it out, thrusting out. . . . I know that Tyler can hate the school, really *hate* it, and also *need* it at the same time. He can mean both." Hawley says he thinks Tyler has learned something here and he sees that, on the one hand, Tyler is even thrilled by it. "He needs to feel important. He likes to feel important. He's looking for his identity."

Tyler will take two exams on this day, and surpass his expectations. This trimester will be among the strongest academic performances of his high school career—he manages only a C in Am Cult, his favorite class, but the teacher is a notoriously difficult grader, and the rest will be solid Bs.

As for the meeting with Dr. Hawley, well, that too had surpassed expectations.

"I was really impressed by Dr. Hawley," he tells me when I call him that night. "I think he's very in touch with the school. He's extremely liberal and open minded. I just couldn't believe it. I'm convinced the problem with the school is not with him. He even *apologized* for acting rashly. . . . I really admire him," Tyler says, "the way he caught himself, the way he reacted. . . . He said I can complain about the rules but I've got to *follow* the rules. I *do*. I've followed the rules all my *life*.

"I felt really comfortable being honest," he adds.

I tell Tyler he didn't look very comfortable either before the meeting or after.

"I was so scared to *death* when I went in," he says.

"Dr. Hawley's honest," Tyler concludes. "You might not like what he says, but you know where you stand." Then Tyler says, "There's delight all *through* this house."

The conclusion of the Soltis Affair has turned out to be entirely predictable. A boy writes a rude letter about the school; the headmaster has a chat with him; the boy apologizes for his rudeness without altogether relinquishing his beliefs, and the headmaster offers a concessional apology of his own. The boy and the headmaster return to their school work. All is right with the world.

This is what happens, but the joints of this drama do not seem flush; the results are not commensurate with the stormy progression of events. Tyler spent nearly forty hours stewing and worrying, and he had to write yet another letter of clarification following his meeting with Dr. Hawley. Yet there seem to be no lasting consequences. Nothing has really changed. Has Hawley, therefore, overreacted? Had he been manipulating Tyler, pulling a psychological power play to bring Tyler, disrespectful but harmless, to his knees? Nearly everyone I speak with thinks that Hawley's reaction to Tyler's letter was extreme, an opinion supported by the fact that little had happened to Tyler until the headmaster returned to school. Hawley had responded passionately for reasons that were clear and unwavering. But do these reasons justify the intensity of his reaction? There is something spooky about it all, maybe genuinely dark. How can this headmaster, who is so even-toned and magnanimous when writing about boys, be so unpredictable and extreme when dealing with them in person? Had the headmaster simply been fatigued, worn down by the year and longing for the heaven of Thanksgiving break? Or was Tyler's letter symbolic of larger problems Hawley felt he was struggling against, a pervasive cynicism of teenagers, a deterioration of language and decency, and a contemporary culture that was in his eyes growing more crass by the day?

The reaction to an event in this school was, as usual, more interesting, more revealing, than the event itself. Tyler's senior speech was neither original, artful, nor illuminating, but the reaction from his fellow students, pro and con, proved to Tyler that he had a voice; it's not an extraordinary leap to suggest that had Tyler not given his speech at that particular moment in the school year, he would have lacked the confidence and strength to answer Mr. Brennan's letter. Kerry Brennan's letter was also a reaction—to Beaverfest and parental uncertainty. Finally, Hawley's reaction to Tyler's letter, in this domino-effect of correspondence, was perhaps the most interesting and complex reaction of them all.

Throughout the year, the events themselves were not unlike small plays, fictions, dramas staged against the backdrop of school, emblems of bigger issues, not quite real or large enough to matter in and of themselves until their meaning is fulfilled by the audience. To know the school, to know the boys and this unusual headmaster, one might only follow Hamlet's advice to himself: *The play's the thing/Wherein I'll catch the conscience of the king.*

7

"I'm so *glad this* is the year that you're here," Hawley had said to me. School is best when it's hard, the headmaster says. That's when you know it's working.

Paul Bailin had almost mastered the unruly seventh period, and hammered away with ancient Egyptians, Buddhist parables, and the Jewish kings three periods a day, followed by a section of tenth-grade Western Civ II and the elective Reason and Rhetoric class, three preps in all. Nancy, though she taught only two sections of English requiring only one prep, had found a way to work harder than most full-timers. Hawley was well into his philosophy course, examining theories of how the mind works, the classroom remaining his haven amidst the travel and endless administrative tasks. The boys, as ever, staggered relentlessly through their language-science-English-math-history days like punch-drunk fighters and lived for weekends.

Hard as school was, though, the cumulative effect was one of smooth industriousness, the massive gears grinding with oiled precision as they had been, more or less, for a hundred years. So it did not seem unreasonable for the headmaster to throw some caution to the wind and exclaim how glad he was. This kind of beginning made him happy. This was soul-nourishing stuff for a man who has spent virtually his entire conscious life in school.

Then November 11 made a *crack* like the backfire of a truck's engine grinding uphill under too much weight.

No one at this school, I would venture, appreciates the power and import of the written word more than its headmaster. I was continually surprised by how much communication began as words on paper—words *caused* things here—and no day throughout the year would better justify an appreciation of the force of written words than November 11. Several acts, which would swirl into a storm front to end the trimester, had their origins on eleven-eleven. It was the sort of a day that might make an otherwise logical person believe in astrology.

On this Thursday, of course, Brad Krupa read the written remarks of introduction that would delight the students, incense faculty, and earn Brad a suspension from school—a clowning, boyish preface to more serious events. Shortly after sending Brad home on November 11, Kerry Brennan wrote the post-Beaverfest letter, or "the blasted letter," as he would come to think of it—words that even some parents found patronizing, words that sent shudders of anger through Tyler Soltis, propelling him into a letter of his own (and then another and another and, following his suspension, still another before the whole affair was finished). Kids were being suspended for what they *wrote*. Finally on this potent Thursday, Tuck Bowerfind, a young faculty member at the lower school, wrote a letter to Paul Bailin. It was a good letter, clear, well-written, from one young teacher to another.

Paul was at his desk in the history office with teachers Rob Thomas and Dick McCrea when he opened it and read it.

"Hey, Rob," Paul said. "Take a look at this." Rob scanned the letter, then focused a serious gaze on Paul and said, "This is *scary.*"

News of the letter spread like fire through parched hills. In all, Paul showed the letter to four people. Within one hour, the entire faculty knew about it and had begun to pull Paul aside to ask in whispers for more details, mumbling dark forecasts for the school and their position in it. Paul was embarrassed, a little baffled, and eventually upset that the day quickly turned bad because of his own indiscretion. "There were all these sneaky conversations in corners and people Xeroxing the letter," Paul says, wincing. Several senior faculty members, after speaking with Paul and seeing the letter for themselves, wondered aloud to Paul if this was the right school for them. Before I even knew about the letter, I spotted Nancy walking the halls with a hair-day-from-hell expression. "I am ready to *quit,*" she snapped.

Needless to say, this is precisely the kind of discontent that most jars the headmaster; for a man who cherishes school and school culture, it cuts at his heart. Some of the best teachers at his school, his friends, were speaking of quitting. It can't have helped that Paul Bailin, a colleague

Hawley not only hired but admired, had spread the letter, an act, no matter how reflexive, that was tantamount to smashing the glass of a fire alarm and yanking the lever. This upset the headmaster, but not because he needs calm routine. Hawley is not a headmaster who locks himself in his office thinking lovely thoughts about boys' schools, stewing happily in the Western Canon, braising himself with Plato and Aquinas, while the good boys and good faculty carry on the business of school outside. To the contrary, this headmaster is the primary agent of change—or, as is often the case, the preventer of it—in his school; and this second crisis, unlike the Soltis Affair, was one that he himself had initiated.

Hawley had little idea what was to come when he sat down one Sunday afternoon to put a few thoughts on paper. He was at home, a large white Pennsylvania Dutch house owned by the school that lies a few minutes walk along a gravel road to the playing fields. He'd read some Alice Munro—"No one writes better short stories," he says—graded some papers, then sat down to compose. The subject was religion in schools, religion in contemporary culture. The day was Halloween, the last great pagan holiday. On this occasion he would announce the year's first Headmaster's Essay Contest. One could say these thoughts on paper were simply words asking for more words. One might also say that in announcing the first essay contest of the year, Hawley had built a teepee of dry kindling.

Then he gave Tuck Bowerfind a match.

"I am going to ask you to indulge me for a moment this morning as I try to work through a problem out loud," the headmaster tells the school. Winter has struck early, and this morning Hawley has worn his warm gray tweed jacket over a navy V-neck sweater. His brown shoes are soggy and water-stained from the slushy weekend snow. "It is an issue that has bothered me occasionally since I started teaching at University School," he says. "But last winter, when we were searching for a new director of the lower school, the problem came into especially clear focus."

The headmaster's addresses, the sound and cadence of his voice, can have a soporific effect on the students. "Every time he speaks, he has that *tone*," says one of Paul Bailin's freshmen. The "tone" is idealistic, didactic, and so earnest it can raise the hairs on your neck. This can work to good effect on idealistic and earnest students, especially those with a literary bent; for the sour and cynical, it's an "off" switch. Regardless of the effect, there's a lack of self-consciousness to student reaction. They hesitate neither to express polite interest nor thorough, crushing boredom. A student once groaned so loudly when Hawley approached the podium that Hawley stopped dead in his tracks. What Hawley says on stage is always so personal he can seem almost naked up there against the deep maroon curtain. Hawley knows this well, and he knows that what boys like best is something concrete, so he always tells a story, links the didactic message to something that actually happened.

The story Hawley tells today concerns an important meeting regarding two job candidates, one of whom would take Kerry Brennan's post as director of the lower school. It's an important position, and various factions—administrators, parents, trustees—formed a search committee. The meeting Hawley describes was one of the committee's last. The field had been narrowed to two candidates, and the committee needed to choose between them. It was here that the group hit a snag. Both candidates were Christian, one of them a Roman Catholic nun. This fact had been making some of the committee members nervous, and one of them had finally voiced this concern.

The headmaster at first found the committee's reaction to the candidates' religious affiliation—at the eleventh hour, no less—surprising, and then irritating. What's the big deal? After all, he explained to the committee, the school has employed a number of faculty who happened to be clergy people. Tony Jarvis, an Episcopal priest, had chaired the history department. One of Jarvis's colleagues at the time, Rabbi Arthur Lelyveld, who taught courses in Jewish literature and history at the school, presided over a local temple. Another Episcopal priest, Tuck Bowerfind, was on the faculty at the lower school and currently held the Religions and Ethics chair at US. Furthermore, Hawley pointed out, "a Christian was already in charge without any disastrous effects, so far as I could tell."

What, he wanted to know, were these people so worried about? Why would they fear hiring a religious person, Christian or otherwise?

"It soon became an interesting meeting," Hawley says to the students in Monday morning assembly.

The committee offered no clear answers to his questions, but they spoke with considerable emotion. After a pause—a sort of dead-end frustration—a parent who was also a trustee tried to smooth feathers on both sides and return them to the business at hand. "They are both terrific candidates with extensive experience," he said. "I don't suppose there's any real harm to their faith, as long as they don't bring it to school with them."

A reasonable statement. The school claims no religious affiliation. It employs people of various faiths as well as agnostics and atheists. If a prospective employee is not religious, this has no bearing on whether or not they're hired; why, then, should religious affiliation carry any weight? So long as no one's toting a suitcase of brimstone and fire to school every day, what *is* the harm?

The headmaster bristled when he heard those words. *Hold* it, he thought. Do you realize what you've said? Those are powerful words made deceptive by peaceful motives. The words remain so revealing, in fact, that the headmaster pauses, gazes out at the hundreds of faces before him in assembly and repeats them: "I don't suppose there's any real harm to their faith, as long as they don't bring it to school with them.

"It was this comment that clarified the religion-in-schools issue for me once and for all," Hawley continues. "I asked this parent, and I am asking all of you: Is it *possible* to leave your religious convictions and beliefs at home? Is it *possible* to take them out of the way you relate to other people in the course of the day, to take them out of your work, your thinking, your decision-making? No religious person *I* know could do that if he or she wanted to, and no really religious person would want to. Religious faith and convictions are not things you can put on hold or in a compartment while you tend to business. Religious commitment is not like a passion for sky-diving or for a favorite form of music—things which you could, reasonably, put on hold for the greater part of a school day. Many of you count yourselves as religious people, and I don't have to tell you that you don't leave that part of yourself at home.

"You *can't* leave it at home, because your religious dimension tends to operate at the very *center* of your thinking and feeling. It determines the style of your personal relationships; it is the fixed point of reference you use in making a decision."

Already, some of the faculty are growing a little edgy; one sighs audibly.

The headmaster, apparently, will get around to the competition in good time. He's been thinking about this issue of leaving one's faith at home, and he's going to vent some of his thoughts—in a sense, enter his own contest before he even announces it. He's the headmaster. He's allowed.

"Beneath that statement," he says, "lies a very modern and very recent attitude. Not too long ago, there would have been great unease in the community if a school leader was thought *not* to be religious. This *suspicion* of religion is a late-twentieth-century phenomenon, a product of our age, and I don't think it represents progress.

"Being suspicious of religious faith, expecting bad things rather than good things from religious people, is the result, I think, of a good idea gone wrong. The good idea was, and is, *tolerance:* tolerance of the passionately held, sustaining beliefs of people who share our community. Tolerance, combined with courtesy and curiosity, actually *expands* our spiritual and intellectual life. Tolerance is quite a good thing, but it is a giant and dubious step to move from tolerating different faiths to being suspicious of *any* faith.

"Yet this is precisely what is occurring in American culture. The logic runs as follows—and though it is poor logic, it is worth noting. Since majority faiths have sometimes been imposed clumsily on minority faiths in schools, we should avoid the clumsiness by banishing the faiths. A related argument goes this way: since some religious practices and styles have been oppressive, all religion is suspect. Examined closely, neither of these modern arguments is very sound, but they are widespread. . . .

"I would like to put the question to you one more time," the headmaster concludes. "In fact, I would like to make it the subject of the first of this year's Headmaster's Essay Contests. For those of you new to the school, the contest works like this. Anyone wishing to compose about five hundred words, two typed pages, answering the question I ask will be a candidate to win one hundred dollars, great honor, and lasting celebrity.

"I will have posters put up to remind you, but the question to be addressed is this: What is the place of religious belief and practice in a diverse and non-sectarian school?

"The essays will be due to me by the Monday after Thanksgiving break. That's November twenty-ninth. Submissions should be typed. Originality, good reasoning, and persuasive prose will be the criteria. Underclassmen are especially encouraged to try.

"I know you are all very busy, but I hope many of you will consider entering. The issue really does matter."

As always, the headmaster receives polite applause. Keith Green, long-time teacher, long-time friend of Hawley's, mutters, "Who *cares?*"

The religion-in-schools issue is an explosive one—Keith Green's response notwithstanding—an issue that is particularly visible in public school systems where debate escalates into drama. The week after the headmaster's religion-in-schools address, a high school principal in Jackson, Mississippi, is suspended for allowing a student to read a prayer over the intercom before the start of classes. For three days, the student council president broadcast these words: "Almighty God, we ask that you bless our parents, teachers, and country throughout the day. In your name, we pray. Amen." Relatively generic, perhaps, but clearly a prayer, something the Supreme Court expressly forbade in 1962.

What gives this story its bite is the fact that the principal was fired for allowing this prayer—despite the fact that the student body *voted* for it— and his dismissal prompted prayer vigils outside high schools and student walkouts across the state. Massive crowds demonstrated at the Mississippi state capitol. A majority, it seemed, favored *increased* religion in school, and the man dismissed for allowing a prayer to be read before classes became a local hero. *The New York Times* reported that the case "is typical of the emotional tug-of-war going on in many school districts in the religiously conservative South between Federal strictures against organized prayer in schools and a yearning to inject more religion in school life."

The issue may be particularly visible in the South, but debate simmers throughout the country. In Bristol, Virginia, the school board voted to use the Bible to study grammar, literature, and history. While this might have gone over well in Jackson, an uproar in Bristol forced the board to abandon the proposal quickly. "This is an extreme example of the greatly increased activity we have seen in this area in the last two years," legislative counsel for the ACLU told *The Times*. A group that monitors church-state violations said they were worried by the activity because efforts such as this to introduce religious teaching into schools were growing increasingly sophisticated, with conservative religious groups searching for legal means to circumvent church-state law.

Increased efforts to pump religion into schools is not relegated to the United States. In January, *The Sunday Times of London* reported, "All children will be expected to study the Ten Commandments, the Bible, and the teachings of Jesus as part of a government drive . . . to revive religious and moral education in schools."

Of the myriad cases each year, whether they regard Hasidic children at a publicly funded school or deaf children at parochial schools who receive public funds, whether the issue concerns mandatory periods of "quiet reflection" in school or public schools discriminating against religious groups who use school facilities after hours, patterns are emerging.

Christian fundamentalist groups have thus far been ineffective in bringing change to schools (a good example of this is a school board in San Diego County, California, whose attempts to open the way for teaching creationism in the classroom were soundly squashed). Yet many districts throughout the country are openly encouraging, and in some cases legislating, looser church-state-separation rules by approving voluntary prayer or cutting funds from schools that forbid it. "Pressed by voters," *Time* magazine wrote in the spring of 1994, "legislators around the United States are probing for loopholes in Supreme Court rulings that have forbidden school prayers. . . ."

The reason for recent acceptance among voters of prayer in school seems partly due to two things: a perception throughout the country that a moral chaos has the nation in thrall, and a growing realization that in a pluralistic society, teaching values to children in school has become so politically loaded that the response has often been to teach no values at all. Many school districts seem to have come around, in a general way, to acknowledging that some values might not be altogether a bad idea in school. However, when values are introduced into a school district, and those values are named "Christian"—in San Diego County, in Bristol—or named any religion, for that matter, voters decry the move. The aforementioned *Time* magazine article put the either/or question succinctly, the answer to which no one can agree upon: Is religion good, or is it a menace?

The bulwark protecting state and church from each other—for so long a seemingly immovable tenet of democratic society—had begun to crumble. And at University School in Cleveland, a headmaster had suggested that this wall was an impossibility, a kind of lie.

Paul Bailin wanders the deserted downstairs commons area. It's not yet five but Paul, glancing through the floor-to-ceiling windows along Monkey Island, can see that evening has already hung itself on the black branches of the trees along the edge of the lake. Language and science exams were completed today, the fall sports season has ended, and not a single boy remains in the building. The last exams are tomorrow, then Thanksgiving, five days of freedom. Paul is here for a meeting. A group formed last year called the Religions and Ethics Committee is gathering tonight at the request of Tuck Bowerfind, whose November 11 bombshell had rocked the faculty. Paul has made several copies of it, and keeps them in a folder with several other Religions and Ethics documents.

"Dear Paul," the letter reads.

"At Dr. Hawley's suggestion I am proposing a two-year plan for the teaching of religions and ethics. The plan seeks to bring the boys as far along in their religious and ethical understanding as possible by means of curricular and extra-curricular offerings that provide information, invite student participation, reach into every corner of the school, promote a spirit of generosity and hospitality, and connect religious and ethical thinking to action. Our goal is for boys to know and respect religions, and make practical and conscientious moral decisions."

Tuck's letter grows increasingly gamey when he suggests the means by which this might be done. As part of a school leadership program, in which upper-school boys conduct discussion groups with seventh and eighth graders, Tuck explains, he has already introduced such topics as "Models of Male Virtue," "The Ethics of Sexual Abstinence," and "The Role of Religion in Conversion of Life."

"With the encouragement of Dr. Hawley," the letter continues, "I am now beginning to put together an assembly series at each campus for the winter and spring trimesters to address the role of religion in daily life." These speakers would address, he says, "religion in business practice, religion and the arts, religion and civic duty" with a general focus on "how religious belief informs our idea of what it is to be a man."

Paul responded to Tuck's letter over the weekend. Paul's words were so strong that the headmaster decided it would be a good idea to discuss it with Paul away from school, and took him to lunch. Tuck in turn had written Paul back; though Tuck had addressed it to Paul, mysteriously, everyone *but* Paul received it, and Paul had to borrow Kerry's copy, further reinforcing Paul's suspicion of sneaky business afoot.

I've come out to school this evening to sit in on the meeting, and when Paul sees me he stops and takes a seat on the stairs.

"How did the lunch go?" I ask. The headmaster had taken him to a nearby Hunan restaurant, a coincidental bow to the East.

"Rick told me he didn't think I was going to hell," Paul says.

I chuckle at this, then realize Paul's raised eyebrows suggest that he isn't trying to be funny but, rather, hopeful.

Nancy Lerner emerges from the faculty lounge, jangling her Lucite butterfly key ring. She looks exasperated but she spots Paul and alters her course. "You had lunch with Rick today," she says. "How was it?"

"It went well, I think."

"Oh—*good.*" She adores both Paul and Rick and it's important to her that they get along.

Paul asks, "Are you here for the meeting tonight?"

"No," she says. "It was suggested that tonight would *not* be a good night for me to be there." She speaks somewhat wryly but she's so worn out that she isn't crushed to be missing the event. "Have you seen Bob Davis?" she asks.

"No," Paul says. "Did you check Deb Nash's office? He might be there."

Nancy's furious with Bob, the teacher apprentice who'd been in her class all trimester. He asked to see her students' exams so he could practice grading. "He was supposed to *borrow* them," Nancy explains, "Xerox them, and put them back in my mailbox."

Nancy looks up and sees Rick trotting down the stairs. He's here for the meeting, too. Rick stops at the middle landing, wedges himself behind the table there, and dips beneath it to pick up some scraps of paper. After hours, the headmaster rarely makes a pass through school without picking up paper.

"I am grading some absolutely *amazing* essays," she says quickly, when Rick has reached the bottom landing.

"I wish I were," he says.

Paul remains seated on the steps, elbows propped on grasshopper knees, fingers clasped at his chin, silent.

"Is this your cause-and-effect paper?" Nancy asks Rick.

"Yeah," he says, clearly mad. "Jason Koo's is perfect, but the rest—" and he trails off. He asks Nancy about hers.

"It's on *Hamlet*," she says. "I gave them five different choices and they're all really different."

Rick asks about Ryan, a student they share.

Nancy lowers her head slightly and says, "He didn't do well."

"He doesn't know that as of this afternoon," says Rick, then asks about one of their favorites, the unpredictable Tyler Doggett.

"I *finally failed Tyler*," Nancy says, her eyes enlarging. "For *once* I'm doing what he wants."

"You finally did it," Rick says smiling for the first time. Earlier in the year, Tyler had accused her of faulty grading—she gave a passing mark to a paper he claimed was bullshit. Tyler's grades are the last thing Nancy and Rick are worried about.

"He talked about Nietzsche and Sartre and—"

"But not about Hamlet."

"But not about Hamlet. For *once,* he'll thank me."

Paul has remained quiet during their discussion, tugging at the tips of his wispy moustache, and appearing not unlike a boy listening to his parents' dinner-table conversation. It was here that, for the first time, the unusual dynamics of this triumvirate became clear to me. These three people formed a peculiar little family. Hawley the dominant father (Nancy and Paul both repeatedly referred to Hawley as a father figure); Nancy, the maternal force concerned first and foremost with people's feelings, wanting all to get along; and Paul, the rebellious son, forging his own identity and voice.

Hawley glances at his watch, then scans the corridor. No one else has arrived for the meeting. Nancy heads off to look for Bob and the rest of her exams. Hawley leaves for the kitchen, hoping coffee and some food have been prepared.

No one had mentioned the meeting, or had wanted to, so it's impossible to gauge how Hawley's handling this. He appears calm, but he doesn't look happy or even at ease with these two colleagues. He has a way of tucking his chin into his collar, as though bridling back, when he's upset—and there had been much chin-tucking during this brief exchange. Just three days ago he'd ironed out l'Affair Soltis and now Paul, whom he respects and perhaps even finds reminiscent of his youthful self, has done some of his own knife-in-the-back work: "I also cannot help but feel that the faculty has been intentionally kept in the dark on this issue . . . and that I have been manipulated," he wrote in his letter to Tuck, a copy of which he'd given to Hawley. "I find myself wondering whether the committee, and its spirit of open-mindedness, was a charade, merely intended to create the illusion that the new curriculum had been thoughtfully considered and widely supported. In any case, I was left with a feeling that the entire process had been ironically and disappointingly unethical."

As he proved last week, Hawley takes written words not only seriously, but personally. To claim that his school is behaving unethically is to say that he himself is behaving unethically.

Paul, too, is serious; this is exactly what he means to say.

And Nancy—Hawley's *friend*—had met with Hawley immediately after reading Tuck's letter, unable to contain her anger. Nancy had told me a week ago, standing in her office before class, that her meeting with Rick was lively but difficult. "It pains me to give him pain, and I *did* give him pain," she said. She had told her boss that she thought he was being "terrifically naive." She confessed that as a non-practicing ethnic Jew, she had to mistrust Christians. She said there was no one she mistrusted more, in fact, than a "good" Christian. When Nancy said these things, she looked at Rick and thought, *He's thinking he doesn't even know me.*

"It is a private school," Nancy told me, "and I know Rick's got a vision. I know he feels that something has gone wrong and that he's got to repair it." She thoughtlessly straightened a row of books on a shelf, stared blankly at them, then wondered aloud whether she wouldn't be better off in a public school. The fourth-period bell was about to ring, she was clearly distraught, and she acknowledged it. But she would not show this to her students, not ever. "Not with this," she said with a determined grin. "Not so long as I have this." She pointed to a button pinned to her lapel—a picture of Shakespeare above the words "Will Power"—and headed off to class.

Rick has found a cart loaded with coffee, soda, and cookies and, hunched, he wheels it up the ramp from the maintenance wing and through the corridor to the boardroom. Paul and I take a seat, surrounded by oil portraits of headmasters and photographs of the businessmen who have served as trustees of this school for more than a century. Kerry Brennan, dapper and coiffed, bounces in, looking suspiciously well-rested. Margaret Mason arrives also, followed by Carol Ulrich, a first-grade teacher at the lower school. Still no Tuck, the keystone wedged between opposing buttresses.

Rick, Kerry, and Margaret talk school to pass the time, but Paul is silent, listening, tugging the ends of his red moustache. Two morning assemblies last week featured outside presentations on AIDS. During the second a woman in her early twenties told the boys and faculty about her life since she contracted the AIDS virus. Most of the boys, those from middle- and upper-class neighborhoods and perhaps overly aware of, and confident in, the sheltered nature of their lives, believe that AIDS is something that happens to gay men and prostitutes in New York City, only rarely to women and never in Hunting Valley. The first morning's speaker was a doctor who discussed the technical side of the virus—what it is and how you get it. Even here, however, even at eight in the morning listening to a guest of the school, Paul Bailin is tuned ruthlessly to mixed messages and undercurrents of bias.

Paul didn't like the tone of this speaker—the doctor's voice carried a sort of antiseptic disdain for the subject—and when the man explained to the boys who carried the virus, Paul would not let it go unchallenged, in very much the same way he wouldn't let Tuck's letter go. Paul sits in the stratosphere of the assembly, in the furthest row of seats, virtually level with the technicians' lighting and sound booth. When the speaker asked for questions, Paul had to work to be seen.

His voice was unnaturally high because he had to shout out his question, which turned out to be not a question at all: "You said that the people who contracted AIDS through transfusions," he called out, "were somehow innocent bystanders. I hope you're not suggesting that the others were *guilty* of something."

The speaker, momentarily trapped, hemmed and hawed—"of course not, of course not"—but this was exactly what he'd implied and Paul, who hears the human side of AIDS terror every Saturday from midnight to four A.M. on the Free Clinic Hotline, will not allow anyone to plant seeds of bias in the kids.

Paul is consistent. Tonight, he is doing the very same thing—calling out from the back row. Just as he had done with his response to Tuck, who is still not in evidence tonight.

In the four-page letter that earned him a lunch with the headmaster, Paul summarized his main contention: "A particular concern," he wrote to Tuck, "with an apparent Western—particularly Christian—slant to the proposal . . . as well as the absence of any mention of Eastern or non-theistic religions, secular humanism, atheism, etc. The list of virtues, for example, is exclusively Christian and Aristotelian. Eastern virtues such as *tolerance* are notably absent from your list. The notion of 'reaching into every corner of the school' also rang rather Orwellian to some. . . .

"If we desire a more ethical school," he continues, "we as a faculty—and an administration—might take a lesson from Matthew 7:1–6 and begin by examining our own ethical shortcomings, which many view as equal to those of our students. . . . While there may or may not be textual evidence for these concerns in the letter, I think they stemmed in large part from the context in which the letter arrived—Rick's speech last week, and a perceived trend towards Christian advocacy, perhaps even religious dogmatism, at US. Based on the reaction Friday, these concerns, whether founded or not, are pervasive and serious."

Paul's letter ("Tell Ann I'm entering the Headmaster's Essay Contest," he had told the colleague who delivered a copy of his letter to Hawley's office) presents an incisive and reasonable argument. Certainly it would not be unusual or untoward had dissent come from a senior faculty member or an administrator or trustee. But Paul is a mere sprout at twenty-four years old, the second-youngest teacher at the school, he hasn't been at the school two years, and he has no teaching credentials beyond one year's work. He was hired "through the mail," and was lucky for the chance. Furthermore, it can be professionally unwise to lash back at something the headmaster has worked hard to create. Margaret Mason suggested that contractual repercussions can result—or at least that is the consensus. When contracts are renewed each year and raises are doled out, intangibles such as how much a teacher gave to the school beyond the 8 A.M.-to-3:10 hours of service, are deciding factors. A contentious letter would not weigh in Paul's favor. Paul, perhaps *because* he is twenty-four years old, senses something deeper at stake than his own position within the school.

From Hawley's vantage point, matters are complicated. He likes Paul; he is, or was, so proud of Paul that when I asked to sit in on a Western Civ class, Paul was the first person Hawley suggested. All teachers are periodically reviewed and evaluated by their peers, and when the headmaster's review came up, Hawley chose Paul to evaluate him. Hawley admires Paul's intelligence, the very gears that Paul had now engaged to undercut an important proposal of his own creation.

The plan had been more than a year in the making. US has endowed special chairs in each department at about half a million dollars apiece. The teacher chosen for the chair receives a salary boost, controls a budget, and oversees work specific to that chair. (They also receive an actual chair, one of the fancy captain's chairs found throughout the school.) Though the school had endowed many chairs, the headmaster felt one more was needed: a chair in religions and ethics. Money was raised and a chair, named after Tony Jarvis, was established. The teacher to be installed was the Rev. Ellis "Tuck" Bowerfind, a graduate of St. John's College, Yale's divinity school, and now a social-studies and English teacher, and leadership counselor.

Last year, the formal installation took place on November 11.

"Each one of our boys—indeed every human being—has a spiritual life," Hawley told guests gathered for the ceremony. "He will either give it voice or not. He will express it robustly and proudly, or he will mute it. He will understand its place in history and current affairs or he will leave it in some corner of his life set uneasily apart from his practical daily business. Each of our boys has a spirit and that spirit must find its voice."

The new chairman will, through various programs, emphasize "the place of common, deeply rooted ethical standards in society," and work with the faculty "to build coherent curricular approaches to religious history, ethical questions, and the determinants of behavior generally."

This is no easy thing in the 1990s, not even in an independent school that is free to do what it wants. The chair's mission statement is 1990s-cautious when it adds that the chairholder will not "promote the establishment of any particular religion or institution. Rather, they would give point to the religious and ethical emphasis already embedded in the school's program, while providing new outlets for student views and questions."

No one, apparently, had a problem with any of this in theory—until, a year to the day of Tuck's installation, when Tuck wrote a letter to Paul changing theory to action. Action was the point. Hawley had told Tuck, You've got a chair, a budget, and a salary raise—there's a reason for that, let's get moving. Tuck did his job. And he got hammered. In the course of an hour during which his letter circulated through upper school, he became the instigator and focal point of faculty anger, and a symbol of invasive Christianity.

It is well after five now, chitchat in the boardroom has ebbed, and still no Tuck. Is he thinking he'll find a pride of lions, lazily licking their chops? Kerry suggests they begin the meeting without the chairholder, and at that moment a rap-rap-rap sounds on the window. The night is black outside and the sudden noise makes me jump. Kerry bounds to the window and pulls the curtain back. There, a few feet beyond, is a white glow, an apparition.

"It's Tuck!" cries Margaret.

The glow, as it nears the window, comes into focus as a white T-shirt, with a US insignia on the breast, hovering in the darkness. No other part of the man is visible from where I sit.

The school is locked. Tuck has been shut out of his own meeting. You can scarcely hear him behind the thick glass. Kerry shouts, "Go around to the doors by Monkey Island," and hurries out of the boardroom.

"It's chained," Paul calls out. "He's got to go around to the dining room."

At last, Tuck enters the boardroom in his immaculately white T-shirt, somewhat out of breath and apologizing for being late. Delayed by coaching, he explains. He smooths his receding brown hair and slides into a seat between Kerry and Rick, across from Paul. In the harsh neon light, Tuck's skin appears pasty—a common malady in Cleveland—and a shadow of beard darkens his narrow face. His eyes are dark brown, also shadowed, perhaps from fatigue, and seem to me vaguely humorless, though perhaps he is simply not looking forward to the meeting. And no wonder. It is his job to launch a plan that one person in this room wants no part of, and who has claimed that most of the faculty want no part of either. But Tuck is the chairholder, and he is determined, at the demand of his boss, seated beside him, to see his plan through.

This is just how Tuck begins the meeting.

"I know Paul has some concerns," Tuck says, then quickly and completely avoids these concerns by sidestepping into the new plan: the need for structure, a series of assembly speakers, and perhaps one elective at the upper school on religion.

Hawley senses immediately that dismissing Paul so bluntly is a wrong step.

"Tuck, can I add something?" he asks. "I think it's important to remember the origins of the chair. There have been concerns on behalf of some faculty, so we need to reiterate the mission. This chair is not a new attachment. We have a program that we really care about. We are an ethical place and we do teach about the world's religions. Religions are part of the data of history. Maybe it's just a matter of improving what we do." He pauses briefly, staring at the table, and continues. "I do want to say that if there were problems, the letter was partly my fault. I think it was my saying, ya know, 'Tuck, let's get off the block.' Tuck was trying to be responsive to me in sending out this letter."

Hawley's taking responsibility for Tuck's letter was an important concession to Paul, and Paul nods.

Tuck begins again by reiterating the mission, which he reads directly from his controversial letter. "The plan seeks to bring the boys as far along in their religious and ethical understanding as possible. . . ."

When Tuck finishes reading, Paul says, "I guess my concern is that if you're the point man in all this, students who wanted to bring this up with you could. But this sounds different for us, as though it was coming from the administration." He asks about the questionnaire passed out to faculty—what were the results? "As far as I know," Paul says, "we got negative feedback and concern. Overwhelming concern about bringing religion into school classes or assembly."

Tuck blusters, raises a flat palm to Paul. "Yes, I understand that, and I think it's important that this is student driven. It *can* be student driven—"

"I'm having trouble seeing what that has to do with what I was saying," Paul says quickly.

Margaret, sensing the tension, says, "Now that you're here every Friday, Tuck, and you'll be a regular presence—"

"A regular presence," Tuck acknowledges. Several boys are actively studying religion, and Tuck drives to the upper school once a week to meet with them. "I can be connected."

"But our concern," says Paul, "is that this seems like an engineered program."

"The faculty responses that we got were for it," Tuck responds.

"With all due respect, that's not what I've found. I've talked to about twenty-five faculty who are not for it."

Tuck nods and smiles. "Yes, I know," he says, determined to remain positive. "The teaching of religions ought to be done at home, and if it's done in school it should be done by example, not dogmatically or didactically. And also, and this goes back to your letter Paul, there's worry of a creeping fundamentalism. But the purpose of all this is opening up a dialogue."

"What were some of the concerns of the faculty that you spoke with?" Margie asks Paul.

"I'd rather let the faculty speak for themselves. I'm happy to express my own concerns, but I don't think it's my place to speak for them."

"Well let me phrase it a different way," Margie says, but before she can continue, Hawley says, "What I want to know, what I don't understand— Paul *teaches* religions. He's a *scholar* of religions. That's what he studied. So here's someone who teaches it, studies it, and likes it. How have we gotten this distance—love and interest to fear and skepticism. I'd like to close that gap."

Paul says to Tuck, "See, I'm really leery of organized religions. I don't see a lot of difference between that and the KKK."

Tuck takes a breath, lets that remark pass. Organized religion is part of his work, his life, and likening it to the Ku Klux Klan doesn't appear to sit well. Tuck remains positive: "I still think we can move in a practical direction. You've presented the case well," he says to Paul, then to the room he says, "Now. How do we introduce this to the school?"

Tuck suggests possible assembly speakers—*The Plain Dealer* film critic might be asked to discuss how religions are portrayed in movies, for instance; he notes other secular figures in Cleveland who might speak on religion as it exists in daily life.

"Do you have any atheists?" Paul asks. "Any Satan worshipers?"

Tuck, exasperated, says, "I don't understand *what* your *interest* in *Satan* is."

Hawley leans quickly in Tuck's direction and mock whispers, "You don't know him as well as Paul does."

Hawley chuckles, but Paul and Tuck, slugging it out in the center of the ring, don't seem to hear the joke.

"Can the faculty get together?" Paul asks. "Is there a time when we could meet so the faculty could express their concerns?"

"This is a personal thing," Hawley says. "I want to know if the faculty feels crowded about this Religions and Ethics chair."

This is precisely why Paul would like an open meeting.

"I've talked to some people at the lower school and my ears were burning," says Carol Ulrich. "I know Charlie wants to talk about atheism. And I've got Mikey Bailin in my class and he's said some interesting things."

"Oh?" Paul smiles. Mikey is his half brother. "What did he say?"

Somehow, Carol says, describing her first-grade classroom, the subject of God came up. Carol grins and says, "Mikey said that God was blue. And another boy said, 'No, God is yellow.' And Mikey said, 'No, I *know* God is blue.' "

Paul grins too and says, "Mike and I had a long discussion on whether God was a man or a woman. Unsuccessfully. He still thinks God is a man."

"Ahhhhh!" says Hawley, as if vindicated.

Kerry has been quiet for most of the meeting, jotting notes on a legal pad, but he now asks, "Is there a *fear* of *teaching* about religion?"

"We teach enough about religion," Paul answers. "As Rick said to me at lunch today, if we taught any more religion in the freshman and sophomore year, this would be a parochial school. There's so much more to teach."

Kerry says, "But boys at this age are really turned on by these issues. These kids are ripe for this stuff."

"The meaning of life," Tuck adds.

"Yes," Kerry continues, "the meaning of life, their place. They're reasoning about it now, and I don't want to ignore these pregnant issues." Kerry notes that schools "are now more responsible for things that had previously been left to other institutions," adding, "It's not our job to make kids religious. I just want to ask the question, What should a boy know about religion at what level?"

"M-hm." Paul nods. "OK"

"We must make some judgments," says Hawley. "We're too compartmentalized. We've been too timid so far about having galvanic people in assembly talk about religion."

Paul reiterates the issue of trust. Everyone pushing for this new injection of religions and ethics are Christians, and that is what's making everyone uneasy.

Carol says, "I don't see what scares people so much about spirituality."

Rick notes, "The cultural climate at any school is going to reflect the culture of the times."

Kerry asks, "How do we continue this discussion?"

The meeting has begun to unravel. Hawley wants to be home. His middle daughter is arriving tonight after her first months at college, he explains, and apologizes for having to leave. He stands and sets his coffee mug on the cart. It's late and people are tired; nothing has been accomplished and it's clear to everyone that little can be done without a more comprehensive airing of faculty views.

Kerry begins making plans for a faculty meeting on the issue, and Paul explains to Tuck that he never received a copy of the third letter. Tuck appears surprised and apologizes, saying he sent it through the normal channels.

"I had to borrow Kerry's," says Paul, still suspicious.

Hawley, standing at the door, tells the room, "Paul, the way we mail things at the upper school is to put them in all the student mailboxes."

Paul grins, but Hawley doesn't. The first trimester is over. In two short weeks, the mood of the school has turned dark, and it's left a bitter taste in the headmaster's mouth.

There will be no immediate injection of religion into school life. The subject, the plans for special assemblies and curricular changes, will drop this year like a brick. A couple of days after Thanksgiving break, after the school reconvened and headed back into business, Kerry posted a handwritten note in the faculty lounge: "Prior to exams," it read, "there was some concern expressed about the nature of the Chair in Religions and Ethics and the school's position in regard to religion. On Tuesday, 7 December (in the Board Room) at 3:30 P.M., there will be a meeting for anyone interested in discussing these issues. Thanks."

The meeting was less a discussion than an effort in stamina for Hawley, Tuck, and the rest of the committee. Hawley arrived early, sat in the same seat, his chin buried in his throat. He knew already what would happen: no one supporting increased religion in school other than the committee members had any reason to attend. The only people who showed, thirty upper-school faculty, were there to say one thing: "NO." Hawley told the faculty at that meeting, "My personal hope for this meeting is to make your concerns clear." Looking around the room—and the room was packed, every chair, sofa cushion, and bare spot of wall was taken—Hawley then added, "This is a case in which the Christians might be thrown to the lions." A tense little chuckle erupted from the headmaster. "And that might be kind of exciting."

He turned out to be only half right. It wasn't all that exciting. Every faculty who wanted to speak did so, creating in the course of an hour and a half a list of every possible objection to even trying to promote religious curiosity in a multicultural community. Hawley would sit there and take it—and while he would not relinquish his own beliefs or even temper them, he was cautious. He sat with right leg crossed over left, hands folded, chin tucked, staring at the table, looking up only when he spoke. As the meeting wore on, he grew tired; it was the sort of fatigue that makes someone appear to age before your eyes.

The final blow came from the students themselves. Their entries for the Headmaster's Essay Contest overwhelmingly echoed the faculty.

"Would it be fair, in a school composed primarily of Moslems, to require a Christian to take part in daily prayers to Mecca, even if he did not believe in Islam?" asked Mike Cohen, a senior who had proved himself a deft Clytemnestra in hockey mask and cape. "If harmony and diversity is the true goal of a school community, then all religious practices must be removed from this environment."

Mike's friend, Andy Kline, wrote, "I think that one can simply look at some of the ideals that this country was founded on to see that there is not much of a role for religion in school today."

Junior Timothy Tseng argued that it was indeed a school's job to develop the moral code shared by the major faiths, and to accommodate the various religious faiths of students, but added, "as a nonsectarian institution, the school's commitment to diversity must stop at accommodation."

Only one student, Shin Lin, argued for something more than accommodation. Shin, a junior, contended that religion could never be completely severed from school life because many students in it were openly religious and therefore "religion would always mingle with school. . . . Because religion will never be eradicated from school and any manifestations of it can only come by individual choice, the school as a whole corporate body must take a totally neutral stand on this issue." Shin concluded, "religion should be allowed to roam around as freely as any other tool used to capture truth."

Shin Lin, perhaps unsurprisingly, was chosen the contest winner.

I was rather enjoying the reaction to this brouhaha that had charged the entire school. I did not enjoy the pain this was clearly causing the headmaster—Hawley was sharply stung by the faculty's response—or Tuck's frustration—he'd been given a job that few wanted him to do. But the energy with which everyone had responded was powerful. The issue galvanized teachers and students alike. They really cared about this one, and apparently cared about the school and how it might be changing. Because no laws forbid religious expression in independent schools, there are few natural barriers to potential benefit or harm. As Mike Cohen wrote in his essay, "It is in a private-school atmosphere that religion can best arouse conflict."

Another side of the drama interested me as well, one that seemed more in line with the darker side of the school that had bubbled up over the last two weeks of the trimester. Everyone pushing for more religion in this school *was* Christian. Additionally, all the proposals mentioned in Tuck's letter, ordered and approved by the headmaster, had an explicit Christian bias. Were Hawley, Margaret, Kerry, and Tuck, all committed Christians, trying to railroad Christian doctrine into the school?

Before the meetings, I asked the headmaster, in the warm, homey glow of his office, if he thought that Christianity, specifically, should be a part of the school, and did he understand the faculty's widespread fear that Christianity would swamp any attempts at a comprehensive religious program? He seemed uncomfortable talking about it and unwilling to let his own decisions and desires be overridden by faculty simply because they were the majority. Given his strong, often surprising, reactions, I had no idea where he stood.

Hawley was by turns elliptical, stuttery when his mouth wouldn't form the words as fast as he was thinking them, cautious—I was beaming the red eye of my tape recorder at him—and, despite the tape, disarmingly personal.

"I think Christian religion *is* part of the school," he said. "I think Christianity is part of the school in that some of the people in it are Christians, are practicing Christians. . . . I think the religious dimension of people's lives *should* be part of the school because the people in it are religious. The thing I'm trying to interest the kids in more, in waking up to, responding to—and I can't say terribly successfully—the thing that's irritating the faculty so much now, is . . . what do you do with the religious dimension of your life in a non-denominational, non-sectarian community? We are a nondenominational school, and we're going to stay that way. My feeling is that, our being an independent school allows us to celebrate that data too. History doesn't make any sense without religious influence. It's been shaped, literally, by religious fervor, religious dread, religious hatred, and everything else. That would include American history. Art history is meaningless—imagine taking religious symbols out of art, out of all Western art. You'd be left with 1890 on."

Such questions and his interest in them have led to the only vocational dilemma he's ever had. "Given what I believe," given that he is, in his words, "irrevocably Christian," he has often asked himself, "should I be working at a Christian school?"

"That's the deepest thing about me consciously," he explained. "Perhaps gender is deeper and some other things. But in terms of the cultural overlays, that's the most central shaft. And when I reference decisions and so forth I reference them to that."

What is important to remember, he said, is that school is a series of value judgments, and to choose is to make a judgment that helps define a school: "I could say, tritely, *Moby Dick* or *Jaws*. To make a choice is really a value judgment. Those are referenced to something, and that value is only a chain or two away from something like," he paused, "a theological conviction. . . .

"But when that standard is challenged, as it is often in philosophy class, you keep backing it up, and what do you back it up to? That's the whole business of philosophy. What is the reference? And I know what my reference is, and I happen to think my reference is in alignment with Western philosophy. I think, like Aquinas"—he holds his index fingers up, then presses them together to form a peak—"that truth and theological things meet at a point."

Didn't he then, given his unequivocal religious convictions, understand some of the concerns that Paul voiced?

"Paul's worried about the creeping Christianity and some sort of crypto-Christian agenda taking hold," he acknowledged. "It's arrogant to interpret another person," he said, "but from my point of view, Paul is a very spiritual person. He's a quester. He's a serious, principled guy. . . . He sensed, rightly, in me this kind of crypto-idealist always trying to turn the world around. . . .

"I think there really is that danger," Hawley continued, "especially when some of the people—including me and Tuck, who's empowered by his chair—the people who are cheerleading for this and trying to get it all going, are Christian, and know their tradition better than they know any-body else's tradition. So there is that danger that it could happen, and that's why I think it makes sense to do this slowly and collaboratively. I'm not absolutely discouraged because Paul thinks it's such a terrible idea, and some others do, that we can't do it. I do think it's saying, whoa whoa whoa, maybe we oughta start with some gentler assumptions, and I think that's fine."

Nancy, on the other hand, brought more emotional and personal concerns to him, ones that speak to larger issues. She had surprised him when she explained that his religion speech offended her.

"I looked her in the eye one day and said, 'Nancy, we've had all these much more vivid exchanges with good humor, deeper penetration than *that*. I thought that was the most accommodating talk I ever gave.' And she said, 'You cannot know what it means to be a Jew at this school. And it really hurts me that you don't see why that's not a scarier thing or Tuck's letter might be scary.' And obviously, I don't. I don't *see*. I'm working on understanding. I certainly understand her position emotionally. I really don't understand it intellectually because again it rests on . . . toxicity and historical interpretation in Western history."

Nancy's insistence that the one person she had to mistrust was a "good" Christian implies "two awful things," says Hawley. "One of them is big-otry. Apart from the data she's experienced about Christians—she did tell me *I'm* OK—apart from that data, she's got an ideology that says she shouldn't trust me. Now turn that around: 'Now, the one thing I've *got* to mistrust is the Jews.' Or, 'The one thing I gotta mistrust is blacks.' It's bigotry. It is bigotry. She doesn't feel it's bigotry because she thinks Christians are so incredibly empowered and safe.

"In fact, Mike," Hawley continued, his voice softening almost to a whisper, "real, practicing Christianity is *feeble*. It is feeble in the late twen-tieth century. There's almost no robust expression of it except these clowns on the television, who are felons." To critics who denigrate Christianity on the basis of the TV felons, Hawley answers, "the fact that mathematics teachers drive badly, cheat on their wives, or do anything like that, does not disprove mathematics."

The other assumption in what Nancy said is the suggestion that there is something "toxic" about Christianity. "It's a little bit like some feminists' view of masculinity," he said. "Males are essentially there, but I don't want them to get together, I don't want them organized, I don't want them to have a club together, I don't want them to have a school together, because males together are toxic. . . .

"A lot of people cross their hands trying not to be offensive," he continued. " 'Oh, I can be a Christian at home.' I'm not a great church man, by the way, but I hope I'm a passionate Christian. I *can* leave that dimension at home but I think it's *wrong* to do that completely. I'm worried by doing that, I'm then empowering that kind of unintended bigotry. 'I've got to mistrust Christians,' she said, 'but especially good Christians.' I think people need to confront, I need to confront, robust people of faith, other faiths than mine. My world gets bigger and better if I do. And they need to confront me, not the, I don't know what fraction of me is Christian, but not the fraction, the whole bit, and not to be afraid of me and to be able to deal with me and things like that. That was my aim, that's what the question was about."

Hawley is not a fundamentalist. He believes, like the philosopher Alfred North Whitehead, whom he studied extensively at Cambridge, that "God is a dynamic." "That if you love God, there's more of God. It's a contingency. You can actually *hurt* God." Hawley goes to church every Sunday and says that he is not a great churchman. He believes that the Bible presents, among other things, a powerful theory of behavior.

"It's not some Tarot pack," he said, "but if the Bible's telling the truth . . . we should be able to make some predictive things about what's happening in history. That's one of the things about having a theory, or a powerful explanation—it should help us predict and help us foresee what's going to happen. . . .

"If Christian imperatives are true," he continues, "like if the love imperative is true, then you literally determine the future of the world by living that way or not living that way.

"If you live well and lovingly with people, you'll thrive and prosper and if you don't, and take away any grounds for doing so, you're going to be divisive and in conflict and live in a kind of material and emotional hell. I believe that is true. I think if we lose this ground, actually denigrate it—the only ground that we have for living well together—don't even allow people to talk about it, I think we're going to have bad times.

"So that's my issue," he concluded. "That's all. That's it. My one life, that's all I think about. . . . That's all I write about. The alignment of what you do with what's true."

8

More than once during the year the headmaster would say, "I will never understand this century."

That last word is revealing. Hawley doesn't bemoan the drugs-and-rock-and-roll post-sixties America. The line crossed is not marked by Kennedy's assassination, nor the passing of the family-values fifties. It's the entire twentieth century or, more precisely, everything that has happened since 1914, when World War I rolled out the bloody, corpse-strewn carpet upon which an age of irony and the antihero rattled into the world.

Indeed, Hawley sensed a pervasive absurdity at work in the culture even as a teenager—a confusion that came to a head in, of all places, his chemistry class. One afternoon at the large public high school he attended in the suburban outskirts of Chicago, frustrated by, among other things, the "embarrassing Tinkertoy contraptions" that supposedly represented molecules, he found himself mixing a solution that would become Butric acid—foul, rancid, and as meaningless to him as the Tinkertoys. He fled the school at the smell of what he'd just made. Sixteen years old at the time, he rested on a door stoop a block away, glared at his high school, just visible above the tree line, and asked, *Why have I been born into such an age?* Later still, in college, he suffered a spiritual malaise so severe that he almost never left his bed until Plato and Aristotle vaulted him onto a new plane; yet even here, methodically studying the "majestic causeway" of the history of Western philosophy, he saw that it ended at the twentieth century "like the frayed ends of a rope."

Few who know the headmaster fail to sense his aching hunger for eras long past—for the magic of the Renaissance, the heroic, questing chivalry of the Middle Ages, the reason of the Golden Age—nor the relentlessness with which he holds this century in judgment against that awesome backdrop. Hawley may be twenty-five hundred years behind his time, and he may be that far ahead of his time, but he is clearly not *of* his time.

"He is the walking, living, breathing example of ultimate idealism," says one colleague, perhaps selling him short. Sometimes, though, this colleague continues, "it's hard to translate that into the day to day."

His friend Ron Powers describes him, with unequivocal admiration, this way: "The aura of a slightly prior time is all about him: in his vocation as headmaster . . . ; in his dress and appearance . . . ; and certainly in the unhesitant moral inquiry that underlies every sentence he sets to paper.

"Hawley the writer and the man," Powers continues, "is a magnificent retrograde."

Powers is a journalist who won a Pulitzer Prize for a Chicago newspaper. The description of Hawley is from an introduction he wrote to Hawley's book, *Boys Will Be Men,* and what is striking about this foreword, arriving as it does from the keyboard of a former newspaperman, is that it's so thick with adoration that even Hawley was a little embarrassed by it. Powers nevertheless delivers some eloquent ideas about the enigmatic headmaster.

Chief among them, Powers says, is irony—a stance or frame of mind that has been, as Paul Fussell argued persuasively in *The Great War and Modern Memory,* the dominant form of consciousness since World War I. In Hawley's writing, in his formal addresses to his own school, to schools across the country, and most recently Australia, the man is utterly without, in Powers's phrase, "the industrial-strength prophylaxis of rote irony" that degrades so much of today's writing.

This should not suggest that Hawley's a hard-boiled preacher, serious as a tombstone as he rails against sinners. Actually, Hawley is funny, and his humor, if nothing else, is ironical, and often flip. (At lunch one day with Hawley, after the debate of whether or not to make condoms available in schools had resurfaced in newspapers, I asked him, "What's your opinion on that?" Hawley looked away and said, "Yeah, just stop by the machine outside my office." Before his students were about to take a test he implored them to write carefully and well. Being a bad writer, he added gravely, "is like going through life with your fly down. You can be a great guy but if you go through life with your fly down, people don't take you seriously.") But when it comes to matters of importance, the big issues—

romance, love and death, work, how one might live well, how people ought to live together—his words and ideas are imbued either with a sweetness that, for many, is unpalatable in this age of irony and skepticism or with portentous warnings against a contemporary culture that most of his students seem to find quite pleasant, and certainly harmless.

"The conditions that characterize our world in the last decades of this century really are different from those in all of previous history," he told the student body during one address. "The world that you and I wake up to each morning is characterized by speedy, almost instant information and by total access to all persons at all times.

"Even the things that once were thought to relax you and to restore your soul—entertainment, stories, music—have become quick and jumpy. We have a popular culture which tries to engage your senses by pulling them to the surface and tickling them. Consider the pace, the elusive messages of MTV; consider video games: prewired programs for your nervous system, instantly engaging but curiously unsatisfying. Again, this kind of culture is new. It is a culture of video and malls. It has not been lovingly designed because it is good or healthy for you. It has been designed to engage you in a very specific way. It wants your attention, and it wants to make you restless to do what it says and to buy what it sells.

"It never satisfies you, never teaches you anything, and it never makes you happy, but it tells you that the answer to the thin, jumpy dissatisfaction you feel is to have more of it. Stay tuned. Bigger, flashier, more comprehensive video-electronics are on the horizon. The next is called 'virtual reality,' and it is a computerized simulation of existence itself."

Hawley is pre–World War I, and virtually everything he laments seems to be post–World War I, perhaps in many cases *resulting* from World War I and its aftermath. So there's an apt symmetry to his life's work as a teacher in, and headmaster of, a boys' prep school, as Powers suggested, one that might even please his detractors. If the man insists on living in the past, they might argue, best that he does it in an institution similarly locked in the past.

This attitude about the boys' school, Hawley has suggested, is a distinctly modern one. He notes that the first anti-school writings emerged shortly after World War I from the pens of Robert Graves, Evelyn Waugh, and George Orwell. The image of the private school in general, and the boys' boarding school in particular, has always been an easy target of criticism, criticism that is not much different today from what it was a century ago—private schools exist to serve the rich and are therefore bad. More than bad. Un-American. Antidemocratic in their nurturing of an aristocratic subculture reminiscent of monarchical England, from which their form supposedly originates. Furthermore, their clientele represents an insignificant sliver of the educational scene. Much of the criticism of elite private schools is no doubt valid. Even educational historians, such as the formidable Lawrence Cremin, have all but dismissed the elite private school in comprehensive histories of education.

What's rarely noted, however, except by the schools themselves, is that their roots extend further back in American history than public schools do. In colonial America, the school scene was so haphazard that in 1647 and for a few years after, various colonies had to enact legislation forcing towns to pay one of their residents to teach school. One such act reasons that "It being one chief project of that old deluder, Satan, to keep men from the knowledge of the Scriptures," every town upon growing to fifty or more households "shall then forthwith appoint one within their own to teach all such children as shall resort to him to write and read. . . ." Cremin, who cites this in his massive history of American education, adds, "By 1650, schooling as an institution had been firmly transplanted to the North American continent, though with varying degrees of enthusiasm." Two current members of the National Association for Independent Schools— Collegiate in New York City and Roxbury Latin outside Boston—were by then already founded. Many of the private schools of that time, Latin grammar schools, which would flourish through the American Revolution, dated to the first century B.C.

More significant than historical roots, though, more significant to to-day's examination of education, is the fact that these schools are and always have been independent—free of the bureaucratic shackles that have re-stricted public schools since their phenomenal growth following the Civil War. The private school, which only superficially aped the English public school, would thus seem, ironically perhaps, to be the most democratic form of education America knows—in structure if not in the student body itself. Certainly, there have been insidious private schools as a result of this freedom. The elite prep schools did for many decades offer all-but-guaran-teed in-roads to the nation's top colleges and universities to people who could pay for that advantage, though this is less frequently the case today.

Regardless of the fact that many private schools have been effective schools, private schools are, by virtue of their independence alone, potential models of innovation in education, never more so than today with so much of public education turned to rubble and ash heap. It is to this conception of the prep school—the opportunity for self-governance and innovation— that Hawley most wants to align his school. It would be easy to compare Hawley to Thomas Arnold, the paradigmatic headmaster of the Rugby School, building an army of rugged Christian scholars, or to Arnold's later counterparts at American boarding schools—Endicott Peabody of Groton or the other legendary boarding-school headmasters. While Hawley wouldn't shy from such comparisons, the analogy is somewhat hollow. He is in many ways more radical than his predecessors, and certainly more so than his contemporaries, in that his range of accomplishments is unusually broad. Hawley has appeared before a United States Senate committee to speak about the effects of psychoactive drugs on teenaged brains. He has published, aside from books of fiction and nonfiction, articles in national magazines such as *American Film* and *The Atlantic,* poetry in *Commonweal.* Now he has turned what for so long has seemed an anachronism—the all-boy school—into a potentially cutting-edge, one might even argue modern, proposal. Later in the year, at a conference for boys' schools at which Hawley will deliver opening remarks, a leading educational researcher, unaffiliated with any secondary school, private or public, will claim that, given what is now known, it should be incumbent upon coeducation advocates to prove the benefits of coeducation, and not the reverse.

While University School in Cleveland has clear links to the Academy movement of the early seventeenth and late eighteenth centuries, and there are several schools throughout the country like it, the school is indigenous to this city on the eastern fringe of the Midwest. Everything about the school, including its all-boy make-up, is in some way linked to, and continues to be guided by, its past. Latin teacher Karl Frerichs, transplanted from a school in Louisiana, once exclaimed to me in passing, "This place could *only* happen in Cleveland." Another time, he drew a deep breath through his nostrils and said, "This place smells of the Industrial Revolution." He was perhaps more accurate than he realized.

In Cleveland, 1890, the sound of railroad cars, steam whistles of ships along the Cuyahoga River, and the roar of factories rang out in a singular chorus: commerce. It was a galvanic era of romance and recklessness as the city dominated not one industry but many—steel making, chemical processing, machine-tool production, ship building, manufacturing, and oil refining. It was during this era that young Clevelanders embarked on careers in business—John D. Rockefeller, Marcus Hanna, Louis Severance, Henry Flagler. That the city would rank among the three or four top producers of one industry was significant; that it was a leader in so many industries fundamental to the sudden growth of the United States was unusual. Cleveland's population virtually tripled during each decade of the last half of the nineteenth century. While the city rumbled and rolled, its outer reaches remained rural, with woods so plentiful Cleveland remained true to its nickname, the Forest City, and vast expanses of the farmland, which had for decades made it a center of raw agriculture production, held strong.

It was a time of unprecedented growth throughout the country. Industry everywhere flourished and people got rich. Between 1870 and 1920, a flood of institutions, organizations, and societies swept the country. These fifty years would build the base structure of an American high culture. Major symphonies, museums, and philanthropic foundations were born. The National Institute of Arts and Letters was established. American publishing reorganized for a more cultivated audience. Professions such as medicine and law defined themselves by establishing standards and governing bodies.

It was during these years too that public schools came to dominate secondary education but also a time when the famous boarding schools came into their own. They were tiny. Endicott Peabody's Groton, for instance, founded in 1884, graduated only forty-one students during its first ten years. Yet during these decades, the elite schools graduated a disproportionate number of the country's leaders. The founders of these schools typically were educated at the ancestral academies and studied at Harvard; they stressed development of the whole boy, with most emphasis put on that elusive, distinctly pre–World War I ethos, "moral character." The success of this movement opened the way for another form of private prep, the "country day" school.

Compared with the noble, wealthy, Protestant gentlemen who founded the elite boarding schools, Newton Anderson, the founder of University School, was blue-collar. Whereas the famous headmasters attended eastern or English universities, Newton graduated from Ohio State College. While the East Coast boarding-school founders were learned men, steeped in classics and theological training, Newton Anderson was skilled in carpentry and blacksmithing. He was a hardware man.

Anderson, formally trained as an engineer, began his teaching career at

Cleveland's Central High School in the early 1880s, though he lasted only a couple of years. He felt the school, then the city's main public high school, was not doing enough to prepare boys for the demands of living and working in booming, industrial Cleveland. So he set up a carpentry shop in a barn in February 1885. Here he trained boys in wood and metal-working. The boys hammered and lathed away with such enthusiasm and success under Anderson's direction that he was able to raise money for a building with expanded facilities and machinery; after one year the school board bought it and incorporated the Cleveland Manual Training School Company, initiating a comprehensive three-year program. Anderson's new school was so popular that public high schools throughout the city created manual training programs of their own. According to a local historian writing in 1910, Anderson had sparked "one of the most significant and far-reaching educational movements in the local history of education."

Anderson's quick success impressed the philanthropists of the city, and he had little trouble raising money for his next plan. Indeed, in photographs, his neat moustache, rimless oval spectacles, and fleshy jowls and neck folding over his starched collar project the air of a banker. Manual training in barns was no longer enough for this stout twenty-eight-year-old high-school physics teacher. He wanted a bigger school in a proper building, one on a spread of land outside the city big enough for athletic fields, and with a dozen teachers. Anderson raised $150,000 from seventy wealthy Clevelanders. A massive fortress of a building with barrel-vaulted windows at its third story was soon under way on nine acres of land, the former site of a gun club, and University School began classes in September 1890. As far as anyone knew, there wasn't another school like it in America.

In Cleveland, few schools prepared boys specifically for universities; the only real option was far-off boarding school. This new school would fill that need. What's more, Anderson had introduced a new concept into the prep-school program: combining classical learning and manual training. Boys, sooty and grease-smeared from tool-and-die work, would be bathed in Latin and other classical studies. The first six graduates of University School, four of whom went to Yale, would be able to hold their own with a hammer and anvil or drill press.

Whether it was important for a Yalie of the time to know how to work a drill press is open for debate, but the new school and its novel program seems to have been popular. Within a year, it was filled to its two hundred-student capacity, and families were reserving places for their sons' enrollment as far off as the twentieth century, one decade away.

Students apparently liked the school, too. One student-run publication states, in October 1890, "University School boys can at the same time with their education derived from books, get a good knowledge of all the ordinary pursuits of the day, such as carpentry, wood training, blacksmithing, and the handling of machinery. This not only gives them a good idea of what the methods of these departments are, but also teaches them to do with their hands what the brain conceives."

The Plain Dealer was likewise generous with praise, writing shortly thereafter that the school was the only one of its kind in the world. Former United States President Rutherford Hayes delivered the keynote speech at the school's dedication, and said the school "would likely be regarded hereafter as one of the notable steps in the educational progress of Cleveland." Hayes also suggested that a similar girls' school ought to be planned. This remark reportedly went over well with the boys. (In fact, there was already a girls school, Hathaway Brown, not far from US. Several years later, Laurel School would be incorporated. These girls' day schools continue to flourish today, a mile on either side of University School's lower campus.)

University School was novel in a second way. It was in the "country"— which its address at 71st Street and Hough Avenue, several miles east of the city, certainly was at the time. Nowhere else could an entire student body prepare for college during the day and be home by evening. It was the beginning of the "country day" school movement, one that would mushroom over the next several decades throughout the United States.

Newton Anderson ran his school for ten years, but for all the hoo-ha about manual training, and iron-masked students toiling away in a shower of sparks, college was the main business. At the time, boys prepared for entrance exams and applied to colleges and universities in the late spring of their senior year. Anderson was so serious about boys attending college that he forbade graduation ceremonies. He didn't want the boys distracted. After two years, he conceded to the seniors' wish for an end-of-the-year dance, but that was it.

The 1890s school day began at 8:45; there was one midday break for lunch (the school had hired a chef from a swank hotel in the city and claimed to be the only school in town that served hot lunches), and the day ended at five. From the outset, "physical development" was emphasized; twice a year, physical evaluations were required of every boy, and sports were big. One of its early football games attracted five thousand spectators.

The days were so busy that most students were too exhausted to get into trouble after school. But not during school. While studies, football, the mandoline club, say, or how many kids got into Yale (Yale was for decades the overwhelming first choice among graduates) may help describe the school, the mischief boys engaged in probably best captures the tone and mood not just of this school but of the era as well. Snuff, for instance, was evidently a popular tool of fun in the 1890s. Placed inconspicuously on a schoolroom stove, it would soon have the whole class sneezing their heads off. Soaked sponges were slid surreptitiously onto desk chairs for the old wet-spot-on-the-trousers prank. During the first school year, it was risky to leave a stiff hat anywhere but on your head; boys were fond of smashing them to pieces. One boy lost five hats in one year. A pair of gym shoes was occasionally stolen, setting off a chain reaction of gym-shoe thefts. Some boys would steal away from school to a neighborhood pub that would serve them beer. Boys whose rubber overshoes were missing did well to sniff the air; their overshoes could often be found melting on a stove. In clement months, large loud insects caught and released in class could prove an effective distraction from work. Punishment for such actions ran from standing in the corner of the classroom wearing a dunce cap to standing silently on a raised platform before the assembled school.

The 1890 prospectus of University School lists four founding principles:

To develop the greatest possible dexterity of mind and body.
To impart to him as much useful knowledge as possible.
To teach him healthful and manly habits.
To aid him in forming an earnest and upright character.

Character has always been a big deal in private schools. The notion that a school can teach a boy moral rectitude became world famous with the popularity of Thomas Hughes' best-selling novel *Tom Brown's Schooldays,* a portrait of Rugby and its headmaster Thomas Arnold.

As James McLachlan points out in his history of American boarding schools, Endicott Peabody, who was schooled at an English public school and then at Cambridge in the mid 1800s, would officially announce that his Groton was modeled on the English public school; Groton would develop "manly Christian character," like the English schools influenced by the Church of England. A trustee of the newly formed Lawrenceville told a newspaper that the school would be modeled on Eton and Rugby. McLachlan goes on to explain that this tie to the English public schools is more superficial than most realize. Boarding schools were more fundamentally linked to the American Academy of the early 1800s, more likely to foster middle-class values rather than those of an aristocracy.

University School, too, followed this path, but the philosophy of molding character had more to do with the ideas of the progressive educational theorists of continental Europe than those of English public schools—most notably, perhaps, those of Swiss educator Philip Emanuelle von Fellenburg, who stressed integration of intellectual, moral, and manual education, and German theorist Friedrich Froebel's then revolutionary notion of "learning by doing." Learning by doing remains one of University School's fundamental principles.

Schools can blather on forever about principles, missions, historical roots, and educational theory and still be ineffective. The private schools that lasted seem to have had in their early years forceful, authoritarian, durable leaders. When Newton Anderson left the school he founded (to found another school in North Carolina), US engaged in a nationwide search for a new headmaster and found George Pettee. Pettee would not be the required great leader.

Headmaster Pettee, a man with a square face and daunting, owlish eyebrows who was previously the registrar at Andover, seems to have done little in his eight-year tenure other than initiate formal commencement ceremonies and tell the board of trustees that they needed a bigger school on more land, which the board did not want to hear. The most lasting move of Pettee's career was, in fact, a fluke that would propel the school for half a century.

In the winter of 1902, having just fired a teacher who could not keep boys from throwing pennies and chunks of coal at each other in study hall, headmaster Pettee passed through New Haven to interview a potential replacement, a law student at Yale. When Pettee knocked on the student's door, a lanky serious young man named Harry Peters answered. Peters had a vast dome of a brow; even then, his fine dark hair seemed to struggle to advance skyward past large ears to cover that brow, never achieving dominance. Peters's jaw was square, his chin strong, his nose straight, and his blue eyes were invariably described as "piercing."

This first-year law student explained that he was not, alas, the one whom headmaster Pettee sought. That would be his roommate, who was out. It didn't matter anyway; his roommate had already found a job elsewhere. This no doubt distressed Pettee, and the two men talked. Peters and Pettee got on well. There was likely an immediate camaraderie between the two owing to the fact that Peters had been a scholarship student at Andover when Pettee was the school's registrar—and Peters, who didn't much care for law school anyway, suggested that he might fill the vacant post in Cleveland. Pettee, having few options, agreed.

The young schoolmaster with a brow the size of a planetarium was evidently a sound teacher of French, Latin, and history. But mischievous boys, sensing a weakness in the neophyte, gave him hell. Peters proctored a study hall of seventy or eighty boys who would slam their desks up and down and generally cause a ruckus. Not responding to verbal threats— boys, if nothing else, are concrete thinkers—they continued to harass the quiet boy-teacher until, eventually incensed, Peters threw the two chief troublemakers out of the room with enough force that he rarely had trouble again.

Life as a schoolmaster was not suitable for young Peters, nor was Cleveland. He had met a girl out west while traveling, and in the summer of 1907 returned to visit her. On the way, he contracted typhoid fever aboard a ship bound for Duluth by drinking water that had been drawn from Cleveland's industrial waterways. The illness, which struck when he reached Yellowstone, nearly killed him. He missed a year of school, convalescing. This gave him enough time to realize that the great western expanse held his future. His schoolteacher days were finished. Peters landed a job managing a gold mine in Montana. Shortly before he began his new life, a telegram arrived. It was from the board of trustees of his former employer. Pettee had resigned. Would Peters accept headmastership of University School?

Peters was twenty-eight years old. He had been teaching all of four-and-a-half years. He had no administrative training. He accepted.

The new position and salary allowed him to propose to the girl who'd brought him west. They married, returned to Cleveland, and young Peters assumed a post he neither deserved nor was qualified for. He would be the school's longest-reigning headmaster.

Peters was not intellectual and he was not eloquent, but he would return the school to its country origins by building a $1.3 million structure with a massive clock tower on a mud-slopped meadow that would eventually become the plush suburb of Shaker Heights. He would lead the school through two world wars, during prohibition and its repeal. When the school was hit by the Great Depression and admissions fell off and boys dropped out, his faculty agreed to cut their salaries by almost half for the duration of the Depression rather than cut faculty and weaken the school.

Peters was elected president of the National Headmasters Association, and he was awarded honorary degrees by Kenyon College and Yale University. He had gained such prestige throughout the country that when, following prohibition, he explained to a local reporter the benefits of boys' learning to drink beer rather than liquor—"it brings friendliness instead of drunkenness," he said, and, "it inspires him to song, to good fellowship, to a feeling that the world is not such a bad place after all"—his remarks were worthy of national attention and headmasters across the country criticized him for counseling his students to drink beer. The sensible headmaster meant nothing of the kind and responded to critics with endearing lead feet: "I'd be an ass to urge my boys to drink beer when I know it isn't good for growing boys."

Peters was a living example of the rectitude he preached most mornings of the school year. He always spoke about integrity, and he once said, "I would have more religion in the school if I could get away with it." Peters was an austere man who did not want to be bothered at home. He was not well-liked by students (and many mothers, as well, one of whom found him so rigid she nearly succeeded in ousting him in his early years as headmaster).

At the end of the 1947 school year, four decades after turning his back on a gold mine, Harry Peters stepped down from the only job he'd ever had. His impact on the school had been profound. In 1908, his first year as headmaster, he had told the boys that "it has always been the primary aim of the school, and it will continue to be, to prepare boys to become good citizens." He did not falter in this aim. Upon his retirement, *The Cleveland Press* called Peters himself one of the city's "finest citizens." The sixth headmaster of University School, Richard Hawley, in his loving, but not bowdlerized, history of the school written for its centennial, would write, "Dr. Peters was US. Hadn't he built it out of mud? Forty-five years in its service, he was not only the link to the Hough Avenue origins of the school, he was a link to the origins of schooling itself."

In the boardroom of the upper campus of University School in Hunting Valley, august oil portraits of five headmasters line the back wall in chronological order. Peters is in the center. To his right are George Pettee and Newton Anderson. To his left are Harold Cruikshank, who ran the school through the 1950s when it languished, and Rowland "BY GUM" McKinley, headmaster for twenty-five years, who, like a successful general, revived the troops and drove the school into a new era. It's probably more than coincidence that, at a school which for so long stressed the building of things, the three headmasters who most influenced it built massive structures during their tenure. All five men, a human time line of the school's history, stare severely out at all who enter this room.

Were Peters to visit the spread of land where he began as headmaster, he would find the school replaced by one of the most crime ridden, burned-out patches of the city. He might even, reasonably, broaden his beer statement. "The *world* is not good for growing boys," he could honestly say if he saw Hough now. His school, however, in its glacial migration east, would change very little. Superficially, it has changed. The school body is bigger, now requiring two separate campuses. The new building is modern. The machinery used by boys is more likely to be a computer than a drill press; the area used for manual training which covered entire levels of the previous campuses has been reduced at the upper campus to a small room in the maintenance wing. Generally, however, the four founding principles in the school's 1890 prospectus could be reprinted verbatim in today's brochures.

Yet, because the culture has changed so drastically from Peters's day, and because that culture is not left at home, the way, as many at the school contend, religion can be, pressures on the school, and perhaps most of all on the headmaster, demand change. Hawley's job is far different from Harry Peters's job. Otto Kraushaar, in his *American Nonpublic Schools,* has some sharp ideas about that change. Kraushaar says that the authoritarian rule of the headmaster, which allowed a boldness and swiftness of action, is no longer possible. "Now that the teachers have become professional and power-conscious while the students tend to question not only the wisdom but the legitimacy of autocratic authority," he writes, "the dictatorial stance is considered an anachronism." The headmaster is expected to *share* his powers with faculty, and it's considered wise to hear the student voice, as well, in decision-making. The headmaster's role thus becomes, Kraushaar writes, "that of a negotiator, mediator, balancer, and compromiser, instead of a charismatic leader whose word is law within his fiefdom."

Kraushaar made these observations twenty-four ago, and yet they seem only to have become more valid over time: "[The headmaster] is less free than was his precursor of even two decades ago to plot his own course. He is drawn willy-nilly into the search for better, more effective education, into the battle of opportunity and against racism, into the religious dilemmas of our time, and as many heads see it, into a struggle for economic survival."

While these changes have made the job more complex, the governing structure remains hidebound—namely, the head answers to the board. They can legally fire him on the spot if they feel like it. "Each of us is on a one-year contract except for me," Hawley said during an all-school faculty meeting. "Mine goes minute to minute."

Another thing that hasn't changed, according to education experts, is that the most important factor in a good school is a strong, consistent leader. A wishy-washy headmaster or principal, or, as is more often the case, a repeated changing of the guard in the top office, does more to weaken a school than anything else; that a headmaster's tenure today averages about seven years makes this the rule for independent schools.

When Hawley headed down the dimmed maintenance corridor and out into a dark cold night after the ineffective and disheartening meeting of the Religions and Ethics Committee, he was not a happy headmaster. He was certainly not a well-liked headmaster at that point, either. Several of his students were tired of his philosophy class, they told me, disappointed in it; they found Hawley overly opinionated and indoctrinating, and they had responded by shutting down. Hawley knew it. Their exams were rotten. Additionally, a majority of the faculty were wary of Hawley. Some did not trust the man outright; others believed that, anachronism or not, Hawley would do what he pleased with regard to religion and discipline and that there was little anyone could do about it except leave. Paul Bailin had become chief troublemaker, and Hawley now knew Paul would be a problem. But what cut at him more than a young teacher's open dissent was a sense that the common ground he and Paul had once shared, the ground on which they could argue productively, was fast eroding. He knew too that some igneous crest had risen up between himself and Nancy. What he didn't know—she would never have told him before a decision had been made—was that she really was ready to quit.

Trouble and tension happen all the time at school. What is unusual about this fall is that the trouble struck all at once, like a bad case of the flu. You can point to the date on the school calendar. Everything that had coalesced into a mood of suspicion and clenched jaws at the school of this backward-glancing headmaster began, ironically, on November 11, Armistice Day, the day America remembers the end of World War I.

■ ■ ■

"This short mini-term between Thanksgiving and the winter holidays can be an especially good part of the school year—if we get it right," the headmaster tells morning assembly first day back from break. Thanksgiving is over, and now it's time to count the days till the real break in just three weeks. "It actually works as a period of thanksgiving, of counting our blessings, and also of conferring a few blessings on those who could use them.

"Like many of you, I found myself very busy, frazzled, and behind as the first trimester came to an end. I'll also have to admit that I wasn't in much of a holiday mood. . . ."

Here comes his story. Necks in assembly go limp. Boys slouch out of view. Hawley describes a Quaker meeting he'd attended a few years back at a private school in Locust Valley, New York. As is the custom at such meetings, periods of silence are broken by someone, anyone, wishing to speak. And at the one he'd attended, a girl had spoken out. The headmaster describes the girl's words fairly completely, and the gist of it is that this girl was feeling depressed on a holiday, and then she looked out the window and saw a blue autumn sky and brilliant leaves and she felt, the headmaster recalls, "very small—and great at the same time."

You can see this thing a mile away. Maybe the gauntlet Hawley had run those last two weeks of the trimester had him addled and weak. Maybe he was losing his touch. Could it be? Was the headmaster slipping, like the culture he so often decries, into greeting-card banality?

"Like the girl in Locust Valley, I found my own mood growing heavy and sour as exams approached. I was feeling behind in my work, behind in my sleep, and small problems and annoyances were starting to look like big ones. A boy had said some mean things about the administration and had employed some mean language to say them, and he had posted this in all the student mailboxes. At the same time I was also made aware that colleagues I love and respect disagreed with me fundamentally on matters close to my heart.

"In my case, a blue sky and autumn leaves did not snap me out of it. What did snap me out of it was a phone call from a friend telling me that one of my headmaster friends, one of the most distinguished boys'-school heads in the United States, had just been diagnosed with inoperable, terminal cancer in his pancreas. This high-spirited, high-energy man, a former Rhodes scholar, a husband, a father, a man younger than I am, is, I now know, dying. He is expected to live for only a few months. It is typical of him that he wants to work on at his post as long as he can, until, in his words, 'I become an embarrassment.' Of course, he will not become an embarrassment. He will become an inspiration.

"Among his several gifts to me will be a vivid reminder of how lucky and graced I am, of how fleeting are not only my troubles, but also the things I count, if I am careful, as my due: my own work, my health, my family, my friends, my colleagues, my students, the phenomenal beauty of this place, this valley, and beyond.

"So I am glad to count my blessings this morning, even to count them out loud in front of all of you. For in fact, you and our common business here are a good part of those blessings. To teach and learn, to work hard and to blow off steam, to agree and to disagree, to try, to succeed, to fail, and to be forgiven here are great blessings, phenomenal and unearned. I hope that I never take them for granted.

"And please know that I mean it when I wish you, too, a happy Thanksgiving."

Part II

WINTER

9

Tuesday, January 4, was the first day of school after the long winter holiday. It was still dark when I started my car and shoveled about a foot of snow off the windshield. Street lights were still on and they lit the great clouds of car exhaust that made it hard to see what I was doing. The inside of the car was so cold I tried to crimp myself up—I thought if I could make myself smaller, I would be less cold. Wind whipped thick gusts of snow across the hood of my car. A radio announcer who sounded cozy said it was 28 degrees, which seemed hopeful to me. The morning traffic report listed about a hundred delays and accidents. As I headed out Cedar Road, the cars in front of me looked like beginner water skiers, kicking up little rooster tails of fresh snow as their back ends swung right and left. Clevelanders are used to driving in snow, and they can be cavalier about it, so I kept my distance as I listened to the long list of schools in several counties that had closed. US almost never closes on account of snow; when it does, it's usually because of the cold and concern for the little kids who have to stand on corners in the dark waiting for buses. Holidays and vacation and everything you look forward to when school starts were gone. Winter was here. You pretty much had to admit that nothing pleasant was going to happen for the next three months.

I was late. When I crept into the parking lot at 8:10, I saw Paul heading up the walk toward school wearing a giant green hooded down parka that hung to his thighs; he looked tiny inside it. Paul hefted his ox box and leaned into the bullets of snow as he hurried up the walkway.

The hike from the parking lot to the school takes two or three minutes,

169

but on mornings like this, you're fairly unconscious the whole time. I don't think I even realized how hard the wind was blowing till one of the faculty made a crack about my hair. It was 8:15 and assembly hadn't started. Music still pumped out of the speakers and everybody was milling.

At about 8:20 Kerry Brennan strode across stage, followed by Mike Costello, an art teacher who heads the ski club, and Hawley, who's not a morning person and shows it. Kerry stood at the podium waiting for everyone to sit down. He'd pulled a wad of announcements from his jacket pocket and flattened them on the stand. He gave the microphone a crank in his direction, and then waited some more.

"Good morning," Kerry says. He glances around at stragglers squeezing into their seats. "I hope," he takes another serious look around assembly. "I hope you all had a good vacation. On mornings such as these when we obviously have weather problems we have to start a little late. There are several announcements.

"First, thanks to all faculty and students who contributed food and/or money to the drive last month. Special thanks to Messrs. Logsdon, Harmon, and Friebertshauser and to those students who helped pack the food and the forty students who delivered it to more than two hundred families on the near West Side of Cleveland. That's a record for us and I think all those involved deserve a round of applause."

Kerry leads the applause which, from the audience, is disinterested, mechanical, though not weak.

"There are the following athletic scores. There are a lot of them so hold your applause." It's probably a good thing that Kerry reads them rapid fire because out of thirteen wrestling matches, hockey games, and basketball games, nearly every one of them was lost except for the hockey team's placing third in the Bowling Green tournament. Kerry asks for another round of applause.

Kerry had written all these announcements himself and now sets them aside for a new stack, squares of white paper; he places each neatly to the right of the stack when he's finished reading it.

"Wednesday's swim meet against St. Ignatius will be held here at Hunting Valley," he says, "not away as originally scheduled. All first trimester health students please meet in lecture room at the break. The Glee Club is asked to convene in the auditorium today, and A through E are reminded to bring their music folders. Mr. Jones's freshman English students are to bring their vocabulary notebooks to class today." He reaches the final sheet and sets it aside. He pauses and looks up. "There's an important result regarding the dress code following a faculty meeting. Starting now and through the foreseeable future, or at least the winter months, boots will be allowed. But this is conditional. They must be neat, laces tied, and cuffs worn over the outside of the boots. The rest of the dress code remains as it was. Belts must be worn, white T-shirts only, shirts must be tucked in, and sweaters, not sweatshirts, please."

Routine is crucial to order in the school. On the first morning after a two-week vacation it's helpful that assembly is a long one so you have more time to get used to being back. Morning assembly—which until only about a decade or so ago was called "chapel" because that's what it had always been called, even after formal prayers were discontinued—is part of the, as Hawley put it, "liturgy" of the day. At mid morning, there's also the Break. Twenty minutes of no classes. Then at around noon, lunch. Two seatings. Here, the school eats together at alternating circular and rectangular tables, in a square, high-ceilinged room, surrounded by tall glass windows looking out to the courtyard and the lake. One boy at each table is designated waiter for the week. He brings the food and clears the dishes. For three months, boys sit with the same people; tables are changed each trimester. On the first day of the trimester a crowd of boys and faculty will crunch against the brick wall outside the dining hall where the lists are taped to see which table they've been placed at and who else will be with them. Mr. Siekman assigns seating randomly so it's rare that best friends or groups of friends eat together; instead, everyone's with several people they might not otherwise even say hello to. No one seems to mind; in the hundred years of the school's history, never has there been a concentrated effort to change assigned lunch seating.

Debbie Nash has a small office between the dining room and the faculty lounge. She's sixty, but hip, wears her blonde hair short and straight and is tan even in January. She's in charge of the Teacher Apprentice Program at the school, and for years was a college guidance counselor here. Before that, she worked at Hathaway Brown, the all-girl school. She's an ace gender watcher, and her past two jobs in addition to her being the mother of both sexes gives her some license. She can talk a streak. I liked to sit in her office during free periods and listen to her. Late in the year—after she said to me, "You're not using actual *names* in this thing, are you?"—she was a lot more cautious, but get her talking about the differences between boys and girls, and she can fly. "Now, I have no proof of *any* of this," she would remind me, and then she was off for a good half-hour on the subject.

"Girls are not risk takers—I had to *fight* with girls to take a heavy class load," she says. "Boys overburden themselves. I told my son Doug that he shouldn't move into the calculus classes. Why do it? He wanted to be in the 'smart' math classes. . . . Girls worry about their grade point average. They worry about what rank, *exactly,* they are in the class. . . . Another thing is, girls cry. It doesn't matter what about, could be anything and everything. Boys can cry, and do cry. But girls just *routinely* cry.

"Girls keep secrets," she continues. "They don't squeal. Guys tell." Here she offers as evidence the infamous Punderson scandal of the late seventies. Debbie worked at Hathaway Brown at the time. During a weekend retreat of US, Hathaway Brown, and Laurel students at Punderson State Park, somebody brought pot-brownies; others brought beer and wine. A lot of people got stoned and it turned into a major bust that was reported in the local papers. Debbie explained that Geoff Morton, who was handling the aftermath at US, was able to find one boy who confessed and then everyone confessed, resulting in the suspension of eighteen boys and the expulsion of six, in all a quarter of the class. The thing is, Debbie says, "There were just as many girls involved as guys, but we couldn't find one person who would say *anything.* Girls will lie to their graves. You *cannot* catch them."

And assembly! Oh! Debbie rolls her head. Boys are so good they're almost like zombies in assembly compared with girls. "Girls are chatty, squirmy, rude. These boys are benign. *Obedient.*" She seems sort of disappointed to report this, as if to say, obedience is fine, but comatose is something else.

Armchair psychology is a great way to pass time; I'd often walk in on heated discussions between faculty as well as between boys about the difference between men and women, girls and boys. No one, other than the headmaster, ever made any claims beyond the in-my-opinion variety. In fact, there was hardly any genuinely serious talk of gender at all, which may simply be because the all-boyness at this school is simply everywhere and will continue to be so for the foreseeable future. It would be like fish attempting a serious analysis of the pros and cons of water.

On the first day back after winter holiday, after Kerry's announcements—he had also asked all freshmen to remain after assembly to discuss a spate of theft running through their ranks, and they do; not one boy moves as the rest of the school files out—Mike Costello advertised the ski club. His main selling point was that there was a favorable two-to-one ratio of girls to boys this year. Dr. Hawley spoke on the importance of making the most of one's time on earth. Then school began, the long slog through winter.

The gloomy tension and uneasiness that ended the first trimester is gone. It had completely vanished by the time everyone returned from Thanksgiving break. There is something peculiar about the air here—it's like a sponge for tension, and everything had a way of feeling heavy. When the school convened after break it was as if someone had wrung the sponge dry and all was lightness. Part of this was no doubt that the boys had all finished their exams and, for better or worse, there was nothing to do now but begin again fresh.

On the first day back, the classes themselves seemed fresh. A change in trimester for many means new books and new directions. One of the most drastic changes occurs in Dr. Hawley's philosophy class, which moves out of the more technical realm of the way the mind works (Freud and Skinner) to the sphere of ethics and the question "Are there objective criteria for judging something right or wrong?" (Plato, Aristotle); Hawley is most in his element here and the boys, who find big abstract issues compelling, are more receptive to his teaching now than they will be at any other time during the year.

Hawley loves to teach. Ann, his secretary, has noticed that on particularly difficult days, when his teeth grind and a sallow, haggard expression hangs on his face like a waxy veil, he will return from the classroom braced, as if from a long walk in cold air. "Teaching *changes* him," says Ann. When Hawley first began teaching he used to write down every word he needed to say the night before class. Now, his lectures—as he does about 90 percent of the talking in his philosophy class, that's what they amount to—are off the cuff and move randomly across centuries and continents, from contemporary America to ancient Greece, from Nazi Germany to Bernard Goetz to the metaphors lost by changing analog clocks and watches to digital. He loves his classroom and his class. He's personally upset when students don't do well; he's galvanized when they excel. When he walks into class and notices that several students are absent, he appears, for a moment, crestfallen. He asks the class where these missing students are. Then, to shore himself up, he says, "Since this is the class in which the meaning of life will be discovered, someone's going to have to take very good notes."

The layout of the classroom, with wall benches running the length of the room, allows for some casual seating arrangements, and Hawley doesn't like casual in his room. Boys rest their feet on table edges to tilt comfortably in their chairs. "Hey, *Rob,*" Hawley says. "Feet off the table in AP class." When Ryan, feeling surly, has turned his chair away from Hawley to rest feet on the bench and face the wall, Hawley, motioning, says, "Ryan. *Ryan.* Join the magic."

Every boy in this class accepts Hawley's brilliance as a given, but they resent it also. They're used to teachers agreeing with them when they make a point, Nancy's saying something like, "That's interesting—I hadn't thought of that." Hawley will more likely demand clarification and then use their definitions against them, or borrow their words to prove his own point. There's a constant butting of heads and Hawley always wins. The boys want to get their way at least once in a while but the only time they do is when they agree with Hawley, which most avoid whenever possible. Hawley never concedes. This can have counter-productive effects when the topic is Christ's Sermon on the Mount or C. S. Lewis's arguments for Christianity, but with Plato's sparkling dialogues, and the astute parallels Hawley draws between philosophy and their own lives in twentieth-century America, the boys are rapt.

This is how Hawley begins the second trimester on ethics, with a discussion of Plato's allegory of the cave. It's among Hawley's favorite pieces of writing, yet when the headmaster enters the classroom to begin this new section, he seems unusually distracted. He stands at the head of the class staring down at his books, wincing.

Earlier that morning I'd noticed an announcement posted in the faculty lounge. A good friend of Hawley's had died the day before and Hawley found out about it this morning. His name was Bob Gilkeson, a psychiatrist, and for several years the school's psychiatrist and counselor. It was this man who had been responsible for leading Hawley in his research on the effects of drugs, specifically marijuana, on teenaged brains; who taught Hawley the scientific methods for evaluating the objective data of EEG results, which helped form the ideas for Hawley's book on drugs and pleasure. Gilkeson had been so influential and original in his thinking that Hawley would later claim that all he had done in the book was to organize and clarify the ideas of Gilkeson. The unexpected and, as Hawley called it, "slightly eerie" death of this middle-aged man, had struck him with particular force.

Now, as he perches at the edge of the table in his brown tweed jacket, paisley tie, green V-neck sweater, and tan bucks, the pre-class chatter circulating in the room, he seems lost in thought—and not pleasant thought, but concentrated, uncomfortable thought—not properly ready to begin his class. Mike Cohen shuffles in late and apologizes. Ryan follows Mike and doesn't apologize. Tyler Doggett, in the chair nearest Hawley, is spread flat on the table like a sleepy dog, arms beneath his jaw, T-shirt stretched over his mouth. Hawley remains silent, chin squeezed into his neck. Then, apparently willing himself out of the reverie, his chin rises, he's off, and he doesn't look back.

"We're going to begin our syllabus of the course today with a consideration of Plato's 'Cave,' " he says, "the shortest but probably the deepest reading assignment you'll ever get in your entire educational careers. I can think of documents in the history of political philosophy that might be called radical in the sense of calling people to action—a radical document really *is* something that proposes a course of action and a view of human conduct that is so different from what it ordinarily is, or historically has been, that it's *disturbing.* If you read this cave allegory, I'm not sure how Kris has read it, we're about to hear, but the way it's been read, when it's been read seriously—it puts the Communist Manifesto in the shade, or certainly even the American Declaration of Independence in the *shade.* The radical call to conduct is a call to such a *different* conduct it's stunning. In a way it's so radical, that one tends to be numbed to its call. It's literally saying that the mass of men live a certain way and as long as they do, they will not realize the human—"

He breaks off there, having in the course of ten seconds gone too far and too wide. He's assigned Kris Fletcher to give the presentation today. "I don't want to steal any of Kris's thunder," he continues, "because he's going to present this in a few minutes. I'm also very grateful to him for agreeing early on to do this. I would like to ask next Tuesday if you, Avery, would present the first part of 'The Apology'?" Avery nods. "I'm going to evaluate you on the quality of the précis, that is, the quality of how you broke down the entire reading assignment; did you break it down into its correct elements; the accuracy of your language; the depth of the reading."

Each class features one boy who synopsizes and evaluates the assignment for that day. Hawley then chooses another student at random to critique the presentation. Before the boys departed for break, Hawley asked for volunteers to present Plato's "The Allegory of the Cave," a short chapter set like a gemstone in the middle of *The Republic,* the first systematic attempt to describe an ideal society. Kris knew the cave allegory, had read it in the original Greek in Doc Strater's class, liked it, and his hand shot up to ask for the assignment. His eagerness is apt, given that he someday hopes to be President of the United States. The allegory asks what is a leader, what does leading mean, who are those led, what is the state of society in which they will be led?

"Would you like me to address from the front of the class?" Kris asks.

"Wherever you think is best," says Dr. Hawley, moving aside to sit against the wall.

Kris, who always sits at the farthest end of the class directly facing Hawley, strolls to the head of the class, carrying a batch of papers. He wears a white shirt tucked into black trousers; his leather mesh belt is about ten sizes too big and the end swings down to the middle of his leg. Slowly pushing his mane out of his face, he says, "I tried my hand at art and drew up a picture of this cave, or at least how I envisioned it. I think it's somewhat difficult to say what the cave looks like without an artistic representation, so I'll pass these around. I'll be the first to admit I'm not an incredible artist." He Xeroxed twenty copies of an ink drawing he put the finishing touches on while working in the library second period. "The first and foremost important thing about the cave is that there is no natural light in the cave," he begins, then moves methodically through a literal description of Plato's allegory.

The cave, of course, represents society, also one of Hawley's favorite subjects. It's a strange cave to be sure, so it's helpful that Kris has sketched an illustration. Inside the cave there are "prisoners." They are chained in a way that allows them only to look forward at the wall in front of them upon which shadows are cast. These shadows are all that they see, all that they have ever known, and are therefore what the prisoners consider to be real. Above and behind the prisoners a fire burns. Between the fire and the prisoners, a little puppet show is going on, casting the shadows on the wall of the cave. The prisoners, not knowing any better, comment on these shadows as though they are of vital importance. Those whose comments are most articulate and perceptive, those who are best able to predict what shadows will come next, are accorded reverence and power by the other prisoners. In this way, the cave situation is not much different from a bunch of guys sitting around watching a football game on TV. Plato makes no reference to chips and beer, but these shadows do elicit from the prisoners all sorts of fervent dialogue, argument, and prediction. Whether or not to go for it on fourth and one is a matter of life-changing urgency to the prisoners. In such a society, John Madden is president. There are all sorts of cute ways to look at the cave, but what Plato really means to suggest is that from the second your eyes focus on the buzzing alarm clock till your last glimpse of the bedside light switch at night, all you've seen all day long are shadows on the wall of a cave, and that's all you're going to see tomorrow.

The second part of the story, as Kris recounts it, concerns the one person who leaves the cave. Plato doesn't say who freed this person, but he suggests, if you were the one unchained, leaving your little spot on the bench would be no fun at all. This is important. First, it's confusing to see the puppet show and realize that's what has been making the shadows; that what you had been watching and talking about, thinking real, was in fact the distorted outlines of strange objects. "What gives?" you might think, anxiously. Also, the firelight burns your eyes. As if that weren't enough, you're then dragged "forcibly," according to Plato, out of the cave, up a "steep and rugged ascent" and "hauled" into the sunlight. The sun hurts your eyes more than the fire. You can't see a thing. It's all very confusing. But eventually you get used to the brightness, and it's rather pleasant once you do. A clear day, warm dry air. You are very happy. Regrettably though, you feel compelled to return to the clammy dark cave to explain what you know. You tell the prisoners that they're prisoners. You tell them what they think is real is actually shadow. No one believes you, which you appreciate because your eyes haven't adjusted to the dark and you're stumbling around like an idiot trying to present your case. Eventually, your eyes adjust, and you find your voice and present some pretty good arguments to convince the prisoners of their situation. Then the prisoners kill you.

This, according to Plato, who had seen the government of Athens kill his teacher Socrates because Socrates would not shut up about what he knew, and he was pretty arrogant about it, as well.

When Kris finishes his presentation, he says, "Are there any questions?"

Hawley jumps up and says, "Can we wait? I want to get a couple responses first before we get into questions, but thanks for that excellent presentation. The Cave is kind of a standard way of starting out this branch of the course. This, by the way," Hawley says to Kris about his drawing, "isn't quite as good as my pigeon but it's pretty good." Hawley had recently drawn a pigeon on the board trying to make a point and it had caused a good deal of laughter. Hawley asks for a few moments of silence for people to collect their thoughts. He finishes jotting comments on Kris's presentation, which will count as a grade. "OK," he says, "will everybody repeat his personal mantra once and we'll get started. Vish, will you respond?"

Viswam is not quite sure what to do, this being the first time anyone's been asked to evaluate a presentation, and Kris's presentation was so thorough there seems little left to offer. Luckily, he doesn't have to mumble for long before Scott, seated directly across from Viswam, rings in with a question and Hawley glides to the front of the class. Questions are the fruits of this allegory and Hawley wants to direct the students along the most productive lines.

"Who are those puppeteers?" he asks. "And what were they doing? And what was their motive? Who ever chained them in the first place? What does it mean to be in chains? There are all these wonderful questions. And who is this founder, this liberator? What would be this liberating force? Someone going against the grain, against his will. That's the problem with the founder. How can we get anyone for the first time to look away from the wall? It could be an accident, a genetic fluke. The nice thing about it is that anyone could be it. Plato doesn't say, an especially smart, well-prepared, bold, physically strong person—just a guy, *anybody*. But in order to do it, an ordinary guy would literally have to turn around, utterly, completely. The nice encouraging democratic doctrine here is that *anyone* can turn around. The only problem is, it's painful." Hawley pauses, then whispers, "It's *painful.*"

Hawley picks up a piece of chalk from the blackboard and shakes it in his hand like a die. "What's our deepest original response to pain?" he asks.

Several students call out, "Avoid it." This is as much common sense as a reference to the Freudian psychology they've recently finished.

"Right," Hawley says. "We try to repeat pleasure, and we try to avoid pain." Hawley begins to pace back and forth, silently rattling the chalk. Unlike Nancy, who pretty much sticks to one spot in the classroom, Hawley's a classroom stroller and covers all available floor space when he talks. "How responsive would we be to this?" he asks, putting the students in the position of the prisoners of the cave when the ex-prisoner returned to tell them of their misfortune. "If I were to say, 'OK, I've got some good news and some bad news. The good news is that I've got a great plan for all of your life. The bad news is it's going to cause you more stress than you've ever felt in your life, at least in the short run. It's not going to be any fun and it's going to be painful.'" Hawley stops moving, holds a palm out to the class and says, "Whaddaya think?"

The class chuckles, but softly, warily. They sense Hawley is up to something, and they have their radar on.

"But what if it's *true?*" Hawley asks them. He pauses again, stands still, looks at the boys, who have turned silent, waiting for him. Perhaps he senses their resistance, and he tacks.

"I think this is *really* a radical document. I'm almost sad that I live during a time in history where the term *radical* got debased. In the 1960s and 1970s the term radical was applied to people's attitudes, applied to hair length and applied to life-style changes, approaches to material life. It was not applied to people who had things of life-changing substance to say. And I want you to consider, what would it mean to pay attention to a doctrine that would literally change the very nature of practically everybody's life?"

Once Hawley begins, he drives through his classes, charges them, jackhammers, sprints. Occasionally, however, it seems even he finds beginning difficult. The class spends a little more than two weeks on Plato and Socrates. On the day they are to move into Aristotle, Hawley seems happy to drag his heels. He congratulates Eric Hermann who has been accepted early to Hamilton College, noting that B. F. Skinner had gone to Hamilton. He pauses a moment, looks at the the table before him and says, "My daughter brought home this book that I think was derived from *Saturday Night Live.* It's called *Deep Thoughts,* by Jack Handey. Do you know this? Does anybody not know *Deep Thoughts?*" A few of the students mumble affirmatively, unsure if this material will wind up on a test. "Does anybody *not* know *Saturday Night Live."* Philipp, a German exchange student, raises his hand. "It's kind of improvisational television," Hawley explains to him. "It's very vulgar American humor. Occasionally, they just roll down the screen these deep thoughts." Those familiar with the show nod, smiling now. "One of them was," and here, Hawley gets trippy, tilting his head back, wagging it like a cynical hipster, and says, "Sometimes, ya know, like when you might drop your keys in a pit of flowing lava? Fergetit, they're gone." The class laughs and Hawley turns serious. "It seems too bad to me that families should be torn apart by something so simple as—wild dogs." More open-mouthed laughter. The students like class when it's like this. Hawley, who delivered one of his lofty morning-assembly speeches today, says, "It makes you hesitate to get up and do deep thoughts in front of the school."

Having softened the audience into willing acceptance, Hawley plunges into the lesson.

"OK! We're making a transition to Aristotle, and Aristotle, though he's one of the twin pillars of Western philosophy, is no fun to read, as you may have discovered, because there's no art to his presentations. He was a teacher and a lecturer. Aristotle is the master of fine distinctions. We're going to take a lot of time on very few pages—I hope you're able to see some of those fine distinctions. But the pleasure in Aristotle is in the construct and the design; the pleasure is not in the reading as it is with Plato. He of course raised philosophizing to an art form. Those dialogues are an art form. Not so with Aristotle."

"For Aristotle the realest reality was the material world." Hawley begins to pace. "For Aristotle the *realest reality* was the *material world.*" When he repeats a sentence, one witnesses something in the classroom that never occurs at any other time: every student taking notes simultaneously. Boys, generally, don't take many notes, and notes in this class are rare, except for Nick Caserio, one of the school's star athletes, who's rarely *not* taking notes. His notebook looked like a court deposition. Whenever I drifted, and this was not difficult during the long double-period class, I would ask Caserio if I could borrow his notebook.

Aristotle and notions of teleology and golden means are indeed dry but Hawley is expert at shaping abstract ideas to engage his students, whisking philosophical theory and teenage zeitgeist into a soft emulsion.

"Say we wanted to develop you, eighteen years old, on your way to becoming educated young men in the late twentieth century" he says, "and we wanted to develop you to your full potential as sentient people, as thinkers, as citizens. And materiality is one of the variables of your life, by the way. You can have more or less things. Clothes, utilities, shelters, and so forth. Now Aristotle would look at this scientifically, as would Skinner. Is there an amount of material things that you could imagine—this is almost un-American to say—but an amount of material things that could impede your ability to develop? Most of you are probably wanting at least one thing. 'Oh, gosh, if I had that Jeep I'd be happier, I'd be a better person.' But can you imagine some material possession that would impede your progress of developing?"

"Sega," Rob Haffke calls out with sinister relish.

"What's Sega?" Hawley asks.

Rob, a big guy with a round head and fine, short, brown hair, explains that it's a video device and says to Hawley, "If I had Sega, I'd never do any work ever again, ever. I wouldn't even think about it."

"Describe, briefly," Hawley says, "the video game, Sega."

"It's not a game," Rob says. "It's a machine that you hook up to your television." He says there are all sorts of games you can plug into this machine.

"How much are they?" Hawley asks.

"About forty bucks."

"The game?" Hawley asks in wonderment. "Forty dollars? You're forty dollars away from ruin?"

"No, no," Rob hastens to clarify, "the machine itself is about a hundred."

"How many games are there?"

"A couple hundred."

"This is a good question. Rob, how many would it take to ruin you?"

"One," Rob says with a grin. "One good one."

"Oh," Hawley says, tipping his head back. "You're cheap. You're *easy*. But let's look at this seriously. We should probably combine materiality with amusement and entertainment. Because there's a mountain of entertainment and aesthetic presentation, there's an amount of stimulation that would overwhelm our senses; it would make us soft, it would make us dependent, almost addicted. Aristotle talked about people being soft, addicted to too much beauty and luxury, and they lose their balance. So there's excess beyond which we stop functioning well as people. There's a golden mean, and it's not the same for every person, but it's always that thing which drives the person toward his or her full nature."

The students now are upright in their chairs, some leaning forward, eyes bright. All except for Kris Fletcher who holds a pose still as a statue, as he does throughout most classes. He tilts against the windowed wall at the far end of the classroom, head resting on one shoulder, chin up, with a half-smile and narrowed eyes. Always on guard.

Most of the students thrill to talk about their lives and video games and when one of them mentions video games in connection with college, Hawley is amazed.

"There are video *games* at college?" he asks them.

"Yeah! Yeah!" several students cry out, delighting in the naiveté of their teacher.

"You guys gotta try reading," Hawley says. "You're gonna love it."

Ryan, with awe, and eager to inform his teacher about the new advances in virtual reality, says, "You can just put on a helmet, and it's exactly like you're skiing. It could end up where, if you want to go skiing, you don't have to go skiing. You just go in this machine, just hook yourself up to this machine."

"Ah!" says Hawley, having herded the students exactly to where he wants them. "Then you will be like some characters we read about on the opening class day. You will be sitting in the cave, unaware of your chains, looking only at shadows of shadows. And that's fine, but who's manipulating that? Who are you dependent on?"

"The designer of the software," Ryan answers, somewhat less excited.

"Yeah," Hawley says. "The designers of the software and the designers of the technology. By the way, the person who is literally brought up in that virtual reality—boy, how Plato would turn over in his grave for that to be called reality, or virtual—but the condition of your doing that, you could never *be* the person who *produced* the software or the hardware. You'd be a complete slave of the product. The person who developed it did not come from virtual reality. The virtual reality of this game is a product. They came from lots of engineering smarts and theories and good and bad motives and who knows what else. But they're going to produce some people who will certainly live in it, and dwell in it, and probably won't know the difference between it and that other kind of reality."

"Say that you enjoy it," Nick Zinn calls out suddenly. He loves a debate, and he lunges and rocks in his chair. "You're having a fun time ins-s-sside this machine. Y-y-you're enjoying it. So what's the matter w-w-w—"

"What's the matter with being in the cave and sitting on the bench?" Hawley asks.

"If you're having a good time, it seems fine to me."

"So you'd stay in the cave?" he asks. Nick nods, smiles tentatively, knowing somehow Hawley's going to get him but doesn't know from which direction. "This is a problem," Hawley says. "Because someone's going to come down and say,"—Hawley's voice grows sinister—" 'Hey, *Nick. This* is not a ski slope. I can *show* you a ski slope.' And you say,"—Hawley swaggers, pushes his lips out, lowers his voice—" 'Oh. *Tell* me about it. *Tell* me this is not a ski slope.' "

The class erupts in laughter. Nick Zinn grins and shoots glances around the room, rocking forward and back in the saddle of his chair.

Between periods when the hallways throb with students changing classrooms or before morning assembly, the crowd-effect obscuring individual boys has one exception: Nicholas Zinn. You can't *not* notice him. He's tall, nearly six feet, with short curly brown hair, and is what adoring mothers are wont to call husky. His chin, so dominant that some of his classmates call him Jay Leno, distracts one from his blue-gray eyes, which are the only peaceful feature of Nick Zinn. It's not so much his physical size as the way he carries this bundle that makes him a tangible, perpetual dynamic in the school. He charges; he struts. His feet pound the floor and his arms swing wide. His large back rolls and crests like a wave within his checked shirts. All this when he's *seated,* a position to which he's disinclined. Chairs are contraptions he's forever struggling to get out of. The only time I saw him seated, except when I sat him down to talk, was in class, or in the computer room writing programs or bashing out letters. At all other times he was covering ground. In the winter, he would often stalk the halls in a zip-up winter coat and large rubber boots (he takes long walks when the school building feels too confining). His boots were rarely laced and the tops splayed wide at his calves. He appeared to me when dressed like this to be the image of a working-man's D'Artagnan.

"I have a speech—" he says. I've corralled Nick into a chair on the upstairs landing during one of his free periods. Occasionally when he speaks, as happens now, his eyes clamp, his lips cement together, and his chin flutters up and down as he fights for the next word. The effort, apparently involving a spasmodic clenching of his entire body, looks exhausting. He gives up, opens his eyes, retrieves a breath, and starts over. "I have a speech—" Again, no sound issues for one, two, three seconds, until, as if releasing a heavy weight from his embrace, he says, *"impediment."* His peaceful blue-gray eyes fix on mine. His body and face relax.

"Every day of my life it restricts me," he says—an unbroken volley of words.

"How?" I ask.

"People can't understand me. If I call somebody and they say h-h-hello, and I don't say anything—if it's someone who doesn't know me—they hang up. When I go into a restaurant and order veal"—his lips clamp, his eyes clench, his chin jerks rapidly—"P-P-P, P-P-P, P-P-P, P-P-*Parmesan,* I don't say Parmesan. People can't understand."

"But Nick," I say, "you're the most talkative person in the school."

He smiles and shrugs cavalierly. "That's my way of working through the problem."

Nick doesn't have to deliver a senior speech to the school. He dodged the requirement the only way he was able. As a junior, he entered the annual public-speaking contest. He was one of six juniors, chosen from dozens who tried out, to speak before the school and be evaluated by an outside panel of judges. He did not win, or even place third, but he'd given it his best shot.

As an editor of the newspaper, Nick is an unhesitant critic of the school. Following the Krupa and Soltis suspensions, he wrote an editorial that chastised the administration—that is, Kerry—for not announcing these suspensions to the school, as they had done with two boys who had been suspended for excessive demerits. Announcements of suspensions to the school, and the reasons for those suspensions, is school policy, Nick argued.

"It is unfortunate," he wrote, "that the administration has been inconsistent in this policy and has chosen to only announce publicly disciplinary actions that it feels are necessary. It is not fair that certain students are subjected to public disgrace while others are exempted."

Before the editorial appeared, however, Mr. Brennan made a special announcement to the school. There had been some "concern," he said, about the school's policy of announcing suspensions and why some disciplinary decisions had altogether ignored the Student Discipline Committee. He explained why Brad Krupa was suspended and he said that the Soltis suspension by fiat "was Dr. Hawley's prerogative as headmaster." He encouraged anyone with questions to see him directly.

After the assembly, Nick was furious and stalked back and forth along the downstairs commons. Mr. Brennan's announcement had essentially negated his editorial before it could appear. It wasn't fair, Nick said, that he had to get his editorials *approved* by Mr. Brennan, allowing the director to pull fast ones like that.

Nick and I talk a little longer on the upstairs landing. But Nick doesn't sit still for long.

"I gotta go," he says suddenly. I say "Bye," he says "Seeyalater," stands, and lumbers briskly around a corner toward the English department. He has some business to discuss with Dr. Lerner.

Like many of the students, Nick grows disenchanted with the headmaster's philosophy class the moment they move into the realm of theological ethics. While assigned reading during this trimester ranges from Plato to Nathanael West's novella *Miss Lonelyhearts,* the notion of a divine being hovers like a beacon a few feet above Hawley's head. The syllabus includes two assignments from the Bible—the story of Job and the Sermon on the Mount—and, later, several chapters from C. S. Lewis's *Mere Christianity.* "I know certain things," Hawley told me one day in the faculty lounge. "I believe certain things. I'm going to pass that on. That's what I do. That's my job."

When the class hits Sermon on the Mount, something not unlike a chemical reaction catalyzes in the body of Nick Zinn.

"Only in Matthew," Hawley says, charging into theological ethics, "does this myth called the Sermon on the Mount happen, and most historians believe that it's unlikely that Jesus actually went up onto a mountain and gave it in one day. But there's something nice, metaphorically, about going up on a rise, going up above, going up high for an audience and pronouncing this way."

This sermon is not, Hawley says, "splashy miracles and stuff," it is rather "the *first great teaching* episode."

"It is really rich," he continues. "I think along with Plato's Cave, Matthew chapters five through seven is one of the most rich ethical treatises that's ever been written. It's very, very compact. . . . Some of the language of the Sermon on the Mount is embedded in culture like the words of 'White Christmas' or something like that, and it tends to blur your ability to look at it analytically. But I'm going to ask you, no matter what your religious orientation is, to look at these fresh, as a bunch of ethical prescriptions about how to live. And look to see how do they hold up, what is the psychology underneath them? Like every other theorist, Jesus is only asking people to do what is in their nature. So one thing we have to ask is what does Jesus feel our natures are? What's really rich in the Sermon on the Mount is what's the relationship between human beings and their nature and the big issues in life? Like material things, law, what are our obligations to others? Those very concrete questions are answered in the Sermon on the Mount."

A presentation is given and critiqued and Hawley talks about some of the qualities of human behavior that the sermon advises, such as humility and turning the other cheek, qualities that don't seem to have a wide appeal among these students. He asks nevertheless, "What would it be like if those were valuable qualities of the world? But let's take a break first. Five minutes."

The class adjourns and Kris Fletcher and Mike Cohen walk side by side down the hall toward the bathroom.

"You've got to be a sucker to believe that," Kris says. "It's like buying real estate in Florida."

"That's good, I like that," says Mike. "It seems so *manufactured* to me."

When class resumes, Hawley picks up in the middle of the sermon where they'd left off, but Mike Cohen, wanting, gently, to expose this sermon as dubious Florida real estate, says, "I sort of seem to notice a negative aspect of—"

Interrupted, Hawley turns to Mike and says, "Please."

"After going through all these Beatitudes, He says that, you know, whoever looks at a woman and lusts for her, he's already committed adultery in his heart. It seems to imply this negative connotation that God is watching you. It just seems to—"

"If there is a god, a sentient god," Hawley clarifies.

"I mean, but *think* about it," Mike says. "If He can read your thoughts and you can't live up to everything that Jesus has just spelled out here, you're *doomed*. You're *screwed*."

The class chuckles and Mike looks around as if to say, Am I right? Who on earth can expect people to follow such rules?

"You're screwed especially—" Hawley says.

"And God *knows* this," says Mike.

"You're screwed *especially* if you're left to your own devices," says Hawley. "If I say, What I have is my wit, my talents, my strength, my reason, my resources, my will, my house, those are my personal human materials and instinctive devices, that's what I've got. And I think you hit it," he says pointing at Mike as if dotting an "i." "Those things, yep, we *are* screwed. With those things alone, we are lost. We have to *do* something, we have to transform those things, and act, a devotional act, according to this. You're absolutely right."

Mike's head jerks right then left then right. That's not what he meant. He wasn't agreeing with Hawley, but here was Hawley agreeing with *him*. Not fair. What happened?

Nick Zinn is causing a silent one-man commotion in his seat. He knows better than to try to argue here. The same thing that just happened to Mike would happen to him, but worse. He needs a different tack to battle with Dr. Hawley. He wants a fight but he wants to be prepared for it.

Shackled by his stutter, Nick won't attempt an oral fisticuffs with his philosophy teacher. When they hit Sermon on the Mount, however, Nick will attempt a dialogue that circumvents his mutinous tongue.

Nick has an unusual class schedule that gives him the first three periods and break free so that from 8:30 to 11, he can lurch and pound through the school freely. Polly and Frances regularly ban him from the library. It is a rare day when Nick does not wear, metaphorically, the raccoon-skin cap he'd donned for Beaverfest night and clutch his thermos of molasses instant coffee. When he's bounced from the library, he'll wind up in the newspaper office to work on the next issue, or hunch in front of a computer screen. Computers are his main interest, and I imagine that the speed with which they communicate, and with which he can answer back, appeals to him.

During second period in the computer room, Nick writes to the headmaster. The letter, returned to him by Dr. Hawley with comments like starbursts in the margins, actually reads like a dialogue between the two. Indeed, at the very top of the page, Dr. Hawley says, "Nick, I am glad to have this reflection—but you say some of the strangest things. (An ongoing conversation?)"

When Nick gets his letter back from Dr. Hawley, he finds me in the library. He approaches with such speed that I have an urge to dive out of the way. "Here," he says, thrusting the letter at me.

"Dr. Hawley," Nick writes, "Several things have come to my attention after reading the New Testament last night. I had never really read the entire New Testament before."

"Nick, *did* you read the *entire* New Testament?" Hawley asks.

"First of all I was surprised by the fact that it is seemingly more difficult to be a true Christian (not fundamentalist), than it is to be an orthodox Jew." Nick was raised Jewish, and in his letter, he notes the gravity of some of Jesus's precepts and wonders how people can call themselves Christian since so many who do clearly fail to abide by them. "There is not a single Christian I know who follows these central religious principles," Nick says.

"Not any of them?" Hawley asks. "Ever? To any extent? (I hope your luck with Christians improves.)"

"The New Testament," Nick continues, "is a religious document. It is not clearly and logically thought out like Plato and Aristotle."

"Is the Sermon on the Mount (your assignment) unclear? Illogical? How so?"

"It is something that people believe in and have faith in. You cannot analyze such a document—"

"Of course you can," Hawley interrupts. "I do. Millions do! All the time!"

"—as being philosophical and compare it to Plato and Aristotle. It cannot be critically examined like Plato and Aristotle."

"Of course you can," Hawley repeats. "I do. Millions do! All the time!"

"I am not saying that you should not analyze Christianity. It should be analyzed historically and sociologically. It is the driving religious force of the Western World. But it is not a philosophical system like Aristotle's and Plato's philosophies."

"Are there axioms about what is fundamentally true?" Hawley counters. "Assumptions about human nature? Related assumptions about human conduct and society? If so, it is indeed a philosophical system."

When I finish reading the letter, or rather eavesdropping on it, I tell Nick I think it's interesting; he takes the letter and pounds away. It isn't the end he'd hoped for. He had intended his letter to be a coup de grace for his teacher, a let's-just-admit-it's-futile-to-discuss-religion-and-politics argument; instead, he had gotten his own words stuffed back at him. And the way he charges off means he isn't finished.

Nor is Hawley. In the very next class, before Nick can respond, Hawley mentions the letter to the class.

"OK, last time, Scott introduced the Sermon on the Mount," Hawley says. "Biblical scholars say it may or may not have been an historical event, where Jesus walked on a mountain, up on a hillside, and gave that particular talk, but it does seem to represent a true batch of Jesus's teachings all in one presentation. And it begins with a call to attention saying the people whose lives are going to be redeemed and fulfilled are going to have certain qualities. And as we discussed, they're not qualities that even now society tends to value. Not many people live for meekness, for humility, or seeking suffering so that right may prevail and so forth. So already He's saying, Jesus is saying, indeed Socrates is saying to the people in the Cave, 'The message I have for you is what you're least likely to understand, what you're least likely to consider as true and take seriously.'

"Also, since that class, I've gotten a challenge from Nick Zinn who says how can we compare religious stuff to philosophical stuff. How can philosophical, classical treatises like Plato's *Republic* and Aristotle's *Ethics* be compared to religious stuff. I believe there certainly is a religious dimension to the Sermon on the Mount; there's also a religious dimension to Plato's 'The Cave' and Aristotle's *Ethics*. Both of them found the whole enterprise of a world moving forward purposefully incomprehensible without theology. They were theological, too, for the same reason. You don't have meaning without a meaning maker. You don't have clockwork without a clock maker. So those philosophers were grappling with meaning, too. Jews and Christians saw that meaning source being the god of their covenanted agreement, the god of Abraham, the guy who started this whole special mission of Jews going, consciously, about two thousand years before Christ. I hope that some of you besides me would have arguments for Nick, and back to Nick, about whether indeed the teachings of Jesus are comparable to the teachings of Plato or Aristotle. That's an open question, but I just wanted you to know the challenge is out there."

Nick sits quietly the entire time, rubbing his chin, his heel pounding like a piece of construction machinery. He lets the pressure build, and over the weekend, he hones his reply.

Dear Dr. Hawley,

I certainly do not mean for you to take personal offense when I criticize various elements of our philosophy course. This being a high school philosophy course, I expect any discourse on philosophy to be entertained and I am offended by you making any mockery of my thoughts whether you intend to or not. Last Thursday, I was offended by the way in which you presented my thoughts. If you are going to present ideas and say they come from me, please allow me the opportunity to present them.

I am extremely frustrated during class and in my discussions with you. When I make a point it is rarely entertained and often dismissed. Rarely do you ever examine what I am saying, and you seem extremely rigid and concrete in your thought. When you do attempt to disprove what I say, it is often in a way that makes me feel like you never really took the time to grasp my point. I feel as if there are a million ways one could defeat my arguments, and you choose the wrong one. I enjoy arguing, I enjoy playing the devil's advocate, but I don't enjoy being always proven wrong through logical fallacy, which I find is often the case. It is extremely frustrating. . . ."

The reason someone accepts Aristotle as the correct philosophical system is because it is logically grounded. The reason someone accepts Christianity is because they have faith and a religious conviction. There is a distinct difference. . . . I understand your point, and I hope that you will attempt to grasp mine.

I am aware that my performance in your class has not been as stellar as I am capable of. I have failed at times to articulate my views. Due to my speech impediment I requested that you be more patient when I express my views. It is very upsetting to me and frustrating when you interrupt me in the middle of a word. I am certainly going to stand for what I believe in from now on. I was somewhat intimidated before, and many things were happening in my life. I am someone with strong convictions; I am very open minded and I hope that will be evident. I am no longer going to be intimidated by the class and respond emotionally to their remarks; I am going to hold firm on my convictions.

Sincerely your frustrated student.

On the Monday Hawley receives this letter, I have lunch with Nancy Lerner. We're late to the dining hall and the second lunch period is under way. Nancy takes a plate and is served some Polish sausage and stewed vegetables and puts a huge glob of mustard in the middle of her plate.

"I'm having a *boy* lunch today," she tells me.

By the time we finish, the dining hall has emptied. I notice Hawley, at the entrance within a pack of boys, answering questions. He looks over at us. He has a word with one of the faculty, then, seeing that we're still talking, gently approaches. He seems not to want to interrupt but he needs to say something. He's dressed in his formal dark gray suit. This morning, he'd announced the winner of the Political Essay Contest and the guest speaker was Eric Fingerhut, an Ohio freshman in the United States House of Representatives. Hawley dresses up for such occasions. He stands at Nancy's side staring down, his hands thrust into his pants pockets.

"I wonder if you could help me with something personal," he says.

Nancy pushes her chair back to suggest, Please, sit. He does.

It's Nick Zinn, he explains. "I just got this letter from Nick that said he was terribly frustrated." Hawley pauses for a moment, then asks Nancy, "Do kids *laugh* at him?"

"*No*," Nancy answers. "I've never seen *anyone* laugh at Nick."

Hawley tells her he can't quite figure it out, and explains the first letter he'd gotten about Aristotle and Jesus, "which also said some *amazing* things. 'I read all of the New Testament last night.' " Hawley's not sure what to do about the new letter.

"He wants you to shoot him down," Nancy suggests. "He expects to get demolished. But you dismissed him. He *wants* you to shoot him down." This is conjecture, but she's known Nick for a long time and has had her own dramas with him.

"Listen to the language we're using when we talk about philosophy," Hawley says. " 'Demolished.' 'Shot down.' It should be a discussion." He tells Nancy about Nick's previous essays and while there were, he says, serious logistical errors, "I loved the fact that Nick was *thinking*." Again, still troubled, Hawley continues, "I'm worried that I did something wrong, made a flip comment." He shakes his head. "But I make them all the *time*. I make them every minute."

"Where are you now?" Nancy asks him.

"We're doing Job."

"I've got a favor to ask," she says. "Will you do Descartes's proof of God? And I want you to do John Locke."

Nancy is now teaching poetry that examines the relations between God and man and man and mind. This had been one of the main ideas in teaching the same class on alternating days, that the two might be able to intertwine their lessons somehow, but it's proving easier to conceive than accomplish.

"I have time for that," Hawley says.

"Tomorrow?"

"Tomorrow," Hawley repeats.

"Yeah."

"You mean *tomorrow*."

"Well, no," says Nancy. "It doesn't have to be *tomorrow*."

"I have time for that," he says, knowing he doesn't.

A long, leisurely pause follows. Nancy leans back.

"I feel so *old*," she says. Then she says she feels like the oldest person on the faculty.

"Nancy, you are not," Hawley says.

"Who's older than I am?"

"Dick McCrea is older than you are, and Rollin Devere," and Hawley methodically lists a half-dozen other names. Nancy isn't convinced.

Dear Nick,
I have taken no offense (yet) from anything you have said or written to me in philosophy.

Nor do I mean to give offense. I certainly didn't mean to offend you by stating—because it was interesting and on the subject—that you had challenged Christianity as an ethical system comparable to Aristotle's. As I said in class, each is a well-worked-out system based on specific (and contrasting) axioms.

I'm also sorry if I have interrupted you while you have been searching for a word—I didn't mean to.

Nick, I don't believe we have a fight or even a *disagreement* going. Your contributions are always interesting to me.

I fear I am not communicating very well with you. Maybe we can do better.

And I assume/hope/*insist* that you will stick to your convictions!

He has signed the letter, as always, "Doc H."

More than two weeks later, Nick Zinn charges into Room 270, five minutes before philosophy class is to begin.

"Hey, Kris," he says. Kris Fletcher is already in his seat at the far end of the room, tilting in his chair, waiting. "I showed Dr. Hawley a copy of my article, and he threw it on the floor!" Nick seems to be feigning outrage, but he's got a big grin on.

Kris lets his chair drop forward with a jolt. "What?" he says. *"Why?"*

"I don't know. He j-j-just threw it on the floor."

Kris shakes his head and scowls.

Following their previous exchange, Nick told me that Hawley had approached him before morning assembly and said, "Nick, we need to talk. We're both going"—he crossed his arms in front of his chest, index fingers pointing in opposite directions—"and we need to be going the right way."

Nick said to me, "W-w-which is going to be *his* way."

The Zinn-Hawley correspondence had subsided after that until this morning when Nick charged Hawley's office and found the headmaster at his desk. Within the stacks of "urgent" and "less urgent" papers and general clutter, Hawley had carved out a small area on which to grade papers. He looked up. Nick shoved the article at him. The article, about half a typed page, titled "Religious Controversy at a Non-Sectarian School?," argued that "The school, while claiming to be nonsectarian, has maintained several overtly Judeo-Christian practices." Hawley read the article, looked at Nick, dropped it at Nick's feet, and returned to grading his papers.

When I ask Nick to elaborate, he does so quickly, before the fourth-period bell rings. Surprised by Dr. Hawley's reaction, Nick apparently told Hawley that he was offending him. Nick tells me that Hawley said, "I don't care about offending you. I care about the *truth.*" Nick utters the word "truth" with bite.

That's all Nick tells me before he says, "Hey, Jason," and launches over to Jason Koo, who's seated, slumped against a wall. "Hey, did you get my letter? Is that all right?" Nick had written Jason, and other newspaper editors, a note about article deadlines.

Hawley enters the room looking grave and distracted. Again, he's wearing his dark gray suit.

"It's been an odd time," Hawley says immediately upon setting his books on the table. Nick Zinn sits immediately to his left. "There have been three deaths this year and as you know Judy French's husband died, and I'm going to have to leave to go to his funeral today at noon." Judy is a long-time employee of the school who works in the maintenance department and this unexpected news had been announced at morning assembly. On two separate occasions, earlier in the year, the deaths of students who had graduated from the school within the past four years were announced. Hawley is teaching now and says, "But we've got a lot to cover today so I really want to focus." He shoots off into the lesson, a continuation of C. S. Lewis and notions of standards of behavior that are common among human beings. "We talked about whether that standard was true," he reminds them, "or whether it was instinctual or cultural. Lewis says it is not. He says if it is a standard then it must have a source; the source seems to behave like a mind; what kind of mind is it? . . ."

It was during this "strange time," during the series of unexpected deaths and too much work with too little time, that Nick had burst in on the headmaster. Hawley was behind in his grading and he had only a few more minutes during which to complete the papers. Hawley explained to me later that he was not in a very good mood, was rushing to keep up with his work, and it had seemed to him that Nick was merely goading him now, not really arguing at all, a presumption supported by the glaring errors in Nick's article. Their encounter had been brief. Hawley confirmed that he did toss Nick's article on the floor with no comment.

Hawley ends class twenty minutes early as promised, but before he leaves, as students push books into backpacks, he leans down to Nick and says, "Nick, I apologize. I think I misinterpreted your smile. And I may have misread your article."

Nick is hunched so far over he is almost a ball in his chair. He does not look at Dr. Hawley but stares numbly at the table and nods OK. Hawley gathers his books and strides out of class, bound for a funeral.

■ ■ ■

"Dr. Hawley," Nick writes the next day,

I think that we have a fundamental disagreement in the way that
we perceive the world. No matter what we discuss, I will always
perceive things differently than you because there are fundamental
differences in our view of our world.

I need to see the world the way that I see it. If I did not, I could
not make it through the day. I imagine that your perception is
necessary for your existence too.

Despite the fact [that] there are fundamental differences in how
we see the world, I believe that in the end, our aims are the same.
Although I arrive at my goals through different methods, I believe
in justice, honesty, and consideration of others. You will never be
able to convince me that my methods are wrong, and I know I will
never be able to convince you that yours are wrong. I don't think
that matters. This is the way that is most logical at the moment.

Although we will never agree on our methods of perception of
the world, I believe that I have much to learn from you.

—*Nick Zinn.*

Nick, clearly we see the world differently. I am not *sure* the differences are 'fundamental' or permanent. We are, however accurately
or inaccurately, attempting to perceive the *same* world. In that, is
my hope that we can communicate, teach, and learn from one
another. Cheers, Doc H.

10

"I'm concerned with, one, justice," Hawley pronounces, "and, two, that you *feel* all right."

Hawley is at his sixth-period lunch table. He has just said this to Brian Walker, a sophomore. Brian does not look happy. Earlier in the week, Brian had unwisely claimed that he could eat a large pizza by himself. Hawley spotted an idle boast from a braggart. Brian insisted it was not idle. A bet was made. At the end of the week, while the rest of the school lunched on ziti with tomato sauce, garlic bread, and pink-frosted cake, Hawley's table, by executive order, ate pizza.

After Mr. Siekman finishes post-lunch announcements, he says, "I hope you all have a good weekend and I hope all the people at Dr. Hawley's table get indigestion." With the boys thus excused, a crowd gathers around Hawley's table. Hawley had instructed Ann to order two pizzas, one for Brian, one for the other five students at the table and himself. Brian is not yet through half his pizza. His expression doesn't seem unhappy because he's full, but rather because he's been tricked. The two pizzas Hawley had ordered are rectangular and measure nearly six square feet.

Hawley sits quietly, hands folded in his lap, watching Brian. This is taking longer than he expected. Brian defiantly grinds away, and Hawley seems to be wondering how long he'll have to watch Brian's losing battle before he can grab his after-lunch coffee and a calm moment in the faculty lounge. A dozen students hover around the circular table, part curious and part hoping to get their hands on some of Brian's unfinished pie. A pile of crusts half a foot high sits on Brian's plate. He's taking fewer and fewer bites from each piece. Hawley gives Brian a hard time about not finishing his crust.

Brian, looking increasingly ill, dumps another crust on the pile and appeals to me: "Come on, help me out."

I tell him that not finishing his crust is like doing wimpy push-ups, which he doesn't find funny.

Brian now begins to pick off the pepperoni and dumps these on his crust heap. The rest of the table, six people in all, has been unable to finish the other pizza, mushroom-and-sausage.

"Come on, Brian," Hawley says. "Ready to throw in the towel?"

Brian surveys what remains—about half—then, sadly, lifts his right hand. Hawley stands, triumphant.

At that moment, a few enterprising boys have discovered in one of the boxes a Geppetto's Pizza coupon listing pizza sizes. What Brian had just tried to eat was not a "large" but rather something called a "sheet" pizza, they say, their voices strident with insinuations of foul play. Hawley, who'd had Ann order "the biggest one they got," took a quick look at the coupon. He then confused the boys with some sophistry about their definition of "large" and scampered off to the faculty lounge.

Brian, leaving the dining hall, not feeling all that well but looking on the bright side, tells me he won't be eating pizza for a while.

I thought about Brian and the pizza all day. Brian is trim and athletic. A guess would put him at five-feet-five or so. The pizza had been impossibly huge—at least the size of two large pizzas and maybe three. Brian must have realized that he'd never finish the whole thing. Why then had he even attempted it? And why had he accepted defeat quietly, obediently even, knowing he'd been hornswoggled? Why had he made himself ill to finish even half of Geppetto's pepperoni sheet pizza?

I don't know. Maybe he really thought he could eat it, or didn't think at all. Maybe it was part of his unspoken code—a bet's a bet, and it was dishonorable not to try given that he hadn't had the sense to define large. Or maybe it was the simple challenge of it. I do know one thing for certain. I know what Sam Woo would say. If only Brian had a duck bill, he could have chewed much more easily.

■ ■ ■

After lunch, Hawley usually pours himself some coffee set out on a little cart in the dining hall and carries it into the faculty lounge. This is the one time of day he relaxes at school. He leans back in his chair and talks with his colleagues about movies, students, his tennis game, and occasionally, this year, the fat content of lettuce. His daughter, a sixth-grader at a girls' school, informed him that lettuce contains fat. This thwarted Hawley's notions of ultimate justice in the universe, and he initially refused to believe it. The issue sparked a small family wrangle and then a wager. Hawley seems to be coming around to his daughter's way of thinking. Chuck, George, Keith, and Phil are also lounging after lunch and, Hawley tells them, "I stay away from the fatty lettuce myself. I only go for the slender lettuce."

Then, and this is not uncommon, the talk turns to students, today one student in particular, Nick Caserio. Caserio is one of the best athletes in the school and is respected by students and teachers alike as much for his prowess on field and court as for how hard he works. By all accounts he should have to struggle to be average, yet he is pushing for first honors. At the end of the year he will make Cum Laude. Yet everyone's worried about him because his SATs are so low he's going to have a hard time getting into a school he wants.

Earlier, at a report meeting on the students, Geoff Morton had said, "This may surprise some of you but I'm concerned about Nick. . . . I just worry that the Ivies, whatever those are," he adds with mild contempt, "aren't going to take him." People who know Caserio as an athlete, hard-worker, and all-around great guy are getting his hopes up.

Hawley tells Phil and Geoff that he's called his friend Karl Lindholm at Middlebury—Hawley wants nearly everybody to go to his alma mater—to say they've got this strong student who's got low boards but is a great athlete and works his butt off. "They said they were very interested," Hawley claims.

Phil is happy to hear this because Nick had been talking about Swarthmore. "Swarthmore sounds like a pack of nerds," Phil says. Nick wouldn't be happy there, they conclude.

Phil then asks Hawley how to handle a kid like Caserio, someone whose test scores don't reflect his ability, with college admissions directors.

"Send them his *essays,*" Rick says. "They say, 'Well he's only got 440s on his boards and he won't be able to do the work at Middlebury.' Just *send* them the papers. He does some *remarkable* work. And then if they say, 'We only admit a small number of kids with boards under a thousand,' I tell them, 'If you only admit *one* kid with boards under a thousand, Nick should be the one.' "

One afternoon, Viswam Nair approaches Dr. Hawley just after lunch and reminds him that he needs to rehearse his senior speech, scheduled two days from now. Hawley forgoes his after-lunch coffee and he and Viswam, or Vish, as he's called, repair to the headmaster's office.

Vish is Indian, has a dark complexion, and is very skinny. His black curly hair falls in ropes. One of his classmates says it's the "coolest hair in the senior class." Hawley sits in his usual chair and Vish stands at a distance, behind the couch, to recite his speech. Vish's family—his parents are both doctors—is comfortably well-off and Vish uses an anecdote about a young man less fortunate than himself, with whom he'd worked one summer, to discuss the college selection process. The speech is muddy, still very much a first draft, and Hawley wants Vish to improve it. Vish clearly thinks this would be an unnecessary hassle, but their talk leads to a discussion about how US views college acceptances. Vish seems to take it for granted that anyone with enough money and connections can buy his way into any college. Seated on the couch in front of Hawley, Vish says to him that all US really thinks about is how many Ivy League colleges accept its seniors.

"Who do you mean?" Hawley asks. "You mean me, personally?"

"The admissions people."

"Do you really think that, Vish?"

"Well, yeah. It's a college preparatory school."

"Right," says Hawley. "People who graduate from here go to college."

Vish tells Hawley that they want kids to go to *prestigious* schools because it makes the school look good.

"I don't care how many people go to Ivy League schools," Hawley tells Vish. "As far as I'm concerned what's important is the number of people who get into the college they choose."

"Yeah," Vish says, tilting his head against the sofa back and looking at Hawley over grinning cheeks. "But if the entire class went to Ohio State, you *wouldn't* be happy."

"I'd be happy if it was the right school for them. As you know Ohio State is a good university, with many good programs now."

Vish continues to criticize US. "It's *elite*," he says.

This rankles Hawley, and he says sharply, "It's elite in that standards are high and you have to work really hard, yeah."

Vish continues to insist rich people can buy their way into schools such as Harvard. Hawley asks Vish why, then, of several qualified candidates applying to Harvard last year, only one person got in?

This silences Vish, who has no evidence to support his claims. Hawley tells Vish his speech is weak and he wants him to rewrite it.

"I hope I'm not repeating myself," he says, "but can you do these things? Make Frank a stronger character?"

"I don't know if I'm going to have time to make all those revisions," Vish mumbles, starting to wriggle.

"Vish, I may see if I can get this speech backed up without any penalty for you so you can work on it." Vish doesn't say anything. "Would you like me to do that?" Hawley waits. Vish says nothing. "Or would you just like to get it over with?"

"I'd kind of like to get it over with," says Vish.

Hawley releases an irritated chuckle, his chin tucked. "OK," he says.

Vish leaves.

Hawley postpones the date of the speech anyway, so Vish has more time to work on it.

Several times during the school day, I would stroll through the administrative wing, whether I had any business there or not. So many dramas happened simultaneously at this school I was perpetually worried I'd miss something. If I didn't bump into anyone or couldn't strike up a conversation, I could always amuse myself by teetering forward and back, hands in pockets, in front of the mug shots. On the wall outside the Xerox room hang four large cardboard sheets affixed with the school photographs of all 370 students, arranged alphabetically by grade, names printed below each. Last year, a student told Hawley that all this talk of diversity in the student body was a bunch of hogwash—this was still a school for rich white boys. Hawley got so mad he hauled the boy in front of these pictures and told him to point to one row of photographs comprising only white boys. The rows run about ten pictures across. You can't move more than five or six

199

frames in any direction without hitting a black, Asian, or Latino face. Confronted with the evidence, the boy remained skeptical.

The student body, after all, *is* predominantly white, and for three-quarters of its life it was exclusively white, like most private schools in America. Thirty-one years ago, a year before the Civil Rights Act of 1964 forbade segregation in public places, and nine years after the Brown decision, the school enrolled its first black student, Carl Stokes, Jr., the son of the man who would become the city's mayor, the first black mayor of a major American city. Today, Asian students are the predominant minority. Ask Ann McGovern, Hawley's secretary, what is the ethnic breakdown of the current student body and she wheels backward in her chair to a file and announces, *"The* most asked question," then, reading, says, "OK. There *are* fifty-two African Americans, sixty-nine Asian Americans and seven Latinos." At the upper school, minorities make up between 20 and 25 percent of each class.

This is fairly standard as private schools go, and many schools, as well as organizations such as NAIS which represent them, make a proud fuss about it. Their self-congratulations are perhaps understandable, an example of, as one social commentator put it, "the defensiveness of the besieged." Private schools continue to carry the baggage of their racist and discriminatory past and must continually defend themselves against, and distance themselves from, centuries of all-white, all-male exclusivity. It *is,* after all, *the* most asked question.

"They're all so pious about it," says Hawley. "It happened. Diversity is true. The nation is diverse, and the schools, frankly, are culling this thing in a good way. All these bright families of these new ethnic groups want their kids to go to your school. So you accommodate. We never said, 'Because we're now meeting the Eastern rim culturally and economically, I think we need to incorporate them into our school.' We've taken the best kids that have applied to the school, and they happen to be, because Cleveland is diverse, diverse."

What was endlessly perplexing to me, though, was that the boys' perception of their school was that of the stereotype. They were more easily persuaded by the opinions of people who had never been to the school than by Hawley or teachers. They, the students who made up the very body they criticized, were the most skeptical of all.

Still, I could stand in front of those photographs as though they were a Vermeer in the Louvre. Each square seemed to contain its own little universe. Also, these sheets of faces changed over the course of the year. One day, Ricky Smith smiled out at you. The next, a large ballpoint X had been gouged into the lamination across the entire photograph. I asked around. No one knew who had defaced the picture or why. It was more of a mystery because Ricky, a sophomore, was respected, soft-spoken, earnest, opinionated, and honest. One day, there was John Gregor, the next he was gone. The photograph had been scalpeled out. John appeared at my side while I stood before the photographs and I asked him who stole his picture? "Well . . . ," he said, blushing and looking down. No mystery here. He had recently struck up a romance with a Hathaway Brown girl in the school play; rehearsals ran late at night, when the administration wing is unlocked and deserted, during which the girl performed a little commando raid to kidnap John's image.

I stood gazing at the photographs on the first day back after winter break when Tyler Soltis staggered by. He had no reason for being in the administration wing and no apparent destination. He looked rather as if he'd just stepped out of a train wreck. "Howya doing, Tyler?" I asked.

Swarthy and bug-eyed, a patch of zits speckling the gap between his thick eyebrows, he looked at me and said, "I'm in shock."

Margaret Mason turned the corner just then and halted. "What are you in shock about?" she asked with immediate worry.

"I got a *scholarship* to *Syracuse*."

Margaret relaxed and said, "Tyler, that's great. But why are you in shock?"

"I don't *know*. I'm just amazed. I just got this letter in the mail over vacation."

Margaret smiled, congratulated Tyler, and hurried on her way.

The $12,000 scholarship spread over four years, he said, was not need-based. Over vacation, he had called Kris Fletcher five times to tell him the news.

Tyler stood there, swaying gently. Then he said, "Well, I guess I've got first period. Is Doc in? Yeah." And he was gone.

I never knew what was going to happen when I stood in front of these pictures. Sometimes I was even asked for advice.

"Mike, can you help us?" Hawley said, stepping out of Ann's office and spotting me. "Come here a second. We're wondering what to put in that thing."

He drew me into Ann's office. Ann was seated at her desk. He pointed to the Mr. Coffee machine behind her, next to the fax machine. The headmaster was evidently displeased with the quality of the coffee.

He whispered to me, "It tastes like weasel piss." Ann heard this in mid-slurp of her diet soda, and it squirted out her nose. She rushed for a Kleenex.

"Dog water," said Hawley.

The headmaster was in a good mood as winter moved along peacefully. He confided to me that, for the first time, "I actually feel like a"—in case God was listening and might take it back, he whispered—"a headmaster."

My attention locks on the exchange *in medias res,* Eugene having just released a staccato baritone HA-HA-HA-HA-HA. Hawley had let the class go for a five-minute break and Eugene is too enthralled to leave his seat, in which he is potted sideways, back against one armrest, legs hanging over the other. He is banging his feet together and clapping his hands. He claps like a manic wind-up doll, palms flat, like cymbals. Hawley is seated at the head of the class, engaging Eugene. For a reason I missed, Eugene has just used the number 3100. Hawley says, "Ah! My *address* is 37100. You just left out seven, a magical number which proves my divine place in your life." This is when Eugene laughs and claps and bangs his feet together, heels of his hard-soled shoes clicking. "Wait," Eugene says, in his thick Russian brogue. Apparently, he thinks he might have another seven connection, and he says, "How many headmasters have there been?"

"I'm the sixth," says Hawley. "That's a *diabolical* number."

"HA-HA-HA-HA-HA-HA!" cries Eugene, clapping.

Eugene Gurarie, who grew up in the Ukraine and Lithuania, is one of two émigrés in the class, both of whom moved to the States about three years ago. Igor, seated across from Eugene, is the other. Igor Lyubashevskiy is arguably the smartest student in the school, but his accent is so heavy that it sounds like he's speaking Russian even when he's not.

Eugene and Igor did not know each other two years ago when both were students at the same public high school. Eugene eventually introduced himself and told Igor about US and said they might apply for scholarships there. Igor got in easily but Eugene was a borderline case. The problem was language. His accent wasn't bad; in fact, Eugene now has a beautiful baritone voice with the rich accent of a chess master, or a Vladimir Nabokov. But his use of English was so wild and error-filled that the admissions department didn't think he'd be able to handle the work, given how much writing was expected of students. Now Eugene wants to get into Princeton, which has deferred his early application.

Eugene is not a budding Nabokov. He is, Hawley realizes, reminiscent of a great Nabokov character, one Timofey Pnin, like Eugene, an immigrant to the States, like Nabokov, a teacher in an American college. Pnin, in the eponymous novel, is a comic butt, awkward in appearance with a giant head, apelike upper lip, huge torso, and spindly legs. In his struggle to master the language (when he rents his first house, Pnin throws a "house-heating" party) and to assimilate American customs within a competitive academic world, he is a pathetic hero, tragic yet representative of the best of Russian emigration.

In looks, Eugene is Pnin just turned seventeen. Especially since he got his perm. Eugene's dull brown hair, neither curly nor straight, is, in its natural state, more of a bad hat than a coif, and Eugene hoped to give it some shape with a perm, tight curls that now rise up and off his great round skull like Eraserhead's. This gives his head a Pninian disproportion to his small body. Pnin had something of a potato nose; so, too, does Eugene, though yam might be more accurate. Beneath this, a downy gray moustache struggles to be noticed. Elsewhere, patches of whiskers sprout. Were it not for his rich, heavily lashed, hazel eyes, Eugene would be a homely boy. Given his appearance and interests (composing music, captaining the chess team, though he's regularly trounced by the one freshman on the squad), Eugene is easy prey for the jocks who idle around a table on the upstairs landing during free periods. One afternoon the hulking Chris Petro locks Eugene's arms behind him and says, "Who's your *girlfriend* Eugene?" The others call out names of girls to make fun of him. In Petro's grip, Eugene goes limp, his eyes blank until Chris, feeling no resistance, releases Eugene, and Eugene wanders off apparently deep in thought. No teenager's feelings can be immune to harassment from other boys, but Eugene seems to do quite well. He has more important things to worry about, such as music.

As recently as two years ago, music bored Eugene, but when I talk to him about music his eyes brighten and his voice drops to the bottom of his throat: "Music tells me the story of my life," he tells me.

I ask him to sit at one of the tables on the upstairs landing, and he describes his difficulties in English by saying, "I cannot express my ideas on a one-dimensional sheet of paper." He points his fingertips at me, flutters them like spider legs, and says, "My ideas are one big *gossamer.*"

Hawley admires Eugene for the very thing that nearly prevented his being at the school. Though Eugene still makes wild mistakes, his use of language is unfailingly original. Hawley only wishes Eugene would work harder in philosophy. Eugene, by appearances, couldn't care less about Plato or Lewis. Most days before fourth-period philosophy, he is flat across a wall bench asleep. He tells me *not* that he doesn't sleep much; instead, he says, "I have lost interest in sleep." He stays up well into the morning composing music, reading, and writing long letters to a girl in the Ukraine.

Not long after Eugene's early application to Princeton is deferred, Hawley is in New Jersey at a headmasters conference. Before he returns to Cleveland, he has time for a quick trip to Princeton to visit the admissions director at the university, Fred Hargadon. Hawley has known Hargadon for years and he has come to see what he can do on behalf of Eugene. Eugene's grades are good but not outstanding; his SAT scores are likewise uneven. Furthermore, Hargadon tells Hawley, Princeton has received a record-high 14,000 applications this year; competition is intense even for students with top grades and scores. Hawley and Hargadon chat, and not unusually, they talk about literature and writing and the subject of Nabokov comes up. Hargadon lights up. He used to teach at Cornell, where Nabokov taught. Hargadon explains that he used to *teach* in a room where Nabokov lectured, and might have used for some of his novels. Do you know the novel *Pnin,* he asks? Hargadon explains that he *lived* in the house believed to be the model Nabokov used for *Pnin,* the very structure wherein Pnin had his "house-heating" party.

Suddenly the connection dawns on Hawley and he exclaims, "Fred, I *have* Pnin in *class.* And I want you to admit him to Princeton."

Hawley leaves Hargadon with samples of Eugene's writing, including the personal essay for Nancy Lerner about an epiphany Eugene had one night in Israel beneath a star-filled sky while listening to Mozart's 23rd piano concerto. Hawley doesn't know if it will work.

On Valentine's Day, about a week after Hawley's Princeton mission, Eugene delivers a speech. Because the presentation for his Strnad project, a year-long independent endeavor, counts as his senior speech, he's not required to address the school, but he's asked to be allowed to do so. Until this morning, I knew two Eugene Guraries. One sat sideways in his chair during Hawley's philosophy class, clicking his shoes together, chewing pen tops till they disintegrated, and, when excited, slapping his hands together rapidly like a child, bursting with a laugh too deep for his age. The other Eugene wandered the school slowly, dressed in synthetic trousers a size too small, white socks, and holding fingers to his mouth, thinking, occasionally playing possum anytime someone put him in a headlock. During the entire week before he was to attend the Cleveland Orchestra's performance of Mozart's 23rd piano concerto, he was useless in school from the anticipation. On Valentine's Day, he explained why, and here was a third Eugene.

Wearing a tie and secondhand jacket, Eugene commands the podium as no student has this year, having been introduced by Greg Coudray as "my permed friend." Despite the awkwardness of a body and head that don't quite match, of being a cultural outsider less than three years in the United States, and apparently having little in common with most of his fellow students, Eugene demonstrates that self-esteem is not a problem. On stage he is Demosthenes, railing at the sea, shouting out his speech, enunciating syllables so precisely that his Ts click and his Os elongate into cello notes as he explains his obsession with music, less than two years old now, and the string quartet he is writing for his Strnad project. Eugene tells the audience, "I would like to take advantage of this unique opportunity to provide you with a brief summary of the composer's biography"—his own, that is.

"My father," Eugene shouts, "will testify that I started singing long before speaking, thus nearly transcending Mozart's precocity." In Eugene's high-calorie accent, the baritone voice pounds out *tuh-ran-SSSEND-ing MOTE-zzzart's pre-KO-city.* "In fact, my father has a tape of my vocal expression at age three. Nowadays listening to this tape over*whelms* me with nostalgia and *self-envy,* for my range at that time significantly surpasses the two octaves of the present.

"Modesty aside, *was-I-a GENIUS?*

"Well. Genius is traditionally defined as a combination of natural talent and an extraordinary urge for putting it to use. The latter quality was utterly lacking in my chemical makeup. . . . The PREEmitive keyboard exercises that I had to *practice* everyday and perform in front of my TEEcher once a week permeated my regimen with boredom and EEN-dignation. I was absolutely sure that I myself could have composed each STOO-pid LEE-tle song that entered my repertoire. . . . To me, music bore as little purpose as rhymeless poetry. Having tried not even once, I saw no challenge in the art of musical composition and therefore disdained all published composers, myself never descending to their activity.

"With such skeptical spirits, my *sixth year* of *life* approached."

It was then that young Eugene was formally enrolled by his mother, against his wishes, in music school. "I am still trying to *fathom*," he explains, "what PREEN-ciple in the world MO-tivated her to couple me with the least likable TEEcher in the entire institution. For six years, following this FAY-tal settlement, I was shedding tears on the *wretched* keyboard, for six years diverting my *wretched* piano teacher into discussions of soccer and poetry, harassing the *wretched* Bach by transposing his B-flat major into A minor and flabbergasting my *wretched mommy* with a five-hour guitar practice on the eve of a final piano recital.

"For the last, seventh year of music school I was fortunate to study with a twenty-year-old student teacher, whose combination of attractiveness and intelligence somewhat intensified my effort. . . .

"During the first year of my American life I suffered a kind of identity crisis. Having apprehended the necessity of replacing a part of my huh-BEE-tual culture with NO-velties, I strove to engage every minute of my day in some sort of improving activity. In order to utilize the daily fifteen-minute time gap between going to bed and falling asleep, I thought, why not devote it to the exploration of music? The day this idea came to me, I moved to the basement so that my tuh-ransgression didn't reach my parents' ears at midnight. I set up a tape player near my new bed and every night before lying down turned on a new Mozart cassette borrowed from the library. At first, the tragic G-minor symphony"—da-da-DAN! da-da-DAN! da-da-DAN-*DAN!* he mimics—"served as a great lullaby." But soon the "music's MEE-sterious PHEE-zics" so enchanted him that he could not sleep, so admiring was he of each new composition he got his hands on. "Still," he adds, "it took a while to suppress my musical self-esteem."

Not until he announced to his viola teacher that he would compose an exercise that would allow them to play a duet did he return home to compose for the first time in his life.

"That night," Eugene says with tragic resonance, "I realized the *depth* of my dee-LU-sion. A week's melancholy transformed into an enormous curiosity for music scores. I would stand there between the dense shelves of the Cleveland Public Library for hours and hours reading Mozart, my opened mouth revealing the cordial amazement caused by a bunch of white and shaded circles called notes."

Thus was his obsession and calling confirmed.

"So this is me now, staying up till three in the morning reading and composing, and then requesting favorites on the radio. This is in no way an exclusive interest. . . . But one thing I know almost for sure: that for as long as my ears communicate properly with the auditory tube in my cortex, suicide *isn't* an *option.*"

The audience loves what can only be called Eugene's performance and applauds vigorously while Eugene falls as if exhausted into the chair beside Mr. Brennan, who is likewise clapping and beaming at Eugene.

On the way out of assembly, Deb Nash asks me if I can believe the school almost rejected Eugene last year because his English was so bad. In the faculty lounge, Hawley, having filled his coffee mug, says, "Did you listen to the *language?*" Chuck Seelbach, hovering pen in hand over a text book, looks up and nods but doesn't speak, returns to his work. Hawley says, "I wish he'd do *other* work though." Tomorrow, when Hawley arrives for philosophy class, Eugene will be prostrate across a wall bench, all but snoring.

Two days after Eugene's speech, Nancy arrives for fourth-period English and unloads her books onto the table. Nick Zinn is unaccountably rambunctious today and he approaches her immediately. She listens to him for a moment, sees what he holds in his hands, and says, "Oh. You want to proselytize?"

Nick mumbles some more, staring at the twenty sets of Xeroxes he's brought to class.

"Go ahead. Nick has something to say," she announces to the class, then to Nick says, "Be subversive. Deviant. *Controversial.*" Then she leaves the room.

"This um-um-um-um-um-um is an essay by B-B-Bertrand Russell," Nick tells the class. "Bertrand Russell is a famous um-um-um-um-um-um philosopher of the twentieth century." Nick hands out an essay titled "Why I Am Not a Christian." He's smiling subversively. When Mike Cohen receives his copy, his eyebrows rise and he says, "Hmm." Nick says no more before Nancy returns with a box of books, two dozen paperbacks of *Portrait of the Artist as a Young Man,* and begins class. Nick's made an appointment with the headmaster after school, and he's bringing artillery.

Nick has found a great comrade in Paul Bailin, who is himself still something of a boy and whose age affords him a spiritual middle-ground between teacher and student. Paul is a model of credible and attainable adulthood that older teachers are less likely to be. Both Paul and Nick picked up Bertrand Russell independently but at about the same time. Paul echos Nick's fatalistic, you-see-it-your-way-I-see-it-my-way reaction to Hawley: "He doesn't think Russell is much of a philosopher," Paul said to me when I noticed the copy of Russell's book *Why I Am Not a Christian* on his desk. "I don't happen to think Lewis is much of a philosopher." Nick in many ways *needs* Paul, a teacher he can bounce ideas off of without fearing those ideas will shoot back at him and send him to the canvas.

C. S. Lewis uses a metaphor that Nick responds to. Lewis argues that some extraneous force has organized the universe; we know this, his argument goes, because we have a conscience. He uses the postal service as a metaphor. He knows that the paper packets the man in blue delivers to all the houses are letters because he has opened packets addressed to him and found letters. He does not need to open packets addressed to someone else to know they contain letters. In the same way, by examining what is inside himself, he deduces general characteristics inside all humans. He does not know what other people's letters contain, only that they do contain letters. These letters describe what is in one's nature as a human to do. He does not expect that other people on the street get the same letters he does. Lewis then suggests that if there is mail, then there is indeed a sender—"a power behind the facts," he writes, "a Director, a guide"—and that in those envelopes lie clues to the identity of that sender.

"Hey! M-M-Mr. Ruhlman," Nick says, barreling toward me. "Have you gotten your letter?"

"My letter?" I ask.

"*Yeah.* Your letter in the *mail?*" He suspirates, his chest heaves, a chuckle rolls through his back, he grins, and barrels away.

A couple days earlier, Paul approached me, his eyes squeezed to slivers of mirth, and said, "Has Nick asked you if you've received your letter in the mail?"

Nothing in the world, it would seem, delights them more than making fun of the headmaster. Nick would let nothing slip past without reporting to Paul.

"Is it true," Paul asked me one afternoon, "that Hawley told his class that he heard," Paul paused, "little voices?" Paul has a look that seems to combine hilarious disbelief and real concern. Nick, Paul explained, described the class as a *revival* meeting.

I confirmed that some of the class did focus on little voices and that Hawley did confess to hearing voices himself. Paul is at once surprised and not surprised.

■ ■ ■

"There are some questions that I'd like to clear up before the bell rings," Hawley says to the class. Eric has just presented the second half of "The Apology," in which Socrates defends himself at his own trial. "Socrates refers to this little voice, this divine voice. He does this in 'The Apology,' but in many of his dialogues he refers to this little voice, this divine voice. . . . John Brown the American abolitionist heard a little voice that said move into west Kansas and kill people, and who knows, Charlie Manson probably heard multiple voices." Vish throws his head back and laughs. "But Socrates was a reasonable man," Hawley says. "He's not above using reason and using it elegantly, but he's also using this other thing that Western seers and mystics and religious people call revelation. A revelation is a pure shaft of conviction. . . . Is that persuasive to you? 'I have this divine voice that does not oppose me at any moment during this trial as I'm making these arguments, so therefore I think they're pretty good arguments.' The divine voice later on tells him, 'It's OK today, Socrates. This is not something you have to worry about.' "

The class is not responding; Hawley pauses, sensing their apathy, then says, "If somebody comes up to you and says, 'I have this little divine voice that tells me what to do' "—he has whispered this, with bobbing, sinister eyebrows—"do you say, '*Good!* Tell me *more* about it because I want to know what to do, too! Maybe it will tell me what courses to take!' " The class laughs. "What do you think about divine voices?"

"I think it's just a conscience," says Kris Fletcher dismissively. "That's the way I view it."

"A superego kind of thing?" says Hawley.

"Yeah, exactly. It's just the way you interpret it."

Hawley wants to keep Socrates, and his claim, in perspective, and explains what an oddball the old coot was, going barefoot all year in the style of neighboring Sparta, Athens's enemy, goading the judges at his trial. "Would you be impressed," Hawley repeats, "if there was somebody among you that was very different, very nonconformist at University School who said, 'Yeah, I'm *this way,* and I hear a little voice'?" Hawley whispers, "He says, 'That is what's *driving* me.' Would you find that laughable, interesting, maybe even dangerous?"

"I think again it's a matter of your definition," says Kris, tilting his head back and peering over his cheeks at Hawley. "Hearing little voices is your interpretation of it. I think everybody's had it at one time or another, it's just how you define it. If you want to call it your *little voice,* that's OK with me."

Undaunted by Kris's derisive tone, Hawley says, "Let's talk about little voices. By the way, you know the story of Elijah, the Old Testament prophet-hero?" Hawley describes for the class one of the first references in literature to little voices. Until Elijah, God had always appeared as a loud, angry, wheeling-and-dealing voice that used lightning, tidal waves, and plagues as visual aids. For the first time, God speaks to Elijah in a new way.

"And Elijah heard a *still small voice,*" Hawley says. "Some people think that this is a way of condensing spiritual experience, that God cannot relate in external distant ways." He pauses. "Do you hear, are you guided literally by, voices? Do you hear, do you get a sense in your head, do you get a conviction that seems to come, in a sense, as voices? Am *I* the only one in this room who hears voices?"

Everyone looks down, though not from lack of attention. The class is silent. Hawley scans the room, seeing nothing but crowns.

"Don't be shy!" he shouts suddenly. "Everybody who hears voices! Come forward!"

Amidst the laughter, Hawley hears a stuttery voice at the back of the room. "Tony?" he asks. "Do you hear voices?"

"Yeah," says Tony, so lacking conviction that it sounds like a question. The class howls.

"I don't think it's odd or creepy," Hawley says quickly. "I remember one time, I was the dean, and a case involved possible expulsion of about four or five students. It was my job to decide. The faculty was divided on whether the outcome should be that severe. On the other hand why should we have a policy? So you had the hardliners saying you have a policy you stick to it, and other people saying wait a minute, we're talking about *human beings.* . . . It had been a seven- or eight-day deliberation, and I remember driving home and a voice said, or it at least came to me in sentences, 'This is not about *pleasing* people—what can you go to sleep with?' This voice was reasoning with me. . . . I think we hear something. We certainly hear some language. We're certainly carrying on a dialectic in our head. Also I think we need to stop short of saying that if we believe that some power, this revelation, whether it's a projection of our own unconscious, which is what I think Freud would say, or whether it is the reception of something reasonable and cosmic and true, whatever we think of it, I think we have to watch out. If we're saying anyone who hears a voice or makes a claim on the basis of revelation is inspired or right—because I think John Brown *murdered* people on the basis of his revelations; I think Charlie Manson murdered people on the basis of his revelations—we have to judge revelations by their fruits. Yes, it came to me in a real way, but what is real, and how humane and right and true is it?"

When the bell rings Nick Zinn bolts for the history office to find Paul Bailin and to tell him that Hawley hears little voices.

It's a genuine battle Nick seems to be waging, one that he's forever losing yet never accepting defeat. At last he finds Bertrand Russell.

The day after Nick's meeting with Dr. Hawley, I'm hanging out with Kris who's desensitizing books behind the desk in the library. Nick Zinn charges through the electronic gates. He's mumbling about Hawley, and Kris, as he usually does when he hears the headmaster's name, smiles wryly, cynically.

"I talked with Hawley for an hour yesterday," says Nick. He tilts his head left, then right, slips his thumbs into the back pockets of his trousers. "He's really not such a bad guy. He's had some bad things happen to him."

Nick's grinning; there's something ironical about his smile, as though he senses I don't trust this magnanimity. He wags his head some more, shifts his weight from one foot to the other then back. "He sees the world one way and I see it another." Nick shrugs. His mouth has not tripped on a single syllable.

The volume of Kris's grin is on loud and he shakes his head. Without a word, he leaves with a stack of books to reshelve.

Mike Cohen enters, a perpetual stout-framed hunchback hefting a forty-pound backpack, large plastic traveling coffee mug dangling from a long gray strap. No sooner does Mike shout *"Hey,* Zinn," in greeting than Mrs. Hanscom arrives. "Gentlemen, could you please take your conversation into the hall?" she whispers. "You can hear this all the way in the silent study area."

"What am I doing?" Mike exclaims to everyone in the library. "I gotta study." Nick and I find a table on the upstairs landing.

He repeats that he spent *an hour* with Dr. Hawley and that Hawley's really not such a bad guy after all. They talked about the news article, Nick explains, the one Hawley had dropped on the floor, and it led to a discussion on the ethics of journalism.

"There are two ways people get readers of the newspaper," Nick says, paraphrasing his philosophy teacher. "One is to take a Howard Stern tack, the other is to tell the truth. Dr. Hawley said, 'Which would you rather be, Nick? Howard Stern or Socrates?' " Nick tells me that he used to enjoy such tactics as planting swear words in the text so students would scour the paper, writing a story, for example, in which the first letter on the left of the column was F, and the line beneath would begin with U, and so on. But, he says, "I've come to a new conclusion." Truth, he says, should probably govern, though he offers this grudgingly.

Paul Bailin wanders by and takes a seat. "How did your meeting with Dr. Hawley go?" Paul asks.

Nick tells Paul that he and Dr. Hawley talked for *an hour.*

After discussing journalism, Nick explains, they moved into Lewis and Russell and the "Why I Am Not a Christian" essay.

"What did he say?" Paul asks.

"He suggested that I *present* it to the *class,*" says Nick. "He actually *suggested* it."

Softly, Paul says, "Did he? *Really?*" Paul seems to find this news surprising.

Nick Zinn, smiling, exhilarated, lumbers away from the table, arms swinging wide, feet pounding the floor.

11

"**D**oes this reveal a theory of human nature? I think that *Hamlet* reveals a theory of human nature. Is Plato saying that humans are perfectible? Plato is saying anybody can do it. He's not saying that there's a special breed of people who can take it, there are two different natures. Is there one nature that's perfectible?"

"One," says Mike Cohen. "I see a real one-sided egotism of human nature. They don't want to be told they're wrong, that their perceived reality is wrong. We don't want to know that our reality isn't true."

"In Freudian terms, what is the human personality always doing?" Hawley asks the class.

"Reducing tension," says Kris.

"Reducing tension," says Hawley. "Now what if somebody comes to you and says, 'The world doesn't work the way you think. I have now seen the light.' What does that do to your tension level? It goes way up. And depending on how well you're set up and how much new data you can take in, that tension is going to go *way* up, and you're going to go into denial to reduce the tension. Tyler made the point that what if this allegory is just a big tension reducer, that all there really is is this cave and we make up this allegory to reduce tension?"

This is the end of the first class that begins Hawley's section on ethics. Kris Fletcher has presented Plato's "The Allegory of the Cave," Vish has critiqued it as best he could on short notice, the class has weighed in with comments. Then something happens I would not see during any other class all year.

Of the scores of wild Hawley lectures, of the tens of thousands of words that cascade from the headmaster's mouth during fourth and fifth periods, in no other ten-minute stretch does Hawley so condense his own core convictions—not simply the spine of his philosophical beliefs, but the intellectual source of that spine, the root, the wellspring, out of which all his passion seems to flow.

"Why do we come up with theologies and new social orders?" Hawley asks. "Because we think there's a better one out there. Even in the shadow world, there's better and worse, there are experts. Tyler used the term a minute ago, about how do you know this isn't real? Maybe this illusion of better isn't just a tension reducer. And this shadowland, this imperfection, is all we've got. What is real and what is not is probably the biggest issue determining Plato's thinking, and the second-biggest issue is human nature. Plato's known for the first great consistent metaphysical system. And this is what we'll get into Tuesday. For Plato, what's real is highly specific, what's real has some qualities. What's real and what's true could never be corrupted, could never be changed. What's real and true must be real and true forever. And so reality, what's really true, does not change with time, does not exist, is not affected by time, it's outside of time, it has no material dimension at all."

Hawley is talking fast now, pacing a horseshoe path around the students. He mostly stares at the table as he gesticulates, motioning sharply with his hands, squaring thumb and index finger to form a box into which he fits definitions. When he speaks at a particular student, it usually is Kris. Kris doesn't know why, but Hawley regularly seems to address him alone, as if Hawley is trying to convince Kris of something, as if Kris's eyes are arguing back. Kris tilts his head and maintains the eye contact at an angle. Eugene, Igor, and Scott Seidelmann watch the headmaster pace the room as if following a man playing himself in tennis; Jason Koo stares blankly at his notebook, spinning a pen in his hand and not missing a syllable of Hawley's words; and Nick Caserio scribbles frantically in his notebook, trying to get it all down.

"Remember what I said about the C chord? Three tones—bum bum bum. Sometime in the past those three tones were played together on purpose, and some people think that the ancient Greeks were the ones who did it. Certain pre-Socratic philosophers were stretching out cat guts for the first time and, bing bing bing, and they named it. And not only that, the ratio of the length of these strings is regular, there's a harmony to the lengths, there's a harmony to the sound, and they believed that there's some reason, that there are celestial, perfect harmonies just waiting to be discovered, and so the code for how to live is the arrangement of all these symmetries and harmonies and so forth—Western philosophy began with this sort of numbers mysticism. And by the way, now that we can actually measure sound vibrations, they are actually symmetrical. And so the C chord, if we nuke ourselves into oblivion, will always exist, will always be out there cosmically waiting to be played. The fact that you can tune your guitar wrong, and don't get it, doesn't mean there's no C chord anymore. It just means that you don't have a tuned guitar. The C chord is perfect. The 360-degree circle is *perfect,* whether you can make one or not, and there are all kinds of things that are perfect, and *that* is what is *real.* But the people in the cave think that, just as Vish said, the things we can touch, the things that are tangible, are real."

"Then a tree isn't real," Scott Seidelmann bursts out, incredulous. *"You* aren't real."

"The tree is not real," says Hawley. "I am not real. I am a form. I'm participating in a form."

He dashes to the board and writes *eidos.*

"This is sometimes translated as 'form' and sometimes as 'idea.' I am a number of forms. I'm a teacher—I'm that form. I'm a man—I'm that form. And so forth. And not only that, I'm sometimes, when I'm a really effective teacher, I'm coming close to what Plato would have said, I'm participating in the form of teacher. And when I'm bad, I'm very little of a teacher. And that's the reality of me. I exist to the degree that I realize my form. But Richard Hawley didn't exist once and he will not exist one day again, and if you watch me, my whole life in one of those speedy animation films, you'd see that I once didn't exist and won't."

Hawley himself is speaking rather like one of those speedy animation films. He returns to the metaphor he'd used of an oil painting of a chair, a painting perfectly representing a tangible object, then picks up the pace.

"We know that the oil painting was a trick, that it was a rendering in two dimensions of what actually exists in three. Well, the relation between the oil painting and the chair is the relationship, Plato says, between the chair and what is true. Now *this* chair," he says, slapping his hand on the backrest of a nearby chair, "built out of hard maple and oak boards. OK, there were these maple forests and oak forests out in the Pacific Northwest. I've got one of these Disney films now, we're looking at the trees. And then we see the lumber companies come in and cut them down. And then we see the logs turned into boards, and those boards are sold to an educational furniture company, and they're made into these fabulous chairs, and they have to put our little logo on it like that, and it becomes a chair and so forth. Now this chair comes to University School last year, it's going to have a life of twenty years and then its slats are going to break and so forth, and when we consider it unrepairable, we'll burn it up and it'll be converted into carbon atoms. So, in twenty-five years it'll go from forest to carbon atoms. For awhile, it's quite sound, for a while it participates in chairhood. Now *this* is not real."

He raps his knuckles on the table.

"What it is participating in is real. The fact that we call this a good table, if it is—it's supporting things, it's upright and so forth—it's a good table because we know something in our deep immortal soul, we know tablehood. Even though we've never seen tablehood, we know. That's part of what's divine, what's incorruptible. As a matter of fact, we could never know, never understand what a table is unless we had that tablehood already ingrained in our souls. That is the immortal part of us. For instance, I can teach you"—he lunges at the blackboard and starts drawing a circle and its components—"I can teach you the geometry of circles. OK, here's a circle; a circle has 360 degrees; it's got a diameter; it's got a radius; the relation between the radius and the circumference is a number called pi. I could go on and on and all of it would be true, but that's not a perfect circle."

He taps the board with his finger, lifting a dot of chalk dust from within the circle.

"There's no instrument in the world that can draw a perfect circle. None of us has actually experienced a perfect circle. But we understand it *perfectly.* And the fact that we can intuit the perfect circle, the fact that we know it, it's in our immortal souls, allows us to say that's a good one, that one's better still, and that's a poor one. We reference every *actual* experience, every shadow of shadows, we reference it to a perfection we already know in our immortal soul. The very notion of *perfection"*—he writes the word on the board—"we will never experience, but the fact that we've got it engraved allows us to say better or worse, not just about physical things but also morally. We know some people are better than others, but how can we know that unless there's a scale for better and worse? The forms for goodness and badness are ingrained in our immortal souls."

Eric asks, "Isn't it one of the traditional arguments, that how can there be a god with all the injustices in the world. And how would we know there were injustices without a god?"

"Exactly. By the way, that's Plato's very argument picked up by C. S. Lewis who uses it for Christian arguments later on. He says if there is in fact no universally true basis for justice—truth, fairness, kindness—what on earth is the sense in complaining about its absence? Why—would you mind child abuse? You certainly might mind if it's your child, or if you're the child being abused. That would make a lot of sense. It's psychologically unpleasant. But why on earth would you ever be concerned about justice unless you expect there to be a standard of justice that everybody knows and intuits. In other words, it's a form of it, like a C chord that's not being realized. It's like when you play bad music, say you're out of tune. You're tuning toward perfection, you're tuning toward an ideal. And *society* is also to be tuned. We certainly know when it's out of tune."

12

"I'm not coming back next year," Paul says.

"You *aren't?*" says Lisa Hauptman, a teacher apprentice in the science department.

"I'm applying to grad school."

They are standing at the far end of the faculty lounge. Third period is about to begin. Lisa's eyes are wide with surprise and excitement. "Dan should know about this," she says, thinking of her fellow apprentice in the history department, who will be needing a job next year.

Chuck Seelbach, head of the history department, strolls in as he does every day at exactly this time and sets his briefcase on the table at his usual spot.

"Oh," says Paul. "There he is." Seelbach halts and looks at Paul. Paul says, "I guess I should tell you."

"Tell me *what?*" Seelbach says, not liking surprises.

"I'm not coming back next year."

"Oh," says Seelbach. "Yes. You *should* tell me." Seelbach pauses, takes a breath, then asks, "What are you doing?"

"Applying to grad school."

Seelbach, poker-faced, nods, then asks Paul if he's been accepted somewhere. Paul says no, he's just now applying, but he's confident. If he isn't, or even if he is, and the school is desperate to fill the spot, he'll gladly reconsider, but as of now, he's in the grad-school market and US should not expect his return.

"My brother wants to teach here," Paul adds.

"Oh," says Seelbach.

"He wants to take my job."

"*Oh?*" says Seelbach with what is for him great emotion.

Language chairman Roger Yedid, happily eavesdropping on the exchange, says, "That's nepotism."

"No," says Paul. "It's only nepotism if I have power."

Teacher apprentice Lisa has dashed from the lounge to find Dan and tell him the news so he can call first dibs on Paul's job. Seelbach, returned to his routine, is already grading papers, the bald dome of his head gleaming between his massive pitcher's shoulders. Paul checks his mailbox again and departs.

Paul had been grappling with the dilemma all fall and made up his mind during the long winter break. On the first day back, I'd been loitering in the library, staring at the snow swirling across the frozen lake. I strolled by the book-checkout station where Tyler Soltis stood talking to Kris as Kris sensitized books to be returned to the shelves.

"You've *got* to come sometime," Kris said.

"I *have*," Tyler pleaded. "I've been there."

"I want you to go *in* one," Kris said.

"I—no. When it comes to swimming in excrement—"

"Come on, where's your sense of adventure? It's not *swimming*."

"All right, *wading*."

Paul, who had been rushing to gather his application materials, approached, leaned on the checkout counter, and told me about not coming back next year. "It feels really good to have made a decision," he said. He explained that these two years will have been productive but that he had reached a point of "diminishing returns." While he'd gotten a lot of encouragement and praise regarding his teaching during the first half of this year, the wear and tear of the work allowed little time for his own reading and reflection. His real desire was more education, a masters, and perhaps a Ph.D. in philosophy. He had few obligations and was young enough to make the jump. Now was the time. Later that day, shortly after ninth period had begun, Paul had gathered his courage and headed to the administrative offices to tell his boss. Hawley was talking with Margaret Mason in his office. Paul informed both of his decision; each expressed disappointment and asked him if this was a final decision. The third year is when things really get going, Hawley told him. Paul assured them he'd made up his mind—his course was fixed. Hawley offered help with recommendations if Paul needed them. Then, according to Paul, Hawley remarked on the bright side of the situation.

"Rick said his life will be a lot easier with me gone," Paul recounted, squinting and chuckling. "He said he's now planning to install holy water in the lobby."

Paul was in fine form, rested from vacation and buoyant with prospects of an exciting and uncertain future. At the all-school faculty meeting the day before, a sort of mid-year state of the union gathering, one of the issues discussed was the recent poll sent to faculty, parents, alumni, and students in preparation for next year's ISACS evaluation about how well the school did what it had claimed to do. During the meeting, Paul scribbled away. When I asked what he was doing, he explained he was tabulating exact percentages of negative responses. A general description of negative responses had been included in a handout, but Paul wanted exact figures regarding who doesn't like what. "I've gone three weeks without being subversive," he said. "I've got to do *something.*"

Knowing he won't return next year also seems to have softened his view of the school. He said he likes the school more now than he ever had before. And he'd changed his mind about the school's being all-boys. "I had a conversation with Carol Pribble and she said she's taught at coed schools and there's just as much sexism there as there is here."

"I'm inclined to blame my latent sexism on US," he continued, "but everyone's sexist. People who go to public school are sexist, too, so maybe it's not fair to blame as much on [US] as I did." He noted also that he can no longer fault the school's single-sex make-up for hindering social development. He had been a student here since he was in fourth grade, he said, and he never had problems relating to women; indeed, he feels more comfortable being with women than with men.

Paul stopped, leaned on his elbows, then said, "Girls are *idolized* here."

This may be true among many boys but not Kris Fletcher, not now at any rate. The biggest thing in his life had been a girl named Sarah: "She dumped me on Sunday," he said.

I asked him how long they'd been going out.

"Not all that long," he said. "A month and thirteen days." Without pausing to think he added, "November sixth, 1:06 P.M."

She was so wonderful, he'd broken up with all his other girlfriends, most of whom he'd met at a mall where he, Tyler, and other friends hang out. Just one week before Black Sunday, he and Sarah had such a lovely weekend together. And now this. He was on the phone with Tyler, who'd also dated Sarah briefly, talking till four A.M. Tyler, wanting to shore up his wounded buddy, said Sarah was "a conniving bitch," but Kris said he knew this wasn't so and hoped to win her back.

What made matters more humiliating for Kris was the way she did it. She was afraid to tell him in person, so she persuaded her friend to call Kris and do it for her. But this friend was too afraid to do so, so the *friend* called Odum, one of Kris's buddies, and Odum, at last, informed Kris of the bad news.

Kris seemed to sense an eternal dilemma and was stoic but also philosophical: "I love her," he said. "That's not something I say easily. . . . It's kind of like God. You can't see it. You can't touch it. But you know it's there." Or would be there, he added, if he believed in God.

He hopes, by ignoring her, she will return. But his hopes are not high. Since she didn't call over break, he sits impassively behind the library checkout counter through the gloomy winter mornings, thinking of spring when the sewers warm up. You wouldn't know a thing was wrong from the looks of him, but the tone of his poems has changed. Verse that had once read, "Now surrender your love to me/ And I yield for eternity," and, "As my life is but one short breath/ I wish to love before my Deth," has darkened. Throughout January, when his reshelving is completed, his hair shrouds his face as he pores over loose sheets of notebook paper, scribbling song lyrics and sonnets.

There was a time that I thought I could care,
And a time that I thought I could get close.
My heart had sprouted wings and kissed the air,
Now I wonder if anybody knows.
The clouds, the birds, all seem to mock me now,
Her leering face stares at me ev'rywhere.
I have to go on, but I don't know how,
No one ever said that my life was fair.
A feeling of tenderness betrayed me,
I loved a woman with Deth in her breast.
She cradled me in darkness; Let me be,
The wicked shall never have any rest.

I can never feel true love, only lust,
Ashes to ashes, always rust to rust.

"OK, gentlemen," Nancy says, having put her books down along with some wads of soggy Kleenex. "Mr. Garrett really enjoyed this class on Monday, and Nick has informed me that it was nice to have a *man.*" Nick's subversive grin expands, he heaves and rocks in his chair, looking right and left. The class noise rises. Nancy waits. "I don't have much of a voice today, so if I can *possibly* have some *pity?*

"Some of the papers were marvelous," she continues. "And the sonnets, those of you who did sonnets, were generally wonderful. On some, I've written 'T cubed.' Totally, truthfully, terrible. Some people just *don't follow directions.* Paragraphs that began, 'Hamlet was wandering down the hall and he bumped into Ophelia,' are just *not* going to work. When I hand out an assignment sheet, it's not to trap you.

"I've also got something else to say. Here is a gender question. Are males more stubborn?"

A chorus of "no"'s goes up, so many it sounds almost as if they are booing Nancy. Tony says, "Definitely not."

"That *astonishes* me," Nancy says. "Really." Nancy presses a palm to her chest. She's wearing a black dress with a gold choker, gold earrings, and, in defiance of winter's gloom, a brilliant yellow blazer—elegant even with gobs of Kleenex and a raw nose. "I'll tell you my definition. This is true of Hawken and Shaker. I can suggest to a person of the male persuasion to do something, but that person will do something else on their own. I've got a number of papers that prove that point."

I had bumped into Nancy a few minutes before this class, not unusually, as she left the Xerox room. Nancy uses the copying machine the way some people use a Stairmaster. She cradled an armful of warm paper and began speaking immediately about how bad the *Hamlet* papers were. And then about boys.

"Nothing I have *ever* done has changed—I'm going to use one of Rick's words—their *trajectory,*" she said. "Boys are on a course of their *own.* That's not very scientific but it's the way I felt even before I met Rick. When I've asked girls to do this or work on that, they generally do it. Not boys." She had gone to some length to warn them, of all the subjects they might write about, not to try to argue that Hamlet was insane. "I wish I could steer students away from Hamlet's madness," she had said to the class. "I tell you, if you try to argue that Hamlet is mad, you're *going* to get into *trouble.*" And what do they do?

"It's the beginning of the end," she said. "If their parents saw this"— their work—"they'd say, 'We sent you to US for *this?*' If I hadn't already seen it before I'd be in a state of *shock.*"

The "it" to which Nancy refers is sometimes called senioritis—the sudden deterioration of effort, care, and work among virtually the entire senior class. Grades from the first trimester are the last that any colleges will see, and while there are no doubt seniors for whom learning for learning's sake is their chief and noble endeavor, a majority would give that idea a raspberry at this point. Nancy told me that the senior shutdown is so inevitable that her colleague Bob Hanson absolutely refuses to teach seniors because of it.

"I'll say one more thing," Nancy continues. "For some of you I'm going to use my ultimate weapon. It's not a low grade because I know some of you who have gotten into college don't care about low grades. It's the incomplete, and it can *keep* you from graduating. I call 'em the guns of Navarone."

A series of raised eyebrows among the boys seems to indicate there were more than a few who had intended to more or less blow off the rest of the year.

Now she begins class, running through several love poems—"To His Coy Mistress," "The Passionate Shepherd to His Love"—and finishes the class with a Shakespeare sonnet that must particularly resonate with the jilted Kris Fletcher, number 129.

"OK," says Nancy. "I would love as we go along to have more of you do some reading but not until you have more preparation. So I'm going to read this one. Because I *love* this one and I'm *selfish.*" Nancy is rarely selfish in this way, but hearing her beloved Shakespeare read by novices is to her like having to listen to a beginner violin student scratching out a Bach sonata for the first time. "This is what I consider a far-out Shakespeare sonnet," she says, and reads it unusually quickly, as if to mirror the subject, in salacious pursuit of exalted language:

> *Th' expense of spirit in a waste of shame*
> *Is lust in action; and, till action, lust*

> *Is perjured, murd'rous, bloody, full of blame,*
> *Savage, extreme, rude, cruel, not to trust;*

and on through to its upending finale:

> *All this the world well knows; yet none knows well*
> *To shun the heaven that leads men to this hell.*

"This is a sonnet as a knot," she says, resting her *Norton Anthology* face down on the table, "an intricate, dense—a black hole where almost everything is so compressed it's not easily sorted out. And yet, if you like couplets, if you like knots, if you like paradoxes, unraveling it can be a great experience. If you want to figure out a Shakespeare sonnet the first thing you do is try to paraphrase it, but I want you to do more than that. OK, what does it mean? The expense of spirit in a waste of shame."

She pauses. The boys look down at their books pretending hard to read.

"What's the matter? Is there a word in this line that you don't understand? What's expense?" She writes expense on the board. "Cost, to give out, expensive."

"It's bad, has negative connotations" says Ryan.

"Always? If you buy a great work of art that's very expensive do you say it's bad? Can't expensive mean valuable in some ways?"

"It can be dear," says Eugene, explaining that in Russian, as in French, there is a term that means both expensive and dear. "Like *cher,*" he says.

"OK, good. The expense of spirit—we usually don't think of spirit, an immaterial substance, to be expensive, we generally think of expensive as something material and valuable for which we pay. There's a paying out. In a *waste* of shame. There's a process in that line, there's a drama. What's the scene? Who's the speaker? Eric."

"Who's the speaker?" he repeats.

"Yeah, make it a little play."

"I don't understand."

"There's a speaker in every poem. That speaker is speaking to you. Look fellas, the expense of spirit in a *waste* of *shame*—wow, that *is* lust in action. Where is he? Where are you? You're in a bar, let's say, maybe you're in a seedy bar in Singapore, like in one of those B movies. He's already been through this, he's expended his spirit, and in this first line he's already had time to feel this waste of shame."

"A waste of the spirit," says Tony.

"What is the waste?" she asks. "Does the addition of lust—well, what does lust mean?"

"I think lust in action is acting out lustful thoughts," says Ryan. "You're acting it out and your spirit is going in the wrong direction. Desire that goes the wrong way, in a sexual connotation."

"OK, what's sexual about it? What is lust?"

"You don't care about the person," Ryan answers.

"Deep physical desire," says Eric.

"One of the questions that's going to come up in one of John Donne's poems is what's love and what's lust? What's body and what's soul? But what is lust?"

"Deep physical desire," Eric repeats. "Idinal desire."

"OK, deep physical desire coming from the id—having nothing to do with someone's personality, or whether they're a nice person or whether you're in love—for a physical experience. Is that the end of it?"

Eugene's voice sounds out. "Could lust," he asks, "be associated with *light?* Like luster, lustrous?"

This halts Nancy. Her head cocks back on her shoulders.

"I don't know," she says. "I never thought about that. I'll try and check that out." She's not sure what to do here, and looks at me, her eyes discs. "There's nothing like a person relatively new to the language to let you look at it in a *completely* different way."

"It's *all* sensual," says Scott.

"Well I don't know," Nancy responds. "Can you lust after great art, or can you lust after knowledge?"

Kris smiles wickedly and nods. *"Knowledge."*

The class continues through the last half of the period speaking of lust, physical desire, orgasm, and the expense of spirit, with the same objective seriousness that they have given to Platonic form, sunlight, and cave dwellers. Physical desire is a perpetual, often tormenting, concern among seventeen-year-old boys but they seem, as they have in all previous classes when sexual subjects were on the table, engaged not so much by their libidinous drives or innate craving for hilarious obscenity as by a sympathy for Nancy's passion for literature and poetry.

"You're swallowing the bait and you're hating reason," Nancy concludes. "So is there any way out of this poem? He tells you lust is terrible, lust is terrible, lust is terrible. The typical ending of the poem would be 'All this the world well knows, but none knows well to shun this *evil* that leads men to this hell.' But he doesn't does he? He ends with a suggestion"—the four electronic pings sound out, ending the class—"that lust might, as hellish as it might seem, might be, *heaven.*"

"Which will lead you to hell."

"Which will lead you to hell. He overturns the *whole system.*" The boys are already gathering their books and zipping up knapsacks. "Hold on a second," she shouts. "For Friday, I want you to start reading the poems of John Donne, and particularly 'The Ecstasy.' "

As the boys file past her and out the door, Nancy's entire frame, released from the spotlight of teaching, sags. She is exhausted. She is exhausted not only from the cold that won't leave her head, and from teaching and staying up too late to grade their rotten *Hamlet* papers which had taken her far too long (untouched on her desk at home the entire break, "they sat there," she said, *"accusing* me"). All this was part of the teaching life she'd known for fifteen years.

But this year, unlike any year before, Nancy had been broadsided by a spiritual crisis. Several events had combined to open a seemingly bottomless gulf that she had struggled all fall, and now winter, to bridge. It had begun early in the year when her most cherished student, a brilliant woman she'd taught at Hawken, visited the school and described to her old teacher her new interests in Islam. This just as the battles between the Jewish settlers and the Palestinians were again boiling to the surface on the West Bank. Then within the school an apparently Christian agenda to inject religion into the curriculum fueled the fire. Outside the school she and her husband had been active in supporting the Holocaust Memorial Museum in Washington, D.C., had attended its opening last April, and, on top of all her other work, she is preparing to address the school about it, though she's not sure why or what she needs to say. The irritating kernel at the center of this spiritual crisis was her conviction that she had somehow harmed friends and colleagues, primarily Hawley, with her statement that she feared "good" Christians and had failed to explain adequately, even to herself, why.

It was coincidental, surely, that *Schindler's List,* Speilberg's powerful drama about a Catholic war profiteer who saved hundreds of Jews during the Holocaust, opened shortly before Christmas, a movie so important that the entire upper campus would take a day off to see it together. And shortly after that, *Shadowlands* arrived at movie theaters, a love story about the Christian philosopher C. S. Lewis. ("Ah," Hawley said to me one afternoon. "We have our own Shadowlands right here.") For some, such a confluence of Jewish and Christian themes can be brushed aside as coincidence and little more, but Nancy is a woman trained to follow themes, to take special note of coincidence in texts, and she has done so in the text of her own life; it has opened a gulf, as she calls it, that has already hurt one of her closest friends, a mystery that she cannot help but explore lest it consume her.

Shortly before Christmas, Nancy delivered her presentation on the Holocaust Memorial Museum, and like everything she did, it seemed to rise from the deepest recesses of her heart. She agonized over it, and she arrived early on the designated morning in a smart navy blazer and long dark skirt, having gotten no sleep because, she said, "the dogs were howling." The neighbor's dogs were no doubt real but she implied a metaphorical threat and menace hounding her night. At eight A.M., she stood at the podium to ensure she could work the threatening slide projector mechanism. She'd brought a small white travel alarm clock to set on the podium but still looked to Kerry, who was helping her with the props, to say, "If I go over twenty minutes," and she drew two fingers across her throat. She was dreading this.

"I'll tell you, Nancy," Kerry said. He pointed to the first row in the second section of seats. "I'll be sitting right there."

Ten minutes later, when the boys were jacket-and-tied and seated, Kerry took the stand and delivered morning announcements, one of which was that the Christmas-tree sale, proceeds of which go toward the after-prom party in the spring, had been extended for one more weekend. Nancy, seated behind Kerry, looked down at her colleague Evan Luzar and rolled her eyes—*hawking Christmas trees before my Holocaust speech.* Then Kerry said, "This time of year we pause to acknowledge that certain people and families observe the holidays in different ways," and he introduced Jeremy Handel, a junior who gave a brief presentation on the historical significance of Chanukah.

Nancy then stood and the hall was silent. The lights dimmed. She fiddled with her travel alarm clock and the projector remote, then bent the microphone to mouth-level with a loud creak.

"This is going to be awkward for me," she said, her voice amplified to unusual proportions. "This is very emotional for me."

Her initial aim had been a simple description of this new, important structure on the American landscape, but as she worked through her thoughts, she told the audience, they did not seem so pressing as *why* she should be describing it to a crowd of US boys.

"It's very difficult to explain what this museum is *like*," she began. She said, "I can't imagine what it's like for young boys to sit here in assembly, listening to tales of the late-twentieth century. Guns and violence, battered women, AIDS"—all of which had been the subject of morning presentations. "You know you're supposed to care deeply, but sometimes you just want to turn it off. This is a prep school and this is prep for the world, and now I want to take you not into a horror of the present, but a horror of the past." The Holocaust Memorial Museum in Washington is indeed, she said, "a *terrible catalogue* of horrors."

But why is she up here? she asked the audience. This has been her struggle. *"What* could I tell you to make you *go* to this? You young boys from caring families." She stopped and looked at them. "I can't *tell* you why. . . . We're taught to mistrust the bias of the speaker, so here's mine," she said. "I was born October 15, 1938."

This to her is everything. Her parents were both born in the United States. One set of grandparents was born here, as well; the other in Russia. She can trace her European ancestry back as far as virtually any other Jew living in the United States today, she says. One generation. There had been at one point records, but all have been destroyed or lost. She has ample cause to believe that she had ancestors who were killed in the Holocaust. And this leads her to the biggest why, the personal why: *why not me?* "It's affected my entire life," she said.

On the day that she and her husband first saw the museum, the season was beautiful, verdant spring, with a crowd of "beautiful people" lined around the block waiting to enter. Young men and women were spread across the grass enjoying the sun, the air streaked with arcs of footballs and Frisbees. And she thought to herself again, *Why?* More than 750,000 people have visited the museum, she tells the audience, 4,200 a day. Thirty-eight percent have been Jewish; 48 percent have been Christian.

"What is it that attracts these people?" she asked. "It's not the rock-and-roll museum. What's in it for all those people that would make them want to visit this again? Why is it in America? Why in the world would Jewish people want it?" There are, she noted, no museums celebrating the destruction of African-American slaves, no permanent national museum devoted to the massacre of the American Indian.

Having presented all that she didn't know, she moved into what she did know, a description of the museum itself, beginning with it's neoclassical façade, a deliberate false front, a lie that reflects the entire horror itself— "architecture designed as a metaphor," she said. Then from inside the museum, slide after slide flashed on the screen in arresting, gigantic detail—"These are terrible pictures; I can't *not* show them." Nancy had turned teacher, leading the student body through this catalogue of horrors, stressing the ordinariness of the objects, shoes and photographs, the homely details of ordinary people who were stripped and ravaged, gunned down in rows and incinerated. She was completely frank, completely objective. Her voice, clear and even.

Then the final slide appeared and remained on screen. It was a photograph of one of the tablets in the final chamber of the museum, an area of meditation called Hall of Remembrance, and Nancy read the words engraved on the tablet now projected on screen: "Only guard yourself and guard your soul carefully, lest you forget the things your eyes saw. . . ."

I stared at the projection reading word by word to myself along with the bouncing ball of Nancy's voice, a deep melody of poetry. ". . . unless these things depart your heart all the days of your life, and you shall make them known to your—"

But, here, in mid-sentence Nancy halted. The spell of her delivery broken unexpectedly, I turned to look at her, along with everyone else, to see that her head and her shoulders were twisted around toward the curtain behind her. She had begun to weep. I turned back to the screen to see which word had stopped in her throat. ". . . children," the line continued, "and your children's children."

And you shall make them known to your children. She had, wordlessly and on view for the entire school, answered the question she claimed she couldn't. To bear witness for the children, her children. And it was clear then, as she collected herself and returned her gaze to the hundreds of children's faces staring back at her—still and gripped by the surprise of her tears—that she was not referring to her own, grown children, but rather to them. *They* are her children. They are why she stood before them, fanning images of horror, then turning her back to hide her tears—they are why she is a teacher. Nancy had told me she knew she was a teacher when she realized that, she said, "I loved *them,*" that this was "a *gift* from *God* that has nothing to do with me." Here were those words in action.

When Nancy's voice returned to her, she finished the line she'd begun and the presentation ended.

Dead silence. Applause was not right, here. Kerry dismissed the assembly and the boys quietly filed out. Nancy descended the steps and sat in the first seat of the assembly, head bowed, solitary and depleted. Hawley had been in his usual seat for the presentation, the last seat in the senior

229

section. He strode immediately toward Nancy, crouched beside her, and cupped her shoulders in his arm.

About midday, I approached Nancy to comment on her address, and then mentioned that I noticed she and Rick talked for an unusually long time afterward. In fact, I was very curious about this; they had sat in the empty auditorium for an hour. Her response was brief.

"He healed me," she said. "He's a healer."

Wanting to know what students thought of Nancy's Holocaust Museum presentation I spoke with, among others, Eugene.

"It's as genuine as a presentation like that can be," he said. "I adore it when people have such genuine feeling. It's quite touching."

On the following Saturday, Nancy sat down to write Hawley a letter. The letter is dated December 11. She would give it to him on January 23, about a week after the love-poems class. It's only half finished, but she can't wait any longer. The letter is her attempt at an answer to the headmaster, a response to their conversation, and a response to his speech. To let that speech go unanswered, she said, "would have been disrespectful of the Jews who came before me and protected me." Her letter is also her hope to bridge the cavern that opened in her this year. It would arrive stapled to twenty pages of Xeroxes, support material from four scholarly texts on the Jews, the Holocaust, anti-Semitism, and also an editorial from the *New York Times* on the issue of prayer in schools.

> Dear Rick,
> I recognize that my feelings and attitudes in recent discussions of the place of religion in the University School community have not been fully understood (even by me initially) and that they have given pain and offense to people I esteem and care for. . . .
> While I cannot share your belief in the divinity of Jesus Christ, I share your deep commitment to the values expressed by Jesus in the Sermon on the Mount. I share your admiration of the thousands of people who have practiced those values as individuals throughout history and who—openly and at great risk—put their beliefs into actions during the Holocaust. How then could I ever have offended people such as you with the statement that I feared

'good Christians'? I should not have spoken as I did, but I believed that you, who share with me a common core of education, would understand what I meant by that term. I should not have spoken so ironically; I should have realized the pain I would cause you personally—but I am as shocked as you that you have not understood my meaning.

Nancy's letter, like her presentation, was both scholarly and emotional and here she was careful to keep these two spheres separate. Her premise was simple and forms the fulcrum on which their differences balanced. A contemporary Christian can be a Christian, can talk about his or her Christianity, she wrote, "in an ahistorical frame of reference." This is not so for a Jew. She, and all the Jews she knows, Nancy wrote, "cannot talk of themselves as Jews except in a collective sense and an historical context."

The Holocaust, she continued, was not an isolated event, and she cites scholars who have argued that it was, in fact, "the culmination of centuries of Christianity." She illustrated this in proper scholarly fashion by citing texts and ticking off a list of evidence, dating from the Apostles, through the anti-Semitic writings of Martin Luther—founder of Protestantism—the Inquisition, and on up to the Holocaust. No shortage of evidence here.

When you are appalled at my reaction, please think of what it feels like to be a Jew with a history—to know that every time Jews felt safe, felt a part of the mainstream, felt they had achieved equality and understanding with the dominant Christian culture, they were destroyed. . . . Whenever I travel in Europe, I am aware of a double consciousness. I am at Chartres, overwhelmed by its beauty, and I remember how the Crusaders massacred the Jews on their way. I am in Florence—and near the Duomo, I see the bullet marks on the synagogue when the Jews were rounded up there. . . . I read Chaucer—and I read a tale that is a diatribe against the Jews. I read Shakespeare and note that one of the ingredients in the witches' brew in *Macbeth* is 'liver of a blaspheming Jew.' I attend last week's concert of *Das Rheingold,* and I hear in my head Wagner's vicious diatribes against the Jews. I read T. S. Eliot and have to endure his anti-Semitism in order to love his poetry. . . .

What I realized after talking with you is that a Christian is not burdened by that omnipresent sense of history. Am I wrong? I somehow thought—when I spoke—that you would understand my consciousness and understand my deepest fears. But I don't think you can, and perhaps the gulf is so great that we cannot understand each other. I hope that is not true. In terms of any offense I have given to people I care for, I deeply apologize. But I cannot apologize for wishing you to understand a history that will not let go of my soul.

On January 24, Nancy is about to give her class a test—the boys must identify three writers, Milton, Shakespeare, and Donne, from three passages of writing and analyze those passages. She tears off sheets from a legal pad and hands them out. "And I don't want any talking," she says. "If I see anyone talking I'll take your test away. That's not because I think you're going to cheat, it's because I don't want any talking." She then hands out the Xeroxed test. Nick Zinn is bouncing and fidgeting in his seat. He can't wait to get at this thing. All morning, he'd been carrying around three scraps of writing from Milton, Donne, and Shakespeare, thrusting them at people and asking them to identify who wrote which one. I excuse myself from class but Nancy stops me once I'm in the hall. As the boys get down to work, Nancy stands in the doorway, half closing the door behind her.

She had been telling me for a month that she was writing to Hawley and there in the hall, she hands me a copy, stapled to the support material. She has apparently given the letter and Xeroxes to a few other faculty. "This letter took me *weeks* to write," she says. "I gave it to him yesterday. *Today,* I get his response." She pinches the letter between thumb and index finger of her fist, sheets of five-by-seven stationery with "Office of The Headmaster" printed at the top and filled with minute black ballpoint script. She presses the letter to her sternum and says, "This is the kind of thing he does—he *binds* me to him with steel *hoops.*"

I can't tell if she's angry or glad.

Three periods later, Paul enters his Western Civ class, sets on the table his books and papers—among which is today's assignment, "The Allegory of the Cave"—and drapes his green tweed jacket over a chair.

He no longer dreads this period as he had in the fall. The ninth graders are now midway through the year and have hit their stride; and while the winter break ended nearly a month ago, they remain refreshed and energetic. All but one, that is, Shawntae, about whom Paul is worried. Tim, a capable student, had been easily distracted in the fall by his classmates, didn't finish his homework, and failed tests he should have passed easily. But after half a year working with teacher apprentice Lisa during free periods, Tim has learned how to organize his notes and keep up with the daily work, which Paul now says is "flawless." With the improvement in his writing, he's near the top of his class by the end of January. Kevin, who at the beginning of the year promised to be Paul's archenemy, still hates Western Civ and occasionally causes an uproar in class—staining his entire tongue deep blue, for example, by chewing a pen too long and distending his tongue for all to see and laugh at—but has settled down somewhat and has been doing his work. Paul sends a report to Kevin's parents that begins with the word "bravo." Then there's Matt, whom Paul calls the "light" of the classroom. Matt works at a level of complexity that is very near Paul's. But Shawntae, a giant of a boy who just wishes he'd quit growing, continues to fail test after test, rarely completes his homework, and often simply loses his books.

At the midwinter interim report meeting, other faculty had described similar stories about Shawntae. These report meetings occur six times a year—two-hour meetings for each of the four classes during which most students are discussed, though problem cases are accorded the most time and talk. The students have been given the last Friday of January off to make time for these meetings, and the faculty, having had a bite of Danish and a mug of coffee laid decorously on tables on the upstairs landing, gathered at 8:15 in the library around tables pushed together to form one large island; class grades are handed out; discussion is typically moderated by the dean of each class, who names the student then looks to the student's sponsor to begin discussion.

"As you know from Kerry's memo," Margaret Mason said, opening the meeting, "we're not going to be talking *only* about kids who are giant concerns."

This was acknowledged by a few stifled groans from faculty. The meetings are long even when they talk only of student problems, and now the new director wants every single boy discussed, no matter what their status is. When I asked Kerry about this new mandate, he told me, "Can you imagine what a parent would say if they found out that their son had never even been mentioned in these meetings?" For Kerry, it's an ethical consideration—each boy deserves to be mentioned, if only to inform all faculty of a boy's solid work. While the faculty is quietly dreading Kerry's directive, none seem to disagree with its reason.

Margaret ran through the class list alphabetically, eventually reaching Paul's main worry. "Jim?" she says, looking to Jim Garrett. "Shawntae?"

"I am very concerned about Shawntae," Jim said, "as we all are." He uses severe "avoidance techniques," Jim noted and told Margaret that he wanted to meet with Shawntae during the break and also keep him out of the gym, where Shawn spends most free periods instead of studying.

Paul cleared his throat and said, "Shawn is the perfect example of someone who protects himself by not working. If he doesn't do the work he can't fail. There is no reason he couldn't do 70 or 80 work." Paul announced his current grade of 51 percent.

Rollin Devere, Shawn's Spanish teacher, said Shawn has "a bad attitude." " 'I'm tired of working, I'm tired of US,' " Devere imitated, then added, "One thing about him is when he *does* do his homework, I try to compliment him and he turns and walks away. He will not accept a compliment."

Paul said, "There's very little chance of his passing Civ."

Another teacher said, "His entire freshman *year* is in danger."

If Shawn doesn't pass Paul's Western Civ course, he'll have to take it again next year. Unless, that is, he fails other classes as well, in which case Shawn might not have a next year at this school. Margaret finished her notes on Shawn regarding problems and what she and other faculty intend to do to amend the situation. Shaking her head, she told her note pad, "Shawn's a *big* worry," then looked to her list for the next student.

"OK gentlemen, we're going to be discussing the 'Allegory of the Cave' today," Paul says and asks if everyone did their reading.

Mild rumbling surfaces along the right ranks of the classroom and Shawn says to Jonah beside him, "If I had a choice between a *Sports Illustrated* or a book, I *wouldn't* choose the book."

Paul hears this and says to Shawn, "Ah, that's what it's about."

"I think it's cool," says Jonah, "but I already heard the story."

"OK, we're going to have a discussion today," Paul continues, "and I want you to see if you can figure out for yourselves what the 'Allegory of the Cave' is about. I'm not going to say anything, I'm just going to be a silent observer." Paul normally sits on top of the table at the front of the room, swinging his legs as he conducts class, but today he takes a seat and tilts against the blackboard. The class is silent.

Paul pushes his glasses to the top of his formidable nose, waiting.

Hen, sitting straight in his chair, raises his hand high.

"You don't need to raise your hand. Hen?"

"Um," Hen says softly, "I think the light was freedom."

A brief spattering of comments follows and then nothing, silence. Thirty seconds goes by. Sixty. Lots of throat clearing. Many of the boys are still winding down from a bracing after-lunch snowball fight.

"The conversation seems to have died," says Paul. "What should you do to get it started again?"

Again, Hen speaks softly. "I think the shadows are what they think freedom is. And the light is freedom."

Shawn says, "You could probably call it self-slavery. They can't escape from the mind state."

"What if this light is knowledge?" Jonah asks.

Shawn asks, "Is it wisdom or knowledge? Knowledge is math, science, literature. Which is it?" And to Jonah beside him, "What do you think?"

"I think you read too much *Sports Illustrated,*" says Jonah.

Shawn smiles his giant's smile and shakes his head No, meaning that would be impossible.

"All right, guys," says Paul, standing to resume control of the class. "Good job. You got the main ideas. What is this story about? What is reality for the prisoners?"

"The shadows," says Jonah.

"Good," says Paul. "It's sort of like a primitive version of the movies. Perhaps this is the first movie theater. It's like sitting in a movie theater your whole life. Or reading *Sports Illustrated.*" Shawn smiles. "Imagine if you watched soap operas and thought it was true, you thought it was the news. You might wait with bated breath to find out if Joanna marries Rodriguez. But then someone shows you the news. You'd probably stop watching the soap operas."

Paul leads the conversation to the idea of the sun. Jonah is skeptical.

"But the sun goes away," he says.

Paul chuckles and says, "Yeah, but say they come out in the daytime. Why is the sun the most real thing for Plato?"

Jonah has been puzzling this out for himself and suddenly blurts out, "Why would he stop at the sun? Why wouldn't he think that the sun wasn't just another fire?"

"*Good question,* Jonah. *Excellent* question. You should ask Dr. Hawley that. I asked him last year. I don't think there's an answer."

Paul is pacing the room. "Why would Plato think this chair is not real?"

"It's a figment of your imagination?" Shawn asks.

"No," says Paul. "If it were my imagination, I could drop it on my foot and it wouldn't hurt."

"It can be changed?" asks Jonah.

"Very good. Permanence is in both Plato and Buddhism. Remember the chocolate bar. Why isn't a chocolate bar real for Buddhists? Right, because you eat them and then they're finished—you can't always be eating them. This chair." Paul places his hands on the backrest of the chair abandoned in the center of the room. "It was once chemicals and metal and plastic. But it will rust and corrode and fall apart. Right now it's made up of molecules which are constantly moving. Plato thought that this couldn't be really real if it changes."

Tim, who's been engaged but silent the entire class, says, "Then *people* aren't real. *I'm* not real."

"You're not real," says Paul. Tim's mouth hangs open—*whoa*—and he looks away from Paul as though this idea is going to require some digesting. "You're soul might be real. Let's stop here," Paul says abruptly. He doesn't buy Platonic form, things hovering cosmically in space, and he returns to the text. "Who is the person who first goes out of the cave? What would Plato call him? Or her, because Plato believed it could be a man or woman."

"A philosopher," says Jonah.

Paul says good and then moves into a creative riff on how the cave allegory can represent the process of education and explain why going to school might be painful but good for you.

"So life is learning," says Shawn.

"Yes, life is this process, and you'll keep rising and rising." Shawn, excited by the discussion, begins bouncing in his seat and talking with Jonah. "Hold on Shawn," Paul says. "Would you want to go back down into the cave?"

He settles and says, "No."

"Why would you?"

"To enlighten others?" Hen asks.

Shawn asks, "Wouldn't it be *scary* for them?"

"Yes," says Paul. "Socrates, as you know, thought democracy was the best form of government. But Plato did not think that. What did Plato believe was the best form of government?"

John calls out, "A philosopher monarchy?"

"Very good," says Paul and writes "philosopher king" on the board. "Plato believed in a philosopher king and the government would be called an enlightened monarchy."

Paul is exuberant throughout the period, even after the bell rings and the boys reload their backpacks and hustle to their next class. This material interests him but it's the last of it that does. "After ancient Greece, I'm not much interested in anything till about 1850," he tells me (Neitzsche was born in 1849). I tell Paul I enjoyed the class but was surprised he had implied that people have souls, since Paul himself does not believe in immortal souls. A look of alarm strikes Paul. "Did I?" he asks. *"Oh."* Paul recovers quickly though and tells me, well, it's only fair to stay in keeping with the philosopher they're studying.

The class had grown lively after a sluggish start, and Paul is happy. He's buoyed further by the anticipation of graduate school next year, when *he* can be the student and somebody else will teach. Yet even with these prospects—a short four months of school followed by a mysterious future combined with the heady dose of romance (his friendship with a woman who teaches at a Catholic school has recently blossomed into something significantly more than friendship)—the unbroken weeks of school wear him down. The paper cuts continue to drain.

Just as it had during the fall term, pressure builds. And now it's intensified by the Cleveland winter. Crawling out of bed into a cold room when it's still dark and returning home in the dark is depressing enough, but this year winter is unusually harsh, with record sub-zero temperatures throughout January. Weeks without an extended break allow the stress no release. This was the tone of winter, similar to that of the fall but with one additional element that proved more elusive than I had at first realized. The headmaster.

In the first term, as the pressure increased, the headmaster became the location of the pressure point and release valve. This had happened, it seemed, coincidentally just before the end of the trimester. When it happened again at the end of the second trimester, I realized that it was more than coincidence. Maybe it was necessary. Maybe inevitable. While the corporeal headmaster was only occasionally in evidence—here in assembly, there at lunch, strolling through the hall on the way to philosophy, stooping to pick up scraps of paper on the stairs' landing—in another sense he never left the school. He was present like garlic in a stew, not always distinct or identifiable but permeating everything.

Jonah had delighted Paul by addressing a key weakness in Plato's cave allegory. Why should a philosopher, of all people, accept the sun as the ultimate light source? Why wouldn't a questioning philosopher wonder whether this sun was but another fire casting grander and more dangerous shadows? But more interesting to me was that Paul had lit up at Jonah's observation: *"Good question,* Jonah. *Excellent question.* You should ask Dr. Hawley that."

Hawley was in that room as surely as Paul was. Hawley was the fixed point against which all things were measured.

When Nick Zinn, waging his own struggle with the headmaster, had told Paul about the little-voices class, Paul had found me to ask if it was true. I can't say he wore an expression of evil interest when he asked, but there was clearly mischievous delight. Paul, though, is among the kindest souls at the school. During the religions and ethics brouhaha, he had expressed genuine concern for the headmaster after he told me that he intended to give Hawley his good-Christian test.

"What's your good-Christian test?" I asked.

"I'm going to ask him if he's a good Christian," Paul said. "Then I'm going to ask him for his coat. He's got lots of nice coats."

Paul clearly wanted to prove the headmaster a hypocrite who preached Sermon-on-the-Mount ethics but didn't practice them.

"What if he *does* give you his coat?" I asked.

"I'll take it downtown and give it to the poor. And the next day I'll ask him for his coat." Paul smiled, knowing that Hawley couldn't possibly give him all the coats he had and said you shouldn't claim to be a good Christian if you don't follow the rules. "Actually," Paul said, pinching his jacket sleeve, *"I* need a nice jacket. Look at this thing I wear." He pauses. "Maybe I should ask him for his tie, too."

Later, when I asked Paul if he'd followed through with his test, he looked sad, and said, No. It wasn't right, he said. The headmaster's addresses to the school had become filled with references to deaths of friends, former students, former employees, their tone persistently dark throughout winter. Hawley was visibly upset. "Maybe Rick's having a really bad year," Paul said.

So Paul didn't feel malice toward the headmaster and could be concerned for him, but there was always the headmaster's presence, appearing and vanishing like the ghost in *Hamlet,* and this Paul fought. He was always searching for weaknesses in Hawley, scrutinizing the sophist armor for chinks; he was, when he approached me hungrily for details on Hawley's little-voices class, even waiting for traces of madness.

Nancy too felt the intensifying stress of the long winter trimester. During the first week of February, one week after the steel hoop of Hawley's letter to her, she told me she would not be returning to the school next year. The choice had nothing to do with the religions and ethics debate—she felt that there had been an agenda, but that Hawley had dropped it when he felt the reaction of the faculty—nor with any criticisms she had of the school. She was tired. She wanted to read and to write. She wanted to spend more time with her husband. She remained devoted to the headmaster despite their differences which were, in the end, a rich source of intellectual food for her. But her decision was final. She would let him say nothing to dissuade her. This was to be her last year as a teacher.

I don't know if Hawley fathered swarms of little families in the school. Demands for his time were constant and intense. Yet the intimate triumvirate of Hawley, Nancy, and Paul remained in my mind a distinct family of sorts, complete with familial care and stress. Paul, the son, thrusting out, straining against Hawley for his own independence, always distancing himself from Hawley without releasing him completely; Nancy, the wife-mother who reached out with enveloping concern—healer and caretaker. At one point, she was so worried that the differences between Paul and Hawley would become permanent, she tried to organize a lunch to re-bind them, but Paul bluntly resisted. Hawley in Paul's mind could demolish him. Hawley always won.

While Paul battled the headmaster along intellectual and ethical fronts, Nancy did so along intellectual and emotional ones, wrestling for more than a month with her letter which, on one level, was not so much an effort to win an argument or even rebut a resolution; it was rather a quest for mutual understanding and a healing of wounds. Hawley, the moral absolutist, was omnipresent in Nancy's classroom exactly as he was in Paul's. When, during the fall, Nancy arrived at an apt line in *Hamlet,* she recited it, "Nothing good or bad, but thinking makes it so," and said, "Tell *that* to Dr. Hawley. How's that for relativism?"

Hawley was never far from anyone's mind.

13

The end of winter seemed like a good time to make a request of the headmaster. The months of January and February had been busy, but again, the busyness seemed smooth industry—Kris Fletcher writing gloomy poetry in the library, Nick Zinn pounding out letters to the headmaster, Eugene Gurarie working long into the night on his quartet for violins, cello, and viola, seniors awaiting news from colleges—as the snow swirled through dark afternoons across the lake and into leafless woods. With days clicking by routinely, with the headmaster feeling headmasterly and happy ("Maybe I'm missing something," he said, "but everything's going beautifully"), I asked if I might spend one full day with him, to see what exactly he did during a normal working day. Hawley didn't seem much to like the idea. He said, "Hm," looked down, then explained that he really didn't do anything worth watching. But he said sure, if that's what I wanted. It was the last week in February and Ann and I chose a date at random, Thursday, March 3.

"Beautifully." I didn't know if February was in fact going beautifully, or if this was again an example of Hawley's relentless optimism. I had asked him how school was because Ann had told me there was a good deal of stress in the administration offices, owing to the fact that it was contract time. According to Ann, this is inevitably a prickly stage in the year of the school. Teachers' egos are intertwined with their salary, one starkly literal indication of their worth. The size of raises—about three-and-a-half percent this year—can differ from one teacher to the next; this increases stress. It's easy to forget that, what with all the beneficent work undertaken here and the fundamental nobility of the teaching profession, an independent school is a business and must make financial decisions accordingly. People's feelings don't come first in such matters. And yet, there's so much talk of this place being a community or a family, employees can be lulled into expecting treatment that's more familial than corporate. Contracts are sandpaper to the baby's-bottom sensitivity of the place.

One teacher won't be receiving a contract. Evan, who had introduced himself to me on the first day of school, the big bear of a boy in his second year teaching, a teacher who could, reciting mellifluous passages from *The Great Gatsby,* rock a classroom's walls, would not be coming back. This was not unexpected. He'd been told he was here to fill the seat of a teacher on sabbatical, and while the school would be needing to replace Nancy, Evan, though a graduate of the school as well as its teacher-apprentice program, didn't have a Ph.D. nor the years of experience that might have weighed in his favor. But what rankled him and his colleagues in the English department was that the school had delayed confirming that he would not receive a contract, stringing him along, some felt. Again, the business-family conflict flared.

Jim Garrett also sat on needles, many felt far longer than necessary. The head football coach was leaving and Jim, along with two dozen applicants from outside the school, had made a strong push for the job, one he desperately wanted. It seemed an easy choice. The school for several years had brought in an outsider as head coach, and wanted to return to the custom of having one of its own teachers lead what is something of a flagship sport for the school. Moreover, Garrett was from a football family—his father had been a Cleveland Browns coach; his brother Jason, class of '84, had this year taken his first snaps as a professional quarterback for the Dallas Cowboys, for which brother Judd is a running back; and brother John works as a scout for the Tampa Bay Buccaneers. Jim Garrett, furthermore, was married to the daughter of Geoff Morton, a former director of the school and now assistant to the headmaster who'd been with the school more than a quarter century. This, though, could not have worked in Jim's favor; his wife was no indication of his talents as a coach. If he did not get the job, it would be a professional setback, a personal disappointment, and would force him to reevaluate his future with the school, of which he'd till now felt very much a part. The field was eventually narrowed to three, but the scuttlebutt was that Jim wouldn't be tapped.

This was the nature of business at the end of February. The configuration of the next school year was created now.

A more immediate, pressing, and unpleasant situation was bearing on the headmaster regarding Geoff Morton, his friend, the man who had Hawley hired twenty-six years ago. Geoff, a tower of a man with giant hands, fierce black eyebrows, and gray-black hair, had given virtually his entire adult life to the school as a teacher, a director, coach, and a director of summer programs. But his own life blood at the school was his work as tennis coach. The US tennis team is a perennial contender in state championships (it would win another this year) and traveled throughout the country to high schools, colleges, and universities to compete. It was Geoff's baby, the passion of his work.

During last year's spring break the tennis team, as usual, trucked down to Florida to begin formal practice. One evening, two players returned to their rooms after curfew to find Geoff not only worried but furious. Geoff is known to have a temper along the lines of a blast furnace, which, combined with his physical power, makes him something of an unpredictable presence. When the boys returned, Geoff exploded, hit both boys, bloodied some lips, and seriously damaged feelings. The incident was reported in the local papers, and eventually a lawsuit was filed by the family of one of the boys, who left the school immediately. The other boy, Andy Kim, stayed.

In the throes of this personal and professional fiasco, Geoff publicly apologized to the school and resigned as tennis coach.

When I brought the matter up, Hawley was, I think, delighted to tell me that advice from lawyers prevented his discussing anything about the event.

He seemed glad to tell me this because the whole thing was painful for him. The situation was nasty and complicated and leagues away from what the business of school ought to be, but here it was, in his face, and there was little he could do about it. Geoff was a personal friend, but the thing that made it most troubling was that Geoff did so much for the school—the school was his life, which he shared with his wife, Emily, who worked in the administrative offices. Of all the things Geoff had done for the school, perhaps the most significant was his contributions on behalf of black students at US. Geoff had done more than anyone in the school to smooth what is almost always a difficult road for African-American students. He had been their chief advocate, counselor, and mentor. Most recently, he initiated a program called REACH, which scours the Cleveland public schools for talented young black kids and enrolls them, if they are willing, in a free three-year summer program at the school. The idea was to locate bright inner-city boys before the streets and deteriorating, increasingly violent public schools consumed them.

The last public word on the matter came from the editorial pages of *The Plain Dealer,* which had covered the story. Each week, the editors run a "cheers" and "jeers" column acknowledging the city's weekly do-gooders and ne'er-do-wells. The paper commended Geoff's resignation from the tennis team, one of the best in the country and largely of his own making, but it did not forgive what he'd done, sending him a "jeer" and concluding that there is "no place for them [his actions] in coaching." When Geoff asks to return as assistant tennis coach the entire incident resurfaces.

So while the business of school progressed smoothly outside Hawley's office, inside there had to be stress. On March 2, when I'd gone to the headmaster about some questions less important than what was transpiring inside his office, he wore the pained grimace I'd seen during the Soltis affair and religions and ethics meetings, and he apologized for being distracted. I'd arrived after two back-to-back closed-door meetings, one with Geoff, and one with John Murray, the current tennis coach who also wanted Geoff's return. Outside Hawley's office Ann sat at her desk, relieved that at least the first stage of business was done—contracts would go out in today's mail.

None of this should have been a surprise to a man who's spent his entire career at this school. Perhaps this *was* "beautifully." On the other hand, maybe he was trying to hide the roots of the *Sturm und Drang* because he didn't want it written about. Hawley was unfailingly, maddeningly insistent that all was sunny. It seemed, at times, that he simply chose not to look at what upset him but rather only at that which he liked and with which he agreed. All *was* going beautifully—by executive order.

I arrive early on March 3, the day I'm scheduled to spend with the headmaster. I stroll through the long entrance lobby, enter the faculty lounge, and hang my coat on a hook. Deb Nash sits in a chair in the corner, blocked from view by the morning paper. Dick McCrea is filling a coffee mug. As I begin to head out, Deb lowers the paper like a sleuth staking a hotel lobby in a Bogart movie—just her eyes are visible. I stop. The paper lowers more and Deb says, "Just *walk* around!" If I could have stopped more than I already had, I would have. *"Feel* the *vibes,"* she says.

"The vibes," I say. When Deb lifts the screen of her paper between us, I ask if she might be more specific. The paper drops and she says, "Some things can't be spoken in public."

Behind me, Dick McCrea is pacing with his mug of coffee. I turn to him. He issues a happy growl and says, "Stay away from the women!"

Kerry is on stage early planning morning assembly as Vivaldi's *Four Seasons* pumps through the speakers and students mill. Mike Cohen, dressed in a tie-dyed T-shirt and jean cut-offs, approaches the podium and says, "Mr. Brennan, I need to get into the music room." Kerry leaves with Mike, fishing for his keys. There is to be some sort of special assembly.

At about 8:05, the headmaster arrives and stands against the wall on the far side of the auditorium as he often does, waiting for assembly to begin. Kerry finds him there and does some wide-eyed talking that the headmaster listens to with interest and then rolls his eyes, apparently concerned, and stretches his chin forward as though his collar is too tight.

The assembly features four Davey Fellows, boys who are working independently on creative-writing projects. Kris Fletcher reads from his short story, "Den of the Metalheads"; Jason Koo reads one sentence from his baseball novel-in-progress, a comic sentence of Joycean length; Tyler Doggett reads a long poem, half of which seems to be in French; and Mike Cohen and Nick Rajkovich act one scene from Mike's play about counselors at a summer camp.

After assembly, I tail the headmaster to the faculty lounge, eager to begin the day. He sits with a cup of coffee and talks about the Davey Fellow presentations, which "interested and delighted me," he says. Moments later, Ann sticks her head in the door and reminds Hawley that he has a nine o'clock meeting. Hawley hustles out of the lounge.

He has evidently forgotten the plan. I remain seated. Chuck Seelbach is hovered over schoolwork as usual; others read the paper. It's very quiet.

Try as I might, I cannot pick up any meaningful *vibes*. I feel rather like an illiterate American plunked suddenly into the middle of a Chekhov drama, oblivious to the nuance of the situation.

The lounge remains deadly quiet, so I head up to the administration wing to find out what has happened to my plan. I turn the corner heading toward Hawley's office. Ann, standing outside her doorway, sees me coming and immediately begins sweeping her arms at me like a referee signaling an incomplete pass.

I go to her office anyway. Before I can speak, Ann says, *"Yes, Frances knew* about the memo before it was handed out."

Ah ha! *"What* memo?" I ask, shrewdly.

Ann halts. "Oh," she says. "I guess I didn't put one in your box."

TO: Faculty

FR: Rick and Kerry

We're pleased to announce that Pat Aliazzi has agreed to become the next Wean Librarian and, blessedly, he'll also do some teaching. Clearly, Pat's academic and bibliographic interests will serve us all well as he continues to advance the worthy mission of what is sure to be a library that supports our work in all academic quarters. Of course, it will be on the peerless work of Polly Cohen that Pat will build and while we will have ample time to celebrate her contributions this spring, Polly deserves our gratitude for her wise and wonderful stewardship over the past twenty years.

Such were the things that tsunamis were made of.

The memo explains both Deb Nash's and Dick McCrea's cryptic comments in the faculty lounge. Frances Hanscom, for years assistant to Polly Cohen, the departing librarian, wanted the job and had put in the work that would seem to make her the obvious and easy choice. But, surprising everyone, the headmaster has named an eccentric history teacher to the post. The history teacher, who has been on sabbatical all year, is by all accounts a brilliant scholar and one of the best teachers in the school, but also a notoriously difficult person who doesn't seem to like people, and who has no background in library science. But the most contentious aspect of the headmaster's choice is the new librarian's sex. Pat Aliazzi is a man. This is seen as both a professional slight to Frances—who does have a master's in library science and has logged years of devoted service with the school— and also an affront to all the women in this boys' world, who feel they regularly get the short end of the stick. There are few women at this school and fewer in positions of authority; now there would be fewer still.

While every woman at the school had a strong reaction to the announcement, Deb Nash's response best symbolized the whole. She was so furious she exclaimed that this was the most ridiculous thing she'd ever seen in her life and began to cry, and when Kerry walked into the faculty lounge, she had some short words with him. That's why Kerry immediately found Hawley in assembly. It seems, he told the headmaster, that there has been a volatile reaction to the appointment of Aliazzi.

Discussion of the memo dominates the day among adults. In Deb

Nash's office, there is talk of little else. By mid-morning several women have gathered there, venting and comparing notes with Deb, who believes that this is a "slap in the face" to women, that it "belittles" them, and smacks of the male hierarchy of the place. Deb tells Nancy Lerner of her emotional response. "I started *crying*," she says. "I probably shouldn't have." But Deb thinks again and says, *"No. Why shouldn't I?"*

"Professional decorum," Nancy answers sternly.

"Men rant and rave," Deb says, "women cry. Why say one is all right and one isn't?" Deb then explains she almost considered staging a women's walkout in protest.

Back in Hawley's office an unrelated tribunal has gathered for the nine o'clock meeting. Jim Garrett, prospective football coach, is pleading his case to Hawley, Kerry, Geoff Morton, and Tom Callow, head of the athletic department. After Ann and I talked about the memo, I reminded her that this was the day I got to see what it was a headmaster did, and pointed to my name penciled into her daily calendar.

Ann glanced at the day's schedule and told me Hawley had several important meetings scheduled, none of which I'd be allowed to observe.

And so the day proceeds. The only time I see Hawley is in philosophy class, during which he seems completely untouched by today's fomentation. But after class, as he heads back to his office, he looks at me and says, "This is a day when it's impossible for *someone* not to feel terrible."

When I mention this to Ann, she says, "Yeah, and you know who it's going to be? Rick."

The students are for the most part oblivious to what is going on among the faculty, but there is one bit of mischief that lends a comic dimension to the upheaval surrounding the appointment of the new librarian. During morning classes, a freshman steals onto the roof of the school, where ceiling-level windows look down onto the group study area of the library, drops his trousers and begins mooning all the people below, pressing his cheeks flat against the glass. This is not, apparently, an editorial on the library discussion; minutes earlier, the anonymous cheeks had said a flattened hello to an art class in a different part of the building.

Once again, a sudden melee had erupted one week before trimester exams and the approaching two-week spring break. Margie and Kerry hustled to isolate the mooner, the women at the school stewed, and Hawley staggered through his nine-round day like an aging George Foreman, absorbing five body blows for every one he landed.

While the football-coach meeting with Jim Garrett was surprisingly enjoyable for the headmaster—because he had led the discussion to the subject of values, the values of winning versus the values of work, competition, and sportsmanship on the field, and perhaps also because he suspected what the outcome would be—the day got sad after that. Deb Nash, coincidentally in the administrative offices while Hawley was between meetings, told the headmaster what was on her mind; this led to an angry exchange, bitter words from the headmaster, and more furious tears from Deb. This was followed by a meeting with the three tennis team co-captains, who demanded a more complete explanation of the Geoff Morton situation and asked for his reinstatement. The headmaster, able to confide neither his personal feelings nor the complete rationale for the decision, could say only that this was his directive and it would have to stand. His next meeting was a one-on-one with Geoff's wife, Emily, who, distraught over the decision and fighting for her husband, also fell into tears. The headmaster then met with a senior's mother; he had agreed to edit and comment on her manuscript about recovering teenage addicts. (Hawley is regularly asked by friends, current students, former students, and parents to read manuscripts, a request he never refuses.) The school day was nearly over. Phil Thornton stopped by the office to discuss matters in the alumni office; Hawley ran down the events of the day for Phil, with whom he spends a lot of time throughout the year traveling and raising money for the school. Shortly after ninth period, when boys headed home or to practice and the school cleared, Hawley met for three hours with a woman in charge of developing, and now invigorating, the entire lower-school curriculum.

It was 6:15 when that last meeting concluded. Kerry remained in his office working. Kerry briefed Hawley on the mooning incident (the boy had been caught; the student discipline committee and the deans would convene tomorrow) and some staffing wrinkles. Emotionally exhausted, Hawley invited Kerry back to his house for dinner. Kerry accepted gladly, having just enough time before driving to Laurel for its production of *Fiddler on the Roof.* During dinner, John Murray, the current tennis coach, phoned. He had just returned from a long run to clear his head and needed to say something to the headmaster. He had been petitioning the faculty, he confessed, asking them to sign on behalf of Geoff; a petition, that is, to reverse a decision the headmaster had already made clear. John explained that he felt rotten about it. Many teachers were for Geoff's reinstatement; many were strongly opposed. John felt that he was dividing the faculty and planned to stop. That was all. He just wanted the headmaster to know about it. Hawley told him not to worry; he was sure that John's motives were good, and certainly not bad.

At 7:30, with Kerry gone, the phone rang again. It was Ann.

"I *dare* you to give me bad news, Ann," he said.

No, she answered. He had been scheduled to spend tomorrow morning at the lower school to discuss contracts with any teachers who had problems, and Ann had forgotten to tell him that the meetings had been pushed back. Tomorrow morning was clear.

I saw little of this, and what I did see was not pleasant. As usual, the most buoyant presence in the school was the boys who were currently anticipating exams and delighting in the mooning incident. But teachers were troubled and tired. Bad feelings coursed through the school. Everywhere I turned, it seemed, secretive meetings were under way. My snooping around didn't help. Adults seemed to bristle with suspicion when I entered a room. When it became clear that my request to spend a day with the headmaster was an impossibility, I began to wonder what it was that people didn't want me to know. Confronted with suspicion, I became suspicious. What others didn't want me to know, I figured, was exactly what I should be after. That Hawley had almost blithely accepted the idea of my observing the inner workings of his day only to ignore it completely, and fail even to explain the reasons for a change in plans, heightened my mistrust. What exactly was so bad that not only should I be prevented from seeing it but I should also not know why I was being stonewalled? Something was rotten here. Hawley gave eloquent lip-service to openness and honesty and truth, but when it came time to follow through on an agreement, he ignored it.

I left the school that day—no doubt like Geoff Morton, Jim Garrett, and fifty faculty expecting their sandpaper in the mail—troubled and a little annoyed, but sensing again that, in the end, reactions, as opposed to events themselves, had illuminated true motives.

I return the next day. The school is standing where it always is.

The morning proceeds as usual. Mike Cohen, who yesterday played out a scene on stage from his play in tie-dye and shorts, today dons coat and tie to deliver his senior speech. " 'Life *sucks*,' " he says loudly into the microphone, pausing dramatically, "used to be my favorite maxim." But no longer, he says, and explains that his discovery of transcendentalism and Taoism allowed him to look beyond petty inconveniences of adolescence to see a bigger picture. Kerry applauds and smiles warmly at Mike when Mike is through, then reads morning announcements, concluding with a disciplinary matter. Even before he announces what this matter is, quiet laughter ripples through the crowd. Yesterday, as many of you know, Kerry says, a certain freshman "engaged in some untoward behavior." The delicacy of Kerry's phrasing brings more laughter. Kerry nods, not smiling, and says, "What he did is generally thought of as funny, but the disrespect it shows is *not* funny." He explains that the discipline committee and the deans will meet to discuss punishment, and he dismisses assembly.

Another day. Having been so soundly thwarted in my purpose yesterday, and not feeling much like being at the school today, I mill about in the commons after assembly wondering how I might spend my morning. Photographs of the stage crew for the yearbook are being taken outside assembly and I stop to watch. I talk with Mike Costello, an art teacher who's eager to tell me about student ceramics. As Costello elaborates on some glazing techniques, I notice that Hawley is standing just off to the side patiently watching us, hands in his pockets. When Costello is called into one of the photographs, Hawley steps up and says, "Mike, as I was falling *asleep* last night, it occurred to me that we had planned to spend the day together."

I honestly don't know what to believe anymore, but I say that it had seemed he'd had a long day.

Hawley begins walking to the faculty lounge. I follow, and he says, "Yesterday was one of the two or three *worst* days of my *life*."

Then he surprises me. He says he has the morning free and would be happy to go through his day, minute by minute if that's what I'd like. We get some coffee and go to his office. I sit and Hawley, having been reminded by Ann that he was supposed to call Japan at 7:30 this morning, tries unsuccessfully to track down a teacher he wants to hire. Then he sits and does exactly as he had promised, goes through every minute of his day from the moment he arrived at school till he went to bed. He then answers every question I put to him.

He does not defend his choice of Aliazzi for head librarian. He calls it "a stroke of genius." It was true that the man was unusual. "Of the nine years he's been here," Hawley says, describing Aliazzi, "he's threatened to quit about eight times. One year he was going to be a Benedictine monk. Then he was going to be a baker." But he is a "dazzling" teacher, the best Hawley has ever seen anywhere; he is also "a maniac of information." Hawley is surprised that contention arose because he was a man. When, after a controversial search for a lower-school librarian, they chose a woman, *"That* was OK," Hawley says. He's dismissive of the issue because sex doesn't have anything to do with being a librarian. I was struck more, though, by the fact that who got to be librarian could create such a furor; evidently, the library was an important place. "Besides being a beautiful shell," Hawley says, "it could be a real hub." He has chosen, he believes, the best person for the job.

Just then Margaret Mason pops into his office with a request form for travel expenses. The school has a three-week exchange program with a boys' school in Tasmania, and Margie's leading the trip this year.

"Do you think $2,000 would be . . . ," she asks hopefully.

"How about $1,500?" says Hawley.

Margie purses her lips, and Hawley signs her form before she's filled it out. "If you run out," he says, "put it on your credit card and we'll reimburse you." Margie makes a joke about all the beer she'll be drinking and departs.

"Live it up, Margie," Hawley shouts.

I then ask about Geoff Morton and the decision to bar him from coaching tennis even as an assistant. Jason Koo, a tennis player and one of Hawley's best philosophy students, has written a long letter on Geoff's behalf. A similar letter from chemistry teacher George Johnston rests open but unanswered on the headmaster's cluttered desk. Hawley insists that the decision is his and his alone, but he's clearly upset about it, and when I ask if it was really the board's decision, he reminds me, "I exist at their pleasure." At my request, he describes the situation in more detail but asks that it remain off the record. I find nothing inconsistent with what I'd already known, except the fact that the headmaster was taking responsibility for something he seemed not to believe in.

Given this sudden climate of openness, I decide to make another request. I ask if it would be possible at some point to read his correspondence from the past few years and this year in particular. I have no idea how he'll respond, what sort of restrictions he'll require. The papers were likely to contain intimate details of the school and also might reveal the headmaster's motives, which some of the faculty had openly questioned.

While I'm wondering this, Hawley is in Ann's office asking her if she has any of his letters handy. She crouches at a file cabinet and removes one of what appear to be several giant manuscripts in disarray, maybe five- or six-hundred pages wrapped in two manila folders and secured by a large rubber band. She asks him if this one will do and hands it to me. As it happens, these are his letters from the 1989–1990 school year, the year the school celebrated its one hundredth birthday. Hawley says, "I have no idea what's in there, but you're welcome to read them."

I say these will do fine for a start. The bundle must weigh ten pounds.

A look of interest comes over the headmaster. "I've never sat down and read them," he says. "I wonder if there's a narrative progression to them." In 1983, he published a novel called *The Headmaster's Papers* comprising the letters and memos of a fictional headmaster named John Greeve. Hawley was Dean of Students when he wrote it, not yet headmaster, but he dedicated the book to his friend and former colleague, Tony Jarvis, headmaster of Roxbury Latin School. The story is a sad one, as the protagonist's surname foretells, until the end, when it becomes sadder still. Hawley now wonders if his own letters form a story.

He returns to his work, phone calls seeking potential teachers for the history department. I sit to read at the table at the far end of his office where philosophy papers on Plato's *Republic* are stacked beside philosophy texts. I've sat with my back to him, as if to give him some privacy.

He's called an acquaintance at another school to inquire about a potential teacher. He says, "That's *OK* if he's eccentric. In fact, this place is *composed* of eccentrics." When he hangs up, Hawley calls out, "Ann, there is at least one honest man in the world."

Feeling like I've stolen into the headmaster's bedroom and rifled his drawers, I begin to read.

14

September 6, 1989

Dear Tony:

It was wonderful to talk to you, even briefly, Thursday afternoon. I am also very happy that your name will be forever celebrated in connection with our Chair in Religions and Ethics.

Enclosed are our back numbers of *The University Series,* for your review. It would be an honor to add a Jarvis piece on "Intimacy Is All" to the series. I have just looked through the alumni magazine from St. Albans. Mark Mullin wrote a fine, very humane response to parents and critics.

We have just had a joyful start on both campuses. I hope R.L.S. is off like a rocket.

Let's talk soon.

September 6, 1989

Dear Mr. Schlesinger:

I am writing in the hope that you might come to Cleveland's University School to give a commencement talk to our 100th graduating class.

We are hoping our commencement exercises will be the jewel in the crown of this remarkable centennial year. I don't know if you know much, or anything, about University School, but let me say briefly that it is both a good and distinctive independent school. We are one of the last boys' schools still flourishing, and we find ourselves agreeably puzzled that it feels so good to be so. Perhaps a great twentieth-century historian could clear up the picture. . . .

Our commencement exercises are 10:30 A.M., the morning of June 8. We would of course take care of your expenses and provide whatever honorarium you feel is appropriate.

I hope you are able to come. My colleagues and the boys would be pleased and honored.

September 7, 1989

Dear Ted:
To the ocean of words that have been thought, worried, and spoken about your schooling this summer, let me add a few more. Now that the decision has been firmly made, you can proceed full speed into this new, very promising phase of your development. The Young Artists' Program is a terrific opportunity, and I hope it launches you into eternal glory. . . .

The good thing about these private schools is that they sink their hooks into you and claim you forever. You are by virtue of your time with us an "alumnus." You can never shake the Prepper claim. Even Jim Backus (voice of Mr. Magoo, also star of stage and screen) has been firmly claimed as one of US, even though he left, I believe, in sixth grade.

Have a best-ever year, Ted. You are more than a promising artist; you are an intelligent, inquisitive, and persuasive young man. The world lies at your feet. Know always that we Preppers are rooting for you.

September 11, 1989

Dear Brent:
. . . It sounds to me as if your own education is continuing pro-

ductively. I have given the Alumni Office your current address and your kind offer to provide assistance to alumni who may need contacts in Asia. So look for yourself in the Alumni Journal.

Thanks also for your generous contribution of $50.00 to the Alumni Annual Fund. With all of your help, we are going to make the Centennial year the most inspiring one in school history.

September 18, 1989

Dear Alice and Rowland:

. . . On another note, faculties on both campuses were delighted more than you can know by the arrival of the "Centennial Celebration" flowers and the warm inscription. We really are off to a joyful start on both campuses. The enrollment is solid (810), the prospects for next year's enrollment even better, I personally and very modestly logged $900,000.00 in gifts this summer, and the response to that has been so warm that no one is being too angry about the fact that the budget doesn't balance by quite a bit. In fact, about $80,000.00. The latter actually isn't a huge worry, for reasons I could explain at boring length, but aren't you glad you are in Duxbury?

Another reason I will remain in my post for at least a few more months is that as I sit here, the football team—no bigger, but shrewder—is off to a 3–0 start, having triumphed over a reconstituted Gilmore (21–0), a startled Talmadge (48–0), and a stupefied Garfield Heights (34–0). That's right; we have outscored opponents 103–0 going into our homecoming game against Warrensville on Saturday. All subsequent games will be very tough, but our scrappy little rats may be up to all of them. Arnold McClain has scored ten touchdowns to date. Aren't you sad you are in Duxbury?

September 27, 1989

Dear Mrs. N———:

Some letters posted in a spirit of pique would benefit from a twenty-four hour moratorium. I suspect your recent letter to me falls in that category.

The *University School Journal* which irritated you is the school's *Alumni* Journal. It is published for the alums of the school, and its primary goal is to underscore the connection between current school business and their own continuing lives. The Alumni Association also pays for the journal's publication. It is sent free of charge to US families as a courtesy.

Nothing, it seems to me, could be more appropriate to the magazine than to celebrate on its cover the fiftieth anniversary of a wonderful class. Nor could anything be more inappropriate than to offer an apology for this gesture of tribute and affection. Aside from the cover picture, the graduating class was celebrated lovingly and amply in that issue—in fact, no graduating class has ever been acknowledged more extensively.

If you would like, I will have prints made of the group photograph of the graduates, and I will give you one. I regret that we are so fundamentally unable to give you satisfaction.

October 16, 1989

Dear Frank:

. . . This Centennial Celebration business is giving us more of a boost than I ever would have imagined. Faculty and student morale is indescribably warm and buoyant, and if we are lucky, we will be able to pull off some school-building feats in the next few months that will launch us into an especially productive and humane second century.

October 16, 1989

Dear Mike:

. . . I am afraid I monopolized your time while you were here, but in the course of all that walking and talking, I feel I got to know you better and, I hope, to share some impressions of the school's current needs and challenges.

This really is a good moment in the life of US. The boys—some of whom you saw at work—have never been better. They prepare, they reach, they think, and they try harder to be decent to one another than they have at any other time in my twenty-two years' career here. The trick is to be worthy of them—and to be worthy in the staggering investments in time they make and investments in money their parents make. . . .

On another note, we are delighted that you are interested in keynoting our Political Essay Prize Contest awards assembly in late January. I will fill you in on the precise date and time before the end of this month.

The philosophy class, and especially its teacher, were honored that you would share our struggle with the question of whether sex drives love or love drives sex. Come back soon.

October 19, 1989

Dear Frank:
I hope you will pardon my bad manners in suddenly coming forward, without sufficient preparation, with an important proposal from University School. I have been deliberating this week with a number of my favorite colleagues and now feel surer than ever of what we need to do in order to realize the best in ourselves and the best in our boys.

You have heard me talk recently about the welcome renaissance in the arts here. Dramatic and studio arts are flourishing, but I think I am happier about our music-making than I am about any other single development in the school. A strong music program here, especially for prodigies and classical musicians, is a very recent development. The synergy of enrolling talented artists and courageous football players and hard-working scholars is difficult to describe adequately, especially so when the artist and the football player and the scholar are the same boy. . . .

Basically, Frank, here is our picture: we have a terrific opportunity to promote the musical life of our boys in an ongoing way. In a way, this opportunity is like the school's opportunity generally. I don't think I am being merely chauvinistic or narrowly parochial when I say that US is on the brink of something great. We are, as you know, a poor, poor cousin to other schools who are up to the kind of things we are. Although we have made some heartening progress over the eighties, we are still virtually unendowed. (My hard-working trustees would weep to hear me put it that way!)

I am in no position to know whether you or your foundation can consider a proposal like this right now. But the more I thought about it, the clearer it became that you are the first person I would like to hear from on the subject.

November 2, 1989

Dear Tyler:
Trina Sikorovsky, who directs our alumni affairs here, showed me a note you recently sent back indicating a disinclination to contribute to the Annual Fund due to the bad aftertaste still lingering from an unpleasant comment you received from a solicitor a few years back.

The remark *was* obnoxious; I can't imagine what P——— was thinking of, except that the terse vulgarity might strike a funny note. This is by no means a new request for funds. I mean only to assure you that the offending note you received is emphatically *not* the spirit in which we want to communicate with our alums. That such a thing ever happened deserves our belated apologies.

November 15, 1989

Dear Kerry:
Thanks again for your logistical help, your off-the-cuff eloquence, and especially for your willingness to indulge me in that Vaudeville foolery. You were a terrific hit and I think we built some new enthusiasm last night.

December 11, 1989

Dear Peter:
Thanks very much for your note apologizing for the "questionable" hockey banner. It is not the worst thing anyone has ever done at University School, but I am glad that you recognize how inap-

propriate the language was—especially coming from such good people and from such a great team.

December 11, 1989

Dear Noah:

Thanks very much for your thoughtful letter about the ways in which we celebrate the holidays. I was especially glad that you expressed concern about a lack of recognition of the Jewish traditions in our various programs and assemblies. . . .

Last Sunday was a "Holiday Revels" program, at which a new medley of Chanukah songs were performed. I played the piano myself at the beginning of that program and I played both Chanukah and Christmas tunes. The tree is a different kind of issue, and perhaps you and I ought to talk about it some more. Holiday trees do sometimes cause confusion in schools and in public places. Pine trees were used to celebrate winter feasts in Europe long before they were taken up by Christians to celebrate Christmas. Using pine trees as "Christmas trees" is a fairly recent development historically, as is the use of some pine trees as Chanukah bushes. Mr. Brennan's hope was that he could use a big pine tree—because they look and smell so good when they are brought indoors at holiday time—to display ornaments and tokens of *all* US boys including Jews and Christians and those of other faiths. I personally think this is a pretty good idea.

Why don't we get together sometime, either before the holiday break or afterward, to review how this holiday celebration went and what you think might be done to make it better.

December 12, 1989

Dear Kay:

I am now able to make official our joyful news that the endowment for our Chair in Religions and Ethics has been fully and formally pledged. The remaining $300,000 has been pledged anonymously by a couple who are great friends of US and great friends of this chair prospect.

258

December 14, 1989

Dear N———:

N———, I am sitting here at my desk irradiated by the glow of three generous checks from you: the $200,000 check toward the Wean Foundation library pledge, the $25,000 on behalf of the class of 1939 toward the library, and your $10,000 Annual Fund contribution. I have never had mail like this. . . .

N———, I have said it before and therefore don't want to labor it, but University School has no one else like you in its history, much less in our current community. The boys and faculty of US are bursting with anticipation, and we have you primarily to thank for this.

January 2, 1990

Dear Jeff:

Thank you for a delightful and thought-provoking luncheon.

We covered ground, I think, in two distinct areas: better ways to air Lower School parent concerns and the desirability of building an endowment to promote great Lower School teaching, coaching, and counseling. Realizing the latter goal might turn out to be the single greatest contribution to the school's progress in the next century. . . .

You and Susan seem to me great parents—deeply and passionately invested in your children's growth. And while it is very chauvinistic of me to say so, your boys are, and have been, enrolled in an exceptionally good school. Good schools are not lumpless puddings, and, as Bob suggested at lunch with respect to his own boys, the lumps turn out to be part of the goodness in the long run. . . .

P.S. I can't imagine what quieted Bob—possibly that I paid for lunch?

January 4, 1990

Dear Debbie:

Once again we gratefully acknowledge your kind donation of four orchestra tickets for Saturday, January 6. These two tickets, in those superb seats, will bring great pleasure to my colleagues.

January 16, 1990

Dear F— T—:

Thank you for sending me the *Plain Dealer* piece on the "Inner Bigot" and for your troubling comment on the bottom of the page.

I can only say that you must be very angry, frustrated, or disappointed in us to say what you did. I would like to know more fully what you mean, and possibly learn from it, but I cannot do this if you are anonymous. Is there any chance that you might meet with me to discuss your concerns?

January 17, 1990

Dear Ann:

. . . We are having a good and lively year here, our 100th birthday. We miss you, however, and the English department misses you sorely. Not that there is trouble there, just a hole. Not filling the hole, but rising like a mountain next to it, is your pal Nancy Lerner, who is an inspiring teacher and a wonderful person to know. She is, among many other fine things, a terrific *reader.* Every day I see her here, I offer a little silent prayer of thanks to you.

January 22, 1990

Dear Mr. Hengst:

I have read your letter through several times since I have received it, and each reading takes me deeper into my understanding of University School's past. Because this is our Centennial Anniversary, I have been working on a history of University School, which is due out in May. Probably the greatest mystery to me has been the seventeen-year headmastership of Harold Cruikshank. I simply couldn't figure out that era. Accounts of much of the teaching suggest that it was dangerously flat, and there seems to have been an unimaginative athleticism (as opposed to glorious athleticism) and even complacency afoot in the school. There is no other period in the school's history marked by this kind of cultural drift. To make what could be an awfully long story short, let me tell you that I figured a few things out, but your letter—a voice from "within"—gave me a terrific boost.

January 22, 1990

Dear Admissions Officer:
. . . Your application requires applicants to note and to explain the circumstances of any suspensions from school. D——— was suspended toward the end of the first term of his junior year. As he explained very clearly in his application, he was disciplined rather sternly by us for an offense most schools of my acquaintance would address lightly, if they addressed it at all. D———'s "infraction" was to enter an exam in physics with information that could have helped him on the test in the back of his calculator case. He did not use the information, nor do we know if he would have done so. A routine check by the exam proctors turned up the paper, and according to our very strict policies, that was a breach of academic trust. D——— was open and straightforward with us throughout the discipline review, which involved a number of other boys, took his lump, and that was that. My point in writing you this head-masterly note is to say that D——— is not academically dishon-est. In fact, his record of service and citizenship here is exemplary. D——— is one of the most humane and generous-natured boys I have ever known in my twenty-two years of schoolmastering, and I heartily recommend him to your consideration.

I am glad you ask students about their disciplinary record, and I am glad we suspend boys from time to time when we wish to put the fear of God into them, but I hope you will not consider this "suspension" as any kind of blemish on the record of D———. He is a boy in a thousand and I would trust him with all my earthly belongings.

January 22, 1990

Dear Admissions Officer:
I am writing to commend T———, one of my former students,

for admission to the entering class. I knew T———— very well in the course of his four years in University School's Upper School, and I have maintained close contact with him since he graduated in 19————.

T———— was a kind of golden boy in the school. Bright, funny, an accomplished, otterlike athlete, and wonderfully personable, he was an honor scholar, president of the student body, and an easy early admission to Duke University. Underlying T————'s surface effectiveness was a special depth, and as T———— will tell you now, there were troubles in those depths. A very humane and passionately idealistic person, T———— wanted inner peace, not mere external success, and he was having a hard time finding it. At Duke, academic work ceased to engage him, and he drifted into destructive socializing and other immediate sensations. Within a year, he was chemically dependent and in desperate need of help.

These stories are usually harrowing and unrelieved, but T————'s isn't. He sought treatment for himself early on, found the sustaining values and the people he needed, and has rebuilt an extraordinary academic record for himself here at John Carroll University, where his professors, one of them a veteran of twenty-three years' teaching, has called T———— the most accomplished student she has *ever* taught. His record there speaks for himself. He is a deep and tireless reader, a sophisticated writer and speaker, and as deeply humane a person as I know. . . . In fact, his illness and courageous recovery have strengthened and deepened him. T———— will be a tenacious and imaginative student of law.

January 26, 1990

Dear D————s:
I am very glad that you came in to talk to me about our decision to dismiss M————, and I am very sorry that we have had to bear such disappointing news.

As we tried to make plain when we shared our concerns in the fall, then again in the December conference, and finally yesterday, M— has exhibited an extraordinary difficulty in keeping commitments.

He has missed so many school days and so much school time that he has lost connection with the life of the school. Moreover, he has *repeatedly* failed to let us know in advance when he was going to be out and to provide requested documentation about his whereabouts and illnesses. Our expectations of him were made very clear both in conferences and in the two discipline letters we sent you. Despite these measures, M——— was repeatedly unable either to come to school or to follow the procedures of informing us of his absence. . . .

I know that none of this is pleasant to hear. Yesterday you were upset that we were being unfeeling and unreasonable in response to M———'s circumstances. To this I can only say again that in my experience the greatest harm one can do to a developing child is to set up expectations for his performance and then fail to maintain them. We have raised these concerns with M——— literally dozens of times since he has been at US. The decision to dismiss M——— was not a hasty response to a single infraction or a recent spurt of them; it was a sad and very reluctant response to an unbroken series of missed commitments.

Mrs. D———, you told me yesterday afternoon that you feared this decision would be devastating for M———. I can tell you quite honestly that a dramatic lump or set-back is often a very positive factor in a boy's growth and development. Significant changes in behavior usually require dramatic circumstances. We know that M——— has the intellectual and personal ability to do good and satisfying things in school and in the world beyond school. While we are of course very sad to lose him, he has our highest hopes in all he now undertakes.

February 9, 1990

Dear Jack:
Because I have been such an erratic correspondent, you may have forgotten that I have this "boys' school" piece in the works. I would be delighted if you would look it over. If you or your colleagues there have any comments, objections, etc., I would be honored to have them. . . .

Otherwise, life here is rich and good. How do you feel about the fact that if we had a single boy who could successfully dive off a diving board into the water we would have licked your swimming team this winter? Did you know that we nipped Hawken in a dual meet, 87–85? Or that we are the number-one ranked swimming team in Cleveland, despite the fact that none of our boys can swim very fast? It is a new era, Jack. I believe I may even get into the water myself.

February 20, 1990

Dear J——— and D———:

. . . I think you and I—and J———'s teacher's—agree on his situation. He has made some progress in English and German and he is currently comfortably passing both subjects. He is still in danger in physics, math, and Western Civilization. He must pass his Western Civilization course for this term in order to be eligible to continue in the school. Nothing but careful, daily preparation is required of him in history, and he simply must prove himself.

As you know, I am strongly convinced that J——— has an innate ability to do University School's work. Whether or not he is motivated to do it remains to be seen. The burden is squarely on J—'s shoulders. . . . His teachers and I stand ready to help him here, but the drive simply must come from him. . . . It is important that J——— see that there are *real* consequences of not getting down to business.

February 28, 1990

Dear Peter:

The Lincoln books have just arrived, and they are as handsome as they are substantial. It will be a joy to catalogue them and to put them in place in a brand new research library this spring. . . .

I am really touched by this gift to us, Peter. Somehow it confirms that your history lights are still on brightly. This really is a wonderful boost to our history collection.

March 5, 1990

Dear Jim:

. . . I have been thinking a great deal about boys and boys' schools, and I believe it is something of a marvel that so little has been said theoretically or positively about the benefits of all-boys' experiences. As you may remember, I did not come to University School from a boys' school background, and I was rather dubious about the experience. This society at large seems to be awfully mixed up about *both* genders, and the climate just may be improving for thinking freshly and clearly on the subject.

Enclosed is a *draft* of an essay I'm working on. I would be grateful to have your thoughts and impressions.

March 5, 1990

Dear Susan:

Thanks very much for the delicious confections conveyed to me recently by Jim. While I have done my best to keep them from my sweet-toothed family, Jim let my daughter Claire know that the candies exist, and I have been forced to share them.

March 9, 1990

Dear Mr. Wilson:

Thank you for your note. Your name is herewith rescinded from our mailing lists. Please convey my apologies to your mother for so many distractions.

March 12, 1990

Dear Donna:

. . . This college selection business can be as agonizing for parents as it is for the boys. . . . What is sometimes forgotten in this tense waiting period is that we and our senior families are allies in this business. We want Matt to make it into the college of his choice just as much as you do. Again, I wish I could promise you some particular outcome, but I simply can't. . . .

In the meantime, please be assured that we continue to work very hard on Matt's behalf. You and I know that many of our greatest souls—and the world's—do not have 700 SATs or rank first in their class or rush for thousands of yards on their way to championship seasons. The great souls include boys like Matt (and Daniel and David). Your boys are the boys they are in good measure because you are the parents you are. I would like to think that University School has played a part as well. But whatever the formula, you have a great deal to be proud of; you have Matt. No college admissions office could ever diminish that achievement.

I am glad you wrote me. I was deeply touched by your letter, and I would like to urge a final time that you take heart.

April 6, 1990

Dear Jim:
I am about to spring into a plane to present my boys'-school paper to a boys'-school heads conference in Baltimore. But I didn't want to depart without thanking you for your wonderfully thoughtful and challenging response to my essay. You have clearly been thinking deeply and very well on these issues, and your ideas were a treat for me.

The questions you raised—about the place of the "sword" in the gently civilizing process of school, about the down side of the "edge," etc.—are excellent, but I believe there are answers. I have been working hard the last few weeks on a developmental sequence which I hope will describe what boys really are up to, what they need, and what cannot be alienated from them without alienating their very humanity. Believe it or not, some of the best data come from Arthurian romance.

I am sorry this must be so brief a reply to so fully considered a letter. Perhaps we can talk soon. Again, I am very grateful for your thoroughgoing review.

April 9, 1990

Dear Peter:
. . . The plans you summarize for the evening of the twenty-fourth seem fine to me. I will enjoy meeting your faculty and special guests. . . .

My real need, however, is a set of clear instructions, designed for a very small, dim child, which will get me to Shady Side. I made every imaginable error getting there for our football game this fall. Do you have a set of very clear, very simple instructions? Failing that, could someone paint a bright blue line between University School and your dining hall?

April 9, 1990

Dear Marilyn:
Thanks very much for your note. Through Steve Szaraz and Terry Kessler, I convinced myself that I am somehow in touch with you, but I really am not, and the fact of the matter is I miss you.

Terry's summary of your position at ———— is that you work in an impressively professional educational setting, but there is so much complexity and scale that it is hard to find much warmth and humanity. Deeply unprofessional myself, I prefer radically home-made schools. If you get them right, they tend to allow people to grow up and into their natural stature. This may be an excuse for being a Neanderthal administrator, but it keeps me happy.

April 10, 1990

Dear David:
The conference material and the *Miss Dove* tape arrived just after we took off for spring vacation, so I am very tardy in sending you my thanks. The *Miss Dove* piece is a find and a treasure. No, we do *not* have cable television—or even much of any television—in the valley where we live. I am delighted to own that document! And what an unexpected range for Jennifer Jones.

I am all set, I believe, for the eighteenth. I will try to do what has worked best before and incorporate some fresh themes as well.

This has been a good, different kind of year. It is our Centennial, and we are getting a boost from the festivities. I am beginning to feel what I believe has always been true: that this is an awfully strong, awfully good school: a male school in the very best sense.

For whatever interest it provides, I am enclosing a draft of an essay I have written on boys' schools.

I will see you soon, and I am looking forward to it very much.

My good wishes, Rick

I read for more than two hours. There were hundreds and hundreds of letters in this bundle. Hundreds more lay in bent-cornered disarray, bound by folders and rubber bands in Ann's file cabinet. I gathered the headmaster's letters from the school's one-hundredth year as best I could and managed to get the rubber band back on without breaking it. Hawley had left his office some time ago and so had Ann. I put the letters on Ann's chair.

The halls were muted, but a soft racket lifted from the dining hall where second-period lunch was finishing up. I went to the library. Here, too, it was quiet. The clamor over the appointment of the new librarian had already subsided, and would soon disappear from view by the end of next week. A freshman would soon spend an entire day in this library, which he'd mooned, in a closed study room, an in-school suspension. History teacher Jim Garrett would be named head football coach. Next week, I would spot Hawley sitting in Deb Nash's office talking for more than an hour, by appearances, comfortably and happily. A few days after that, the halls would jam with students in jeans and sweatshirts, frantically poring over textbooks as the final moments before second-trimester exams ticked away. When exams were done, the school would empty. Classrooms would go dark. The halls would remain barren. And for two weeks, the school would breathe.

I walked to the giant windows and looked down at the quad and beyond the lake to the woods. Time seemed out of joint. The bitter cold of winter had at last lifted. The temperature was above freezing, but snow still covered the ground, and a mist had settled everywhere so thickly that earth and air were indistinct from one another. The school seemed to be enveloped in cloud, with damp dark tree branches poking through the cottony air like thorny, skeletal fingers.

Part III

SPRING

15

The reason for the sudden visibility of romance in spring has a lot to do with, among other things, the weather, which affects the entire tone of school. When students and teachers return from spring break, school is literally brighter. The morning of Monday, April 4, is clear and frigid; a crust of ice has turned car windshields opaque. Drivers heading east shield their eyes to see traffic lights. The day before school resumed—Easter and the beginning of daylight savings—the city woke to a fresh blanket of snow and today, the morning is stiff with cold. But clocks were turned back yesterday and boys file out of buses, tumble out of cars, stream from the parking lot and into school with the sun at an unusual height.

Teachers are noticeably refreshed. Karl, the new Latin teacher who during the stressful winter had begun to wonder why he'd taken this job, has returned from a trip to his old school in Baton Rouge to visit friends and former colleagues. "I made the right decision," he tells me with a relieved grin. Also, he learned that he'd received an NEH grant to study in Rome this summer. English teacher Craig Lapine has received a Klingenstien Fellowship to study at Columbia University. Paul Bailin returns having been rejected at all grad-school programs except the University of Maryland and Duquesne University in Pittsburgh, and those two are unable to offer the kind of financial aid he needs. "So it's either take a student loan," he tells me, "or become a park ranger in New Mexico." He says New Mexico is looking awfully good. Mr. Green and Mr. Johnston are back from the trip to Germany with a dozen German students, Mr. Yedid is back from a similar school trip to France, and Margie is back from Tasmania.

Nancy Lerner is back, as well, but she didn't go anywhere and is mad at everyone who has a tan.

"Good morning and welcome back," Kerry says into the microphone. Kerry is freshly pressed and beaming. "I hope everybody had a good break. I hope everybody's rested." Then he says: "There are only forty days of school left, and even fewer than that for seniors." This is well received by the audience. Eight short weeks to go, and only five weeks for seniors who spend the last three weeks of their high school career on independent projects away from school. The finish line is in sight.

But there is an ominous presence on stage that subdues unequivocal delight. The headmaster. He's wearing an extraordinarily white V-neck beneath his tweed jacket, offset boldly by a red, blue, and gold striped tie, but few seem fooled by the springlike attire. He's up there because he's written another one of his speeches. And it's all about working hard.

Kerry, particularly bubbly this morning, introduces the headmaster to morning assembly by saying, "And, in the manner of throwing out the first ball, the most famous southpaw to come out of Middlebury. . . ."

Hawley takes the podium, welcomes the school back, and says, "I hope your break was restful, and stimulating and renewing. Even more than that, I hope the vacation provided you an opportunity to see something or read something or learn something that you didn't know before. Because that, in my opinion, is what vacations are for: they are for changing pace, changing place, slowing down, stopping, getting an altogether fresh perspective.

"I had that kind of vacation, but the fresh perspective I got was on something I thought I knew all about."

He launches into his address on rigor. No stranger to perpetual work himself, the headmaster frequently worries whether or not the school is hard enough for the boys, whether enough is asked of them, whether he demands enough work from his own students. Oddly enough, he also worries about the reverse.

"I think, overall," he says, "that it is a good idea to be concerned about rigor, but since I've been headmaster, I have also been concerned from time to time about whether US is not, sometimes, *too* rigorous: that more work is assigned in more subjects than can realistically be digested and stored and used. I've often asked myself—and asked my colleagues—couldn't we do less, *better?* Go more deeply into fewer things over longer periods of time?"

His answer: *Don't make me laugh!*

The worst thing you can do to a growing student is to demand too little, he says, and he supports his claim with a pithy anecdote and one interesting observation. Over vacation, he traveled to the west coast to drum up support at alumni gatherings; the people who showed for these gatherings, those who still feel strongly about the school and want to know what is happening there now, he says, are not always the high achievers and stars of yesteryear. A large number of "the weakest and most desperate" former students attend.

"In a way," he concludes, "it may seem strange to launch this new trimester by wishing you all great effort, stress, uncertainty, occasional frustration and discomfort. But that is exactly what I wish you. Because I no longer need alumni gatherings to tell me that the road to genuine personal fulfillment lies this way.

"And so I wish you a great, hard rest-of-the-school year. Enjoy it and enjoy one another in the process. And for those of you able to go, please do your best to spur the Tribe on to a new era in their glorious park."

Yes, it is true. Almost immediately after the headmaster's speech on the importance of rigor and misery, the entire school will adjourn so that a chunk of the school body can attend the Cleveland Indians' home opener against the Seattle Mariners in the new ball park called Jacobs Field. A parent on the commission that developed the pristine structure in downtown Cleveland has bought tickets for the entire freshman class and a score of faculty. President Clinton is scheduled to throw out the first ball at 1:06 P.M. The headmaster may be an omnipresent force, but springtime is indomitable.

Kerry rises from his seat as polite applause for the headmaster subsides and, without microphone, calls out, "It's a great day for Cleveland and America to . . . sing a song!"

The boys groan long and loud. Huge dimples pucker in Kerry's cheeks, he begins to bob and sway in giddy anticipation, and Hawley takes a seat at the upright piano which had materialized to the left of the podium.

"Take . . . me out . . . to the ball game. Take . . . me out . . . to the park!" Kerry sings, and the entire school sings with him, though not so heartily. Virtually all students respond as though this is an unjust imposition, something along the lines of being ordered to bring your little sister with you on a date—all of them but for one boy, a junior named John Gregor, one of the most unusual teenagers I have ever met. John jerks with the force of his own voice. When the song is done, the boys exit assembly to the rousing chorus of the Harry Simeone Singers' version of "It's a

273

Beautiful Day for a Ball Game"—Kerry's choice. Classes will dismiss at 11, and the temperature on this perfect day will reach the sixties as more than one-quarter of the school bakes in the sun along first-base line. The Tribe, hitless for six innings in their new ball park, thump the Mariners 4–3 in eleven.

Classes have been reduced to about twenty minutes apiece, and during second period Kris Fletcher is behind the checkout counter in the library looking surly. Kris will spend more time on public transportation today than he will in school. "The only reason we're here is so they can give us more homework," he says bitterly. Then a fatalistic smile comes over his face. "Kathleen doesn't have school today," he says.

I know exactly what this means: the early-dismissal break in routine isn't a complete tragedy because Kathleen won't be on the Rapid no matter when he leaves school.

At last the all-but-unimaginable has happened. The girl with the long dark hair and confident manner whom he'd watched every morning for two-and-a-half years, the West Side daughter of Filipino immigrants who had sweetened his tedious daily travel simply by existing, has given him her photograph, a demure but devilish wallet-sized portrait and signed it "love." While Kris's hair has grown long and heavy past his face to the edge of his shoulders (Mr. Lagarde and Mr. Brennan *still* hassle him about this), and while he remains the skeptical and silent focus of Dr. Hawley's gaze during philosophy lectures, there is a new edge to his countenance, one of ecstasy subdued.

Boys' love affairs rarely break the surface before adults. Boys know that adults can't possibly understand; but also, the intensity of emotion often contradicts a boy's external persona. Kris, for instance. It would be unthinkable for Kris, West Side metalhead and classics scholar, hanging out with his buddies or with me, to exclaim that his heart had sprouted wings and kissed the air. But the effects of these powerful underground currents swirl the surface of conversation.

Shortly before school let out for spring break, Kris and I sat at a study table in the library. I directed the conversation to the big issues that had been so much on the minds of the people I'd been following this winter; I liked to hear teenagers' convictions on spirit and God, liked to hear them say, "This, I believe." As always, Kris spoke openly and certainly, often staring out into the bright cold afternoon with his head cocked back skeptically.

"I believe there's a higher force," he said. "I don't believe in *a* god, in the Christian person sense. I believe there is a realm of power which is beyond the mundane but I wouldn't necessarily call divine." It's more a force, he said, like in *Star Wars.* "I believe in powers of the mind and I believe in ghosts and I believe in magic."

I asked Kris why he believed in such things, and to what end they existed?

"Power," he said. "Power over oneself. I think before you can start thinking about having power over other people, you have to be able to control yourself. You have to know every millimeter of your body and of your mind. When a man masters himself he can master anybody else. And I think magic, if nothing else, is a discipline. A lot of it is a faith in oneself and a faith in the power of the earth. I believe in the world—sort of like the energy of the world. It's not divine, it's just the world; there's energy in anything, whatever makes it alive. Being able to tap into that. To tap into what you are, to be able to reach that deep inside of you and know what you are. And then if you know what you are and can handle everything that you are, then everything else is trivial. The outside world really doesn't mean anything compared to what's inside your head. Or not necessarily your head but what's inside you.

"To learn the most, is just to sit there thinking," he continued. "I mean I've figured more out when I'm sitting around in the woods just looking at what's around me, reflecting and everything, than studying for a psychology test or cramming for a chemistry final. A lot of it's internal. It's just being able to control yourself. The aphorism for tomorrow is 'The growth of wisdom can be accurately gauged by the drop in ill temper.' " (Kris has started a "Sophists Club," a group of students and a few teachers who meet to discuss philosophy; everybody has been so busy, the club has not been productive, but Kris slips an aphorism into Mr. Brennan's morning announcements every now and then as part of his job as head sophist.) "It's so stupid to get angry," he said.

I asked him if he still wanted to hit people. He said, yeah. "It comes from that Neanderthal in me."

"We're all just raping the earth," he continued. "There can be a balance. You have to give back. We're not giving back. There's just too many people. The overwhelming mass of humanity, it's just so unimaginably vast, it's too cumbersome and it just destroys everything. Like some horrible war machine, that just keeps rolling and rolling; whatever gets in its way, it's going to take down. . . . Man is inherently destructive." Kris stopped to clarify. "When I say man, I am speaking chauvinistically—I mean humanity. My girlfriend would kill me. She's a liberated woman. She goes to HB."

Life force, the earth, magic, those are fine in their place, but more consequential by far are females. My ears prick up, as much at the mention of a girlfriend at Hathaway Brown as by the fact that it's singular. Kris and his buddies are not one-girl guys.

"It changes *everything*," he said with a voice and smile that seemed at once light-hearted and casual, but also loaded. Kris admitted it was entirely physical at first. "I always was attracted to her. . . . I was never ready enough to make a move. It was never the right time. I was thinking of asking her to homecoming, but Odum asked her. *That* was a match made in hell."

I asked Kris to go back a little further and describe the evolution of this new romance. He'd always watched her, I knew. They would make brief, benign conversation with each other waiting for the Rapid. His heart leapt when he saw her in the back seat of the driver's-ed car last summer; he remembers she said to him, "We seem to be bumping into each other a lot." Yet he was never quite able to "screw up my courage to talk to her." And things got worse before they got better.

As Kris talked, in the quiet of the library, I was returned to high school more surely than at any other time during the year till then. The complexities of teenage love were vast indeed, and it came back to me like a gong in my head as Kris talked. It began with Sarah, Kris stated as dryly as a witness under oath.

"I was going out with Erin. I met Lacey. And I was going to go to Erin's homecoming with her. And I was going to take Lacey to *my* homecoming. Erin started getting curious why I hadn't asked her to my homecoming. Tyler was trying to hit on Lacey, so Tyler told both of them everything. *Thanks, Ty.* He told both of them everything, and the two of them basically said, 'Yeah, *choose.*' So I chose Lacey, and it turned out she wasn't *allowed* to go to homecoming. So I didn't think I was going to go to homecoming. Then Bill—Bill was going out with Jacqueline, Sarah's best friend, and he was like, 'Yeah, I need a big favor. Go to homecoming with Sarah.' So I did."

Odum is a Cambodian refugee who lives alone with his younger siblings, for whom he acts as surrogate parent, not far from Kris on the West Side. He is one of Kris's good friends, and his asking Kathleen to the homecoming dance was torture for Kris. "The *dress* she was wearing," Kris recalled with a lusty far-away gaze. That was when he knew he had to make his move.

"The whole way I went about it was sort of screwed," Kris recalled. "I tried to ask Bill to get information and everything. I just wanted to find out what she thought of me. If she ever considered me in a nonplatonic"— Kris cleared his throat—"manner. As a freshman, Bill went out with one of her best friends, so he was going to talk to her. So to make it seem like it wasn't a blatant inquiry—like 'I want to know because Kris says he wants to know'—he said he had a *bet* going with his friends. And so Kristin, that's who Bill was getting all his information from, told Kathleen. So Kathleen wanted to talk to Bill. She was really mad at Bill. Kathleen called him up and bawled him out, saying, 'Next time you want to know something about me, ask *me*. You and Odum can take your bet—' she just assumed it was Odum, and all this."

Kathleen eventually got to the bottom of things, Kris said, shaking his head at his own folly.

"One night she called *me* up and said, 'We need to talk,' " Kris continued. "And we did. She said she really valued my friendship and didn't want to risk it by taking it any further."

Any teenager who's been on the receiving end of those words knows it's not a good sign, but a teenager also knows that the only practical option is to agree vigorously.

"When she called up, everything was told. I got Bill off the hook, told her what it was all about, both of us sat down, and we laid all the cards on the table. We came to the conclusion that the friendship was the most important thing and that now was not the time to try to take it beyond that, risk the friendship. Because all this time we did talk on the Rapid and had a good friendship. And then—this was right around Valentine's Day and I had written her—I was going to make my move around Valentine's Day. . . . I had written her a couple Shakespearean sonnets. Somebody who could appreciate them, somebody who wouldn't think they were just normal poetry, because her name—first, middle initial, and last name, are fourteen letters, straight down the side. I did ten like this." He states her first name (which includes a troublesome double E), her middle initial, and last name, which begins with a K. "I can't tell you how hard it is to come up with two lines that begin with E one right after the other, a line that begins with a B and two lines that start with K. There are not many words out there that start with K. I was racking my brains." He stopped and smiled. "She brings out the romantic in me," he said. "I consider her to be my muse. I'm constantly writing her poetry."

So Kris was writing her poetry before they were officially going out—a fairly bold move. She wrote him one poem, a sort of satire of his—"It was a funny poem," he said. "That was the point of it." Kris's poems persisted, and Kathleen grew impatient. There is only so much poetry a girl can take. Finally she wrote Kris a letter saying, Kris remembers, "she was going to put the ball in my court. And we decided that we would start seeing each other more often. We never really saw each other outside the Rapid, and we would just start seeing each other as friends, but leaving it open to what-ever happens, leaving most of it open to time and fate or whatever, and it sort of—it, it, it progressed."

The winter of 1994 was one of almost unrelieved bitter cold but for one strange weekend in the middle of February—a false spring with tempera-tures in the sixties that melted snow and freed hordes of suburban bikers and rollerbladers, donning windbreakers and neon Spandex, to cruise among the swampy black mats of decaying leaves left over from fall. This was the time and fate that Kris had waited for. He and Kathleen went to the Cleveland Museum of Art to see an exhibit of landscape photography (Kathleen is an aspiring photographer). Afterwards the day was so mild—providence in the center of the coldest winter in a decade—they spent the rest of the afternoon talking at the edge of the large lagoon that fronts the great neoclassical museum. Kris and Kathleen's foundation crystalized.

"I'm quite the monogamist now," Kris said.

I asked why this was unusual, why would he ever go out with more than one girl.

"I guess because I was expected to," he said. When he told Odum about his "change of heart," he explained that Odum said, " 'You can't do this. You give us West Siders a bad rap. We're supposed to be players.' "

Kris suggested that some of his friends think it's powerful to go out with more than one girl. "I guess I do it for the stimulation of it, not physical," he said. "Emotional and mental, I guess, because it's hard to find—I've never had a girlfriend I could really *talk* to. I guess I had four girlfriends. I could talk to each one a little bit and the conversation wouldn't get dull or dreary and without all those stupid moments of silence. I've had girls call me up and they don't say a damn thing.

"After you learn a little bit about a person it's like what do you ask about?" he went on. "Most of the people you ask, 'Oh, so how was school?' And they're like, 'Oh it sucked.' Or, 'It sucked, my teacher yelled at me,' or something. A five-minute topic at most. And beyond that there's nothing to talk about.

"It's different than—I mean, I thought I loved Sarah, and I'm not sure. I don't know if I could admit that I love Kathleen, but with Sarah my only thoughts about her were sexual, or mostly sexual. But with Kathleen, she's smarter than most of the people I interact with around here. Tyler and Bill and Odum, they're smart in their own ways and everything, but I can't call them up and discuss Donne's Holy Sonnets with them. But I can with her. We discuss Shakespeare and Donne. We were discussing *Gatsby*. The other weekend we went to the *art* museum. I don't have *any* friends I could do that with, who would take it at all seriously. The only person I've ever gone to the art museum with is my sister.

"I ask Kathleen about school, we go on forever about the theories of teaching and what's the best way to grade a paper and how you should grade a paper, how you should read a book, how many times you should read a book, what you should look for in particular books."

I asked Kris who was smarter.

"I would say she is, but if you asked her, she'd probably say I was. I'm better at Latin and Greek. She's better at French and Spanish. She's more scientifically and mathematically oriented, but she's just as strongly oriented in literature as far as I can tell. We talk about science. This morning we talked about physics. We were discussing the physics of light waves refracting. . . . I can talk about the *Etruscans* to her." One of Kris's goals is to translate the language of this ancient society. "I can't talk about Etruscans to my friends. They don't even know who the Etruscans were."

He had just finished *Tess of the D'Urbervilles* because Kathleen had suggested it. The next book she gives him will be *Dragonslayer*.

Inevitably, Bill—Bill Shepardson—is not happy with Kris's new love. Bill said Kris has changed. "His take on the world now includes Kathleen," he told me. "It used to be just Kris." Bill doesn't like Kathleen. He said she's snooty, above him. Bill said Kris agrees that Kathleen *is* above him. "There's no more talk of getting girls," Bill said sadly.

Bill didn't realize it yet—he was counting the days, marking them off boldly on his calendar, till graduation, and cavalierly talking about "getting" girls—but he, too, was soon to be smote.

■ ■ ■

"There are always a couple of romances," Carol Pribble says.

"Romances?" I ask.

"Always."

Carol Pribble is the drama teacher, and she is referring to an inevitable result of the spring musical. Carol has a long, narrow face, bright blue eyes, and thick, straight brown hair which, tossed across her brow and curling at her shoulders, looks preppy. She seems to have retained no traces of her hippie days at Ohio State University except for an occasional those-were-the-days lift of her eyebrows. She's a wife and mother now. When her son Jason's history grades slip, she doesn't have to call for an appointment or wait for parent conferences; she can find Paul Bailin in the history office. There are only a few weeks of the year when one of her plays isn't going on. In the fall she directed *To Kill a Mockingbird,* in the winter, *Early One Evening at the Rainbow Bar and Grill.* This spring, it's *Big River,* a play she's been wanting to put on for four years, ever since Eric Myricks was a freshman. She began producing high school plays twenty years ago and has been at this school for a decade. Most of the kids who've worked with Carol say she's awesome, don't fool around when she's pissed off, and call her "CP." Jason, of course, calls her Mom, though mother and son did have a discussion regarding protocol here.

The spring musical is a big deal. It will involve about seventy people, more than forty of whom are actors, singers, and musicians; about a third of the actors will come from other schools; fifteen roles will go to girls. It's the climax of Carol's year. It's also, every spring, the only thoroughly coeducational situation in this school.

Romance is not a seasonal occupation for teenagers, but at this school, love affairs are commonly subterranean bulbs until spring. Sometimes romance, or more often its end, is apparent—in Kris Fletcher's poetry, for instance, or in Carol's drama workshop, which is the only class for which girls from Hathaway Brown and Laurel cross-register. Cross-registration was popular between the three schools in the 1970s when talk of going coed was on everyone's mind, but the novelty of it seems to have worn off. Because it requires a lot of driving, it's considered more an inconvenience than an opportunity, except by aspiring actors—there is only one Carol Pribble. Sometimes cross-registration worked and sometimes it didn't, Carol says. This year it didn't. The girls missed too many classes. And one couple broke up mid-year; the tension in the room was so palpable it distracted from the work, something that had not happened in ten years of her classes here. "I'd forgotten about that from public school," she says.

You can't watch the evolution of romances at this school because there are no girls and therefore no romancing, which is done on different turf and at a different time than school hours, away from adults in the no-trespassing zone of mall and movie theater and park. But now, with girls showing up every night for rehearsals, with a spate of dances and outdoor sports events on their way, and with the weather itself encouraging blooms, romance for the first time could be seen to sparkle, flare, then disappear.

Rehearsals for the spring musical, however, are work. One might argue that more school work is done here on a single project over a longer time than work in any classroom all year long. The spring musical requires careful reading of a text; character analysis; scrutiny of nuance; script memorization; singing; choreography involving dozens of other people who don't know how to dance either; the obligations and responsibility of showing up on time having finished your work and relying on everyone else to have done so, too; that all-purpose tonic and American ethos, teamwork; and, of course, acting. Boys and girls together.

One night before rehearsal, Carol mentioned that she had been to a music program at Hathaway Brown. She's so used to this all-boy world, she said, "I had to remember that I was female."

I asked her what she noticed about the tone of the place. She said she'd never seen so many people arm in arm. Then she said, "Kids touch each other a lot. That's one thing I've learned working with adolescents. . . . If I told boys they touched each other a lot, they'd say, 'What, are you *crazy?*' But they touch each other all the time. They punch each other, they jump on each other, they grab each other around the neck"—Carol mimics a full-arm choke hold—"they roll around. And they're laughing like crazy beating the crap out of each other."

As Carol waits for the cast to arrive for rehearsal, boys and girls cluster around her; tall, thin, and casual in a black dress, straps looping over the shoulders of a white blouse, Carol has some sort of gravitational pull on kids. She laughs and jokes easily with everybody, but at seven o'clock, she's all business. The students find seats in the back-center section of the auditorium, and Carol, having deposited her legal pad and notebooks and script on the railing, runs through attendance. "OK, Mike Cohen's not here—I know about Mike." She runs down her list silently, looks up. "Jessica? Does anyone know why Jessica's not here?" Carol tells Chip, a tall lanky junior who's been cast as Tom Sawyer, to call her. She shakes her head and finishes running down the list.

Carol directs the students on stage to begin dialogue scenes from Act One. The cast is now about four weeks into rehearsals; most dance numbers have been blocked off, songs have been rehearsed separate from dialogue. Dance, song, and acting will be synchronized later. This is the first week back after the two-week spring break, and students are sloppy in their return to routine. The stage, normally cut from view by a thick maroon curtain, is a mess of sawdust and nails, sticky balls of duct tape, and scraps of wood. The skeleton of Huck's and Jim's raft sits on wheels in the middle of the stage like an inept go-cart. The play requires two rafts, the painting of a vast backdrop, and numerous set changes.

Carol stands over the unfinished raft. "Let's put this up-right, coming down on a down-left angle," Carol begins. "All right, the backdrop will be the Mississippi River." She explains the concept of the outdoor set, how it will work, the intended effect, and the various set changes involved. At Carol's instruction, a few boys carry benches off stage to make room; the girls stand aside.

"OK, let's get started. Let's see if we can get through the first scene without scripts." Carol has become serious, terse. And now her voice has a sharper edge because Jessica is in the first scene, so Carol must read Miss Watson's lines from her seat in the fifth row. Her voice has a speaking tone, but theater volume. "Please, read your schedules. I'm getting too many questions about what we're doing tonight. Every night for the next four-and-a-half weeks you *know* what you're doing."

The rim of the stage where Huck delivers his opening words is shadowed. "Who knows how to work those lights?" Carol asks.

"I do," says Bill Shepardson.

"Get rid of those shadows," she says.

Bill is dressed in black jeans, black T-shirt, and has tied a blue bandana over his head. He shuffles down to Carol and takes her keys for the tech booth.

I'm surprised Bill Shepardson is even here. From his looks and demeanor, his eagerness to get out of school and "get" girls with his buddies, his weekend work as a DJ spinning rap LPs and lip synching Beastie Boys tunes, he has a toughness about him that suggests he wouldn't bother with high school song and dance. When I saw him at tryouts and asked why he was here, he gave me a longing smile and said, *"Big River* is my *favorite* musical." It was OK that he didn't get the part of Tom Sawyer, even though he wanted it like nothing else. He's glad to be here, particularly because the absent Jessica is part of the show.

Bill, high above in the booth, sends spots onto the front edge of the stage and Mike Seelbach as Huckleberry begins: "You don't know me, without you have read a book by the name of The Adventures of Tom Sawyer, but that ain't no matter. . . ."

When you see Mike Seelbach on stage, you think here certainly is the US Boy everyone keeps talking about. He has fine light-brown hair, blue cat's eyes, a pale smooth complexion, rosy lips, and a fine tenor voice. His slender body is proportioned like a gymnast. Of all the students at the upper school, Mike most resembles the bronze statue of James Goodwillie in the lower-school foyer. But he's not an athlete and he's not a scholar. He hates science and math. Though his father, Chuck, is history department chairman, Mike's history is so bad that a teacher apprentice tutors him during afternoon free periods. Then there's Mr. Harmon's zoology class— "I'd rather not *know* about all those stupid little creatures that Mr. Harmon gets so excited about," says Mike. He'd rather keep them "mystical," he explains. He would apparently like to keep math and history "mystical" as well.

Chuck says Mike was always "an odd loner," growing his hair long and letting it hang in his face as if to distance himself from people. Mike always had a good voice and in seventh grade, his first year at US, Chuck tried to get Mike to try out for the glee club. "He cried the whole way there, and would not get out of the car," Chuck remembers. I ask what happened then. "He *didn't* get out of the car," Chuck says, "and he *wasn't* in glee club."

The next year, in eighth grade, Kerry Brennan encouraged Mike to try out for a spot in *Damn Yankees*. Mike refused. Kerry all but dragged Mike to the audition. Mike got the lead, and his destiny was then determined. As a junior, this odd loner and acknowledged rotten student, has become the de facto lead in every play, so acute are his skills. Carol doesn't choose a show to suit Mike, she says, and she doesn't cast a show in her mind until after auditions, but she always chooses the best actor for each part, regardless of how many leads they have or haven't played in the past, and Mike, this year and likely next, gets the leads in all four of Carol's plays.

". . . but that ain't no matter," Mike says to an imaginary crowd. "The book was written by Mr. Mark Twain, and he told the truth. Mainly."

"Ya know, Mike," Carol calls out from the fifth row. "You can stroll around at ease, but it's more effective if you finish a point before you move." Mike continues, standing still to speak, strolling, and stopping to speak again: "Now the way the book winds up is this—Tom and me found the gold the robbers had hidden in Injun Joe's Cave, and it made us rich."

"Noelle! That's your cue!"

Noelle strolls from stage right, out of her role as Dolly at Brush High School and into Widow Douglas, now carrying an imaginary tray of cookies. "Huckleberry?" Noelle calls with a sonorous twang. *"Huckleberry!"*

Carol shouts out the absent Miss Watson's lines. When Mike tells Widow Douglas, "All I meant was, I want to go somewhere. I want a change—," Carol stops the scene. "Let's share with the audience your dream of going off into the world," she tells Mike. "Part of the pleasure is the audience wants to go with you. *If* they like you. This play won't work if you don't like Huck."

"Then the widow'd give me a whipping," Mike intones, center stage. He bends over, the Widow swats him three times with a switch, Mike looks up at the audience, smiles, and says, "Which cheered me up a little."

Jessica arrives just as they finish the scene. Carol twists darkly in her seat and holds out one flat hand—*well?*

"I—" Jessica says.

"What?"

"I don't know," Jessica says, and mumbles that her friend told her she only had practice Monday and Wednesday.

"Don't let *anyone* tell *you* what you're doing that night," Carol says, turning back to the stage. *"You're* responsible. *Everybody,* read their schedule."

Jessica hustles on stage, long blonde hair lifting off her back, and the three actors run through the scene again, but Jessica's very first line—"Not likely—he played hookey and went fishing"—falls soggy into the dust and nails at her feet.

"Jessica, do you want to try that again, and try to give me a *strong character* voice like you did in *audition?"* Carol can use her voice like a blade when she wants to. Jessica pouts, whispers "All *right"* with her own edge, stopping just short of giving Mrs. Pribble a salute and heel click. Jessica then delivers with audible emotion—perfect—and Carol settles back in her seat.

The cast is not rehearsing the musical numbers tonight, but if they were, Noelle and Jessica and the chorus would at this point move into the song that opens the show, "Do Ya Wanna Go to Heaven?" This seemed to me rather appropriate, given the debate that had been rumbling through the school all year. The next number is called "The Boys," featuring Tom Sawyer, Huck, and their band of robbers and killers, singing *All together now, we are the boys. All together, forever and always.*

SIMON: Do we always kill the people?

TOM: Oh, certainly. It's best. Some authorities think different, but mostly it's considered best just to kill them.

JO: Do we kill the women too?

TOM: Jo Harper, if I was as ignorant as you, I wouldn't let
on! Kill the women? No—you fetch 'em to the cave, and you're
always as polite as pie to 'em, and by and by, they fall in love
with you and never want to go home anymore.

The scene features Josh Krembs, a short taut senior with a bush of curly red hair and freckles, who executes a standing back flip in the middle of the song and springs to the top of a boy pyramid. The pyramid tumbles to the stage to conclude the song.

Once they have the pyramid and the fall blocked off, and the boys stand brushing themselves off, Carol reminds them that choreography for the scene is tomorrow.

Josh says, "I've got a lacrosse game tomorrow in Cleveland Heights."

"When do you usually get out?" Carol asks.

"I don't know, to be honest."

"Be honest."

"I guess about six, six-thirty. I guess I'll just fly out here."

"Don't fly *too* fast."

"I may have to shower."

"Don't shower if you're just dirty," says Carol. "We don't care. If you smell, take a shower."

"I may have to play hard," Josh offers, "because my girlfriend's coming to the game."

"Ah," says Carol. Then she says let's do the scene again, and the boys shuffle off stage to restart. "Gentlemen!" Carol shouts. "The way you walk *off* stage is part of your character, too!"

While this all-American boy story seemed the perfect choice for a boys' school, Carol had her own reason for choosing this play: Eric Myricks. It's rare that she picks a play specifically because of one actor, but she loves the show, it's a great boy story, and when Eric Myricks moved from the lower school to the upper school, she was tempted to do it that year. But as a freshman he was still too young to handle a lead. Two years passed, and Eric, a tall, handsome black student with fair skin and short brown hair, grew as an actor and his voice developed into a rich baritone perfect for the role of Jim.

I'd heard about Eric well before I met him. He was known throughout the school for his voice; this year he spent half of every day at the Cleveland Institute of Music in classical voice studies. Carol told me that Eric's voice was professional caliber—"or at least," she said, "when you hear professional singers, that's how they sound when they're a teenager." She added, "It's not often you get a baritone like that." Mike Seelbach, who's also intent on a career in the performing arts, told me, "It's an honor to be singing with Eric, because he's one of those legendary voices of the school."

Eric is that rare student whose presence is big enough to fill a stage. Even when he's not singing, dancing, or acting, when he's standing in a hallway, you sense he's there. Shortly after school began I asked a teacher about Eric, and the teacher said, "You haven't met Eric? He will *charm* you with his *smile.*"

Eric is not yet here tonight, held late at the Institute which is about a twenty-five-minute drive from the school. He will spend all afternoon singing, sometimes intensively when he's preparing for a recital, and then his mother will drive him back out to US where he will sing some more.

I spent a lot of time at rehearsals for the spring musical. I'd planned to do this because it was the only time I'd be able to see boys and girls together at this school for an extended time, but as it turned out, some of the most interesting kids at the school had something to do with the play. This has not always been the case, apparently. Not long ago, if you went to a boys' school and were involved in *thee*-ah-ta, you didn't shoot your mouth off about it. I asked Dick McCrea about what the theater department was like when he was a student here in the 1940s and 1950s. First he scowled, then he laughed. I asked him what it was like for kids who did act in plays back then. "Harargh!" he said. "It didn't do you any *good,* I can tell you that!"

286

These days, earning a part in one of Mrs. Pribble's plays carries a distinct cachet. A number of her students have gone on to performing-arts schools, decisions Carol neither encourages nor discourages. An inspiring teacher and one or two students each year who have set their sights on professional acting, and who therefore bring a seriousness and intensity to thespian pursuits, draw a number of unusual teenagers to the stage. One such student this year is John Gregor.

John is shy, so shy that he makes being shy seem vast rather than diminutive. Hawley told me that John would fall down if you even looked at him.

John is in the mid-five-foot range. He walks delicately. His feathery brown hair parts naturally just off-center and lifts away from his ears in little wings. In the wall of photographs, John is the only student wearing a bow tie—until that photograph is stolen, anyway. His large round face is pale, circles flushing whiskerless cheeks, and so puffy that it seems to squeeze his eyes closed. John and I were once talking in the middle of the crowded downstairs commons, and I discreetly informed John that his fly was down. Blood spread through his face like a stain, his closed mouth formed an O, and he departed wordlessly on his toes, springing like a squirrel through snow, away from me, up three steps, and into the locker area, where he vanished. Moments later he returned, casually, as though we'd never been talking. *"How embarrassing,"* he whispered.

But put John on stage—he will take any opportunity he can to get there—and he is an uninhibited parody of a nineteenth-century Shakespearean actor. While some people have what is called perfect pitch, John has a similar sense of high camp.

At a holiday show planned to conclude school before the winter break. John was stumped: what could *he* do for the show? Kerry Brennan had an idea, and John was game. Mid-show, John raced to center stage dressed in a little-boy sailor suit with floppy bow tie and short pants. Hugging a teddy bear and clutching a giant lollipop, John sang, "I Wish Santa Were My Daddy." The laughter and applause rocked the hall.

Afterwards, when school reconvened, John was upset about his act. A girlfriend at HB told him she'd heard about it. Now John thinks he should *never* have listened to Mr. Brennan. "People thought it was *dorky,*" John told me one afternoon, seated on a ledge by the lockers.

I told him the crowd seemed to like it. He glared at me.

Brad Krupa wandered up to us. After Brad's masturbation introduction, I didn't think he would be highly tuned to John's style. Brad handed me a book called *What Men Know About Women,* a paperback filled with blank pages. He smirked knowingly as I flipped through it. I asked him what he thought of John's "I Wish Santa Were My Daddy" number.

"It was good," Brad said. "I liked it."

"People thought it was dorky," John repeated.

"Yeah, it *was* dorky," said Brad. "But that was the fun of it."

John looked away, not buying.

John, clearly, is not a child of the nineties, nor a budding member of so-called Generation X. In fact, he seems hardly a child of this century. His grades remain dismal, he's failing math, and his position at the school is tenuous. Weekends will find him at the library for hours, not studying, but instead rifling the stacks for sheet music from obscure musicals.

About a week before auditions for *Big River,* I was wandering the downstairs commons when I noticed the faint tinkle of piano keys lofting in from the dining hall. This school was funny with pianos—they seemed to pop up everywhere. Perhaps this is because the two top administrators were musicians: Kerry's specialty is in choral music; Hawley, who used to play piano in bars for money during his college days, remains an avid and versatile pianist. Walk through one of two standard-sized doors into the lecture room, and you will see a beat-up baby grand piano, which creates a sort of ship-in-a-bottle effect. All the pianos seemed to be in pretty sad shape, nicked and scuffed all over, maybe because the school considers them portable.

Curious as to who was playing piano during free periods, I strolled to the empty dining hall to find John Gregor rattling off "Once Upon a Time." When I sat to listen, he paused to slide a milk glass containing a dollar bill from the far end of the upright-piano top to the end nearest me. He gave me a solicitous lift of his eyebrows.

"I sang this song in the summer musical," he told me and, like a world-weary barroom crooner, he sang, *"Once upon a time, a girl with moonlight in her eyes, put her hand in mine, and said she loved me so . . ."*

Spring is here, and the boys can feel, almost as if from an internal clock, that school is in its last stages. Play practice will live here through the first week of May. The routine does not take long to establish. John Gregor has won the part of the Duke; he sings the opening number in Act Two and is on stage for half the play as a character very much like himself, or so he makes it seem. John is in heaven. Acting and singing, school moving into its final weeks, the weather warming, and the other Jessica in the play. There are two Jessicas. One is tall and blonde and plays Miss Watson; Bill Shepardson is typically sidestepping in her direction when the cast gathers to begin rehearsals. The other is short with frizzy brown hair and a cherubic face; she plays Sally Phelps. John Gregor is typically in the back row giggling with this Jessica when Mrs. Pribble takes role call.

Mike Seelbach remains silent and attentive preparing for his most difficult role ever. He is on stage virtually every moment of the play and he has focused completely on that task. His performance develops so solidly so quickly that midway through rehearsals Carol will sometimes leave the auditorium when Mike is performing solo on stage to attend to other business because there's nothing more she can tell him. And Eric Myricks strolls casually into rehearsals by around 6:30, dressed in jeans and a worn baseball cap, after afternoons of singing.

On the first Tuesday after spring break, with Miss Watson present and Carol Pribble clicking off the acting scenes from part one, the scripts are about three-quarters memorized. Only Carol seems to realize how little time they have before opening night.

When Eric Hermann, Pap Finn, finishes his scenes for the night he asks Mrs. Pribble if he can leave.

"Do you know your lines?" she asks, knowing he doesn't.

"Yeah," Eric mumbles at the floor.

"Eric?"

"Pretty well," he says. He looks up brightly. "I'm going to rehearse at home."

"All right," Carol says.

Eric, free, bolts from the auditorium.

"What are you doing tomorrow?" Carol shouts, having turned back to the stage, where Huck and Jim are beginning a scene.

Eric slinks back to the auditorium. "What?"

"What are you doing tomorrow?"

"Uh, I don't know," he says nervously. Then he smiles. "I've got to look at my *schedule.*"

"Good," says Carol. A cluster of boys and girls are laughing and talking in a back row. "Guys!" she says, eyes still fixed on Huck and Jim on stage. "This is a rehearsal room. If you want to talk, go outside. Eric, you're correcting your English again. 'I *creeped* to the door.'" Eric Myricks nods and begins again.

16

The second week of May, with the senior class dispersed on independent projects, with the building itself muted because of their absence and the juniors now the eldest students in the school, I spotted Margaret Mason at her desk staring at the wall above her desk. She was rarely still. I asked her what was going on—was spring always like this?

She nodded slowly. "This time of year can get a little spooky," she said.

I returned her nod and wandered on my way. You couldn't fail to notice it. Things were happening now that didn't happen at any other time of year. The final weeks of school had a peculiar floating feel that was distinct from either the fall or winter trimesters. And it wasn't because of the teachers. Teachers were predictable; happy and smiling upon the return from break, their perky countenances drooped like warming wax as the weeks wore on, work piled up, and grading deadlines approached. The boys were what made the spring so obviously different from vigorous fall or dark winter.

Certainly, the brief spring trimester could not have started more hopefully. A morning that began as shockingly bright, cold winter transformed minute by minute into genuine spring. After the headmaster's speech on the value of rigor, the school adjourned so that the entire freshman class, and a couple dozen others who had wangled one of the toughest tickets in the city, went to a ball game. The headmaster himself, though a tad churlish at some faculty who commented on the irony of his welcome-back address, was soon in fine fettle strolling along Ontario Street to the new Jacobs Field with 41,000 other fans and hundreds of stadium workers, protesters (the Tribe and its mascot, Chief Wahoo, are not uniformly loved), journalists, the President of the United States, and attendant Secret Service agents.

Hawley saw a couple of former US boys in the crowd. One spotted him not long after he'd arrived and called out, "Rick!" Hawley had just come from the concession stand where he'd bought a Diet Pepsi and two hotdogs, slathered with Ballpark mustard and chopped onion, one of which he stuffed in the pocket of his brown overcoat.

"Hi, David," said Hawley, holding up Pepsi and hotdog, unable to shake hands.

It was David Modell, heir apparent of the Cleveland Browns. His father, Art, the Browns' owner, stood just behind David. "I may come out to Alumni weekend," David said.

"Have you been out there?" Hawley asked eagerly. "Have you seen the new library?"

David said he hadn't.

"When was the last time you were out?" Hawley asked.

"The last time I was there," David said brightly, "was probably the last time you kicked me out."

Hawley chuckled, but it came out partly as a grumble because his chin tucked abruptly.

"Did you really kick him out?" I asked.

Hawley, striding away, said, "Yeah. *Twice.* He never graduated."

After what he called a "perfectly scripted" game, heading out of the stadium with Geoff Morton, Hawley stopped and turned back to see Geoff talking with a short young black man, the member of a news crew carrying a massive TV camera. Hawley waited for Geoff then said, "Wasn't that—?"

"Yeah!" said Geoff.

"He's a former Western Civ student of mine," Hawley said proudly.

After that fine day, it was back to school to begin a new section of his course and a branch of philosophy that may be even nearer to his heart than ethics.

When Hawley enters room 270 with new books and a new syllabus, Eugene is clicking his heels and howling at Nick Zinn's April Fools issue of the *US News.* The one-page Xerox reports, among other things, Hawley's departure ("In a surprise announcement, Dr. Richard Hawley will be leaving US to become commissioner of major league baseball"); a "barroom style brawl" between Nick Zinn, "known for his incredible hulklike strength," and Kerry Brennan; an article on the dress code ("Apparently

Tyler Doggett favors the institution of a uniform consisting of typical Scottish Kilts. 'Men's legs are just not displayed enough in contemporary society. Why should women be the only ones allowed to wear skirts?' Tyler told the *US News"*); and the announcement that the *US News* had won a Pulitzer Prize. "Eet's hilarious," says Eugene.

Hawley scans the classroom with a look of increasing disappointment. He counts the number of students and says, "Do you know what the story is?" No one responds and he marks several absences in his book.

"Folks! This is an unbelievably short term," he begins, wasting not a moment more. "We look at a single issue in philosophy called aesthetics, and it's structured in some ways the way ethics is. And the opening question is, 'Is there an objective true standard for calling something beautiful or fine, or for that matter calling something ugly and coarse?' Or is that simply a matter of subjective taste and personal experience? In other words, it's the same relativist-versus-idealist issue that's brought up in ethics and large questions in philosophy—very, very important. Certainly in aesthetics, which is technically a branch of philosophy that deals with the question of what is beautiful—certainly, in aesthetics, we can be purely subjective. . . . Some people like *Jaws* and some people like *Moby Dick*. Some people say one's fine art and one's popular art. People who like heavy metal and people who like Mozart—we have people who advocate both in this very room. And why do we have to put them in any sort of hierarchy and so forth? That's an agreeable, tolerant position to take, and in most areas of aesthetics it will probably have to stand because it's such a hard branch of philosophy.

"But you watch. One day, even the most socialist of you will probably live in a house somewhere and if somebody puts up a neon sign and some pink flamingos and they're next door, you're going to be irritated at that. One day somebody's going to do something in your community—the way they organize the roads or the way they organize property—that's going to offend your eye and your heart. And you're going to want to have criteria for saying that doesn't go."

Hawley pauses and shrugs.

"Or maybe the world *should* just be one wall-less, endless, continuous Los Angeles, which is basically low-slung retail signs and wires. But if you think there's any objective reason for preferring the way something looks, sounds, feels, and is to another, then the branch of philosophy called aesthetics may have something to say to you. It's the hardest branch of philosophy in which to make clear distinctions, and this is what we're going to do. It also raises great questions. If we get it right, if I get it right—we only have a month—we'll at least be able to raise some of these questions. I'm going to ask one big thing of you in this term. It's a paper of about the length of the last one you gave me, and it is to present and justify the aesthetic value of an experience you had."

This is a great idea for a paper and most of the boys seem to begin thinking about it as soon as Hawley describes it. With less than five weeks of classes left, the excitement and fear of leaving this familiar world somewhat dampens the drive to plunge into, say, Kant or Schopenhauer. Hawley's assignment allows them to choose something they're passionate about and to justify their response. But the last weeks won't be all fluff— Hawley assigns difficult essays arguing for objective standards for saying one thing is beautiful and another is not by such writers as Mortimer Adler and, of course, C. S. Lewis, but the main text they read is *Romeo and Juliet*, combined with occasional scenes from Zeffirelli's film version. Thus the spring term, filled with discussions of love and beauty, is fast and light and accessible.

Hawley hands back last term's papers in which the students were to defend one of two theories of democracy—either Plato's from *The Republic*, or Frank Capra's theory of democracy as portrayed in the movie *It's a Wonderful Life*.

"It's very hard for a teacher to judge," he says, "you know when you're teaching seniors at the end of the second trimester—the way people look, the way they come to class—it's very hard to judge whether anyone has anything left. Judging from your last tests and these papers, you had something still left in the barrel." When he reaches Tyler Doggett's paper, he looks at Tyler's usual seat immediately to his right, now empty, then around the room, and says, *"Tyler's not here today?"*

Several people shout out that he is in fact in school.

"Is he in the SDC?" Hawley asks.

"Yeah, he is," says Nick Zinn.

"They're meeting?"

"Yeah," says Nick. "Mike's suspended."

"Mike's suspended?" Usually Hawley knows when someone has been suspended.

"He's at the SDC meeting, too," a voice in the back calls out. This is followed by a good deal of snickering.

"Can anyone tell me what Mike did?" Hawley asks.

Wilkie, seated next to Kris Fletcher and leaning back against the window, scowls and says, "He drank a glass of wine."

"He was in that, that—I heard about the event." Hawley begins class with no more discussion on the subject.

The curious spate of spring disciplinary actions began outside the school when Mike Cohen, along with a few other boys who had joined the spring-break trip to France with Mr. Yedid, stopped in a bar in Paris, ordered a glass of wine, and were nailed by one of the trip's chaperones. All students on these trips are required beforehand to sign a form stating they will not drink alcohol and acknowledging that to break this trust will result in punishment. The first full day of school after break, the SDC meets, as do the deans, and in-school suspensions are delivered to Mike Cohen and three other boys—two full weeks of solitary confinement for each.

The suspension of Mike Cohen has significant repercussions for Carol Pribble and *Big River*. Mike, cast as the King to John Gregor's Duke, has a principal part, but he is not allowed to rehearse during his suspension. Spending ten school days in a closed study room in the library by himself, however, gives him plenty of time to learn his lines.

"It's been a bizarre year," Carol tells me. First, she says, directing her son had complications she hadn't anticipated. "I've never directed any student who wasn't afraid of me, at least at first," she says. She would tell the actors to get in a line, for instance, and everyone would do it except for Jason, who would say, "I'll do it later, Mom, I'm going to get a Coke." Carol sat down with Jason, and they had a very long talk. Because winter was harsh, she often had to call off rehearsals at the last minute. "I live under a perpetual winter-storm watch," she said. But mainly it's the boys who are the unpredictable element in the equation. They hurt themselves and they get into trouble.

Kevin Casey, the Civil War scholar and one of the best actors in the school, agreed to enter an out-of-state drug-treatment program shortly before the winter production of *Early One Evening at the Rainbow Bar and Grill,* in which he had a part. While no one ever caught Kevin using drugs, Kevin's deterioration throughout the first half of his senior year had become so pronounced that several of Kevin's teachers, including Kerry and Margie Mason, met with Kevin to express their concern and support. But Kevin remained unchanged, and the school and Kevin's parents decided to go with professional help. Kevin was sent away. He lasted a month in the program before he snuck out, hopped a Greyhound to Chicago, eventually called his parents, and was able to return home and to school, clean, sober, and with all intents of staying so.

A small school has many advantages, one of which is that desperate kids stand out like gaudy neon signs. Though Kevin left the program early, he had returned to something near his former self and was determined to stay off drugs on his own. Carol Pribble knows Kevin well and once he was back and apparently recovering, she reminded me that he had a significant role in the winter play and departed the school at an inopportune moment. "Kevin doesn't go into treatment, he goes into treatment *two weeks* before the show." And of the Mike Cohen suspension, she says, "I don't get him *back* until two weeks before the show."

It is only after Chip, who plays Tom Sawyer, appears in school one day with his arm in a sling and a bandage wrapped around his hand (he'd gotten mad, slammed his fist into a door), does Carol pull out her don't-do-anything-*stupid*-before-the-show speech. Things happen to girls that knock them out of a show or throw a wrench into rehearsals—awhile back the lead in *Cabaret* got laryngitis—but boys typically do something to themselves, Carol says. She has known boys to sprain joints, break limbs, jump in front of cars, cut up their faces, and get suspended from school right before the show.

While Carol is immediately affected by actors who damage themselves, it isn't just the actors who do it. Suddenly I begin to notice a preponderance of injuries and accidents. Redmond Ingalls, in Hawley's class, appears with his arm in a sling, damaged when he fell into a ravine during a weekend paint-gun war. Hen arrives in Paul's class with his hand swollen and bandaged days after Matt walked in holding an ice bag over his hand, both gym accidents. Jason Pribble gets a black eye in a fight in the gym. Ben, a sophomore, loses control of his car on the winding school driveway—a sunny Friday afternoon was the reason for his speed—and careens onto the grass up a short hill and into a utility pole, unharmed but badly shaken. The phenomenon is so striking I would not be surprised to learn that sales of bandages, plaster, and crutches sky-rocket during April and May in Cleveland.

One incident involved adhesive tape but not for any medical purpose. A small group of sophomores bound a fellow classmate to the benchpress in the weight room, turned out the lights, shut the door, and abandoned the kid. There were a lot of SDC meetings during the spring. What added to the strangeness was that the kids being suspended were the most productive and respected members of the school. This was partly why Margaret Mason used the word *spooky* when she described to me this time of year.

So Carol Pribble has more than simply rehearsal stress and strain to contend with. If you break your arm you can still go to class; if you're suspended, the class can go on without you; but if you're in a play in which everyone depends on everyone else, you can really mess things up. Because Mike Cohen, the King, is suspended, John Gregor and Mike Seelbach must rehearse on Friday, a day the cast normally has off. Carol has delayed rehearsing many of the King's scenes, but John and Mike Seelbach still have to rehearse dance numbers and Gary, the choreographer, takes the King's place. I happened to be at school late, well after the hallways had gone dark. I thought I was about the only one left, but passing the auditorium I noticed that dim stage lights were on. I walked to the doors and saw Mike Seelbach, Gary the choreographer, and John Gregor on stage, arms locked over each other's shoulders, sashaying from stage right to stage left and back again, Gary calling out directions for little Rockette-style kicks. There was just enough light to silhouette a figure seated on the floor about ten feet in front of me. The figure was so still, my heart did a little jump when I realized it was human.

It was Mike's father, Chuck. Chuck is a serious guy; all the ribbing he gets from the students seems mainly caused by the fact that Chuck doesn't react to anything. But the boys, and particularly athletes, gravitate toward him, which seems odd to me because his demeanor could be downright stony. He would tell funny stories in the faculty lounge, but he was all work otherwise. So I was surprised to see him there, watching his thespian son so intently that he didn't notice me. He was completely rapt, seated in the dark, out of view as much to avoid distracting his son, it seemed to me, as not wanting to be spotted watching his son with such pure adoration. With people hurting themselves and being suspended, it was an unusually peaceful moment. Such things were more likely to happen when the school was resting.

"**M**r. *Bailin,*" Jonah exclaims from his seat in seventh-period Western Civ. "What happened to your *face?*"

Paul enters the classroom gingerly and rests his books on the table as though the books themselves throb. Paul's eyes are lidded and watery, and the left length of his face from temple to moustache puffs beneath a wide

296

white bandage running diagonally across his cheek. Beneath the bandage, adhesive sutures create perpendicular hash marks. The class is silent.

"I got in the middle of a dog fight," he whispers. He is trying to move his lips as little as possible. Even wincing hurts.

"*Real* dogs?" asks Jonah.

"Yes. And because of that, I'm not going to be doing much talking." Paul directs them into tight study groups to discuss last night's reading among themselves.

Over the weekend he and his girlfriend, Brigitta, were looking for a friend and fellow dog-owner who would this summer take care of Brigitta's dog, part German shepherd, part labrador, while Paul and Brigitta are in South America. The prospective dog-mate and Brigitta's dog got immediately into a fight and Paul, forsaking himself on behalf of Brigitta and her dog, dove into the knot of teeth, dog muscle, and saliva to separate the beasts, successfully but for the two-inch gash on his cheek. He feels a little ill and achy today, but he's looking forward to the scar, which he hopes will give his bookish appearance some menace and authority.

Aside from the dog fight, Paul's spring term begins so well he's thinking maybe he'd like to return to teach after all. Dan, a teacher apprentice, has asked to take over his eighth-period Western Civ II class, reducing both prep time and class time for Paul. Without this class of sophomores, his schedule is delightful, and he has made an appointment with Hawley to discuss a part-time teaching schedule next year that would also allow him to begin grad school at Cleveland State University, a possibility Hawley is glad to entertain. In fact, once his face stops throbbing, Paul has only one main concern: Shawntae.

Shawn is still failing Western Civ. While this happens to a few kids each year, Shawn seems on the edge of either making a real go of passing or giving up entirely, and Paul is conflicted about what to do to push him. More significantly, Paul worries what it will mean for Shawn's future if he begins a pattern of falling behind and giving up. Today, before Paul entered class, while boys dropped their homework on Paul's desk, Shawn, six feet four inches and 250 pounds of boy, lingered, flipping through his essay booklet, opening and shutting the rings of his binder. He would not leave his spot until he knew Paul had seen him turning in his homework. Of course, if Shawn did his homework every day, he wouldn't need to make a show of turning in assignments.

Shawn's situation is part of a larger, ongoing struggle: being black at US. Without doubt, blacks at US have more obstacles to success than any other students. One of those obstacles is the fact that there aren't that many of them. Each grade includes between five and ten African Americans out of a total of eighty-seven to ninety-seven. Shawn's Western Civ class is unusual in that he is one of two black students; most classes have only one black student, if any. Leaving aside the fact that many blacks at this school, though by no means all, come from disadvantaged families and the complex effects this has on scholastic performance—focusing, that is, solely on life within the school—the common response among African-American students I spoke with is that the initial difficulty in entering this school is a culture shock so severe that some black students feel they must become different people in order to exist here and at the same time maintain their identity, an identity still in the process of forming.

Shawn expressed it this way: "You've got to change the way you act," he told me, "the way you dress, sometimes even the way you *talk*."

Most black students realize that US is a good school, are glad they're here, say there is little racial tension among students, but also say that doesn't mean they have to like it. Kofi Anku envisions a time when cities like Cleveland have private schools of this caliber for blacks so that they won't need a school like US. Another says, "It started without blacks, and it can end without blacks."

Teras Herring, a junior and a co-captain of next year's football team, says that he doesn't know if Brush High School, where he'd be were he not here, is any better. Nevertheless, "When I leave this school, I'm not coming back. When people call and ask for money, I'm not going to give. I want to distance myself from this school." When I ask if he would send his kids here, he does not hesitate to say yes.

Some students feel guilty for being here. Shawn, who lives in what is perhaps the most blighted neighborhood in Cleveland, says, "I know people who could be here who aren't and are in gangs."

"I don't feel guilty," says another, new to the school this year. "I know people who turned this place down. I didn't."

I ask him if he thinks his choice was a good one.

"I don't know yet," the boy says. "The first two months, I didn't want to be here. Now I'm not so sure."

There is only one black faculty member at US, though this school and others like it throughout the country search with an effort verging on desperation to find black teachers. The only blacks who have remained at the school for more than ten years are in the kitchen or maintenance wing.

"Is that going to make a kid uncomfortable?" asks English teacher Kevin Kay. "Yeah."

Kevin is the adviser for the Cultural Awareness Society and heads REACH, a three-year summer-school program designed not only to encourage inner-city boys onto a track toward higher education but also to lure young black professionals into high school teaching. Modeled on the Summerbridge program, it's one of few programs in the country for middle-school-age African-American males. It's a good, growing program, but not without critics who argue that it will drain talent from inner-city schools.

When I ask Kevin Kay if he thinks US has done enough as far as paving the way for more African-American students and teachers here, he responds with his own question: "How can you put a time frame on something that shouldn't have been a problem in the first place?"

"There are people who will say that this place is racist," he continues, "and there are people who will say that it's no different here than anywhere else. I think the truth is somewhere in between. It happened too late, and it's not far enough along as it is."

US began admitting African Americans in 1963; thirty years later, it is for the first time seeing graduates of the school, in significant numbers, become business and community leaders, a few of whom return this year to speak to the school.

I had not come to examine issues of race. To claim to understand completely what it means to be black at this school would be presumptuous; but to ignore race altogether would be to miss an important facet of this school. When I read in the weekly calendar of events that Tony Peebles would be speaking to the Cultural Awareness Society during the break, I hoped I might learn something. Tony and I graduated in the same class and went on to the same university, though I don't remember ever having seen him there. When I last saw Tony, he was twig thin, short, played bass guitar, and had a large afro. I scarcely recognized him standing in the hall outside room 270 before his meeting. His hair was short, he wore a gray suit and suspenders, and had the beginnings of a paunch. Tony had become a public funds officer at a Cleveland branch of Fifth Third Bank, financing public works in cities and townships throughout the county. But the biggest change was that his bearing had become substantial. His arms and neck were thick, his voice clear and confident, and his bright smile was almost constant.

We said hello and I sat in the back of the classroom as about a dozen boys filed in. Tony removed his jacket and put it on a chair at the head of the classroom. He sat and leaned back confidently. Kevin Kay and I were the only whites here, which was a heady change from what I'd been used to during English and philosophy classes in this same room.

Suddenly confronted by a dozen stony gazes, Tony looked nervous for a moment—you don't realize what a daunting thing it is to sit down and try to say something meaningful to a group of teenagers until they're staring you in the face, waiting. He began stiffly: "The black alumni of US are trying to get a little more involved in what's going on at US, a lot of us who are back here in Cleveland working here as professionals. We want to get more involved in helping to recruit more black faculty or other minority faculty for the school. We want to get involved in networking with you guys in terms of career opportunities and college opportunities."

In their silence, the boys were impossible to read, except for the few who put an elbow on the table and smashed their cheeks up into their eye.

"Because I can definitely tell you it *did* give me an advantage in the work place in terms of being competitive, being well prepared," Tony continued. "When I was at US, we used to call this the Black Unity Society. Most of us had more hair, *afros* and what have you"—and right there, as laughter rose and smiles passed among the boys, Tony loosened up. His voice livened. "But that's comin' *back!* I *like* that. My hair's thinnin' out now . . . ," he patted his head. Suddenly the boys were with him—all it took was one sentence to let them know he'd returned to talk, not to give a speech.

"But we also had some of the concerns that some of you guys have. Obviously, we were concerned about the racial tension that does happen at any school like this, we were concerned about what type of opportunities we would have after we finished US. And the biggest thing we were concerned about was: *was* US *worth* it?"

A wave of nods ran through the circle of boys. They nodded at Tony and they nodded at each other. He had hit the perpetual question, what they had been asking themselves all along.

"And I can definitely tell you that it is. You probably won't appreciate this place until you're about twenty-five years old, until you're out here in the—I'm *serious*—until you're out here in the work place. A couple things are going to happen. First of all you're going to realize that some of the training you got here and the type of work load that you've got to handle here is going to help you when you're in college, and when you're in the work place working twelve-hour days because you *need* that *pay*check. The second thing that you will find is that you will have a great network when you come out of here. Networking has really been a blessing for me, having gone to US, because what happens is, oddly enough, despite some of the racial tension—I don't know how it is here now—but when I call up my white counterparts who were my classmates, I get responses. We do business together, we network, and I know that may be hard for you to believe now, but that does *happen.* I keep my US directory on my desk, and flip through it, and if I want to find somebody in banking or in law, I can call them and say, I'm a US grad, and they'll say, well, hell, let's grab some lunch, let's talk about doing some business.

"Probably the worst thing about coming out of US when I got to college was I was so used to being disciplined, when I got to Duke University my time was all my own and I didn't know what to do, so I must caution you, when you graduate and you go on to college, try to stay focused. 'Cause no one's going to tell you to be in assembly at 7:30 with your *tie* on. You're going to have to do all that yourself. Coming out of here, sometimes you think you're *too* prepared and you get a little bit lax.

"I would venture to say that what you guys are doing is very important from the standpoint of multicultural diversity, sharing African-American culture with your white counterparts. One is 'cause you want them to understand you a little better, get along with you a little better, and that's important too, you know—in sports and in school and in other activities. But the other reason that's important is because that's what's *happening* in the *work* place. . . . It used to be talking about folks getting along because it was the right thing to do, and because it was a moral issue and all that type of thing, and that's as it should be. But now, companies, corporate America, is realizing that by the year 2000 only *one* of every seven people that enters the work force will be a white male. So that means the rest of them will be either female, Hispanic, black, Asian. OK? So what does that mean? In order for companies to make *money,* in order for companies to be *profitable,* they've got to be able to reach out to a different type of human resource, because a human resource is a commodity, and if their applicant pool is more African Americans, more Asians, more Hispanics, more *women,* they can't make their hiring decisions and their promotion decisions just based on some of the biases, racism and sexism and things of that nature, of the past. So now what's happening is corporate America is getting to be a bottom-line issue." Tony paused and leaned forward. "How many dollars do you guys think African Americans earn annually in this country? Can anybody give me a guess?"

Eric Myricks asked, "As an average?"

"No, I'm talking about everybody, your family and my family—"

"Even big multi—"

"Including Michael Jordan and Michael Jackson," Tony said.

"Bill Cosby?" Eric, who plans a career on the stage, asked.

"Bill Cosby, *all* those."

Now Tony was talking and the kids sat up, alert, leaning forward. This was concrete. This was not history or math—this *meant* something. They called out "a few billion," "twenty-four billion," and Kareem, a freshman, shouts "a trillion!"

Tony smiled and said, "It's not a trillion. We're good, but were not *that* good yet."

"Yeah, about thirty billion," said Eric, finally.

"Other than the trillion—we'd be running the world if we had a trillion dollars," Tony said, "the total earned income for black Americans in 1992 was two-hundred seventy-six *billion* dollars, two-hundred seventy-six *billion dollars*. That's including Michael Jordan and me. Now two-hundred seventy-six billion dollars is a lot of buying power. That's part of the American economy. These are demographics I got from a target-market news source.

"Corporate America, they've gotta say, hey, two-hundred seventy-six *billion* dollars of earnings, they can buy *our* products. We spend thirty-four billion on food, twelve-point-seven billion in automobiles, fifteen-point-six billion in clothing, health care eight-point-six billion dollars a year. So what you're talking about multicultural diversity is more than just getting along and understanding the black white thing. It's about dollars and cents, it's about the bottom line, it's about whatever career you can go into."

These boys had locked their gazes on Tony Peebles so hard it seemed as if no one had ever spoken to them this way, and maybe no one had. The atmosphere in the room was electric with the ramifications of what Tony was telling them.

"In the *Cincinnati Enquirer*," Tony said, "there was an article about the changing demographics in the work force. It said by 2005 the number of women and minorities in the work force are expected to total ninety-three million or sixty-two percent as compared to fifty-seven percent in 1990.

And that's from the Bureau of Labor Statistics in Washington, D.C. These statistics are not coming from the NAACP. These are statistics that the corporate establishment, the government establishment, are looking at. And they're saying, how do we deal with it? So we've got a lot of work to do in terms of letting folks know about our culture and our contribution and about what we're about. Because we're going to be more and more counted on to drive America, just by the numbers—if for no other reason, by the numbers.

"US prepared me to compete on the highest level, but it also allows me to be a messenger, to say hey, this is the deal, and the deal is, it's the bottom line."

Tony paused and took a breath, tilted back in his chair.

"I didn't have a lot of prepared notes," he said, "I just thought that this was something that's kinda important, because *you* guys are going to *be* that twenty-first century work force, and that's the environment that you're going to be working in. And that's why you need to be that much better prepared. I'm not here to *sell* US to you, but while you're here, take advantage of it, take advantage of *every single* opportunity you can get out of this place."

The boys had just heard a speech, and they didn't seem to care a bit. Tony smiled and said, "I want to learn a little bit more about what you guys are doing here, how this place has changed now that *afros* are coming back, what's going on out here?"

"I'd like to get back to the numbers," said junior Kofi Anku. "Exactly what those mean as far as advancement as a collective group. We seem to have all this buying power, but what are we doing with it?"

"See, that's the deal, *that's* the *deal,*" Tony said. "We have this buying power, and the issue for me is how we use it, how we collectively come up with some strategies to use our collective buying power to its advantages. The numbers are *there.* Do we buy from each other? Do we support black businesses? Do we go to companies that we buy from and say what are you doing about hiring us? Beer companies, they sell forties to brothers *big* style. You see Ice Cube on TV and they're marketing that to *us,* because they know we're going to spend a lot of money on it. . . . In the sixties it was about the laws—do I even have a right to drink here, eat here, ride here, stay here, OK, *vote?* We have all that now. Now it's about how do we change our focus to the economic piece. How can we take the resource that we already have, two-hundred seventy-six billion dollars, how do we translate that into power, how do we translate that into access to the decision makers that run the corporations, that run the universities, the government?"

Eric said, "I think the average black family has their *hands* tied behind their back."

"What would happen," Tony asked Eric, "if every one of us were to, say, every time we get our teeth cleaned we would only go to a black dentist?"

"I live close to an orthodox Jewish community," said Eric, "and they keep everything in their community. If there's a person, they need someone to fix something, they will get a Jewish person. That money just keeps cycling through their system. And the thing is, is that in the black community, a lot of the time brothers are scared to have another guy come in and fix their pipes because he might steal their *pipes.*"

The boys laugh raucously.

"Or he might do a real good job and save you some money," said Tony.

"Right," said Eric, "and I think we need to have the confidence, and give other brothers a chance, because I think sometimes we look down on guys who aren't on our level, who are trying to make it just like we are. The other thing is, in Cleveland, why can't we buy a block, and then buy another block, form black communities."

Teras Herring said, "I think a big problem with that is the Jewish community does it, but when a black community does it, it's reverse discrimination. Because black people have fought to get all these rights and then when they go back to seclusion, start their own community, and want to give all these things back to their community, white people—I can't say white people—but other people turn around and say you can't do that after you've fought for all those rights."

"I agree with that," said Tony. "There's a perception that whenever we do something collectively, it's against white establishment. That's not true. If we support each other, and make ourselves stronger, then we're more productive members of the population. There are more African Americans going to *jail* than going to college. So if we buy from each other, and I got a dental practice, and all you guys come and I clean your teeth and I put your braces on, then maybe I send my kid to US and he doesn't go to jail. So that's positive and we gotta take the responsibility to say that *this* is why we're doing this, and it's not because we don't want to be with white folks, but we're going to be about us."

"But that's the perception people get," said Teras.

Eric turned to Teras and said, "But we can't *worry* about that."

Tony said, "When we do come together, it's not that were trying to negate white society, we're trying to uplift ourselves."

Kareem, at the back of the room, minute beside the enormous Shawn, said, "I see what you're saying, but how do we convey this message to the brothers in the 'hood? Where they see no way out, and I gotta shoot someone to be better than them."

"It's about being a role model," Tony answers. "For example, I'm chairman for the Urban Scouting Committee for the Boy Scouts of America, and we're trying to make Scouting chic, so I can get these kids to become a Scout instead of joining a gang. It's gonna happen one on one. It's not going to happen overnight. There's a lot of despair in the city, in the 'hood, a *lot* of despair. But all they need is some little inkling of hope and they can be just as successful as you guys."

Shawn said, "I know what you're talking about, because I live in East Cleveland and it's getting really close to that." All heads turned to Shawn. "And he's right—down there, you've got barbecue places and clothing stores, but you don't really have a strong company down there, a strong black entrepreneur down there, who everybody can look up to and try to be like. And they've got *police* down there who don't give you-know-*what,* and you've got a mayor who doesn't do anything until election time and you don't look up to him because he just *sits* there. And there ain't much you can do about it. Either you make yourself motivated or you just—like Fred knows, over here, because he lives just around the block, Fred knows what I'm talking about. Either you motivate *yourself,* or there's no hope."

"Another thing about the business thing, though," Kareem said. "You're saying, yeah, bring black business into the community and give them a chance and stuff, but there's a lot of situations where you don't know who to trust. People will try to cheat you. And I'm not saying it's only black people that will try to do that, but it's a lot of people out here saying come on and support black businesses, come on, and then take your money."

"A black business person has got to be professional," Tony said to Kareem. "They gotta be about excellence. *We* gotta be about excellence. OK? We gotta start being examples. *You* guys are going to be the *best* qualified leaders to come out of college, because you've gone here and you're all going to go to good colleges. You talk to some of the black alumni at US in this city, we are some of the best qualified—and I'm not saying that to be arrogant—we *are.* But what we have to do is continue to fight that struggle, just like our parents and grandparents fought the struggle to get the right to vote. In 1950-something, they were saying we're never going to get the right to vote. Same things you're saying about economics they were saying about social acceptance."

"You're saying we're the best type to lead," said Teras. "But who are you going to lead when a bunch of people come out of school can't even read, who have no education? Every time you turn around, the government is taking money away from schools and putting it toward some kind of bond or something. Who are you going to lead? You're going to have a bunch of idiot people—I'm not trying to put anybody down—you got a bunch a people who don't know how to read, who don't know how to make educational choices."

"Not necessarily," Tony responds. "We're spending time working within those communities, don't you think?"

"Right," said Teras.

"It's not going to happen overnight."

"Right."

"But if a young black kid that's like seven years old sees one of you guys, maybe he says instead of being that gang member, I want to be like you."

"But he has no chance to do that," said Teras.

"You don't *know* that," Tony said.

"He has the chance to make himself better but the school systems don't support him."

"And yet there are African Americans that come out of those schools and do well."

"But the schools are getting worse and worse."

"I agree, I agree," said Tony. "My parents taught thirty years in the school system. It gets worse. But what are we going to do? Say it's never going to change? We're not going to be involved, we're not going to use our talents to be about leadership?

"You got an example now," Tony continued. "Mayor White's trying to do that. Whether he'll be successful or not, that's your opinion versus mine. But when I work with younger kids, I say who's your role model, they say, 'My role model's Mike *White.*' Little five-year-old black boys. 'Mike White, he's the *man.*' How many more of us, how many more of you guys when you get out there, are going to be in those positions, to be those role models? I don't think there's any blanket solution, and I'm not saying

I *have* the solution. I'm saying, you guys have the tools, you guys have to start thinking about the solution."

"I've got three questions I need to address," said Kofi Anku. A tousle of short dreadlocks drooped over Kofi's brow; his serious gaze was all but lethal. He spoke in a low soft voice. "One thing, as far as the discourse of economics solving the problem. That's not going to happen. Because if you gotta spend forty-thousand dollars to keep a brother in jail, all right. If you were thinking in a rational economic mind, you would take that kid, put him through US, and he would be a productive member of society before he even had the opportunity—"

"So how do we keep that kid from going to jail?" Tony breaks in. "That's what you gotta ask yourself."

"No, no," said Kofi. "The thing is, if people wanted him out of jail— see, that's why black nationalism didn't work in the first place. We can't buy from each other because we don't get loans to open up businesses. You can see in California how the Koreans came in and they got the loans and they opened up businesses in black communities. When blacks tried to get the loans, they didn't get the loans."

"But what happens," Tony asked Kofi, "when somebody like you gets an MBA and becomes a vice-president of a bank and you're in a position to start that process?"

"Well the thing about that, me being allowed to come to US and then going out, see that's good for other black middle-class people, but the thing is that's not *enough.*"

"I didn't say it was enough. Did I say it was enough?"

"It's not enough to initiate the kind of thing that we want to happen," Kofi said.

"In 1963," Tony said, "they said the march on Washington wasn't going to be enough. Three or four years later they had their clear objectives. They wanted the Voting Rights Act, they got it. They wanted some other things, they got it. We gotta sit down and get some *clear objectives.* I'm not saying there's a panacea, you can wave a magic wand, we're all going to be about economics, we're all gonna buy from each other and all that. But we have to set some *goals.* We have to say, 'How can we better educate ourselves and better give ourselves access so that we are in positions where we make the decisions?' "

"Well the thing is, the enemy isn't the white people," said Kofi. "The white people don't inherently want to keep us down."

"I didn't say that."

"I'm *not* saying you *did.* But I'm *saying,* going through the school system, having the education, thinking about the way—see, that's why I stop at multiculturalist; it's not like they think we have our own culture and they just don't understand it. They've been taught to see things in a certain way, you know, and it's not just about cultures, it's about race."

"Sure," said Tony.

"So if we can change the curricula in the school system, whether it's US or in the 'hood, or any other school system, where people can see it clearly, you know, how race functions, because this, I think that, where—"

"I understand where you're coming from," Tony said. "I understand *exactly* where you're coming from. But what *I'm* saying, and what I'm *suggesting* is, if in fact every generation of us is better prepared, guys like us, then we're going to be in some of those positions, we're going to be the school-board president, we're going to be in the position. And *then,* when we *get* there, we're going to have to have the moral courage and take the responsibility to make the incremental changes that we have to make."

Eric Myricks looked at Kofi and said, "You can't deny the fact that there *has* been progress."

"Yeah, well, also black mortality rate is twice that of whites," said Kofi.

"Right, but the number of people who go to US now is higher than the number that went twenty years ago," said Eric. "So the difference is more people who can influence a society."

Kareem said, "But if we all die out before that happens, it's not going—"

"That *won't* happen," Eric tells him. "We won't die out."

"At the rate it's going now, that *is* going to happen

"*No,*" said Eric, sounding discouraged. "It *won't.*"

"If we keep killing up each other, and stuff like that," Kareem said, "it's going to happen."

Shawn said, "I think one of the problems is like you have this attitude if I give you something, what are you going to give me, and that's a problem with schools. Like these tax levies that started to show up. The school *needs* the money. But you've got parents who say my child doesn't go there so why should I pay this money? But they don't understand. You're paying the money to help some *other* child to get their education. And also there's not a lot of black kids out there that know about University School, Hawken, Gilmore. The number of people who come to US could be higher if we could get the word out and some of us don't really get the word out."

"Most of 'em can't pass the entrance exam," said Teras.

Eric said, *"Not* necessarily."

"I know a *lot* of people who could pass," said Kareem. "They just don't know about it!"

"That is *not* true," Eric said to Teras. Teras lifted his eyebrows and tilted his head back. "I think the bottom line—the conversation is about excuses," Eric said. "You *can't* be making excuses. You can't feel sorry—you have to see the problem but you cannot make excuses. You have to say, *this* is the problem, *this* is how it's *been,* and I'm going to *change* it.

Kevin Kay stood from his seat along the wall and said, "Guys, we're going to have to—"

"And you *can do* it," said Eric.

"They're giving me the wrap up sign," Tony said.

Kareem looked at Mr. Kay and said, "Oh, you can't stop us *here."*

Mr. Kay said, "You're going to be making excuses to your teachers why you're late for class, so—"

"Let me just say one more thing," Tony said. "I appreciate you guys taking a little time with me because I got a little better perspective about what's happening at US and what you guys are thinking about. I graduated in 1981. And my classmates, we sat in a classroom like this and talked about some of the same issues, so some things have changed and some things have not. I think the fact that you're at the table talking about it, and the fact that you're preparing yourselves from an educational standpoint—bar none that is the most powerful tool you're going to have, however you decide to address those problems. All I'm saying is, when you talk about US, loyalty, responsibility, consideration, you all have a responsibility to maybe make that change in some way, and we're all going to do it in different ways. I think you have to be loyal to each other and also to the overall classmates of University School, to be plugging into that network, because *that's* where diversity happens."

The meeting was over. The boys, as always, hustled off to classes in which they would be, most of the time, the only black student in the classroom. Kevin thanked Tony for taking his morning off to be here.

I heard a lot throughout the year about the importance of finding good black teachers, from Kerry, Hawley, Kevin Kay, and a number of administrators from other independent schools—but the subject has become such a given that people seem only to be frustrated by it. Kerry, feeling so besieged by the question, once said to me in exasperation, "No one says to us, 'Where are all your *Asian* teachers?' "

That is an important observation. All minorities struggle with questions of cultural identity, how to maintain solid footing in two camps at once while simultaneously forging their individuality as American teenagers. But African-American boys carry the weight of a history defined by a holocaust of their own ancestors, the mass destruction of a race which demands the same constant witness as the holocaust of the Jews, and the effects of which continue to destroy huge numbers of people, most visibly and horribly African-American boys like themselves, in some cases, right outside their front door.

None of this, however, changes the fact that Shawntae is failing Western Civ. If he doesn't pass the course, his future at the school will be in jeopardy. Margaret Mason acknowledged that boys on scholarship, black or white, are expected to live up to their potential or they may lose their spot to a boy who will. For Shawn, the strain of reconciling his identity as an African American with the social and academic constructs of the private boys' school, not to mention plain growing up, has no release. Except for meetings like the one with Tony Peebles, African-American boys have little opportunity to voice concerns with adults who have been where they are now.

I never saw another meeting or discussion that had the same edge as the one Tony led. Even Tony was surprised by the force of the comments and questions. He has been to a couple of career-day meetings and he says, "They're usually looking at the clock waiting for the bell to ring."

It seemed to me after that meeting that the African-American boys here need black teachers not as role models—they are constantly confronted by dozens of outstanding role models, black, white, male, female—but rather to remind them why they are here.

Paul Bailin makes a last effort to alter Shawn's future. Shawn and another of Paul's freshmen are destined to fail the course without a drastic change in their work. It's easy on any given day to push Shawn to work; but it's impossible to be there every minute of every day pushing him. Shawn needs a 75 percent average for this trimester to raise his overall grade to 60 percent, which is passing. So Paul types up two contracts spelling out exactly what Shawn and his classmate must agree to do—complete every homework assignment, attend a set number of tutorial sessions and pre-test preparations. If Shawn does everything spelled out in the contract, Paul in turn will do everything he can to ensure that Shawn passes Western Civ. Below the agreement, Paul has typed four blank lines to be signed by himself, by Shawn, by Shawn's sponsor, Jim Garrett, and by Shawn's mother.

When Paul asks the boy in his earlier class, does he want to pass Western Civ and is he therefore willing to sign this contract, the boy answers absolutely and signs immediately. When Paul does the same for Shawn, Shawn looks up and down and away, and says he'll give it a try and see. Paul tells Shawn a contract requires more of a commitment than "I'll see." Shawn does not sign it.

A day goes by. Shawn has shown no signs of wanting to pass the course. This is the first time Paul has used such a contract with students, and he doesn't know what's going on in Shawn's head, if he's even thinking about it. By the end of the week, Shawn appears at Paul's office and tells him he's ready to sign the contract.

Nancy Lerner thinks she has made a mistake. She has always saved *Heart of Darkness* and Francis Coppola's *Apocalypse Now* for the end of the year because she's found that this story of the wilderness is the only material that can engage a senior in springtime. But this year she taught Conrad's novel in the last weeks of the winter term and now she's fighting with her AP English class to get them to read *Portrait of the Artist as a Young Man.* "I'm smarter than that," she says, shaking her head. Springtime's effects are powerful. Even the best reader in the class, Kris Fletcher, has to force himself through Joyce's novel. Using the blunt language of teenage literary criticism, Kris says, "It makes me want to vomit about every two pages."

One day after class, Nancy stops Kris at the door and asks, "Are you liking it any better?"

"No," he answers.

"*Aaw,*" she says.

"It's getting *worse.*"

"*Why?*"

"I just can't *stand* to read about *God.*" Kris is just finishing Book III of *Portrait,* in which the protagonist has a religious epiphany.

"In the next book he's going to throw that off," says Nancy, hopefully.

Tyler Doggett walks in with a poem of his that she'd asked to read, several pages so rumpled he might have retrieved them from a trash can. She carries around a "Doggett" file and stuffs the papers in. She thanks Tyler and he shuffles away.

Kris tells Nancy he doesn't like Joyce's style.

"In *Ulysses* he changes his style each chapter. Maybe you should read that." Hoping to appeal to his taste for the ancient Greeks, she adds, "Joyce uses the *Odyssey* as a structure."

"I don't know how anyone could improve on the *Odyssey*," says Kris, apparently skeptical of everything by Joyce.

"He doesn't," Nancy admits. "Tyler could tell you how he does it, though, how he uses it as a structure. You should talk to him."

Kris nods, turns on the balls of his feet, and is gone. "Hey! Tyler Doggett!" he shouts.

Nancy's teaching career is almost over and she's kicking herself for jumping the gun with Conrad.

Tuesday morning in the library. Boys sit around a group study table with books open. Matt Jackson strolls up to the table with a grin, the sort that's often described as shit-eating.

Nick Zinn rises in his chair and says, "You gotta tell me what Fioritto said."

Matt laughs, flips hair out of his eyes, and says, "He came to lunch yesterday and said, 'You're never going to *believe* this.'" Matt grins some more and says, "His girlfriend said her friend said *you* were *stalking* her."

Nick pushes himself away from the table, slumps in the chair, rubs his chin hard, and sighs through his teeth, both embarrassed and mad, one big *Geeeez*.

Ryan Alexander says, "Uh-oooooo. Nick's upset."

"I wasn't even *here* this weekend," Nick says.

"She said you called her *six* times on Friday," says Matt Jackson.

"I wasn't even *here* on Friday. I was in West *Virginia*."

"Tell it to the judge," a boy at the next table calls out with a grin much like Matt's.

"I was in West Virginia visiting my *grand*parents." Nick releases a gust of breath. Then he pauses thoughtfully. "How would you stalk? How *would* you stalk? I don't even know how you'd go *about* it."

．．．

Nick admits he *did* have something of a crush on this girl. And, true, matters were somewhat complicated by the fact that when said girl mentioned a classmate of Nick's, Nick informed her that the guy was a "nerd," after which he began to receive threatening anonymous notes, such as "You better watch your back, Zinn" in his mailbox. (The girl had informed the other suitor what Nick had said about him.) But whatever crush there was has now been taken care of by the stalking accusations. *Stalking.* Geeez.

It doesn't matter anyway, though, because Nick has a date this Friday with a different girl. And it may, *may,* lead to a prom date in a couple weeks.

The following Monday, I pass Nick in the hall and ask how his date went.

Nick's shoulders twist right, twist left. He seems unsure which way to run. "It's a long story—I'll tell ya later," he says, then says that she cancelled. He makes a one-man commotion in the hall and explains that the reason she canceled was, she *said,* because a "friend" had "suddenly" come into town. Nick did not believe her. He says he had a fit. He says he told her she was lying. And the girl cried. "She told me, 'I think you're a r-r-really neat guy,' " Nick tells me, adding that he proceeded to make her feel worse by refusing to believe her even after the crying.

Now, Nick says, he feels *really* bad. He found out from "several sources" that she was telling the truth.

Bottom line: no date, no prom.

The weather is warm enough now for Nick to take long comfortable walks during the first three free periods of the day. Nick brings a book on these daily walks. It had been Kafka's *The Castle.* Now it's D. H. Lawrence.

I arrive early to philosophy class and find Eugene alone in the room, pacing. He has just been in a car accident. All winter, I'd enter to find him stretched out along the wall asleep. Now he's burning a track in the carpet.

"I had a personal expeeerience with the cave!" he tells me. His eyes are huge and he's shaking his wide-open hands at me. "You know? The cave?"

I say yes and ask him what happened.

"I was driving along South Woodland. But that doesn't really matter.

What matters was *the sun* that was *out* there. It's dee-vine! The ex-*halt*-ing light was just *beaming* into my eyes. And then I had this little blackout, you know, when you come back from exhaltation, you know, you sort of—I don't know, if you believe Freud that blackouts must be induced by some deeper unconscious desire to go back to the light. But anyway I didn't go back to the light. I went into the car that was in front of me, and the car in front of me hit another car. You know where the trouble comes from," Eugene says. "It comes from the sun."

I ask Eugene what the repercussions will be.

"My eeensurance will go up twenty-five percent, probably, and my licence is going to be suspended because two days ago"—he's rubbing his hands and grinning like a maniac—"I exceeded the speed limit and got my *first speeding* ticket."

I ask him was anyone hurt? He says no. Eugene shares the car with his mother and father, and I ask him what kind of shape the family buggy is in.

"My car is the best of the three!" he says happily. Then he says, "It was just this over*whelm*ing light in the morning, when I'm fresh and open to refreshing experience."

Hawley enters the class, and Eugene practically knocks him down. "Doctor Hawley! Doctor Hawley! I had a personal experience with the cave!"

Eugene, gesticulating wildly, tells the story to Hawley, whose eyebrows remain fixed at the top of his forehead.

Nick Zinn has entered and sits on the table, his feet on a chair, and, glancing at Eugene, says to me, "I feel bad for him."

Nick had a summer job interview yesterday after school and I ask him how it went.

"It was *long*," he says. "It was for an hour and forty-five minutes. The guy liked to *talk*. I think that if I g-g-get the job his productivity will fall because he'll spend all his time *talking* to me."

Kris Fletcher sitting on a table at the back of the room says, "You had your interview yesterday? How'd it go, man?"

"It was very *long*," Nick repeats. "It started at four and I left at five-forty-five."

"What kind of job is this for?"

"Um, um, comp, c-c-computers."

"Coolness," says Kris.

The second bell rings and more boys file in. The atmosphere is lively. Even the way classes begin seems different in spring. People stand around and talk as if around a table of hors d'oeuvres. When all are settled, and Eugene is fastened into his seat, Hawley says, "Men, can we go on quickly? I need a sense of what experience you'll be presenting in the big and terminal paper that we have."

This is the aesthetic experience paper—the boys will attempt to define a passionate experience by objective criteria. Hawley wants to make sure they're all on the right track. Inevitably, some of the boys will choose a favorite song, and he doesn't want anyone turning in twenty-five-hundred words on how awesome Jerry Garcia is.

"There is an illegal date beyond which I can't assign a paper," Hawley says regarding the due date. "I think it's May 2, maybe a little later. But Nick, have you thought about what you're going to present?"

Nick Caserio, seated off to the side, says, "Um, I think so. Probably the beauty of the jump shot."

"Which is fine," Hawley says quickly. "Does it involve any videos or—"

"I could, there are videos that I could look at."

"Nick?" Hawley points at Nick Zinn, directly to his left as always.

"I'm-I'm-I'm I'm caught between two, OK?" Nick rocks back and forth in his chair. "And the first one I'm not sure because it's on e-e-experience more than on o-o-object.

"What are those two things?" Hawley asks. There are a lot of people to get through and he's trying to hurry Nick along.

"Well I-I-I was thinking, um, to explain, on Friday um-um-um I went and sat o-o-on the dock outside, ya know? And I had a transcendental m-m-m-m-m-m—"

"You had a transcendent—"

"Transcendental moment," Nick finishes with a burst.

"Thoreau!" Caserio shouts out.

"Either that or the part right before the explosion of music in Beethoven's ninth."

"OK, either one of those will be fine. OK. Igor?"

"Probably do like a powerful laser beam into space."

"Is it an image that you're going to reproduce or—"

"Probably a concept."

Hawley points at Jason Koo. "Jason, have you thought?"

Jason hasn't looked up from his notebook all year and he's not about to start today. "It's sort of, I don't know," he mumbles, "it's sort of spiritual." He is barely audible.

"OK," says Hawley. Jason, brilliant though he is, clearly needs to hone his idea a little as far as Hawley's concerned, and Hawley does what he can to direct Jason. "One of the greatest theories on the source of aesthetics is that they come from the All, they come from the godhead, they come from the source of all being. Radiant shafts of light. And then to connect with those is what aesthetics is. That's a powerful view. What experience are you going to describe?"

"Well," Jason says to his notebook, "light and stuff."

"Light is . . . *involved.*" Hawley waits. "You're being kind of cryptic, Jason."

"It happened at five in the morning," he says.

"You mean the dawning? The appearance of light?"

Jason nods. He knows exactly what he's doing and wants to be left alone.

Hawley continues around the class.

Tony says, "I'm going to do the beauty of flight. More specifically—"

"Bird flight or plane flight?"

"Bald eagle."

Eric Hermann says, "I think I'm going to do a Beatles song, 'A Day in the Life,' and I thought—"

"It's a song I know," says Hawley, an avid Beatles fan. "It's very episodic as you know, it's almost a little opera, it's got all these different phases and rhythms."

"I'll just do the, uh, crashing before the end and the crescendo going up."

Mike Cohen says, "This may be a little chauvinistic, but I think I'd like to do *The Graduate* when the audience first sees Katherine Ross."

Kris Fletcher says, "I'm going to do a song. Obviously. Um."

"I bet you're going to do *Mozart,*" Hawley says.

"No," says Kris. "It was a toss-up. I think I'm going to do a song by Sabotage."

Wilkie says, "Well I've got two. A car I drove the first year I had my license. A seventy-two green Mercedes, or um—"

"That's actually a project close to my heart," says Hawley.

"Either that or an experience I had while sitting by a brook."

"When will you resolve these? Is it the car as a sculpture or the experience of driving it?" Hawley asks, mildly directing. Apparently he's not too keen on the brook idea.

"The whole experience."

Rob Haffke, who once confessed that he would trade his soul for one good game of Sega, says, "The last passage of *A River Runs Through It.*"

"I'm glad somebody's doing a literary project," Hawley says and points to Scott.

Scott says, "A Rothko painting."

Vish says, "I'm not quite sure. I might do the sky."

"The idea of it or a particular one you have in mind?"

"Just the sky," he says and chuckles.

"Eugene?"

"*Well,*" Eugene says. "The experience that I had this morning has actually complicated my choice. I was going to do it on—"

"Was it an aesthetic experience?"

"I was going to do it on dawn in the desert."

"Israel?" Hawley asks.

"Yeah, but now I'm thinking of doing just the sun. You look at the sun, and I got *so fascinated* I got into a car accident this morning."

The class laughs.

"You almost *joined* the sun," says Hawley. "Did you tell that to the arresting officer?"

"I was thinking about the sun," Eugene says, nodding.

"He probably gave you a breathalizer," Hawley says.

"The problem was that I *stopped* looking at the sun," says Eugene, "and I looked at the road but I had this blackout. You know how he returns in 'The Allegory of the Cave,' how he returns from the light? But I'm going to do that. It was a very aesthetic experience."

"The aftermath was not very aesthetic," says Hawley.

Eugene, nodding vigorously, laughs, HA-HA-HA-HA! "No, the aftermath was not very aesthetic. No."

17

Carol Pribble wanders the empty auditorium a few minutes before rehearsal. The weave of her steps along the middle aisle is so slow that she appears to be happily lost. These moments, with her theater empty and silent, are among the most peaceful she will have all day. Minutes later, at 6:33, the cast arrives. Something has happened. The boys and girls do not appear as individual entities, straggling in to take their seats as they had as recently as a couple of weeks ago. They arrive in the auditorium as nothing less than a rabble. They have been rehearsing together nightly since well before spring break and now cohere. The boys are particularly noisy. Carol has addressed this. "I think it's *funny*," she said recently, "that *you guys* talk three times as loud as when I ask you to talk on stage." This is true. Put a few boys on an empty stage and, if they haven't acted before, you've got to wring volume out of them. Put four hundred boys in a school, and what you mainly hear is a hush. Put twenty boys in an auditorium with half as many girls, and the volume needle slams into the red zone.

The only one not talking is Mike Seelbach, the lead, who perches on the uppermost point of the banister beside the center section of seats where the cast gathers. He is saving his voice, occasionally drawing sips of water from the orange straw in his University of Miami container.

"OK, let's get started," Carol calls out.

Justine and Jessica, twinlike with their long bodies and long hair, sit on the front rail a few feet from Carol, arms draped like scarves about each other. As Carol runs through her notes for tonight's rehearsal, Jessica rests her head on Justine's shoulder. Justine smooths Jessica's hair. Bill Shepardson lies immediately below Justine and Jessica, across the center aisle and propped against a seat back. It's difficult to sense whether or not he hears Carol speaking, so fixed is his gaze. He thinks Jessica, who goes to Laurel, has asked someone else to her prom. "I want to go to the Laurel prom," he had told me a day or so before with a look of hunger advanced to the point of illness. "I reeeeeally want to go to the Laurel prom." He doesn't know that she's asked someone else, he only suspects it. At the moment, he appears to be willing the words *Bill, will you go to the prom with me?* into Jessica's head.

Carol asks where music director Marty Kessler is. Marty's daughter, Sue, says they had a problem with their hot-water heater at home. "He made us all go outside in case it blew up," Sue says.

"See?" Carol says. "That's *just* what I was telling you. Don't *do* anything like that before a show." She looks at her notes, and says, "Something that just came to my attention. The biggest rehearsal, the tech rehearsal, when you get costumes, the orchestra is here, is the day after prom. This is a *major* rehearsal. I *don't* want to know who went to the prom and who didn't. Do you understand what I'm saying? Short of using drugs, I want you in full force on Sunday."

Mike Cohen is back in action, out of the penalty box following his untimely glass of wine in Paris, and Carol says tonight at some point they must block off the tar-and-feather scene with Mike Seelbach and John Gregor the Duke. John, as always, is in the back row with little Jessica. John has asked her to the prom. The two are almost always whispering and giggling secretively.

Sophomore Colin Fishwick arrives late dressed in a junior varsity baseball uniform two sizes too big, and stockinged feet. When he sees that rehearsal proper has not begun, he dashes away, not to shower and dress but to find food. Nick Rajkovich, Judge Thatcher, sits on the steps eating Keebler cookies out of a bag and drinking from a quart carton of whole milk.

"OK, we need the piano brought down here, then we can get started," says Carol. Bill and Jeremy jog to the stage to roll the upright piano out of the Mississippi River.

Justine and Jessica remain entwined, chatting on the rail, as Carol begins what will be a four-hour stretch of work. I sit beside them and ask them what they think of the boys here. They respond without a moment's thought.

Justine: "They don't teach the boys here anything about girls. They ask

319

such stupid questions. They think feminists are these women running around burning bras."

Jessica: "They look at you with X-ray eyes." Jessica cross-registers for Carol's drama workshop and is therefore here during school hours. "On the other hand," she says, "you do find cultured boys, intelligent boys."

"They look at you like a piece of meat," Justine tells Jessica.

"Not all of them," says Jessica. But she insists that the boys here don't know a thing about girls. "You should hear their views on abortion," she says.

Justine: "Come on, they're all pro-choice."

Jessica: "Walk around."

Marty Kessler, water-heater problem under control, arrives and Carol runs through the opening number of Act II, a lively song called "The Royal Nonesuch," led by John Gregor and involving most of the cast. Everyone is sloppy and when the number is finished, Kessler turns to Pribble and says, "I've got about three things to say."

"I've got at *least* that many," says Carol.

About fifteen minutes of directions follow. Eric Myricks, dressed in baggy jeans, a T-shirt, and a baseball cap, strolls into the auditorium. He's been rehearsing for a May recital all afternoon at the music institute. When Carol and Marty have finished, Carol starts from the beginning.

John Gregor strolls affably up to three boys playing townspeople and says, "Gentlemen, gentlemen—"

Carol halts the scene immediately. John is late with his line. "Start again," she says. Carol is gradually moving from big problems to moments. John starts, strolling affably on stage again, and before he can open his mouth, Carol shouts out, "Gentlemen, gentlemen, give a listen!"

John, cheated out of his line, looks up hurt at Mrs. Pribble, who's standing at the foot of the stage.

"Hear the difference?" she asks John.

"Yes," John says petulantly.

"What is it?"

Repeating a line he's clearly heard a hundred times, John says, "It sounds like I'm walking over here before I'm getting into character." Carol turns and walks from the stage up the aisle. John glares at her. You can see his jaw set.

"You *never* want to remind an audience that they're watching a play," says Carol. She's getting cranky. Carol knows exactly why she got that reaction from John, but she does her best to ignore it. Little Jessica is in her seat watching and Carol has just embarrassed John in front of her. She knows he took her words as insult. That's when the guy-girl thing gets to be a pain, Carol told me. "It's much easier to direct all guys," she said.

They run through the entire opening number again, and the conclusion of the scene when all the characters leave the stage except for Huck; Carol allows its course, though she looks like she's sucking lemons as she watches. She takes it out on Mike Cohen, whose last line is, "We're leaving tomorrow," after which he trots merrily off stage.

"When you say 'We're leaving tomorrow,' *get* off that stage!" Carol shouts. "And take that gum out of your mouth!"

Opening night approaches and the pressure builds. Carol strolls the middle aisle as the cast prepares for the next scene. Colin Fishwick is in the front row, elbows on the rail in front of him, devouring his dinner. He stops in mid-bite when he sees Mrs. Pribble approach. She hovers over him. It looks like she's going to take his head off. She stares at his food, a massive roast beef sandwich and a mound of Pepperidge Farm Goldfish.

"Whatcha got there?" Carol deadpans. "Surf and turf?"

Colin gives her a big grin, mouth stuffed with roast beef. Carol chuckles and returns to her notebook.

The next scene is just Huck and Jim, and John takes this time to sit beside his Jessica in the back row. As Huck and Jim sing "Worlds Apart" ("I see the same skies through brown eyes, that you see through blue," Eric sings, "but we're worlds apart . . ."), John is oblivious to rehearsal. Huck and Jim finish the scene efficiently. John waits till the last possible moment to tear himself away from Jessica, then dashes out of the auditorium and onto the stage, breathless, pushing hair out of his face.

"John, you're doing this *way* too often," says Carol. "We have one week and three days till we open. We can't be doing this anymore. There's too much racing on stage. I don't know how you can just burst onto stage in character. Give yourself some time. When you know your scene is coming up, get up there, give yourself a couple minutes to get ready."

"Yes, Mrs. Pribble."

When they're between scenes, cast members often hang out by the front doors in the main commons where they can talk. When I walk out to see what's happening here, a group of boys and girls cluster around a table pushed over on its side. Justine is attempting to hurdle it. Justine looks athletic in a short school skirt, field shoes, and a red bandana headband. Her legs are long and slender. After a successful leap, she lifts the table upright and slides a bench in front of it. She commands the group's attention by wondering aloud if she can leap both these objects. Everyone eggs her on except Brandon, a voice of caution. Carol's don't-do-anything-stupid-before-the-show speech still fresh in his mind, Brandon's worried that she'll break a bone if she misses. "That table will still be there when the play is over," he says.

Justine ignores him. She stands at the table and steps backward with long strides to measure the distance. From ten yards away, she looks determined and everyone is quiet. It will be quite a leap if she makes it. More often than not, guys are the ones jumping over something or off something or onto someone. Here it was a girl doing it, and a boy trying to dissuade her. Justine charges the table, but something seems to anchor her to the ground. You can see as soon as she begins that she'll never make it. Justine balks at the bench and table like a horse before a jump, then walks around them to the other side. "But wouldn't it be great?" she says. "Wouldn't it be great if I could do it?"

A few moments later, Bill Shepardson senses Justine is game and initiates a small competition to pass the time. Who can touch the clock? A large round clock hangs from the ceiling at about the height of a basketball net. Bill does not look athletic; what weight he carries seems to be packed mainly at his haunches. Furthermore, Justine has a few inches on Bill. Justine accepts. Bill goes first. He stands back, looks at the clock, finds the spot directly below the clock, then glides along a sloping path, plants his right foot, sails upward, hovers momentarily, and lands a solid swat on the bottom of the clock. Justine follows immediately. She strides beautifully to the clock and plants her foot, but she doesn't sail. She seems barely to leave the ground and misses the clock by more than a foot. The difference is dramatic because Justine is graceful and Bill is not. You'd swear they were working against different laws of gravity. Bill makes a fist, squeezes his elbow into his side, and says, *"Yes."* He's psyched.

I return to the auditorium and sit on the center rail. John Gregor finishes a scene and hustles off stage, but when he returns to the seats, he spots Mike Cohen beside his Jessica.

"Damn," John whispers. His eyes narrow and he grits his teeth. He sits on the rail beside me, his back to Jessica and Mike, who are laughing and carrying on. "Why is he *sitting* there?" John says. He casts angry, surreptitious glances over his shoulder. "Why doesn't he *go away?*"

John is more anxious than usual tonight. Jessica has given him a note, he tells me. They went out to dinner last night after rehearsal and they talked on the phone till well after midnight. The note reads, "My sleepy boy, don't call me tonight."

What is she trying to tell me? John wonders. *What does this mean?* John continues to glance back at Mike and Jessica. When he can stand the sound of their laughter no longer, he stalks up the steps and plants himself in the seat beside Mike. John's crossed arms and his silent scowl make it clear he's not on a friendly mission. Eventually, Mike stops talking, looks to Jessica on his right, then to John on his left, grins, says, "Oooookay," and departs by stepping over the seat in front of him. John moves immediately into the vacated spot and smiles at Jessica, once again returned to the heaven of her attention.

It's nine-thirty and they've still got to get through more scenes.

Eric Myricks is acting. "And I treated it so," he says in the low drawl of Jim, the runaway slave.

"More regret on that, Eric," Carol calls out.

"And I treated it *so,*" he tries.

"You're beating yourself up."

"Huh?"

"You know how you beat yourself up over things?" Carol says.

Eric thinks, winces, and says, "And I *treated* it so."

"That's it," says Carol and the scene concludes.

John Gregor is sure to be ready before the following scene with Huck, Jim, and the King; unfortunately, he forgets that he has the first line. Huck waits, and waits. Then John says, "Oh!," which isn't the line.

"John," says Carol, "what would you do if an actor did that in a show?"

"Walk *out,"* he says, humiliated.

"Good answer," says Carol. "You know, during a show, when there's a silence on stage? My heart *stops.* My heart is too old for that. All right. Again. Mike *Cohen,* get rid of your *gum."* She turns and shakes her head. She looks at me and says, "I recommended him for gum rehab. I talked to Dr. Hawley."

Rick Hawley is never not busy, but in the spring he's really busy. One thing he doesn't need to worry about, though, is the keynote speaker for this year's upper-school graduation.

Nancy Lerner will address the graduating class of 1994. Hawley's upset that she's leaving; she brought "a real intellectual edge" to the school, he says, and was "an important female influence." He's trying to find a way to keep Nancy connected to the school by securing funds with which to offer Nancy a scholarship to teach students independently next year and deliver a few school-wide presentations on various topics, such as the heroine in literature. Her remarks at graduation will be an elegant way to conclude her brief tenure here: Hawley wants her to go out with a punch that is commensurate with her impact on the school. "It may be a historical first," he adds. "The first woman to speak at commencement."

Nancy began to regret her decision to speak as soon as she was outside Hawley's range. She said Hawley puts a spell on her and she becomes stupid. When the spell wears off, she thinks, "Oh my God, what have I done now?"

Nancy addressed the subject with a former colleague shortly after the spring term began. She'd asked Peter Scott, who teaches English at Hawken, to conclude her classes on *Heart of Darkness* and *Apocalypse Now*. Peter is a Vietnam vet and was recruited by the CIA to join a counter-terrorist group that would sometimes venture into Cambodia, just as the Martin Sheen character did in *Apocalypse Now*. Peter, a big guy dressed in black jeans, work boots, and a dark knit tie, added some blunt verisimilitude to the fictional narratives the boys had been studying. When the class was over Nancy and Peter remained in the room, talking, and Nancy told Peter that she'd decided to renege on her agreement to be the commencement speaker.

"Why?" Peter asked.

"I don't know if I'll be able to keep from crying," she said. "I cry at the drop of a hat." She told Peter about her presentation on the Holocaust Museum.

"But what's wrong with that?" he asked.

"I don't want to be 'The Woman Who Gets Up There and Cries.' "

"Right," Peter agreed, "You could do it if you were a guy, but—"

"I don't have anything to *say* to the boys," she added. "What I have to say to them, I say in class. I meet them at the text."

On Tuesday, May 3, Nancy Lerner's Radio Flyer red wagon returns to school. She'd kept it on blocks, as it were, all winter, as if to spare it harsh weather and salty roads. Her last AP English class is tomorrow, and it's time to start cleaning out her desk and unloading shelves of books. It's a full day's job, and Nancy will take more than a month, almost up to graduation, to complete it. Because Nancy teaches only seniors, who will be at work on independent projects after Friday, her only school obligation is a second trip to the Holocaust Memorial Museum (she led the first in April). She has no need even to be at school. For Nancy, who has complained all year about the strain of teaching and the demands on her time, these weeks might have provided an early start on the solitary reading and writing she's been longing for. Instead she offers to take Bob Hanson's first-period English class for the rest of the year. It's a break Bob can use, and the class is studying *The Odyssey,* one of Nancy's favorites. It doesn't make her feel good to be doing this for Bob and for herself; she feels neither kind nor helpful. She feels guilty. All the moaning she does about being overworked on a two-class schedule, she thinks, and here's Bob handling four sections of sophomores and juniors all year and never saying a word. But that's Bob, aged and gray from thirty years of teaching, and rather than weathering to statuesque apathy he remains the soul of cheerful professionalism. He has recently taken to dressing in Black Tie on the day that he introduces his juniors to *The Great Gatsby.*

Nancy is leaving the profession, and I wonder if she's taking Bob's class because she fears not teaching. "I'm confident this is right," she says. She adds that this class has been great and that it pleases her they were her last students. But she's still kicking herself for saving Joyce till the end. She knows it's a difficult text the first time around, and the boys did not read it the way they would have had she assigned it earlier in the year.

The following day, Nancy enters Room 270 matter of factly in her white blazer and long white skirt; a pink, yellow, and green, neo-sixties striped pullover blouse glows within like the inner petal flush on an exotic orchid. She carries today's quizzes and her tattered Penguin paperback of *Portrait of the Artist as a Young Man,* which is so worn and flimsy its back cover is inserted into a maroon backing for support and the front cover is gone altogether. The pages are filled with pink and blue highlighting and black underlines, words like "Heavenly God" circled in her ornate sweeping pen.

Kris Fletcher is sitting on a table rapidly clicking his fingernails against the wood. This stimulates growth, he says. He had cut them for Kathleen and the occasion of the prom. When Nancy enters, he takes his seat. Tyler Doggett arrives, having discovered a good existentialist-black shirt, and he's smiling for the first time all year. He and Nick Caserio trade jibes about baseball.

"Hello everybody," says Nancy. "Everybody ready?"

She hands out the quizzes with no further preamble, and for the first five minutes of the final class, the room fills with the sound of pencils clicking on table tops. Nancy, intensely scanning their faces, can't figure out who's missing and runs through her attendance book. Eric Hermann and Mike Cohen are on stage in the first performance of *Big River,* a full-scale preview for the lower-school boys before tomorrow night's opening. When Nancy says time's up and circles the room collecting the quiz, everyone whines about how hard it was.

"How many of you read?" she asks. All hands go up, except for Eugene's, which bobs up and down at ear level while his eyes dart shiftily back and forth, and he bites his fingernail. "I didn't mean the quiz to be hard," Nancy says. "Really. Do you want to tell me anything on the back about why you didn't do well? Can I tell *you* something? The thing that I care about is that you read. I'm not interested in doing a great mathematical analysis, and dragging it out, I'm just interested in your reading, and you should be interested in the fact that such a primitive tool as my giving you a quiz has gotten you to read.

"Would you now—I want to ask you a couple things," she begins. Ken Sable, the attendance taker whom Nancy has verbally assaulted all year pokes his head in the door. "Hi," she says. "Mike Cohen and Eric Hermann." Ken hesitates an instant at Nancy's cheerfulness, smiles, and departs.

"Yesterday," she continues, "I had a very, very emotional day, and I told my second period the truth about how I felt, and afterwards I sort of felt that it had been rather manipulative. I didn't do it for that reason. It was the anniversary of my father's death and I was already upset to begin with. But the way I put it to them is the way I'm going to put it to you today. I hope not in a manipulative way but, um, I'm smarter, I think, about teaching than I have allowed myself to be in this last week. I know how seniors feel. I've been teaching them for fifteen years, and you've done as well as or better than any group I've *ever* seen."

Nancy is standing, not at the head of the class as she has all year, but instead at the back of the class, near the windows overlooking the courtyard.

"I've never done Joyce this way before, and I'm feeling bad about it. I'm feeling bad—I'll never teach Joyce in high school again, as far as I know, as far as I have plans to do. I don't feel bad for you. You're going to go on, and if Joyce is going to mean anything to you, you'll read Joyce again, you'll

326

encounter Joyce again, or you'll do something equally glorious. I feel bad for *Joyce,*"—Nancy smiles sadly—"who I somehow feel is up there in the heavens looking down on me saying, 'Why didn't you do a *better job?* Why did you drag out this *great moment* in my book on the last day?'

"I often think about the difference between high school teaching and college teaching, and to me it always comes down to where a teacher's first obligation lies. And in high school, I think the first obligation lies with your students. You feel something very personal and important about sort of knowing who the students are and doing the best for the *students.* That wasn't how I was going to teach, because when you teach college and you have a specialty, like modern literature or Joyce, your obligation is really to the writer, to Joyce. If you care about the students that's nice, but the attitude I would take if I were teaching Joyce in college is, tough, sign up for the course, take it, get what you can. My job is to do the best I can for Joyce. So I'm sort of stuck in between feelings that I've *let* Joyce *down* in some way."

What she would like to do, therefore, is ask them "the favor" of allowing her to examine aloud Book IV, the penultimate chapter of *Portrait,* when the hero casts off God and his boyhood chums and becomes the Artist, the moment when Stephen Dedalus sees a woman lift her skirt and dip her toe into water, one of the great epiphanic moments in literature.

Her lecture is clear, efficient, and insightful and very much in the style of lectures that the boys will be hearing in college English courses. She speaks for nearly an hour, virtually unbroken by comment or question, drawing on Greek mythology, Dante, Yeats, and Helen of Troy.

"Even though Stephen descends again and is deflated in Book Five," she concludes, "you ought to look at his diary. I really think some of you might want yourself, as you go into July and August, perhaps keep a diary—having arisen out of the great course of your high school years about to embark on whatever flight you're about to embark on. What he says at the very end, he starts counting the days to leave Ireland. He allows his mother to bathe him one last time knowing that it gives her pleasure, but of course the bath she gives him is again a rebirth and he says 'Mother is putting my new secondhand clothes in order.' " Nancy's reading of the final words of the book is clear but without emotive inflection. " 'She prays now, she says, that I may learn in my own life and away from home and friends what the heart is and what it feels. Amen. So be it. Welcome, O life! I go to encounter for the millionth time the reality of experience and to forge in the smithy of my soul the uncreated conscience of my race. Old father, old artificer, stand me now and ever in good stead.' " Nancy pauses, closes her book.

"Anyway. Tomorrow. I think some of you will read from your own poetry, you will also read your own 'portrait' and . . . have a good*bye* party."

And she is done. Tomorrow, Nancy will join Hawley for his final class, which will lunch in the boardroom, and the boys will read from their own imaginative writing, copies of which Nancy has Xeroxed and bound prettily in booklet form with staples and back-and-front cover page.

As the room drains of students—Rob Haffke says to me, "It's too bad she's leaving; she's awesome"—Nancy lingers over her papers and books. She thinks about college, where these boys are headed, with an appealingly breathless nostalgia. She tells me what an incredible life college was for her, and may be for some of these boys—to understand in your heart that a life with literature alone can be a rich one, she tells me, to dwell in a purely intellectual world. For her it was to be, she says, "overwhelmed with joy."

Nancy stops fussing with her papers, looks up and says, "Some never want to leave that world. And they become teachers."

Kris leaves the classroom expressionless, as though it were any day. In addition to being de-clawed, his head has an unusual roundness to it. He has cut his hair for the first time all year, and while it remains longer than most of his classmates', it has been sculpted to form what would be in caricature a perfect sphere. He doesn't mind. He just won't be able to "thrash" for a while.

On Monday, two days ago, the first day of school after the prom, Kris had been shelving newspapers and magazines as he had been doing at that hour virtually every morning since school began. Nick Zinn was in the library too, lurching about.

When Nick spotted Kris, Nick's mouth hung open. He said, "Hey, *Fletcher*. What *happened?*"

Kris held his hands out and shrugged all the way up to his now-visible ears.

"*What happened?*"

"It begins with a K," Kris said and strolled away, casual as could be.

"You did that because of a girl?" Nick said. "You did that because of a *girl?*" Kris attended to more shelves farther away. "Oh, man," Nick continued, in anything but a library voice. "That is *wrong*. Kris, I g-g-gotta *talk* to you."

Kris and Kathleen had stayed out till 7:30 Sunday morning. Kathleen's parents are no exception to the fact that Asian parents are notoriously strict with boy-girl relations, but Kris and Kathleen managed. All Kris would tell me was that they had a good time. There is clearly more to tell, but not to me. Kris did say that Kathleen had agreed to go spelunking, though she didn't want to venture into sewers where the water was up to her neck. That was OK, Kris said, because he knows some clean ones.

Nick Zinn continued to bounce off the walls of the library. I stopped him long enough to ask him what he did Saturday night while the prom was going on.

"Um, um, c-c-computer programming," he said with a shrug. I must have had an unhappy expression on my face then, because Nick added, *"Hey,* I had a good *time."*

The following day was the tech rehearsal for *Big River.* Everyone who had something to do with the play was there and they seemed to be so many, I wondered who would be left to watch the show. The day, May Day, was cold and wet and gloomy. Hawley was in his office with the doors closed, working. John Gregor looked wiped out from last night and sniffled from hay fever, but he still found time for Jessica. A special booth had been built out of wood to hold amplifiers and tape decks and equalizers. Two rows of seats at front-left had been unbolted and removed to make room for the band, featuring teachers and students, including Johnny Lee, a delicate freshman and violin virtuoso who plays with the Cleveland Orchestra's Youth Orchestra, and Andy Kline, who's hand was for some reason swollen like a blimp so that he could barely pick his guitar. The stage, which should have been filled with the set, was instead a mess of sawdust and wood. Boys and girls donned their nineteenth-century attire. Girls switched costumes back and forth. Mike Seelbach left the men's bathroom, his face tanned with make-up; he smiled and said, "I'm a cover girl now!" In the auditorium, Carol saw that John was still in street clothes and said, "Johnny, are you dressed?"

"Well, *yeees,"* he answered.

"I didn't mean as opposed to nude."

"What *evil* ideas were going through your *mind,* Mrs. Pribble?"

Carol rolled her eyes and moved on.

When the cast was complete, Carol gathered them in the lobby. Boys and girls spread out across the carpet. Their cohesion seemed complete; many of them propped themselves against each other—a girl used Bill Shepardson's shins for a pillow—all of them casual and apparently unselfconscious of how much they touch each other.

Carol had a lot to say—that "this is the rehearsal from hell," how long she would keep them today, how they were not allowed to say a word in complaint, technical notes from previous rehearsals, and a warning.

"We're having a serious prop problem," she said. One gun and three knives have been missing, she said, and there wasn't a knife for Chip when they performed "The Boys" number for the Tower Society dinner last week. "My guess is that you're not stealing props to take them home so you can *play* with them on the weekend. You're picking them up and playing with them and then you just drop them or leave them someplace. These are all kinds of weaponry toys. This may sound sexist, but those of you who are most likely to play with weapons"—she pauses as both the boys and the girls chuckle—"stop it, stop it, *stop* it. You are going to *ruin* the show. If someone has to go out there and the knife is not there, it will ruin the moment. It is not worth ruining the show so that you can play. You are not children, you are actors."

Thus chastened, the cast listens to Carol's itinerary for the day and her notes regarding actual scenes and set movements.

Because he wasn't on till the end of the first act, John Gregor spent his free time with Jessica. The two of them looked like nineteenth-century school children as John led Jessica by the hand up the steps to the highest, darkest corner of the seats. I sat on a rail to watch rehearsal, and a few minutes later, I noticed two shapes on the other side of the auditorium, in the darkened wing. It was John and Jessica again. They were moving about the place like silent creatures in the woods. They were shadows. Jessica put her arm over John's neck. John dipped and lifted Jessica in his arms. Their silhouettes kissed.

Fourth period, the day after Nancy's final English class, Hawley's philosophy students file into Room 270. Vish strides in and raises a fist in the air. "One-more-day!" he says. Finding his seat, he says, *"This* is a *good* day."

Nick Zinn says, "Why?"

"No more philosophy!" says Vish.

330

Nancy enters in a white skirt and blazer, turquoise necklace, white boots, and holding a copy of *Franny and Zooey*. She announces the day's agenda—"I know Dr. Hawley has ordered a special lunch," she says. "I hope it's not mystery meat with gravy." Before lunch, she informs them, they will be writing an evaluation of the course.

This elicits immediate comment from Mike Cohen and Kris Fletcher, seated next to each other at the back of the room.

Kris: "I think we should *not* read C. S. Lewis."

Mike: "Abolish him!"

Kris: "Excommunicate him! Read more Plato and Aristotle."

Hawley enters dressed in a light gray suit and wearing a tie with the colors of US's rival Hawken. He had been to a reading by Bobbie Ann Mason last night at Hawken and had been given the tie as a gift. The crimson and silver stripes go nicely with his suit.

Hawley doesn't even pause, begins immediately with a question: "How old do you think Friar Laurence is?"

The class has finished *Romeo and Juliet* but Hawley and Igor got into a long discussion yesterday about the character Friar Laurence. Hawley is passionate about the subject. Seven years ago he wrote a novel, based on Shakespeare's tragedy, in which a school administrator becomes so infatuated with two teenagers that the man becomes an agent in their romance and subsequent suicide attempt. He sent the manuscript to one of New York's best literary publishers; it was discovered in the slush pile and bought but never published. He had called his book *Lawrence.*

"How old do you think he is?" Hawley repeats.

The boys shout ages, forty-five, fifty, and Kris Fletcher says, "A hundred and twelve."

"Forty-five years old," Hawley repeats. He's standing perfectly straight at the head of the room. "Sixty-three, somebody said. Probably *not* a hundred twelve. Given a life span, how long did he live? Sixty-five? . . . I was involved in a discussion—I can't stop thinking about it.

"If there were only two cards in life's deck facing you right now, where you are now—you're seventeen, eighteen—and one is the Romeo card. If you play it, you get to love as intensely as Romeo, but with the same short script. There are six days of it, and then *adios.* But you *have* it. The other card is the Friar Laurence card, where you get longevity. You get a whole life span. You get," Hawley wags his head cavalierly, *"philosophy."* The class laughs and Hawley pretends to be stunned.

"As Igor pointed out to me," he says, "there's actually quite a good outcome in *Romeo and Juliet*. Granted the lovers are dead, but there is peace in Verona, which there hasn't been before, and the only reason Friar Laurence did something as impulsive—he was no idiot or a bad citizen—is in effect, 'I'll perform a sacrament of marriage secretly on you two people, enemies,' because he said he perceived a plan that could put these households aright. And he did. There was peace in Verona. You can be Friar Laurence. You can be Romeo. Igor would be Friar Laurence, right?" Igor nods, confidently—no doubt. "What card would you play, honestly?" Hawley asks the class.

The very first voice is Kris's. "Romeo," he says. A couple kids mumble responses, then Nick Zinn says, "I-I-I'd be Juliet."

The class laughs, and Vish throws the long black ropes of his hair back howling.

"That," Hawley says to Nick, "raises too many questions to answer by the time we get out this morning. Seriously." Hawley points to Nick Caserio.

"I don't know, I'd have to think about it," he says.

Rob Haffke says, "I don't think you could answer that unless you had—"

"You've got a life," Hawley cuts in. "I mean, if longevity and philosophy and all those things are the highest, Friar Laurence is the right answer. If having love in all its intensity is the answer, then Romeo is the right card. Kris would be Romeo, Igor Friar Laurence. Eugene?"

Eugene says, "I don't think that it's the right question."

"You think the very premise is faulty?"

"No one wants to have fear in their life. But fear is a part of life, is an anxiety of life that makes life, life. It's our heart to wish for absolute peace, but if there were an absolute peace—"

"*Oh!*" says Hawley, tipping back on his heels and closing his eyes. "You'll *love* death. Rumors are it's really even. Very peaceful, uneventful."

Nick bursts in. "Why wouldn't you just move on to someone else? Don't go *shoot* yourself over Juliet."

"Romeo could *not imagine life* without her," Hawley says to Nick. "Maybe it's an unfair question because not everyone's had a Juliet moment in one's life." Hawley moves through the circle of boys, pointing to them for their answers. A total of five people, less than a third of the class, choose the card of brief, intense love.

"I don't know what this means historically," Hawley says when he's circled the room. "This could be, this is the *least* romantic—"

"I don't want to *die*," says Nick Zinn.

"That's what I *mean*. That's the least romantic—you're *scared* to die."

"I'm far more scared of dying than I-I-I am—"

"Desirous of love?" Hawley finishes for him.

"Desirous of love, yeah."

Nancy enters the room and Rick, genuinely baffled and dismayed, explains what he's just done and says to Nancy, "You tell me. How many Friar Laurences and how many Romeos in class?"

"Oh, put me on the *spot*," says Nancy. "After that do I get to answer whether truth is objective or not?"

"You know these guys," says Hawley. "Look them in the eye, and tell me, how many Friar Laurences and how many Romeos?"

Nancy runs through the circle, hitting Nick Zinn first. "Friar Laurence," she says. "Igor, Friar Laurence. Philip, I'm not sure, I think Friar Laurence. Tony, Romeo. Ryan, possibly . . . Romeo. Mike, Friar Laurence." She blows her perfect score on Kris, gets Eric right, and at the silent Jason Koo, she stops, looks sideways at him, points and says, "That one, I bet, *says* Friar Laurence but underneath is Romeo." Jason, who *had* said Friar Laurence, doesn't look up, only smiles. Bingo. And she continues—Rob Haffke looks to me and says, "She's *good*"—concluding with Nick Caserio: "I don't know, did Romeo play football, basketball, and baseball?" she asks Hawley. "How about you?"

Hawley says, "I declared myself as Romeo yesterday."

It is significant that Hawley is dismayed by his class's response. For all *his* philosophizing, his constant claims to beloved philosophy's impact on matters of urgent daily life, his own Laurencian behavior, Hawley is mad at the boys for not choosing love.

Today's class is not really a class, but rather a farewell. Hawley passes out two batches of papers. One is a recent *New Yorker* article about a contemporary philosopher examining the question "What is mind?," and the other is the course evaluation. The first question on this evaluation—before ones that ask what reading was most/least valuable, and did you progress as a writer, what kind?—is this: "Do you believe some kind—any kind—of experience is true and therefore objectively knowable? Or do you believe 'truth' is relative to each individual's thinking?" Hawley knows that relativists greatly outnumber him, so his second question is, "Do you believe what you said above is true?"

At the end of the evaluation are three stanzas of verse called "A Valedictory Poem for the '94 Philosophy Class." Hawley describes his poem to the boys and, as is his fashion, the explanation takes him into a rapid rush of white water, a description and explanation of process philosophy, Whiteheadian philosophy, and the philosophical question of identity. Nancy stands and rings in with Joycean explanations of mind, and, for a moment, the two of them, Dr. Lerner and Dr. Hawley, mother and father, engage in a dialogue of philosophy and literature. For the first time all year, their idea of jointly teaching a class crystalizes, then evaporates.

Hawley instructs the boys to fill out their anonymous evaluations—"Maybe you can disguise your handwriting by writing legibly," Hawley mutters—and ten minutes later they leave the classroom for the boardroom where a cart of dishes containing baked chicken with gravy, wild rice, and green beans is waiting beside the tables laid with tablecloths, dishes, and silverware. Nancy hands out the booklets she's put together titled, "Portraits of the Class of 1994 as Young Men." The booklet is filled with "Once upon a time there was a moocow" stories and over a long leisurely lunch the boys read from their own writing. Nancy leads the group, and Hawley does nothing but listen, delighting, he says afterward, in the abundance and quality of the language Nancy has coaxed from them.

Hawley's final words to the class are in fact themselves written ones and only partly his own. His valedictory poem, which he'd published earlier in an educational journal, concludes:

> Like close "relations" let's convene
> In a spirit of cosmic fun
> And topple and spin our mysteries
> Like worlds around an approving sun.

Beneath the poem are four quotations:

> Know Thyself.—Socrates
> What a piece of work is a man.—Hamlet
> Life is the joyless quest for joy.—Leo Strauss
> I wish but for the thing I have.—Juliet

And after these, simple parting: Adios.

■ ■ ■

The morning of Friday, May 6, is cool but gloriously bright. In some ways, the vast downstairs commons is reminiscent of the first day of school. There's an unusual energy today. The air is festive. Kerry has chosen New Orleans marching music, as he had done the first day of school, and it's cranking. Boys are moving about much more quickly than they normally do at eight A.M. Tyler Doggett has worn his kilt, along with a white button-down shirt, high white socks, and black hard-soled shoes. Doc Strater wears a red bandana tied around his neck on behalf of *Big River*'s opening. Some teachers, many students, and Mr. Brennan wear goofy grins—as though they're about to start giggling at any instant.

The teachers attribute the unusual charge in the air to its being the seniors' final day of classes. Graduation is not for another month—the seniors all have obligations during the next four weeks—but this is truly the last day of school as they've known it here for the past four years.

A couple of teachers pick up clues that something unusual is afoot. One of the boys has covered the piano on stage with a large blue cloth. Track Malone, president of the senior class, is spotted striding, with an expression that combines purpose and extreme silliness, from the athletic wing through the crowded commons and into the senior lounge, concealing a large object awkwardly beneath his brown corduroy blazer.

But this is a place of routine and no matter how odd the mood, all head to assembly and their seats by 8:10, when the music dies and Kerry launches onto stage pulling a fold of announcements from his jacket pocket. Once this happens, the day seems like any other. There is even a prospective student, a stranger to the school, seated beside his parents in the front row of the juniors' section, as there had been regularly throughout the year—guests who have read the brochures but who have come to see the school in action. When Kerry bends the microphone, scans the auditorium, and says, "Good morning. There are a lot of announcements today," it seems an anticlimax to the festive prelude. What had once been days that students counted on calendars has been reduced to seven hours, but it's still school. The Asian Association will meet at the break to elect next year's president. The Environmental Awareness Society will also meet, as will the staff of *The Record*, the school literary magazine. Seniors are reminded to return any state-funded books they may still have. Then Kerry reads yesterday's sports scores.

When he's finished, he says, "This is a special day in the lives of you seniors, and in a way the end of an era for you. Fortunately we don't have to say goodbye to the seniors just yet, but while the seniors go off on their senior experience, foreign exchange students will be going off on trips throughout the United States before they return home." Kerry then reads a brief citation of each exchange student, calling them one by one on stage to receive a certificate acknowledging their year's work here and, as always, a round of applause. Following this, he thanks the teacher apprentices who have earned master's degrees while working here and calls each on stage to receive two parting gifts: a US coffee mug, with their name printed on the bottom to hang in whatever faculty lounge they find themselves in next year, and "the book that everyone's been trying so hard to find at bookstores, *Hail University!*, by Dr. Hawley." Applause follows each apprentice, and when the last recipient has left the stage, Kerry pauses, looks out over the assembly, and says, "Are there any more announce—"

"Get your hand out of my pocket!" a senior named Brian Buckner shouts, standing. He tears out from beneath his blazer a giant water gun. Instantly the entire senior section is on its feet brandishing all manner of water artillery. Neon pink, green, yellow, and purple plastic explodes from within blazers and from underneath seats. The air fills with water, arcs of water, lines of water, seniors rotating in their seats, firing circles of water at the scattering crowd. Chaos. Hawley darts from his seat and is gone, ducking the whole way, a blur of speed. Teachers stuck in middle ranks head to the back of the assembly out of range. And Kerry, only half protected by the podium, finds himself an easy target. A dozen water rifles train on him and fire. He's ten and twenty feet away so the streams are weakened by the time they reach him. Somebody nails him in the face, another traces his jacket. Kerry winces, a sort of "Come on, guys" look of annoyance, when suddenly a cylinder of water, as if launched from a bucket, smacks him in the chest. Then water balloons drench him. Surprised into laughter, he tries to remain for a moment—to take it like a good sport. But the water keeps coming and, drenched, Kerry stumbles away from the podium as if wounded, catches his balance, and jogs out of range. Shouts and cries of victory ring out, and the auditorium clears, all weapons having been discharged.

The visiting boy and his parents have—bravely, perhaps, or perhaps like deer paralyzed in headlights—remained in their seats throughout. Doug Lagarde, senior dean and head of admissions, has rushed to explain and apologize if they were caught in the cross-fire. They nod nervously, and

Kerry appears in the aisle. He looks as if he's just arrived from a full-submersion baptism. The visiting parents stare stone-faced at Kerry. Kerry strides at them, his hair matted, his shirt and jacket soaked, water dripping off the tip of his nose. "Welcome to University School!" he says, beaming.

"Awesome," says Eric Myricks, standing on the steps of the locker area. Wilkie, beside him, says, "Awesome." This is the unvarying evaluation of morning assembly.

I, too, am impressed—that the senior class has managed to do something in unison for the first time all year; but I am also impressed by their weapons. What were once called squirt guns are now called Super Soakers and have specific names such as XP150. One is called a water cannon, a five-foot-long bazooka requiring two people to fire. Some guns apparently contain as much as a liter of water; others come with water backpacks, obviating annoying trips to the bathroom and water fountain to refill.

"They have completely revolutionized the industry," says Rob Haffke, shaking his head reverently.

When boys discover devices through which to propel copious amounts of water, they are not easily persuaded to do anything else. Add to this the fact that many of the seniors have no classes because of AP examinations today, give them a pack of helpless freshmen clustering warily on Monkey Island and you have a small war on your hands. It is not long before such primitive tools as buckets from the art wing and two-liter Coke jugs arrive on the scene. The day becomes one long water fight.

It begins slowly. First-period classes are under way and the seniors congregate in the senior lounge and on the steps of the locker area. Water balloons smash against the windows enclosing their lounge. The fight spreads into the locker room, and soon several boys are rushing Monkey Island to nail freshmen. Doug Lagarde makes a patrol. "Hey! If I see it, it's mine," he tells them, beginning a series of Super Soaker confiscations that will last all day. He sits on the steps facing the commons, waiting and watching. Somebody spots Mr. Harmon's science class heading into the woods toward the trout hatchery. A commando unit is quickly organized and dispatched for an ambush.

There is more cause for jubilation. *Big River* opened last night and Carol and Eric Myricks are in the early stages of success dizziness. "It was a packed house," says Carol, elated. "They got a standing ovation. They *never*

337

get a standing ovation Thursday night." The ovation that followed Huck's and Jim's rousing "Muddy Water" in the middle of Act One went on so long, Carol says, Mike Seelbach and Eric didn't know what to do.

John Gregor caught a cold.

Upstairs in the lecture room, Nancy's AP English classes and others are bent over exams which can count toward college credit. Kris Fletcher's grin lights the room when he sees that two of the poems on the test are about Helen of Troy. He knows he's perfectly prepared.

Outside the administration wing, two lists of final college choices, by student and by college, have been posted, and seniors crowd to see them. Kevin Feder knows every student's pick and his classmates call out names to test him. "Do you think it's sick that I've memorized every college choice?" he asks.

Another boy says, "Only one stinking Harvard."

Wilkie, wanting to know which of his classmates he'll be with next year, says, "Where's Kenyon?"

"Only two people are going to Penn?" says another.

Eugene Gurarie has been accepted at Princeton.

Kerry, toweled off, strolls past the crowd, once again the natty administrator but for his tie, which is curled and ripply from shrinkage.

The commando unit reconvenes after a successful mission. One sophomore now waits in the reception area. Attempting to escape the ambush, the boy slid down a hill through damp dirt and leaves. He now sits soaked and caked with mud in the reception area, waiting for a ride home to shower and change.

Downstairs the number of seniors is increasing ominously. Polly Cohen says, "It's like *feeding* time at the *zoo.*"

Kevin Casey darts through Monkey Island, spraying freshmen, with a quickness that would have been unimaginable during his cannabis-saturated fall trimester.

"Why don't we send them all *home?*" says a nervous Spanish teacher, Gus Pla.

Margaret Mason relieves Doug Lagarde. She strolls to the seniors, who are gathering for a major offensive against the freshmen, plants herself in front of them, and crosses her arms, a one-woman wall.

A pile of weapons grows in Lagarde's locked office. Outside, a band of boys fire water balloons from an immense slingshot—two boys must stand thirty feet apart and lean back to hold the contraption taut. The balloons explode against the brick wall into a great rainbow mist sparkling in the sun. When they tire of the wall, they sneak chairs out of the dining hall and set them in a pyramid for target practice. When the pyramid grows dull, they find willing human targets who try to dodge the streaking projectiles.

Shawntae is not thinking water fight and he's stayed away from Monkey Island all day. This morning on the shuttle bus from the lower school to the upper school, he was not talking with his buddies as he usually does, but instead cramming for the last major Western Civ test before final exams. He has honored his contract; he has completed his nightly homeworks and he has met regularly with Mr. Bailin, but if he doesn't do well on this test, his chances of passing the course will be shattered.

As the chaos downstairs continues, Shawn is in the classroom before seventh period begins, using every available moment to study. But when Mr. Bailin enters the room, Shawn makes what could be a permanent error. He informs Paul, as if needing confirmation, that he heard there are twenty objective questions on the test.

Paul halts. "How do you know that Shawn?"

Shawn is silent.

Paul feels his stomach sink. He knows that Shawn has been talking to someone in one of the previous classes to find out what is on the test—a breach of academic honesty, the repercussions of which have been continually and clearly spelled out. Such acts are invariably punished by suspension—a handful of boys have been suspended this year for plagiarism and for cheating on tests—and by the automatic failure of the paper or test in question. Paul has no choice but to report this to Margaret Mason. He excuses Shawn from class. Shawn doesn't even get to take the test.

Afterward Paul shakes his head in frustration and says, "Shawn doesn't edit his thoughts before he speaks." Shawn had been so concerned about the test, so dreading the possibility that he might fail, that he had asked people who took the test first or fourth period and found one classmate who would tell him that there were twenty questions on the objective section of the test and that they included the permanent vocabulary words "bureaucracy" and "hierarchy."

"But bureaucracy and hierarchy are *always* on the test," Paul says.

No matter. As Hawley has said, there is always a great argument for mercy, and a great argument for standards. Shawn's fate will be decided next week.

During ninth period, just before the end of the day, Doug Lagarde opens his office and begins to return the cache of confiscated weapons. The water fight thus resumes, but it is weakened by the fact that school is letting out, and the downstairs commons teems with people.

Whitney Lloyd, who heads college admissions, stands at the bottom edge of the steps facing the downstairs commons, dressed in preppy blazer and slacks. Ten feet behind him is Jim Lester. Jim smiles, descends to one knee, takes aim with his Super Soaker, and fires a bull's-eye. A large circular stain forms in the seat of Whitney's khakis. Goosed, Whitney jumps to his tiptoes, turns at a laughing Jim Lester, then scurries off the battlefield. Jim dashes off firing a last shot into the shirt of Nick Fletcher, Kris's little brother. Little Nick looks at his shirt, scowls, and says, "And they call *us* frosh."

Mike Cohen, one big smile, is wandering through the crowd. He's aced the AP test, tonight will see the second smashing performance of *Big River,* and it is the last day of classes. "This," he says, "is a *great* day."

18

The seniors had their last day, and University School's population decreased by one-quarter on the following Monday. Rather than empty of people, the building seemed instead to fill with space—space one could now move through, use, breathe; one could stretch as if stepping out of a car after a long highway journey. The juniors, now actually the largest individuals in the school, were moved ritualistically into the seniors' center seats during Monday morning assembly. The freshmen, too, were larger and more distinct, having in effect grown from one-quarter to one-third the school's population. The sophomores, as in everything else, remained the most innocuous and least visible batch of boys—that is, they continued to be sophomores, middlemen, neither here nor there, biding time and passing their classes.

The effect of all the seventeen- and eighteen-year-olds' abrupt vanishing cannot be understated. The school changes. The dining hall is quieter during fourth and fifth periods, as though everyone has decided at once to mind their table manners; the halls are more hushed than ever; the increased sunlight enhances the sense of space and openness. It's a little eerie. There is no Nick Zinn lurching in the library, nor a Eugene Gurarie wafting through the upstairs commons within the bubble of his singular imagination. And the weight of Kris Fletcher's ironical silence behind the library checkout desk has disappeared.

The juniors, while unused to this new dominance, this appetizer of next year, are nevertheless more visible, and none more so than John Gregor who, Monday morning, swings along the downstairs commons on the armpit support of crutches, his right leg in an air cast up to mid-calf. This might have been more surprising in the fall, but in the spring of discipline and accidents, it was almost to be expected that crutches would appear on either side of someone. Normally, it would have had few repercussions, but the injury occurred Friday night during the second performance of *Big River*. John leapt from a platform and badly twisted his ankle. Adrenaline temporarily hid the seriousness of the sprain, but in the morning John could not walk. At eight-thirty A.M., with the final show less than twelve hours away, John's father called Carol Pribble and told her that John would not be able to perform, that he was taking him to the emergency room. The show, standing-room-only last night and sold out again for Saturday night, could not run without the Duke. Carol is so self-assured and confident, not to mention experienced, that it's difficult to envision her crying. She hung up the phone, and her mind flashed in an instant through the possibilities, all of one: Kerry Brennan, the only one who knows the lyrics to John's songs. Kerry can stand in for the Duke, Carol said to herself, and tears cascaded at the thought.

But the worst was not to be.

The doctor recommended an air cast, which might fix John's ankle so that it would not move and would reduce the impact of walking. It would limit his actions, but he could stand unaided and traverse the stage for part of two hours without aggravating the damage. John called Carol from the medical supply store and said he could go on, but that he'd be limping. Carol told John, Mike Cohen, and Mike Seelbach to arrive at school early so they could revise John's dance numbers, and wrote one line to inform the audience of the slight changes ("I think I hurt my ankle escaping!"). The show went on, successfully. In fact, once the adrenaline kicked in, John stopped limping altogether. During intermission, Carol said, "John, I've given you theatrical permission to limp. Limp!"

Even with the seniors gone, dramas flared at school, both serious and comical. In an empty classroom, Brian Walker, who had three months ago been unable to eat an entire Geppetto's pepperoni sheet pizza, stripped to his underwear—"my tightly whities," as he calls them—hooded his head in a Freddie Kruger mask, bolted to the window looking into Doc Thomas's history class, and performed a wild, hopping voodoo dance, naked but for mask and skivvies. Thomas, incensed, pursued him, but Brian fled to the humanities stairwell where he'd stashed his duds and vanished.

■ ▪ ■

For the first time all year reflection seemed possible. While I'd come to the school hoping to observe the role of gender in an all-boy school, I had all but forgotten about it; a male myself, I saw nothing else; how could I freely observe what I was immersed in, what contained me?

The abstract issue of single-sex education and boys' schools did come up explicitly a few times throughout the year, notably in two gatherings designed expressly to address the issues facing boys' schools today. Six years ago, Hawley and his friend Tony Jarvis, head of Roxbury Latin, organized a small group of boys' day-school headmasters for the purpose, Hawley told me, of "identifying the mission" of boys' schools. They now meet annually.

"There's a distinctive culture in the boys' school," Hawley explained. "We have a great form, and these things are going to blink out of existence. The purpose was to become self-conscious about something that was un-conscious." At the time the group formed, in 1988, girls' schools had marshalled themselves with considerable force and apparent ease, given a political climate that was addressing the ways girls are "shortchanged," as one well-known study put it, in American schools. But boys' schools, Hawley said, remained silent, not wanting to be aggressive.

In April 1994, the day-and-a-half gathering informally called "Boys' School Conversation," was hosted by Doug Blakey, headmaster of Upper Canada College, a private boys' high school in Toronto. Hawley and Jarvis were there, along with Richard Melvoin of Belmont Hill School near Boston, Jacob Dresden of Collegiate School in New York City, Damon Bradley of Landon School and the Rev. Mark H. Mullin of St. Albans School, both in the D.C. area, Douglas Paschell of Montgomery Bell Academy in Nashville, and Arnold Holtberg of St. Mark's School in Dallas.

Before the conference, I heard Ann McGovern talking to her colleague Eileen Perkins about it. They were in the faculty lounge, and Ann was delivering the day's mail to faculty mailboxes, her most loathsome chore as administrative assistant to the headmaster.

"What conference is this?" Eileen asked.

"It's a boys'-school conference—where they sit around and talk about how great they are," Ann said. "No, I don't really mean that." Ann moved to slide a letter into a slot, but withdrew it and turned to Eileen. *"Yes I do,"* Ann said. "There are no coed people to convince them of anything *else.*"

I had been invited to the small conference and arrived early at the Park

Plaza Hotel in downtown Toronto for the ride to the college and dinner with the group. In the bookstore adjoining the hotel lobby, four of the books on the main display table were *The Courage To Raise Good Men, Life After God, The Book of Virtues,* and *Men Are from Mars, Women Are from Venus.* In the lobby, Hawley introduced me to everyone as "Exhibit A." I would forever remain, it seems, the headmaster's dim ninth-grade history student. But Hawley was in fine form. In the car, stuffed with headmasters, Hawley grumbled about his flight to Toronto. Perturbed that his plane had propellers, he said, "I have a very crude way of evaluating airlines. There are two kinds. Those with computer terminals announcing arriving and departing flights, and those that use Velcro labels. Mine had Velcro."

There was a posh dinner at the headmaster's residence, and the following morning all convened at the school for a day-long meeting. I'd secretly been hoping that the gathering would be filled with unintended silliness, stodgy headmasters spouting the virtues of tweed and manly-men ethics, the sort of meeting that would make for colorful anecdote, but the conference was all business, with only an occasional aren't-we-great observation. There was no need for that; that was a given, the reason they were here.

Blakey had sent a memo to the heads suggesting topics for discussion: how can boys' schools address issues of gender and develop greater appreciation for women (a topic Kris Fletcher and John Gregor would have no problem addressing had they been invited); collect data comparing numbers of boys involved in the arts versus boys in athletics; coordinate programs with girls' schools; and analyze research supporting single-sex education.

The nine sat around a table in Blakey's office exchanging stories about their own schools and discussing issues such as homophobia, the hiring of more women, discipline, ethics. Though Blakey said the perception of boys' schools in Canada remained much what it had been in America during the 1970s and '80s, all the American headmasters reported steady to excellent admissions.

"We've had a record number of applicants, too," said Jarvis. "It's not that we're doing a better job, we're benefited by our enemies. . . . The wonders of coeducation turn out not to be wonders." He said parents were now asking him, "Are you sure you want to be a boys' school, because we want you to be one, and if you're not sure, we'll go elsewhere." He looked to Blakey at the head of the table and said, "Doug, I remember you at the first meeting. You were depressed, wondering if there was a future for us."

Blakey, a young, handsome, studious-looking man, a ringer for actor

Kevin Kline, nodded and said, "I was weary of constantly defending the school. I felt like a dinosaur. . . . Parents would say, 'Why are you *here?* You seem like a good guy.' It's been very pleasant not to have to do that."

Blakey said that there was still the problem of perception in Canada, however. He had even been part of a group that called itself Leaders of Single-Sex Schools of Toronto. Blakey chuckled and noted its acronym: LOSSST.

"Unlike you," he continued, "the question of coeducation comes up all the time. There's still the 'Oh, Blakey, when are you going to see the light?'" He told the group that "old boys" and parents still want his school to go coed, including an influential board member who argued, "If UCC is the best school in Toronto, why exclude fifty percent of the population?"

"Ooooh," said Jarvis. "I wonder if it occurred to him that the reason it's a good school is *because* it's a boys' school." Jarvis paused, the soul of confidence. "I think it's the future."

Blakey added that he has a recurring nightmare in which he meets the influential alum and has to convince the man every time not to go coed.

The question of how boys' schools are perceived is probably not so rosy as the headmasters suggested at their conference. Though more parents than ever are looking for schooling options outside the public sphere, applicants to boys' schools remain a splinter from a sliver of the entire school-going population. This is, in part, an indication of how deeply embedded the cultural notion of single-sex schools are: the assumption that they are elitist, snobbish, and Victorian, or oppressively severe, frigid, and scarring.

Yet the research continues to describe more benefits of single-sex education than of coeducation in terms of academic achievement and social adjustment for boys and girls. The benefits are pronounced for girls, but taken as a whole, the data overwhelmingly confirm benefits of single-sex education for everyone.

Valerie E. Lee of the University of Michigan has studied the subject for a decade. In 1986, working with Anthony S. Bryk of the University of Chicago, Lee wrote, "What has been considered by some to be an anachronistic organizational feature of schools may actually facilitate adolescent academic development by providing an environment where social and academic concerns are separated. Perhaps a second look at this disappearing school type is warranted."

Their study described benefits and asked, "Is secondary education in America enriched or impoverished by the gradual disappearance of the single-sex school?" They do not suggest that all schools become single-sex—an impossibility, not to mention illegal—rather, they conclude that if the benefits they've found are "intrinsic to the single-sex form, then the practical issue is to find ways to preserve existing single-sex schools and to encourage their development in contexts where the option does not currently exist."

Four years later, Lee and her colleague Helen M. Marks, noted a second wave of schools changing over to coeducation and reiterated early findings: "Recent research on the issue of single-sex education has provided substantial evidence of its effectiveness, particularly for young women."

Half a continent away on the east coast, Cornelius Riordan was conducting similar research, and his story is groundbreaking as well as emblematic of reaction to that research. Like Lee, Riordan was situated outside the sphere of single-sex institutions. He had, he said, "no ax to grind." As mentioned earlier Riordan, a professor of educational sociology at Providence College in Rhode Island and an educational researcher, knew very little about single-sex education in 1983 when he stumbled on a discovery that has directed much of his research since then.

I met Riordan in Belmont, Massachusetts, a plush suburb outside Boston and the location of the Belmont Hill School, a private boys' school that hosted the second event I attended that addressed boys'-school issues. The group comprised 120 people from seventy-two boys' schools, mainly from the United States but including one from England, two from Australia, and three from Canada. Riordan had come to observe and to visit with his friend and former teacher David Riesman, the Harvard social scientist.

Riordan, an affable fifty-four years old, with curly brown hair lightened by gray, bright blue eyes, and a heavy New England accent, told me here, and during subsequent telephone interviews, of the evolution of his thinking about single-sex schools. The way he described it, it seems almost like a detective story.

In 1983, Riordan explained, he and a few other educational researchers were addressing what was then a hot question. Catholic schools regularly outperformed public schools: what were the elements within Catholic schools that contributed to their effectiveness? Riordan doesn't do actual field work. He sits at his desk and pores over statistical data from large-scale surveys, comparing and controlling for countless variables. Numbers only. Plus point-one differential, negative point-one differential. Anyone who works with numbers knows that they can be made to perform remarkable tricks, and educational researchers are trained to make them behave.

The data Riordan studied had been gathered from about twenty-five hundred students attending eighty-four Catholic schools. Wandering through these documents, he made an unusual observation: many Catholic schools, which were outperforming public schools, happened to be single-sex: 42 percent of them. "I just sort of found this and said, *geez,* this is *very* interesting," he recalled. "And I began to do some thinking, most of it was just thinking, you didn't have to go too far. I said, gee, it must be a different environment and maybe there are some different things going on here, let's take a look at it." He talked to his colleagues and told them what he'd found. They told him, "Yes, that's interesting but not what we're looking for. Get back to work."

Riordan sensed something unusual, something that had not been much discussed or written about. A couple of people had produced large studies on the effectiveness of single-sex colleges and universities in the 1970s, but no one had addressed the issue in elementary schools and high schools. He continued to teach and write scholarly papers and to study the factors that seemed to make Catholic schools better. After examining thousands of students from about nine hundred schools, he could thoroughly document what he'd suspected the previous year. In 1984 Riordan presented a paper called "Public and Catholic Schooling: The Effects of Gender Context Policy" to the American Educational Research Association and later published it in the *American Journal of Education.*

It was an "important finding," Riordan says, the first major paper in the 1980s that pointed to single-sex benefits in high school. Yet he was not excited about the results. He was, he said, "uneasy." His study flew in the face of commonly accepted notions about gender and school. Single-sex schools, what few were left, were uncool, politically incorrect before most people knew that term existed. And everyone knew from stories that single-sex Catholic schools were weird, grim, oppressive places with sadistic nuns and buggering priests.

But the results were definitive. Single-sex Catholic schools, Riordan found, were nearly twice as effective as both mixed-sex Catholic schools and public schools. Riordan was so uncomfortable about these findings, and so political was the world of academia, that he tempered his conclusions—softened them so much when he read them to the AERA that he now chuckles, embarrassed by his timidity. Because single-sex Catholic schools outperformed mixed-sex Catholic and public schools to such an extraordinary degree, he concluded, research comparing Catholic schools and public schools should be limited to mixed-sex Catholic schools only.

Riordan had avoided the obvious as one would a dog pie on the lawn.

After delivering his paper to the conference, he discussed his true feelings with a colleague and she scolded him. "She told me I need to be much less apologetic in terms of arguing the case for single-sex schools," he recalls.

Riordan remained uncomfortable about broadcasting what he'd found. It was still too dangerous, and still too iffy—more research was needed, yet few were interested in doing it. Not until he sat down with his former teacher did Riordan commit himself. "Riesman had the biggest effect on me," he said.

David Riesman, author of *The Lonely Crowd* and one of the foremost social scientists in the country, is not intimidated by uncomfortable truths, and he told Riordan two things. One: If you don't say this, nobody will; *is it important to you?* "And it *was,*" Riordan said. Two: Riesman asked Riordan to look down the road beyond gender discrimination in schools and beyond the passing political brouhahas of the 1980s. Once we get there, Riesman warned, we may have abolished the most effective form of education we have.

Over the next few years, while engaged in postdoctoral work at Johns Hopkins, Riordan examined and evaluated hundreds of studies and warehouses of data. Two studies, for instance—"High School and Beyond" and the "National Longitudinal Study of the High School Class of 1972"— each provided Riordan with scores and evaluations of tens of thousands of students.

The resulting book, *Girls & Boys in School: Together or Separate?,* published in 1990, was the most comprehensive evaluation of data that bear on the "single-sex versus coeducation" question. Yet it was only a launching point. The book said, in effect, this is the information we have, this is what is known so far; it's not nearly enough, but a design is emerging.

"There are three groups for whom there is a clear and consistent pattern, a pattern that relates well to previous research," Riordan told me. "The clear and consistent pattern is that school effects have consistently been shown to be greater among those people who have a greater need for schools to be good."

"Minority females profit most from single-sex schooling," Riordan wrote in his book, "followed by minority males, then by white females in the regular Catholic sampling. I estimate that white males in single-sex schools in the regular sample score lower than their peers in mixed-sex schools, after controlling for initial ability and home background."

Riordan evaluates possible reasons for single-sex benefits. They are complicated and not fully explored, but Riordan and others have suggested that one reason may be that because single-sex schools separate teenage social culture from academic work, they are generally more effective academically. No surprise here. James Coleman was the first to address this in his 1961 book *The Adolescent Society.* Teenage social culture, what Coleman termed "adolescent subculture," has a negative effect on studying and learning; there is less pressure from this social culture in girls' schools. Riordan, though, found that this teenage social culture is high in boys' schools and yet it was *positively* related to academic achievement. He postulated that boys' social culture in boys' schools required "a high level of discipline, which in turn facilitates a high level of learning." He saw a clear difference in the environment of the boys' school and the girls' school but with the same results: better grades, smarter kids.

Riordan documents in his book that in some studies white males from single-sex schools are slightly edged out by their coed counterparts. There were many contradictions of this sort—why does it appear to be worse for white males when it benefits everyone else?—and numerous controlling factors to handicap white males in single-sex schools. Nothing was conclusive. Riordan admits that he knew very little about the primarily white, independent boys' schools. Everyone's concern, Riordan's included, was for women and minorities who were getting shafted across the board, and the evidence to support this and suggestions to amend the problem seemed irrefutable.

As years passed, the evidence in favor of girls' schools mounted and experiments in schools for African-American boys were attempted in Baltimore, Milwaukee, and Detroit. The American Association of University Women issued a report called "How Schools Shortchange Women," and researchers Myra and David Sadker published *Failing at Fairness,* documenting gender inequity in public schools, and toured bookstores, high schools, and the talk-show circuit—all the research confirmed and reiterated Riordan's conclusion: single-sex schools work for girls. Period. *The New York Times* and other papers reported the Women's College Coalition's announcement of an unprecedented rise in applications to girls' schools and women's colleges in the 1990s.

Early in 1994 I called Riordan to find out where things stood for boys. He said the research remained inconclusive. Findings were for the most part null, he said. He was careful to point out that null did not mean negative, it simply meant that there was no advantage either way. He noted that many people construe null findings as an argument for coeducation, which he said was wrong.

I also called Valerie Lee at the University of Michigan, who was more outspoken on the subject of boys. She's a straight shooter, laughs loud and often, and I couldn't help but imagine as we talked that she was wearing army fatigues. If you found yourself at a dreary dinner party with a lot of boring guests trying to be polite to each other, you would do all you could to find a seat near Valerie Lee. She had continued her research—"she has a minefield of data," Riordan said, "she's going to scrutinize the hell out of it"—and her thoughts on boys' schools were clear.

"I wouldn't say it [research] necessarily favors boys' schools, that's for sure," she told me. "My own research has essentially found that, I guess what I'd call too close to call for independent schools. . . . My own research has not really had a lot of favorable findings for boys' schools." She said when you looked at the longitudinal data, what positive effect there is "kinda washes out."

Lee was at work on a book—a massive undertaking attempting to build on her own work and to find more definitive conclusions—called *Is Gender Equal?* She was frustrated at the time because the bottom line, she said, was "pretty wishy-washy." She herself is not. She had just finished a study on sexism at coed and single-sex schools that found girls' schools and mixed-sex schools to be occasional offenders, but boys' schools were the worst of the bunch.

"What we found in boys' schools was actually pretty shocking," she said, noting rampant stereotyping of females and demeaning language regarding females. "We were shocked that this kind of thing was allowed to go on or tolerated or not noticed as being inappropriate. . . .

"We are in the last decade of the twentieth century," she continued, "and there are certain sorts of behaviors that seem to be pretty unacceptable, and yet they don't seem to be unacceptable in this environment, which really suggests to me that an all-male environment is not a very good one."

I told Lee a little about what I was doing and it turned out she knew Hawley. She called him "a militant believer" in the boys' school, and laughed. "It's kind of like defending the *aardvark!*" she said. When she settled down, she was more forgiving.

"I'm very sympathetic to what Rick Hawley says," Lee told me. "He's a very elegant spokesman for something that, really, very few people have been willing to stand up and talk about, and his school may be real special, but I don't think it's the all-boysness of it that makes that the case. . . . The argument for single-sex for girls is a lot easier to make. . . .

"What I think—*honestly* think—is that the gender grouping is not the dominant force in the school. I've seen some very fine all-girl schools, ones I would love to send my kids to, and ones that I don't think are very good. So I think there are a lot of qualities about a school that make it a good school that are probably more important than gender grouping. I think in order to have a really gender equitable coeducational school, you have to be very attentive to the issues of gender. But I don't think all single-sex schools are good and all coed schools are bad. . . .

"One of the things that one does find," she continued, "is that a lot of people who are involved with single-sex education—mostly in girls' schools, but Rick Hawley would fall into this category also—are so passionate about the missions of their school that they make them fine places because they care about them so much, and if other issues about schools could engender this kind of passion, I think we would be in really good shape. . . . And one thing I do believe, at least in the private-school world, is that it's very important to have a lot of different options to choose from, so I'd be very sorry to see all these schools die out."

In 1992 Diane Ravitch, then secretary for Educational Research and Improvement and counselor to the United States Secretary of Education in the Bush administration, responded to the growing research in support of single-sex education and the concomitant disappearance of single-sex schools by convening in Washington a group of sixteen Federal officials, educational researchers, and educators to evaluate the situation. Among these sixteen people were Hawley, Riordan, and Lee. The expressed purpose of this gathering was to reexamine perceptions of single-sex education and ask the question, "Should our society reevaluate public policies contributing to single-sex education's decline?"

The resulting report remained consistent with what was now becoming a growing body of research—definitive benefits of single-sex schools for girls and minority males.

I reached Ravitch by phone at New York University, where she is a senior research scholar. Ravitch, the author of *National Standards in American Education: A Citizen's Guide* and other books, is by most accounts a brilliant, if controversial, thinker on education and educational policy, attended a women's college, and is adamantly in favor of educational diversity and choice.

A perpetual concern dogs researchers studying single-sex education: because virtually all schools in the United States are coeducational, and because they are prevented by law under Title XI of the Educational Amendments enacted in 1972 from changing, shouldn't one try to determine how *coeducational* schools can become better? What does it matter that single-sex schools are effective—why take time to find out how they are effective—when for the vast majority of students they don't exist? It's like trying to prove that Alaskan Eskimos should start developing mango orchards because mangoes are good for them. I called Ravitch to find out what the potential ramifications of all this research might be on education in the United States.

The conversation was relatively brief, because the answer was *nada*—at least for the moment, given an educational system, Ravitch said, "that acts on the premise, 'Stamp out diversity in the name of diversity.' " Yes, she was discouraged, she said, but not without hope.

"I think it's symbolic of the change that has to take place in American education," she said, "not just determining whether to permit single-sex education but permitting any kind of diversity. . . .

"I believe in diversity. I believe the choice should be available to parents. I'm not saying that everyone should go to a single-sex institution. But it should be a choice that's available. And it's available to almost no one. . . .

"My perspective is that I really don't see that it ought to be necessary for single-sex schools to prove that students do better in order to justify the existence of single-sex schools. . . . There's a lot of ineffectual schools now that ought to be put out of business and no one says to them, 'Prove you're effective or go out of business.' They can stay in business forever. *Why should single-sex education have to prove itself when coeducation can't?* . . . Why shouldn't the burden be on all these failing coeducational schools? And, no, it's not about to change. If you were to try to create a single-sex school, it certainly would be very difficult because everything would be against you."

Ravitch mentioned the FT-500 tables published in England each fall by *The Financial Times*. The tables rank the country's independent schools according to A-level exam results, an indication of how effective the schools are compared to one another. Single-sex schools overwhelmingly dominate the top of the list. There has been only one coeducational school in the top thirty in each of the past four years.

"Most of the countries of the world have single-sex education," she said, "and when you try to make a case for single-sex education [in the United States], people act as though you're trying to impose it on all the kids. But if they want to impose *coeducation* on all the kids, that's just fine. The issue is, can the United States' educational system tolerate diversity? And the answer is, at this juncture, no."

David Riesman also rang in on this subject: "Once they [single-sex schools] are gone, the law forbids their recreation," he told me. "We need to have all kinds of experiments to see what works, because what we have now is not working."

I had talked to Ravitch in June, a few days before going to Boston for the big boys'-school conference at Belmont Hill School. It's a gorgeous, made-for-a-boys'-school-movie campus, with sprawling athletic fields—summer lacrosse was under way—and red-brick buildings with white trim scattered across a rolling tree-filled lawn. The weekend sky was summer blue and the air was so still the heat pressed down on you.

When I met Neil Riordan, he told me that he almost didn't come this year because he was disappointed in the tone of last year's conference. There was too much let's-celebrate-boys'-schools and not enough discussion of the research. He felt, he said, "an absence of meaning: *what* are we celebrating?" Once again, the conference had been conceived and organized by the admissions directors of two schools, Belmont Hill and The Hill School near Philadelphia. Would this year be any different? Riordan wondered.

By this time, Riordan's own thinking had solidified.

In 1984, he had been so shy about finding single-sex benefits that he all but directed his colleagues away from that data. This is understandable, perhaps; the idea was unfashionable and if he were for some reason wrong, his reputation as a researcher in the field could easily have been damaged. And in his book, *Girls & Boys in School,* he had remained extremely cautious, cautious to the point, he later felt, of error. He had sold boys' schools slightly short.

I asked how, and he walked me through some of the data, saying things like, "OK, you see Table five-point-seven on page one-eleven? That minus point-one is saying this—despite what I wrote before. It's saying there's really no difference after you control for background and initial ability among white males. There's really very little difference in outcomes between those males attending single-sex and those males attending coeducational schools."

I pressed him on this because on the previous page in his book he wrote, "One is led to conclude from this that white males attain healthier attitudinal outcomes in mixed-sex schools, whereas all other groups are better off in single-sex schools."

The negative findings, he told me, are "too small to make that conclusion," adding, "This is really a mistake on my part." A mistake not with the data but with his evaluation of it. Again, because white males have had, relative to girls and minorities, all the breaks, you've got to counter those advantages—that is, you remove what makes white males effective in order to measure their effectiveness against other groups. Riordan acknowledged, "It is not at all clear what's going on when you do that with the white males."

Furthermore, he would eventually postulate, the benefits of gender and racial bias that white boys now enjoy exceed even the benefits of single-sex education. By this reasoning—and it's all but impossible to prove—as we work to diminish the racial and gender prejudices embedded in our society, white boys—just like everyone else—will increasingly be shown to benefit from the single-sex environment.

Caution is necessary, but there comes a point when you tire of bending over backward trying to defend the weaker argument. As the cases involving the Virginia Military Institute and the Citadel were heating up, when Riordan saw that judges were being forced to decide whether or not to eliminate the single-sex status of two publicly funded schools, he wrote his strongest defense of the single-sex form. The essay appeared in the February 23, 1994, edition of *Education Week* under the headline, "Reconsidering Single-Gender Schools: The V.M.I. Case and Beyond," and it is so confident and authoritative in tone, it's hard to imagine it was written by the man who had shied away from the same conclusions a decade earlier.

"Single-gender schools generally are more effective academically than coeducational schools," Riordan wrote. "This is true at all levels of school, from elementary to higher education. Over the past decade, the data consistently and persistently confirm this hard-to-accept educational fact. There are some studies which have reported null effects—that is, no differences in educational outcomes—but there are very few studies (none in the United States) which demonstrate that coeducational schools are more effective, either academically or developmentally. Moreover, just about everyone *knows* this is true, despite the fact that most people have attended coeducational schools and continue to send their children to coeducational schools. . . .

"Single-gender schools work. They work for girls and boys, women and men, whites and nonwhites."

A̲ll of this, the entire past decade of research, would seem to have boded well for single-sex schools and, particularly, for the private boys' school, the most maligned in the country. Now they had *proof* and an outsider willing to say so in public. I would have expected all these school people to be running around the campus of Belmont Hill waving Riordan's article in the air and patting each other on the back.

This did not happen.

The boys'-school faction was missing something. The task at hand wasn't as simple as pointing to a study or an essay. The problems were far larger, the issues infinitely more complicated than simply addressing who learns more in what kind of school. The negative stereotypes of the boys' school seemed immovable. News stories about the Citadel and other all-male institutions supported these stereotypes. The anthropologist Judith Shapiro, for instance, in her inaugural speech as incoming president of Barnard College, adapted by the *New York Times,* noted the abundant support for single-sex schools for girls, then briefly addressed the question, "Does this mean that we can make as compelling an argument for all-male schools?"

"[G]enerally," Shapiro said, "the link between all-male groups and misogyny is fairly robust, whether you're looking at it in the United States or in such places as lowland South America and Melanesia, as we anthropologists are in the habit of doing.

"Moreover, research to date does not show that boys and men benefit academically from single-sex education in the way that girls and women do. Clearly, the rationales for women's and men's institutions are not parallel."

The phenomenal success of the girls' school did not translate into help for boys' schools. Girls' schools, moreover, were expertly organized into a group called the Coalition of Girls' Schools and had a central office to collect and disseminate positive information; they had built a durable, efficient network.

David Riesman said there was something "weird" about it all. "Boys' schools carry the onus, an odd onus, of being good for boys," he said. "Since boys are already privileged in patriarchal society, something good for boys is bad for the country. That's not a happy milieu in which to defend oneself."

Thus, boys' schools, punch-drunk from years of anti-male sentiment, wandered around lost, trying to figure out what had happened and why they didn't have any friends. They were still the little boys at the dance, alone in the corner in droopy bow ties, sticking their fingers up their nose and wondering why nobody liked them.

A remarkable thing really, considering that so many of them were good schools, considering they had sufficient research to explain why this might be so, and had at last, after years of declining enrollment and attrition, decided they should get together and talk this thing out. They lacked a leader, a voice. One-hundred twenty people from seventy-two schools registered in the driveway of Belmont Hill School in June, 1994, mingled comfortably among their own people, smiling in the hazy heat, but wondering if this were going to be anything more than another "celebration" of boys' schools. Certainly, the red-white-and-blue helium balloons tied to a split-rail fence and table legs didn't help to counter the atmosphere of a party.

Hello-my-name-is tags lined the table at the entrance along with sign-in lists, information folders, Belmont Hill School pens, and books for sale written by some of the authors brought in to speak (a little marketing never hurt anyone). There was also plenty of food. Acquaintances and old friends said hello, caught up, and talked about the heat.

At precisely 10 o'clock, a young boy appeared in the window of a small brick building to pull a rope connected by pulley to a large old bell which sounded out the hour. Guests wiped the crumbs from their mouths, threw back a last gulp of orange juice, and strolled down the path and across the lawn toward the chapel. This slender structure was the size of a church, had a beautiful steeple, and was for a long time actually called a chapel, but was now referred to, neutrally, as an assembly hall.

Guests squeezed into the pews, filling the place to the back rows. Windows had been opened to encourage a nonexistent draft; people fanned their glistening faces with info folders and brochures. Rick Melvoin, the young headmaster of Belmont Hill, took the pulpit, welcomed all "on this glorious morning" to the second conference, and as host made a clear show of taking off first his jacket, then his tie, to let everyone know that the 90-degree heat permitted a relaxing of the dress code. Melvoin spoke briefly and was followed by the originators of the conference, John Farber and Ed Kowalchick. They explained that they hoped this gathering would be "a framework for asking questions" and also a chance "to dream," or some such claim that doesn't go over well in a stifling church.

Rick Hawley was seated in one of the front rows, hot and exhausted, waiting to deliver the opening address. Ann McGovern later told me that he was more nervous than she'd seen him before a conference. She said that while he was comfortable addressing his own school, she wasn't sure how he was handling a group composed mainly of strangers. People tend to react strongly one way or another to his speeches, he knows, and how he would go over here was anybody's guess. What he didn't seem to realize was that the people who had heard a hundred of his speeches were enormously grateful for his work, and those who didn't know him had heard of him and maintained enormous expectations, a sort of hope that verges on waiting for a personal savior for their school. Hawley sat stewing in his khaki suit, tie knotted into the collar of his white shirt to keep the juices in, the twenty-three pages of legal paper on which he'd scratched out his remarks wilting in his wet hands in the airless chapel.

Hawley was formally introduced, strode to the pulpit, spread his speech on the stand—and the moment he opened his mouth to speak, something like an engine went off at the back of the chapel. So great was his concentration, Hawley spoke for three or four seconds before he realized no one could hear a word. A boy had flipped on a giant standing fan—a caged airplane propeller—and now managed to shut the thing shut off, apologizing with his eyes to a hundred heads cranked in his direction.

"Can you hear me now?" Hawley asked.

Scattered yeses sounded out.

"Do you like it?" he asked. The laughter seemed to calm him and he said, "Thank you, Rick, for hosting us. Thank you, John, for putting this together. First, as I am standing up here, you will be warm and uncomfortable. Then again, this is a New England chapel, so you should just endure it." More laughter followed, and Hawley launched into his speech.

Hawley didn't pull any punches. He began by mentioning the work of Neil Riordan, seated in the very last row with David Riesman, who had made a special effort to be here for Hawley's speech. Hawley noted meeting Riordan in Washington to testify at a Department of Education conference called by Diane Ravitch, and he read from Riordan's essay in *Education*

357

Week, then stated what he hoped this group's mission would be: "to conceive of good and great schools." None of this dreaming business for him.

"Schools are not good because they are composed of boys," he said. "But a good school could not be better composed. This is a crucial distinction. If we lose our vision of what good schooling means, and if we close our eyes to what the best evidence says is really true of boys and girls, then we are running blind."

Hawley's first task was to dismantle the boys'-school-as-dinosaur charge. It rests on a fallacy, he said, in which such schools create "misogynist behavior, destructive aggression, and arrogant entitlement." The fallacy, he said, was this: "If the gender composition of schools is a causal factor in these social outcomes, then the coed schools must be the culprits, since they have educated more than ninety percent of this nation's schoolchildren since our founding."

Hawley has a good deal of grim observations of the effects of the coeducational system, as well as ways boys' schools might address certain social problems, discussing, for example, recent attempts to create boys' schools for African Americans. But he can't help addressing the critics.

"There is a radically unexamined—and actually silly—conclusion about boys' schools drawn by some feminists," he said, "and I have seen it in print this year in American, British, and Australian publications. This is the position that says, 'Single-sex schools are better for girls; coed schools are better for boys.' Think about that for a second. If the first premise is true, the second damns some girls, the unlucky ones who have to attend coed schools, to a fate of mitigating the problematic effects of males.

"But there is a far more harmful premise implied in this position, and this is that males are by their very nature toxic. If you let them express themselves freely, if they band together, they will make trouble. I do not believe I am overstating this. This assumption, sometimes tacit, sometimes not, pervades a good deal of late twentieth-century popular culture. But it's a false assumption, let's be clear on that. To propose anything of the kind is straightforward bigotry, however stylish and widely held the position may be. As a barb, or a politically charged gesture of complaint about current gender inequities, it can be taken, I suppose, as one takes other beeps and honks in political traffic, but the assumption of male toxicity is seriously bad for children. No child should be made to feel guilty or ashamed of what may be his most essential element.

"Again, we must confront this kind of dismissiveness and bigotry when we hear it. We will forever argue about school structures and child development, but school people must premise those arguments on an almost unreasonable love of and respect for children—of both genders. . . .

"Our more urgent business requires that we get off the defensive and set about making the case for the great, humane, and socially necessary boys' school. Here, what we actually do in our schools matters more than winning words. . . .

"Biology, anthropology, and all manner of social sciences confirm that we are deeply gendered; gender runs more deeply than culture; more deeply, I believe, than even biology. Moreover, the research supporting innate, rather than culturally formed, gender is growing. And if gender is turning out to be more than a mere cultural imposition, the futility and arrogance of imposing unisex conventions—from toys to bedtime stories to courting protocol—are becoming clearer. Even well-meaning attempts to neuter male children weaken, demoralize, and confuse them. Sanitizing children's environments of gender evidence and nuances is in effect a deceptive approach to gendered children. In certain elementary and middle-school environments of my acquaintance, a boy could not possibly locate himself or his kind. Schools like this have not, incidentally, produced nicer, socially compliant children.

"Rampant, unapologetic aggression and misogyny do not stem from intense male culture. Rather, they are sad, sometimes dangerous over-compensations for the absence of male culture. The much-publicized abusive and criminal behavior on the part of suburban California high school boys last year or the infantile misogynist vulgarities of an Andrew Dice Clay do not derive from patriarchal, chivalric codes. Chivalric codes, you will recall, revered women, decent behavior, and courteous speech.

"No, it is the anomic, relativist era of the seventies, eighties, and nineties, in fact an era of unisexual marketing and coed conversion, that has produced this current wave of unrepentant misogyny. Skinheads do not derive from the Western heritage; they derive from a popular culture that has forsaken that heritage. That popular culture has given us plenty of gender ideology, but precious little gender understanding.

"We have work to do."

Having thus dispatched the anti-male feminists and delivered another thrust of his lance to contemporary culture, Hawley could now address the thing that mattered most to him—boys and girls in school, their different learning tempos, different pace of physiological development, the "gender-specific contours in their skeletal, motor, and neurological development." Neither gender, he clarifies, "has an intellectual or moral edge over the other. Gender differences are not social entitlements." But given that boys and girls develop at different rates, he said, trying to teach to the middle ground can easily shortchange both boys and girls.

The most obvious—that is, commonsensical—benefit of single-sex schools, that they are without the romantic and sexual distraction of the other sex, would seem hardly worth arguing: generally, boys will spend more time studying and pay better attention in class when no girls are around, and girls will do the same with no boys around. Yet here Hawley has received some of the sharpest criticism of all.

"This point, however delicately stated, always puts my colleagues in coed schools in a terrible mood," Hawley told the group. "Some have said and written really rude things to me in response, and one Midwestern school head read certain published words of mine on the subject to his assembled upper school, punctuating the reading with derisive laughter."

Hawley is well aware that his detractors abound; some are perhaps more mature than others, and he's galvanized by a really formidable foe. There were no foes in this chapel, however, and while it was important for the group to hear how one defends certain criticisms of boys' schools, and while it may be great fun to pillory invidious claims, the main reason for his being here was to explain the potential of boys' schools. "The case for the goodness and even the necessity of boys' schools must, again, be a humane and progressive one," Hawley reminded them. "It must be based on data, and the data must be true." This, more than celebration, is the reason they are here, and he wanted to make sure the big picture was clear and fully understood.

"Finally, and very personally," Hawley concluded, "I see boys' schools at their best as an antidote to much of what has gone wrong with Western culture in the aftermath of this century's appallingly destructive wars and dislocations. The sheer scale of the losses and carnage and waste, including the lives of so many millions of young men at the hands of millions of others, has eclipsed the heroic vision of boys and men. In place of that vision has arisen the antihero: the boy who, racked by doubt and despair, refuses to become a man. He is more or less sympathetic, and his brooding image sells products, but he is neither whole nor strong nor socially helpful. He is Holden Caulfield, not young Abe Lincoln, or Romeo, or Alexander, or David.

"The antiheroic age bespeaks a culture that does not like or trust boys and men enough. But every loving parent and every committed teacher knows the necessity of doing otherwise.

"To be that kind of school, to recognize and bring forth the best and truest of what is in these boys—what a generous offering to humankind that could be."

He was done. Hawley answered questions from the audience till he got too hot and then suggested they all head outside and into the shade.

One school person who had attended last year's conference told me everyone was crestfallen when they heard Hawley didn't plan to show, and I saw why. The catalyst, the voice, this group needed was Hawley. These people were clearly passionate about their schools, defiantly so in the face of a culture that belittles them, but inarticulate passion is easily dismissed. Hawley could give them language they could use.

The conference went on for two-and-a-half days, heard various speakers, dispersed into focus groups, and lunched on fried chicken, steak, and potato salad. Speakers ranged from a Harvard professor of statistics to a marketing consultant to Dr. William S. Pollack, author of *In a Time of Fallen Heroes,* who discussed psychological models for male development. Neil Riordan spoke briefly at lunch about the importance of getting the single-sex question debated in public forums and noted a new amendment proposed by John Danforth, the senator from Missouri, that would allow the creation of experimental public single-sex schools. But none had the electric effect of Hawley. Even David Riesman, the aged Harvard social scientist, had accolades for Hawley that verged on superlatives. "I thought it was fabulous," Riesman said of Hawley's speech. "He has a weight, a profundity, an understanding that's truly impressive." Clusters of conference goers begged Hawley's attention. Copies of Hawley's *Boys Will Be Men* were widely available. At one point, two women approached Hawley. Fawning over him like rock-star groupies, they asked would he sign their book. "I'd be happy to sign that book," he told them. "But you *do* know that it's not mine." They had bought the wrong book and departed giggling with embarrassment.

Before the conference was half through, Hawley had been appointed executive director of a new group—Boys' Schools: An International Coalition.

"As a consequence of missing a meeting yesterday afternoon," Hawley told the conference goers on Sunday morning, "and having had a glass and a half of wine on the *Charles II,* I have arisen to this new dignity."

The first conference of this newly formed coalition, it had been decided, would be held next year in Cleveland, Ohio.

Conferences are all well and good, necessary even, but for an outsider such as myself, school *people* were more interesting than theories of male development and marketing strategies. And of those people, women at US evoked the most riveting conversation, such as Deb Nash, rattling off boy and girl differences as if from a grocery list. Carol Pribble could get fiery on the subject, particularly when I asked her about boys' occasional rude behavior. In the faculty lounge one afternoon, I addressed the issue commonly used to argue against all-male schools—that they elicit misogynistic, sexist behavior—with Carol Pribble. Carol looked at me as though she were mad at me for being an idiot. She's taught at coed schools and this boys' school and insisted there was equal sexism at all of them.

I mentioned a story told to me by one of the women in the teacher apprentice program. Teacher apprentices are informally called TAP students and this year three of the five at the upper school were women in their early to mid-twenties, all of them attractive and self-assured. One of them told me she was standing in the dining hall, minding her own business, when she heard barking noises directed at her from behind. She snapped around to find four or five boys seated at a table looking blankly at her. She told them she didn't care who made the noise, but if she heard it again, they *all* got demerits. Nothing more was said. Another TAP student had been oinked at in similar fashion.

Carol rolled her eyes and nodded her head. She'd heard the same story in many versions. "TAP students say, 'Oh, a boy said something repugnant to me. It's the boys' school.' Well, *no.* The boys here aren't any different from boys anywhere else in America. It's just that in school when there are girls around, they have someone to say those things *to.*"

The TAP students all had strong feelings about the boys' school, mostly unfavorable. Toward the end of the year, when I asked one if her job prospects for next year included US, she said, no, it doesn't pay enough, and then she whispered, "And I would *never* want to teach in an all-boy school." She made a frightful face and hurried off.

Another said she thought the entire idea of a boys' school was unnatural, that schools should reflect society. A boys' school, she contended, "retards them socially."

It was always sort of funny, then, to ask them what they liked best about this school. "Oh, the *kids!*" they all said. The woman who suggested social retardation, for instance, added, "They are phenomenal."

Yet another TAP student, Karen, said, "The boys can concentrate on learning when they're without that girl pressure. . . . It's a normal place. They're normal boys." I mentioned that some people think schools should mirror society, and Karen, eyebrows raised, said, "What's society? Society is a *mess*. If you have a school that mirrors society, what do you *have?*"

Undeniably, effective women at a boys' school exert a force that is disproportionate to their small numbers. Nancy and Carol are obvious examples; so is Margaret Mason, dean of students. I could learn more sitting for a half-hour in her office, haven to many a distressed adolescent, than I could in days of conferences.

"I think that every role is played by a boy—boys are more free to be sensitive and caring, more free to cry, to take on the role of nurturer," she said one spring afternoon. "Again, I don't know because I only know this school. I went to a coed high school a thousand years ago, but I wasn't interested, I wasn't looking at it from that point of view, so I don't know how it's different. I mean you could go look at Hawken, but the tone of Hawken is different, and the fact that it's coed is partly what makes it different, but also the whole way the school operates is different. So what about US is because we are all-male, and what about US is because we have this particular kind of philosophy and particular kind of structure to the building and everything?

"I think I particularly like teenage boys," she went on. "I think there's something guileless about them, something refreshing, something what-you-see-is-what-you-get. They're easy, if you're interested in psychology, they're an easier read, and they're pretty forthcoming.

"I do honestly think that going to a single-sex school, with a lot of male teachers around, helps make that happen, and it teaches something about maleness. And I also think if you really learn about your own maleness, then you can connect well with women. And I don't think—I think it's the opposite—you know, some people say, 'Oh, then they get out and they don't know how to have friends.' But that's not what I see and that's not what I've experienced. . . .

"To the extent that we're successful, which is helping you to see all the aspects of what it is to be a man, which includes the chucking each other on the shoulder or discussing poetry or all the other things, it makes you a whole person. And I think in our culture, for whatever very complex reasons, I don't think we've done a great job of raising our sons in the last generation or so, and if we can do that, then we'll make the world a better place."

19

June 10, 1994, begins overcast and cool. The glass front doors of University School have been rubbed to perfect transparency. At nine o'clock, giant bows of maroon and black ribbon are hung at the front of the school. In an hour, a quartet of kilted bagpipers will arrive to usher in the guests. The gymnasium now contains a giant platform to seat more than a hundred people; collapsible bleachers have been extended from the facing wall, and in the center of the gym, an island rises from a uniform sea of folding chairs—a small platform for video cameras and sound equipment. In the dining hall, a dozen or so mothers of the junior class deck the walls with ribbon and a congratulatory banner, fuss with flower arrangements, and set tables for reception refreshments. Kerry, dressed in a dark suit, boutonniere stabbed through the lapel, hustles down the stairs carrying an ornate silver trophy cup that will rest on the table as decoration beside diplomas and awards. I ask how he's doing. "I'm a little nervous," he says, not stopping. "It's my first time." A few seniors have arrived early and sit at tables on the upstairs landing, frantically reading and rereading speeches they're about to deliver. Igor is there, too, looking calm. "Eet's graduation," he says with a smile. "I'm out of school—what could be better?"

I stroll into the silent administration offices to see if Hawley is in. The sun has come out and lights up the leafy trees and sparkles on the lake outside the vast windows of his office. Hawley is seated in the large red leather chair at his desk, reviewing his remarks and the day's schedule. He wears a dark suit and buckskin shoes that are so white they seem almost to glow. There isn't really much to say, but figuring I should have some sort of acknowledgment from the headmaster of the importance of this day, I ask for comment.

"We're going through with it," he says. "We thought about it, and we said, what the hell." Then he went back to his work.

May had passed in a wink, bright, warm, and relatively uneventful.

Paul Bailin, though, did have a final and unfortunate run-in with Hawley. He will not be returning to the school next year. The encounter was brief.

Paul had been speaking with Hawley about the possibility of teaching part-time and Hawley had been happy to consider it, one of several hiring decisions that needed to be made before the end of the year. Paul likewise needed a decision one way or another; he and Brigitta, who teaches at a Catholic school, had to plan next year, decide whether they would stay in Cleveland or move to the southwestern United States. Paul and Hawley set a date by which they would let each other know their situation. When that date arrived, Paul had yet to hear whether or not he would be kept on for the following year. The day, the last Friday in April, was a special work day for faculty of both campuses, a busy one. Paul stopped Kerry in the hall and asked if a decision had been made regarding his future with the school. Kerry told him no, and one wouldn't be made until the middle of next week at the earliest.

Paul felt they'd been stringing him along. Not only his plans but Brigitta's as well were contingent upon the decision; Brigitta needed to inform her school on Monday whether or not she'd be returning next year. Paul explained this to Kerry, noted that this is why they'd set a specific date for the decision, and said that he thought it was unethical for the school to ignore him this way. Kerry grew ruffled and said, "You made the deal with Rick. You should talk to him."

So Paul went to Hawley's office. Paul hates confrontations, and he was hyperventilating. Ann told him that Hawley's day was completely booked, but anger made Paul adamant. Chest heaving, he explained that he needed to speak with Hawley today. He had arrived by chance between meetings. Hawley appeared and said he had *two* minutes.

Paul sat on the couch in Hawley's office and reminded Hawley that they had agreed a decision would be made by today and told the headmaster that he thought the school was acting unfairly. Hawley said he'd been patient all year with Paul's questioning his judgment. Paul said if they couldn't let him know one way or another, they should have at least made mention of that. He told Hawley that the way he and others had been treated was unethical.

Hawley grew furious, and he said so. Then he strode to the door and held it open. Paul walked out and Hawley slammed the door. The white sheet of paper taped to this door, the quotation from Aristotle—"We are not conducting this inquiry in order to know what virtue is, but in order to become good"—quivered from the force.

Paul was rattled. He found Riney, a former teacher of his and now a colleague, to tell him what happened. Riney told Paul that perhaps "unethical" was not *le mot juste.*

"But that's the way I feel!" Paul said to me later that day after describing the events. "You can't tell people one thing and offer them another. I felt that he wasn't listening to me, that he was dodging me. I think it needed to be said. I think Rick needs to hear things like that, but he doesn't listen."

Paul said it was all something of a blur to him now, but he felt a cathartic unburdening. "It's sort of a relief," he said with a quiet chuckle. "It's sort of like standing up to your father."

Later, Hawley confirmed the unpleasantness of the meeting and his own anger. "I was *really* mad," he said. Hawley does not like to be accused of being unethical. He said he thought Paul "had played that card once too often."

When Paul calmed, he was less worried about not returning than that the rest of the year would be unpleasant, but neither Paul nor Hawley seemed to retain their anger for very long. Given the natural diffusiveness of spring—outdoor classes, an eclipse of the sun, the woods filling with deep green leaves, and the increasing warmth—the air in the building no longer held stress and ill will as it had in fall and winter.

Paul went on with his classes in his reflective meditative fashion, working to fathom some sort of ethical system that would explain, he said, "what the relationship is between the good and the happy." Happiness in the Aristotelian sense, he said—a human flourishing. "To me that's all you need. We all want to be happy in the broad sense, and if our being happy is somehow inextricably tied up with our being good, then what more do you need? . . . You want people to be happy, you want people to be good, and it would be nice if that wasn't this constant *struggle.*" He paused thoughtfully for a moment, looking off, and said, "I think I'm going to have the kids read some Saint Augustine."

The kids, by far, were the best part of his spring. He had always thought he favored sophomores, but Hawley told him, just you wait, you're going to adore the freshmen. "And he was right," Paul said. His seventh-period Western Civ class had transformed into the very best section he had. They had been his nemesis, and now they were his pleasure, "the ideal," he said. They had grown before his eyes. Late in the spring Tim, a husky blond boy, led the class in a full-period round-table discussion that was courteous and acute and productive in its analysis of symbolism in *The Book of Revelations;* Tim was so confident in leading that he even appointed his classmates, with jokey pomp, to read passages aloud the way Mr. Bailin did. It made Paul so happy he had to do something—something that would be part reward and part thanks.

On Monday, Paul entered the classroom, removed his jacket and took a seat on the table at the front of the room.

"OK," he said. "You guys need your notebooks out. Today is May twenty-third. I've got a couple announcements before we get started." The boys pulled out their notebooks and waited. "First, congratulations on the dialogue on Friday. You did an exceptional job. I was very pleased with how you did."

The room filled with smiles as the boys looked at each other then back to Mr. Bailin. Tim, completely unaware that anything unusual had happened, said, *"Really?"*

"Yes," Paul said. "You got through more material than any other class. And because of it, I'm going to give you one or two extra points on the final exam."

The news elicited several "wow"s and dropped jaws.

"If you think back to the first day," Paul said, "we didn't get along, and I thought it was going to be a *long* year."

"Mr. *Bailin,"* Jonah cried, "it *is* a long year."

Paul chuckled and said, "I know, Jonah."

Paul's next announcement was a peculiar one: he will shave off a section of his moustache for each class finishing the year with a combined average of 80 or above. "This class represents the middle section," he said, brushing the red bristles directly beneath his nose.

The boys fired all sorts of questions at him regarding procedure and details to confirm that he really meant it. Paul said it was possible that he'd be walking around with only part of a moustache after results were tabulated.

Shawntae began to giggle at the thought and bounced in his seat while leaning close to the desktop. "That's going to look *so stupid,*" he said, voicing everyone's happy hope.

Then Paul began the day's lesson—the Black Plague, the last moment of history that they're required to know. Shawn settled immediately into the work. He had come through the cheating episode relatively unscathed. It was decided by the school that the infraction was minor and that he would not automatically fail the test and thus automatically fail the course. He was allowed to take it and he did well. The punishment was a three-hour detention during which he and his accomplice wrote essays on their actions. Shawn's essay might easily have been a made-for-adults list of the evils of cheating, but the way he began it was more genuine, even artistic. He flashed forward to next fall to write an imaginary journal entry in which he describes his first day at the crime- and drug-choked high school in his neighborhood. Paul was surprised and even touched by the essay. Now the cheating incident was behind him; all that mattered was the final exam.

Throughout May, the seniors returned each Wednesday morning to check in with their adviser and report progress. Kris Fletcher and Tim Watkins composed music in a spare room at Tim's church; they worked four or five hours, which left time on clement days to explore a few sewers. Tyler Doggett wrote short stories. Nick Zinn sat at a computer creating a program that would mimic Darwin's theory of evolution. Eugene Gurarie completed his string quartet and began rehearsing it with orchestra members.

The month passed so quickly no one seemed to believe it when June actually arrived and the preparations for graduation were set in motion.

Hawley has scarcely had time to breathe. On top of the daily work, he's had to write two commencement addresses, one for the lower school and one for the upper, and he's agreed to speak at Middlebury's commencement in Vermont a few days before his own. He must write thorough evaluations of the four administrators with whom he shares these offices, as well as an address to the board of trustees on the state of the school. He hasn't even thought about the address to the Boys' School Conference in Belmont the following week, nor prepared for the day-school headmaster's conference in Philadelphia immediately preceding the Boys' School Conference. The end of school, he says, "is a little like going over Niagara Falls in an inner tube."

But no one can remember a better spring. It seems the entire nation is swathed in sunlight. *The New York Times* writes an editorial imploring readers to remember not only the brutal winter of 1993, but also the spring of 1994. Garrison Keillor opens his *A Prairie Home Companion* radio program by suggesting they cancel the show so everyone can go outside. On Friday, June 10, the overcast morning sky clears to pure blue and the temperature rises to the high 70s. The cities of Pepper Pike and Hunting Valley, which abut each other on S.O.M. Center Road, have hung small American flags on all of the telephone polls along the road so as I turn off S.O.M. Center into the US driveway on graduation morning, with the flags gently luffing and the smell of cut grass pouring through my car window, it seems like the Fourth of July. The deep tire ruts, cut into the turf by a boy who lost control of his car zooming away from school on a recent sunny Friday, have hardened to tawny dirt, but the lawn is otherwise neat as carpet. By 9:30 the senior class, dressed in white slacks, white shirts, and blue blazers, mills in the library, waiting.

Kevin Feder, class comedian, is looking shifty but washed, hair still damp but combed. "I can't believe I'm *graduating*," he says. He looks wistfully at an imaginary horizon. "First one in the family."

Senior dean Doug Lagarde strides into the library carrying two bolts of ties, maroon and black stripe, and begins handing them out to the boys and checking off their names. "Make sure you line up to get your boutonnieres," he tells them.

Mike Cohen scorns the ties for being too conservative.

Lagarde says, "Hey, these will come back into fashion."

I ask Mike how he's doing. He says, "Fan-*tastic.*"

Wilkie, thinking only of his diploma, says, "I'm not going to believe it until I have it in my hand."

Librarian Polly Cohen, leaning lazily on the checkout desk, says, "Neither is the *audience.*"

Jason Koo is lamenting the Indians' ninth-inning loss to the Brewers last night. "*I* should manage the team," he exclaims in a rare burst of emotion. "If I were manager, we'd be in first place and ten games ahead."

Tyler Doggett leans against a table, in a crowd of friends. Long blond bangs droop over one eye. "I'm sad," he tells me, then smiles and looks at his feet as though terribly embarrassed. "I think commencement is a good word," he adds. "Ambiguous."

I ask him why he hasn't buttoned down his shirt collar. He says he's missing one of the buttons. I tell him they are both there. "Oh," he says, fastening his collar. "I suppose on a different day I'd be able to find them."

Lagarde calls out, "Guys, we've got some pictures to take." And he sorts out the groups—lifers, ten of them, legacies, eight, and Davey Fellows—each of which will line the stairs of the library stacks, ties tied, boutonnieres in place, for photos.

The room is crowded with blue blazers, white slacks, and conservative ties. Kris Fletcher strolls nonchalantly around the tables, cracking his neck occasionally. This is no big deal for Kris. When I ask how he's doing, he more or less shrugs "fine." (He had been more forthcoming after the awards ceremony on the last official day of school, during which he was presented with two awards for his classics studies. He and his friends were exchanging yearbooks to sign and I asked Kris how it felt to be graduating. "I'm glad *and* sad," he said. "Both. I'm ready to leave, but you gotta admit, it doesn't get much easier than this.")

Kevin Casey, who remains chemical-free and determined to stay that way, arrives late to the library, hugging a huge yellow envelope containing his forty-page study of the Battle of Monacacy, a graduation requirement completed just before dawn. Kevin has been up for the past thirty-six hours. "I'm just exhausted and overwhelmed with everything," he says. The headmaster appears suddenly: "Kevin, can I talk to you a minute?" Hawley never uses these words happily. He pulls Kevin aside and upbraids him for not turning in his community-service journal, the other graduation requirement Kevin needed to fulfill. He tells Kevin that they could keep him out of the ceremony today because of it—but they won't. Hawley elicits a promise from a delirious Kevin that he will turn in his journal after graduation, and departs looking peeved. Kevin says, "I'll have to make something up."

Wilkie says, "Right down to the wire, Kevin."

Kevin is not the only one. The diplomas of several boys are on hold because of delayed completions. For Margaret Mason and Ann McGovern, the morning is filled with trying to finalize these details. Margaret says she can't remember when so many kids were on the verge of not graduating on graduation day. "It's a way of not dealing with what's coming up," Ann says.

Eugene Gurarie, in the corner of the library, jabbers excitedly in Russian with Igor. Music Director Marty Kessler has just delivered an anonymous gift to Eugene: a new blue blazer. All year he'd worn a ratty, scuffed jacket, a size too small, and Marty handed Eugene the present with the instructions that the anonymous giver wanted to ensure that Eugene looked dazzling when he walked on stage to conduct his string quartet, which he planned to do later in the month. Eugene's mouth hangs open and he shakes his head, incredulous, staring at the new jacket.

"Gentlemen!" Lagarde calls out. "We're going to take the group picture now out in the courtyard." The class lines up to file out of the library. Fran Hanscom waits at the exit, holding a wastebasket, and says, "Throw out your gum." The boys drop gum into the basket on their way out. "Last job I have," she says. "One more tacky job for me. Gum. Gum, please. Gum." Eugene is the last in line. Fran looks at him with disappointment and says, "Your tie's not right."

"Yes it is," he says.

"No, it goes down the *center* of your shirt." She straightens it for him.

The senior class marches past the tables on the upstairs landing and out to the sunny courtyard to have their class picture taken. The freshmen look at the seniors with longing. Jason Pribble, at school to watch the ceremony, says, longingly, "It seems so far away." But for some boys, graduation to the next level can feel just as momentous.

Only a few days before, Shawntae had completed his final exam for Western Civ and he went to the first table on the upstairs landing to begin studying for the next exam. Mr. Bailin's test was hard and Shawn knew it was close. Paul was so nervous for him, he graded Shawn's test immediately. Shawn's exam was one point shy of the grade he needed to pass the course.

Paul grinned. He had promised to give everyone in Shawn's class an extra point on their exams; with this extra point, Shawn had passed the course, no fudging required from Paul, who had seen Shawn work so hard this last trimester he would have felt compelled to boost Shawn the extra point anyway. Paul left directly to find him.

When Shawn saw the red-bristle hair, and then the head, and then the body of Mr. Bailin ascending the stairs, he very nearly swallowed his throat. He knew Mr. Bailin was coming to see him.

"Congratulations," Paul said. "You passed."

Shawn looked everywhere around him on the landing and asked, "You talking to *me?*"

Paul smiled and said, yes, *you* passed, and Shawn was soon back at work—he had more exams to get through before he could rejoice. Shawn began the year at six-foot-three, 250 pounds; he was now nearly six-five.

■ ■ ■

The downstairs commons fills with guests and teachers. Nancy Lerner is on the downstairs landing. She returned last night from a trip to New York, where she had quietly slipped into a hair salon. Everyone is complimenting her on the new do.

"Everyone," she says, "except my husband and me don't like it. My husband and . . . I and my . . . my *husband* and *I.* Listen to my grammar!" she says, aghast.

Nancy loves graduation, but she's mad about one thing. She had argued with Rick that Margaret Mason should be on stage. "They really should have a woman up there," Nancy says. Immediately, she gives me a don't-remind-me look, and says her decision not to be the commencement speaker was the right one.

Nancy tells me she had a dream last night. "I was missing graduation because I was teaching," she says. "I was teaching a class with Rick, and I was leaving, and I was teaching. And it was *breaking* my *heart."*

The seats and bleachers begin to fill and many parents wait by the door to watch the senior class file into the gym. The mood is one of hushed excitement. Nancy departs to join the faculty who are beginning to assemble.

At 10:30 A.M. the faculty, arranged in two files according to tenure, stride into the gym and take their seats in the first rows. From another entrance Hawley, Kerry Brennan, board president Tim Treadway, and other ceremonial adults take their seats on the platform, which runs the length of the gym and is decorated with abundant ferns and ficus trees. The seniors file in last, grave with ceremony and dapper in their blazer-and-white-slacks uniform. Hawley is always amazed at how the boys can be so scrappy and irascible all year long, then suddenly transform into models of decorum.

Before any welcome is spoken, Dr. Mason, Margaret's husband, stands to deliver the Invocation, then Hawley takes the center podium.

"Mr. Treadway, colleagues, parents, families, friends, and boys of US, welcome," he says. "We are here this morning to celebrate the collective experience and achievements of these graduating boys. They are the one-hundred-fourth class to have passed this way and this ceremony not only honors them, it serves as a deep and resonant reminder of the mission of

University School. If there is any theme at all to an occasion like this, it is continuity. The continuity of learning, the continuity of school, the continuity of boys to men. . . .

"The value of these boys' experience lies in the difference it has made in their lives. And what is that difference? *Are* they more durable, deeper, more generous, more loving, more effective than they otherwise might have been? What has come of this strange business of plucking these boys out of thirty-one different communities and combining their different experiences of life so intensely for so many hours and for so many days? They have been exposed by design to the greatest ideas, lives, technical feats, and artistic creations the world has produced as well as to many unsolved and vexing problems. Literally and figuratively, these boys have been tested, and this morning we celebrate the joyful passing of those tests."

Hawley and Brennan still know how to throw a great ceremony. Class president Track Malone and student council president Brian Boukalik deliver sentimental reflections of the year. Kerry reads citations for five awards given to top athletes and scholars. Hawley has prepared his own reflection of the year in which he mentions not by name, but by action, each of the ninety graduating boys—". . . the class has also produced one of the deepest Latin and Greek scholars the school has ever known, a boy who is also, perhaps with a kind of weird compensation, committed to heavy-metal music" . . . "one senior is fond of mailing sensational, angry letters to everyone in the school, then looking back with wonder on what happened"—and he even manages to slip in part of a Beaverfest joke, which Kerry, at the ready with vaudeville antics, prevents him from completing. Dr. Dale Adler, class of 1972, delivers the keynote speech. Finally, diplomas are awarded. Hawley stands at the podium and reads the names off in groups— . . . Henry Clay Aalders . . . Ryan Bruce Alexander . . . Alfredo Michael R. Alonzo . . . Alvin Creed Anthony, Jr. . . . Ryan Fredrick Bartell . . . Juan Carlos Bigornia . . . Adam Howard Blumenthal . . . Brian Christopher Boukalik—and the boys file to platform-left where Kerry waits to shake their hand before they cross the stage—Brian Patrick Delaney . . . Eric Raymond Dina . . . Tyler Carrington Doggett . . . Andrew Geist Eakin . . . Fadel Shukri Elkhari . . . Kevin Michael Feder . . . Charles Thomas Fiordalis . . . Michael Sean Fioritto—for the slip of paper, enclosed in a hard maroon binder, that officially ends their high school career—Omair I. Hafeez Toor . . . Richard Edward Waldo . . . Timothy William Watkins . . . John Fredrick

Webb . . . O. Lamont Williams . . . Samuel Joseph Woo . . . David Maxwell Young . . . Levi Ken Zimmerman . . . Nicholas Savage Zinn. Nick strides big and heavy across the stage, his formidable jaw set, a huge grin on his face, his arms swinging high, takes his diploma from Tim Treadway, shakes Hawley's hand vigorously, and it is done. Loud long applause, screams, hoots, and whistles fill the echoing gym.

Picture-snapping parents, girlfriends, and smiling boys pour into the sun-shot courtyard. More fill the dining hall drinking punch and munching cakes. I stand around in the sun not really sure what to do with myself. The year is over. Carol Pribble is standing around too, and she says, "I guess this was kinda like a graduation for you, too." I hadn't thought about it till then but she was right. Math teacher Terry Kessler stops to talk to Carol. He looks sad. "I *am* sad," he says. Then he issues a small squeak of a whimper. "But it's time for them to leave."

I hadn't thought of *that* either. These kids *are* leaving. *I* am leaving. I am sad, too. It doesn't feel finished—the stories aren't finished. How can they leave now?

I take a pass through the dining hall, shake a few hands, say goodbye. Kathleen has come to watch Kris graduate with the rest of his family. I say hello and goodbye, meet a few parents, and then everyone is gone. The school empties. I stand around looking baffled. I don't want to leave but there isn't really anything more to do. I take a last stroll upstairs, hoping to bump into anyone at all. It's deserted. On my way downstairs, Kerry appears and invites me to the faculty bash that evening at the pavilion overlooking the football field, closure for the faculty.

I accept Kerry's invitation gratefully.

On my way down the stairs, I spot John Gregor loitering in the commons. We'd had some long talks over the previous weeks, and he still looked bad. Jessica had broken up with him, and there were times when he just didn't know what to do with himself and moments when I thought he was about to start weeping right there in the middle of school, but he never did. For two weeks, he simply could not admit to himself that it was over.

I ask how he's doing.

"I'm still here," he says, shyly tucking hair behind his ears. He is wearing his school tie. "At least I don't have to tell my mom to get off the phone anymore."

Margaret Mason appears at his side. When he wasn't talking to me about Jessica, he was talking to Margaret about her. Margaret gives John's shoulder a good squeeze, and John looks at the carpet. "I'll be here Monday," she tells John. "And we're going to talk, right? About *academics?*"

"Yes, Mrs. Mason," says John.

Reluctantly, I leave. My car is the only one in the parking lot, and the day, afternoon now, has gotten hot.

As I start my car, cruise up the driveway, and turn right onto S.O.M. Center Road, heading away from school, I think about the boys, the end of whose stories I probably will never know. I'm feeling pretty peculiar, leaving high school for the second time.

There's a novel by Julian Barnes called *Staring at the Sun* which opens with a situation parallel to the one I'm in. A pilot is flying alone in the night sky, very high up. He's flying east, and he watches the sun rise. Then he descends thousands of feet into darkness, continues to fly east, and watches the sun rise again. He sees the sun rise twice in one day: an actual miracle.

Almost exactly thirteen years ago, I had driven away from my high school on a day very much like this one, sunny and hot, alone in my car. There are times when you do not want to be an adult, and today is one of them.

Hawley once addressed this at a reading he gave from his book *Boys Will Be Men;* in response to a question from the audience he tried to define boyhood. Boyhood isn't a "phase," he said, something that transforms into young adulthood and then maturity. Boyhood is something more durable than that, more real even than male adulthood. In fact, Hawley said, masculine adulthood is very likely an illusion. A "husk," he called it, designed to conceal boyhood. Male adulthood, he suggested, may be successful only insofar as boyhood is integrated into the man. But boyhood is real, it stays in the man, and *keeps* staying there. When he said this, I knew instantly that it was true.

All year people kept asking me how had the school changed? I could never answer. Eventually I stopped trying to say anything because it hadn't changed. When I arrived in September for the first day of school, the sense of ghosts was so strong I almost expected to see my old classmates drifting in and out of the locker area. And during the year, I would at times halt in the downstairs commons to look around at various clusters of boys. They could seem, from my distance, out of time: they *were* my old classmates. I could look around at the boys and say, "There, in the corner, you see Mike? That's my old classmate Tom Hamilton. See, Nick? He's Carmen Ilacqua, who went on to play football for Yale. There's Norm Siegal, now an investment banker in town. Over there, the boy vandalizing a text book? That's Dave Kovacik—he just married a native of Guatemala and is teaching in Harlem."

The school *has* changed in that the boys change every year.

Only boys. And so it will remain, I imagine, as long as the school exists. Given what I'd seen, this did not seem a bad circumstance. The boys I'd watched, departing seniors, had obviously thrived here; students like Shawntae had successfully leapt huge hurdles and were approaching even higher ones. The very best of what school might be and do had happened here. It had happened, not always easily and not always with grace, but under ideal circumstances—kids from caring families at a school with smart, committed teachers, a comfortable, safe, and well-endowed school. How could kids have failed to thrive? They had succeeded in a world designed specifically to promote that success.

What then did this say about education in general during a time of general despair over education in America? And what might it offer educators in their attempts to understand the benefits and drawbacks of single-sex education? American education has been primarily coeducational since the mid-nineteenth century, and it had become so not because coeducation was deemed better for children but rather because coeducation was more economical than teaching boys and girls in separate buildings. What single-sex high schools had formed and lasted were independent—either small, rich, private schools or religious, and largely poor, schools. These lasted for decades unquestioned, largely ignored—anomalies in an otherwise democratic, religiously free country.

Then the country's mood changed. The great wave of conversions from single-sex to coeducation which began in the 1960s and continued well into the 1980s occurred not because researchers and sociologists had scrutinized the single-sex form and found it harmful to children, but rather because it seemed like a bad idea to separate boys and girls, to keep them away from each other in separate schools. Because the mood changed, single-sex schools found it difficult to attract enough students to fill their schools; most could stay alive only if they became coeducational. American independent schools, more than half of which were single-sex, did what public schools had done a century earlier—again, not out of concern for the students but rather economic necessity, a move further enforced by the belief that coeducation was more egalitarian.

By the time I arrived at University School in the fall of 1993, 9 percent of independent schools—of about one thousand monitored by the National Association of Independent Schools—remained all-boy. Just a few years earlier, this figure, a mere speck on the entire American educational landscape, seemed to represent the last breath of this old form. The administrators who cared about these schools walked gingerly, listening all the while for a phlegmy death gurgle.

Yet the schools that had survived did so because they were strong, and when the winds, slowly, began to turn again, these schools sailed—girls' schools, in a political climate dominated by feminist thinking, leading the way. Backed by research, organized into a strong coalition, and bolstered by reports of intractable sex bias within coed schools, girls' schools no longer needed to justify their existence, and enrollment boomed.

Boys' schools followed the girls' schools, first in a sort of dim-witted, hey-wait-a-minute recognition that they didn't have to sit in the corner anymore, and then in a stumbling, pro-active way, in which they began to promote themselves as actually being good for boys. Finally, in the spring of 1994, boys' schools found their voice. Following the Belmont boys'-school conference, a new group would solidify—Boys' Schools: An International Coalition. Its goal: to understand and promote "the development of school-age boys." In a matter of months, the newborn coalition, led by Hawley and organized by Ann McGovern, would comprise 140 schools from the United States, Canada, England, Australia, and Japan. Its mission statement would be lofty enough to support its physical size: ". . . Boys' Schools aims to insure a future in which humane and capable boys will bring their gifts to bear on the creation of a just and livable world."

"I think the mood is better," Hawley would tell me not long before the first official conference of Boys' Schools. "I think the mood is actually inquiring, and really honestly, robustly inquiring, 'Are boys' schools a good idea?' And while we have that climate, I think what we need to do is lay out boys'-school narratives about what it's like. Honestly ask, 'Are we turning out piggish kids? Are our kids unable to contend with modern females? What can we do better?' No end of good things can follow from that, as opposed to the battling—'Our math scores are better than your math scores, our boys are less wimpy than your boys.' *Forget* the other context of 'compared to girls, or compared to boys in coed settings,' and then winning because we do it better. Just get the stuff out there to observe and also to criticize. I think that's where all the excitement is right now."

I asked Hawley if he thought the issue of single-sex education in the private sphere had any relevance to the broader picture of American education.

"We have national learning deficits to catch up," he said. "The typical American secondary-school student is in the bottom fiftieth percentile of learning in all major areas compared with other developed nations. So there are some big learning deficits to repair, and I hope we focus on repairing those. And I also hope, as we do, that we look at gender as a factor and then design things that are good for those genders."

These new winds would blow through what had once been the most cloistered boys' world the country had known, the United States Senate, in the summer of 1994. These lawmakers—entrusted to propagate democratic government and life, the creators of Title IX ensuring no gender injustice would be allowed again within American education—debated an educational amendment that would pave the way for experimental single-sex classes in the public domain. The amendment was introduced by Senator John Danforth, who proposed that grants be awarded for the creation of ten experimental single-sex programs for "low-income, educationally disadvantaged students," and that Title IX, which since 1972 has prohibited the creation of public single-sex schools, be waived in such cases.

Senators Ted Kennedy and Carol Moseley-Braun stood in strong opposition to the amendment, arguing that it would undermine two decades of work toward ending discrimination in schools. Danforth cautiously told the Senate, "I am not saying we should just take the cork out of the bottle. I am just saying that in a limited number of cases we should try it. This is not the repeal of Title IX." A vote was taken that day, August 1, 1994, and, to the surprise of Danforth and his entire office, the amendment passed 66 to 33.

Research in academe continued to support single-sex education, and researchers hoped the gathering data might translate into more experiments within the public sector. Ravitch, a champion of diversity, had written to Senator Danforth in support of his amendment: "This is an important amendment, for it will expand the educational diversity and opportunity that is so badly needed for children who are now at risk of failure." Riordan, who also supported the Danforth amendment, maintained what he had always argued for, exploratory and experimental programs—"the most promising of these programs," he had long concluded, "give students some measure of access to single-sex education."

The debate would continue; and in the public sector, debate focused on programs that would help the children who needed it most, girls and minority boys. The debate on the Senate floor was a strong indication that honest evaluation was now possible, though not easily accomplished. The House would eventually toss out Danforth's amendment after strong lobbying from groups such as the National Organization for Women, the American Association of University Women, and the Women's Legal Defense Fund. "The concept's not dead," Danforth's legislative director said. "It's going to come back. It's just too important not to."

Indeed, as the 1996–97 school year approaches, boys' schools, though limited by three decades of erosion, appear to be enjoying something of a renaissance. "It seems as if many, many of them are reporting that they are at absolute capacity and all-time high enrollment," says Peter D. Relic, president of the National Association of Independent Schools. Moreover, Governor Pete Wilson of California expressed in his "state of the state" address this year his hope of offering $5 million to districts that wanted to create single-sex schools for at-risk kids. Senator Dan Coats of Indiana intends to introduce into Congress a plan to offer a total of $300 million for the same purpose, only on a massive scale. The climate, as Hawley has claimed, does seem to be open; at last questions could be effectively debated.

As I drove away from school on graduation day, though, I thought only about the boys. Somehow, they overshadowed the numerous questions and arguments, pro and con, regarding single-sex education. From my vantage point, the boys I'd watched were rocketing toward the horizon. I tried to invent the hopeful end to their many stories. Kris Fletcher, I told myself, became a heavy-metal star and the first person to translate the Etruscan language before his election as President of the United States. Tyler Doggett, a tortured artist during his undergraduate years at Princeton, founded a new genre of poetry called Sentimental Existentialism. Tyler Soltis became a prominent lawyer specializing in First Amendment rights. Eugene Gurarie, the composer, was ubiquitous on the concert circuit. Nick Zinn, renowned religions scholar, had gone on to make a fortune in computers. And Shawntae had become a teacher.

I did sporadically keep in touch with these boys in their first years as college students, though we soon lost contact. Kris headed to Wesleyan in Connecticut. I phoned him to see how he was doing and to ask some questions. One of the main questions I had was how he, and his US classmates, had made the transition from a boys' school to a coed college or university. None of the boys I spoke with said they had any problem going to school, and socializing, with girls—and the strength of their answers made me feel a little silly for asking in the first place. Kris lived in a coed dorm; he said it was kind of weird heading to the showers in the morning to find a girl in her bathrobe brushing her teeth, but, generally, he loved having girls in the dorm. "They're like sisters," he said. There were two consistent responses by the boys: first, going to school with girls was *fun;* second, friendships with girls exceeded those with guys. "My best friends here are girls," and, "most of my friends are girls," they almost invariably said. Indeed, I wondered if this weren't a fairly common result of the boys'-school environment; it's not that they don't know how to relate to women when they leave, but, instead, that they relate better to women than to men.

Tyler Soltis, happily ensconced in his dorm room at Syracuse University, expressed similar thoughts on going to school with girls—"I have more girl friends than guy friends," he said—then reflected on his final year of high school. I still retained an image of Tyler, standing bolt upright against the window to Ann McGovern's office, eyes bugging out, waiting for Hawley to call him into his office and decide his place at the school. Looking back, there was neither a self-deprecating chuckle nor scratching-of-the-head wonder, but rather dead seriousness: "It was a *very* important time in my life," Tyler said.

And so it would remain always, I have no doubt, for all of them. Hawley had been correct: boyhood wasn't something one went through, some layover station on the journey to one's final destination of adult malehood; boyhood was the essence of their being, the animating force, the rocket fuel propelling them through life to an end that was at best solitary, and inevitably tragic, if only because there *is* no satisfying conclusion. This is why school, school days, school stories, and memories of school remain so powerful. It would be true for Kris, as he cruised through Wesleyan. For Tyler Doggett and Eugene Gurarie, off on different paths through Princeton. For Mike Seelbach, who would graduate the following spring and attend the Cleveland Institute of Music for one year before winning the lead in the touring production of the Broadway musical *Tommy,* a role he'd play in cities throughout the country. The boys were shooting off in all directions, speeding farther and farther away from the source.

It is more important, of course, to be a good school than to be a single-sex school. I had seen that at least this school for boys had created a rarefied example of what school might be. As a boy, I had known it too. These boys this year were no different—a thousand variations of the same thing, boys themselves. I headed away from school hoping to remember what they would become.

Sources

Of the various studies measuring the effects of single-sex education—and there are relatively few—I have quoted from the following:

Lee, Valerie E. and Anthony S. Bryk. "Effects of Single-Sex Secondary Schools on Student Achievement and Attitudes." *Journal of Educational Psychology* 78 (1986): 381–95.

Lee, Valerie E. and Helen M. Marks. "Sustained Effects of the Single-Sex Secondary School Experience on Attitudes, Behaviors, and Values in College." *Journal of Educational Psychology* 82 (1990): 578–92.

Single-Sex Schooling: Perspectives From Practice and Research. A Special Report from the Office of Educational Research and Improvement, U.S. Department of Education, Volume 1, 1992.

The most useful book I read on the subject, one which gathered and evaluated all known studies through 1990, was Cornelius Riordan's *Girls & Boys in School: Together or Separate?* (New York: Teachers College Press, 1990)—a level-headed, even-handed book. Dr. Riordan deserves a personal acknowledgment for his efforts to lead me through this data. On the history of coeducation, I know of no more comprehensive or intelligent book than David Tyack and Elizabeth Hansot's *Learning Together: A History of Coeducation in American Public Schools* (New Haven: Yale University Press and New York: Russell Sage Foundation, 1990). Myra and David Sadker's *Failing at Fairness: How America's Schools Cheat Girls* (New York: Scribners, 1994) was also very helpful.

Chapter 8 was informed by many books about Cleveland and about the history of education, some of which are noted in the text, others not, but all are mentioned below:

Akers, William J. *Cleveland Schools in the Nineteenth Century* (Cleveland: The W. M. Bayne Printing House, 1901).

Bluestone, Daniel M. *Cleveland: An Inventory of Historical Engineering and Industrial Sites* (U.S. Department of the Interior, 1978).

Campbell, Thomas F. and Edward M. Miggins, eds., *The Birth of Modern Cleveland* (Cleveland: Western Reserve Historical Society [Associated University Presses], 1988).

Condon, George E. *Cleveland: The Best Kept Secret* (New York: Doubleday, 1967).

Cremin, Lawrence A. *American Education: The Colonial Experience 1607–1783* (New York: Harper & Row, 1970). [The following two volumes of Cremin's enormous study were also helpful.]

Kraushaar, Otto F. *American Nonpublic Schools: Patterns of Diversity* (Baltimore and London: Johns Hopkins University Press, 1972).

McLachlan, James. *American Boarding Schools: A Historical Survey* (New York: Scribners, 1970).

Orth, Samuel P. *A History of Cleveland, Ohio, Volume I* (Chicago: S. J. Clark, 1910).

References to Vladimir Nabokov's *Pnin* were informed by Gerald Boyd's biography of that author.

For historical information on University School, I relied mainly on Richard Hawley's *Hail, University!,* a history published by the school in 1990. This is a remarkable book in that it is both an institutional history *and* readable. Other books of Hawley's I used were these: *The Headmaster's Papers* (Middlebury: Paul S. Eriksson, 1983), *Seeing Things* (New York: Walker & Co, 1987), and *Boys Will Be Men: Masculinity in Troubled Times* (Middlebury: Paul S. Eriksson, 1993).